The *Giallo* Canvas

Also by Alexandra Heller-Nicholas

*Found Footage Horror Films:
Fear and the Appearance
of Reality* (McFarland, 2014)

*Rape-Revenge Films:
A Critical Study* (McFarland, 2011)

The *Giallo* Canvas
Art, Excess and Horror Cinema

ALEXANDRA HELLER-NICHOLAS

McFarland & Company, Inc., Publishers
Jefferson, North Carolina

Library of Congress Cataloguing-in-Publication Data

Names: Heller-Nicholas, Alexandra, 1974– author.
Title: The giallo canvas : art, excess and horror cinema / Alexandra Heller-Nicholas.
Description: Jefferson, North Carolina : McFarland & Company, Inc., Publishers, 2021 | Includes bibliographical references and index.
Identifiers: LCCN 2020057298 | ISBN 9781476675398 (paperback : acid free paper) ∞
ISBN 9781476640761 (ebook)
Subjects: LCSH: Horror films—Italy—History and criticism. | Motion pictures—Italy—History—20th century.
Classification: LCC PN1995.9.H6 H456 2021 | DDC 791.43/61640945—dc23
LC record available at https://lccn.loc.gov/2020057298

British Library cataloguing data are available
ISBN (print) 978-1-4766-7539-8
ISBN (ebook) 978-1-4766-4076-1

© 2021 Alexandra Heller-Nicholas. All rights reserved

No part of this book may be reproduced or transmitted in any form or by any means, electronic or mechanical, including photocopying or recording, or by any information storage and retrieval system, without permission in writing from the publisher.

Front cover: Poster art from the 1970 Italian film
The Bird with the Crystal Plumage
(Universal Marion Corporation/Photofest)

Printed in the United States of America

McFarland & Company, Inc., Publishers
 Box 611, Jefferson, North Carolina 28640
 www.mcfarlandpub.com

This book is dedicated with all my heart
to Jan Napiorkowski (1975-2020);
author, dreamweaver, visionary, plus friend.

Table of Contents

Acknowledgments   ix
Introduction   1

One—Art, Cinema, Horror, Excess   7
Two—*Giallo*: Italy and Beyond   27

Famous Paintings

Three—Girls Asleep, Girls Afraid: Vermeer in *The Forbidden Room* (*Anima Persa*, 1977) and *The Psychic* (*Sette Note in Nero*, 1977)   52

Four—Swan Guts and Screaming Popes: Salvador Dalí, Francis Bacon and *A Lizard in a Woman's Skin* (*Una lucertola con la pelle di donna*, Lucio Fulci, 1971)   70

Five—The Medusa's Warning: *The Stendhal Syndrome* (*La Sindrome di Stendhal*, Dario Argento, 1996)   80

Clues, Presence and Painting

Six—Misreading Clues: Dario Argento's *The Bird with the Crystal Plumage* (*L'uccello dalle piume di cristallo*, 1970) and *Deep Red* (*Profondo rosso*, 1975)   94

Seven—Haunted Portraits: *The Red Queen Kills Seven Times* (*La dama rossa uccide sette volte*, Emilio Miraglia, 1972) and *Your Vice Is a Locked Room and Only I Have the Key* (*Il tuo vizio è una stanza chiusa e solo io ne ho la chiave*, Sergio Martino, 1972)   105

viii   Table of Contents

Eight—Paint Death Clearly: Saint Sebastian and *The House with Laughing Windows* (*La casa dalle finestre che ridono*, Pupi Avati, 1976) — 117

Painters

Nine—A Portrait of an Artist as a Mad Drunk: *The Red Headed Corpse* (*La rossa dalla pelle che scotta*, Renzo Russo, 1972) — 130

Ten—The Myth of the "Mad" Genius: Vincent Van Gogh and *Blood Delirium* (*Delirio di sangue*, Sergio Bergonzelli, 1988) — 136

Eleven—The Ghosts of Capitalism: Art, Labor and Exploitation in *A Quiet Place in the Country* (*Un tranquillo posto di campagna*, Elio Petri, 1968) — 141

Other Art Forms

Twelve—Fashion and Photography — 154
Thirteen—Filmmaking — 168
Fourteen—Theater and Performance — 177
Fifteen—Hybridity — 188

Conclusion: Style Is the Substance — 207
Chapter Notes — 211
Bibliography — 231
Index — 243

Acknowledgments

I'd like to thank McFarland & Company, as well as the following people: Bill Ackerman, John Atkinson, Anton Bitel, Dean Brandum, Michelle Carey, Hélène Cattet and Bruno Forzani, Sally Christie, Cinemaniacs, Martyn Conterio, Samm Deighan, John Edmond, Giles Edwards, Kat Ellinger, Evrim Ersoy, Lee Gambin, Jack Geary, Dan Golding, Ian Gouldstone, James Gracey, Cerise Howard, Robert Hughes, Kier-La Janisse, Alexia Kannas, the Keylight ladies, Dave Koenig, Clare Leaver, Ramon Lobato, Michael Mackenzie, Anne Marsh, Ernest Mathjis, Michael Mackenzie, Donna McRea, Jennifer Merin and the Alliance of Women Film Journalists, the Miskatonic Institute of Horror Studies, Gary Morris, Luke Mullen, Angela Ndalianis, Phil Nobile Jr., Amanda Reyes, Dominic Richard and Dorothy Lawrenson, James Shapiro, Neil Snowdon, Peter Strickland, Julian Stringer, David Surman, Emma Westwood and extra special thanks once again to Josh Nelson. And, of course, love and appreciation for the unceasing support of my family; Richard, Lorraine, Max, Fiona, Robert, and especially—as always—Christian and Casper. You guys can have the TV now; the "screaming movies" have finally stopped!

This book revisits films and ideas I explored in earlier publications listed below, here used with the generous permission of the original publishers:

"A Brutal Nobility: Painting Death in *The House with Laughing Windows* (Pupi Avati, 1976)," *Bright Lights Film Journal*, June 30, 2014, https://brightlightsfilm.com/brutal-nobility-painting-death-house-laughing-windows-pupi-avati-1976/#.XedGD5MzYRY

"Cannibals and Other Impossible Bodies: *Il Profumo Della Signora in Nero* and the Giallo Film," *Scope: An Online Journal for Film and Television Studies* 22 (2012) https://www.nottingham.ac.uk/scope/documents/2012/february-2012/heller-nicholas.pdf

"Subversive Frames: Vermeer and Lucio Fulci's *Sette note in nero,*" *Refractory: A Journal of Entertainment Media,* 17 (2010) https://refractory-journal.com/subversive-frames-vermeer-and-lucio-fulcis-sette-note-in-nero-alexandra-heller-nicholas/

"The Violation of Representation: Art, Argento and the Rape-Revenge Film," *FORUM: University of Edinburgh Postgraduate Journal of Culture & The Arts,* (December 2011) http://www.forumjournal.org/article/view/676

Introduction

In 1926, upon having attended a screening of Robert Weine's 1920 silent horror classic *The Cabinet of Dr. Caligari*, pioneering English modernist author and iconic proto-feminist Virginia Woolf wrote an article called "The Movies and Reality" for *The New Republic*. One particular passage casts profound light, even today, on widespread assumptions that the consumption of screen media is largely an intellectually passive endeavor. Wrote Woolf:

> ...the ordinary eye, the English unaesthetic eye, is a simple mechanism, which takes care that the body does not fall down coal-holes, provides the brain with toys and sweetmeats to keep it quiet, and can be trusted to go on behaving like a competent nursemaid until the brain comes to the conclusion that it is time to wake up. What is its surprise, then, to be roused suddenly in the midst of its agreeable somnolence and asked for help? The eye is in difficulties. The eye wants help. The eye says to the brain, "Something is happening which I do not in the least understand. You are needed."[1]

While an avid and proud horror film fan—indeed, an avid cinephile more generally—it was not until I first encountered Italian *giallo* cinema that I felt the full extent of this experience Woolf described. It was these films where I first felt that itch, that quiver, that near-overwhelmingly intense tectonic critical shift as my eye demanded of my brain exactly this; "Something is happening which I do not in the least understand. You are needed."

The first *giallo* I ever saw was Umberto Lenzi's *Spasmo* (1974),[2] although at the time I had no idea that was what these types of movies were called. It was the 1990s and I was in high school, where much of my social life hinged around hanging out with my friends and watching videos. There was a clearly established ritual built around this practice; as was common in the Australian suburbs at the time, my local video store had a permanent "seven videos for $7 for seven days" deal that was perfectly suited to our binge-viewing routines in this pre–Netflix era. Each of us would choose films individually and then—by committee—we would prune it down to that week's seven videos of choice. Largely these decisions were governed by what in retrospect can best be defined as performative irony; we prayed in the church of "so bad it's good," practicing acolytes of the "guilty pleasure," card-carrying members of the smug teenage brigade for whom sincere engagement with culture was the least of our concerns. Our aim was the optimum degree of eye rolling and the laughter possible, results that came less from a place of generosity than of cynicism. We were, in short, idiots; but to be fair, we were also kids, and for better or for worse this is the context where my burgeoning film literacy more broadly began to develop in earnest.

But then something curious happened. Somewhere along the way, all those phrases I now so passionately despise—"so bad it's good," "guilty pleasures"—faded into the background, replaced by something altogether more enduring and, in relation to this book in particular, critically rigorous. The more so-called "bad" film I watched, the more I felt the magic of neuroplasticity take over. These films began to rewire on what felt like an almost physiological level *how* I experienced cinema. I found new pleasures, new ways of engaging with film in the most unlikely places; *Revenge of the Nerds* marathons, Shaw Brothers double bills, and—most of all—the seemingly unending treasures housed within the video store's Horror section. It was here that I learned the jewels of the *Halloween, Friday the 13th* and *Nightmare on Elm Street* franchises were to be found in the more-often-than-not oft-derided sequels as much as the more broadly beatified originals in each series. It was here I discovered Troma Entertainment and Redemption Films. It was here I unknowingly took my first informal lessons in auteur studies as I purely by accident stumbled upon the films of Tobe Hooper, George A. Romero, David Cronenberg and John Carpenter. And it was here—most of all—where I discovered *gialli*.

Spasmo made a frequent appearance in our weekly haul of rented videos; at first, we thought the title was funny and got a kick out of the fact that the mannequin on the front cover looked exactly like Tori Amos (she *really* does).[3] But—week after week, viewing after viewing—something happened in my brain: this film that I encountered initially from a place of smug condescension suddenly revealed itself to me as almost indescribably beautiful. It was an old tape, whose ample wear manifested most visibly in the worn-out packaging and the ground-in tracking lines on the VHS tape. And yet somehow this only added to its materiality, its richness, its tangible status as a near-sacred artifact. I loved the film for its aggressive color and wild *mise-en-scène*, its delirium and hysteria, its fearless determination to titillate. And most of all, I loved it for its undisguised *weirdness*.

This was the pre-internet era and I was far too suburban (and as a young woman, possibly, even further excluded because of the "boys' club" nature of horror fandom at the time) to be aware of—let alone involved in—zine cultures or other subcultural collectives or networks, however how informal, of fellow fans. I didn't know *Spasmo* was part of something bigger, and it wasn't until discovering more of these movies on Australia's SBS (Special Broadcasting Service) that I was able to give both a shape and a name to cult film as a definable category. In her compelling love-letter to Dario Argento's *Deep Red* (*Profondo Rosso*, 1976), fellow Australian film academic, writer and cult film fan Alexia Kannas writes about her experience as a teenager watching the regular Friday or Saturday night cult movies SBS would screen with her family, where she first discovered the films of Jesús Franco, Ngai Choi Lam and Camillo Mastrocinque. As Australia's international broadcaster whose content spanned everything from foreign language films to broadcasts of nation-specific news services, as Kannas notes, "In retrospect, I can see that SBS was a place for all kinds of otherness: a home for tastes, languages and cultures that fell outside of whatever dominated the mainstream."[4]

This is important to my story, too. It was through SBS's cult movie nights and my inadvertent indoctrination through my video store's informal status as an alternative film school that I developed my first tentative sense of what in critical terms has been coined "oppositional taste."[5] While I suspect that sex-and-violence heavy Italian genre films weren't exactly what French social theorist Pierre Bourdieu had precisely in mind when he wrote those famous words "taste classifies, and it classifies the classifier,"[6] the initial allegiance my video-store friends and I had was in large part to establish our identities through tastes that were notably different to that of our peers; it made us different, wilder, more interesting (or so we thought). We didn't have a grasp on the theory, sure, but we were beginning to define the things we liked by virtue of how they differentiated from what was dominating the mainstream, the multiplexes, the video store's "New Release" shelves. But something else was happening; it was here, recalling Woolf, that I felt those very first pangs on an almost urgent level as my eye demanded of my brain, "You are needed."

As will be explored elsewhere in this book, there have been a range of ways *giallo* cinema has been critically approached, all of which have undeniable merit and all of which will no doubt only continue to steadily grow as sites of rigorous academic and critical research. While I both acknowledge and engage with this growing field of work, this introduction seeks to underscore my personal experience of discovering *gialli* not as an attempt to diminish or speak over these other essential approaches, but rather to frame precisely where and why my are of interest has developed in the way this book will largely explore. Because so many of these films had English-language titles and Anglicized the directors' names, to begin with at least I confess I didn't even readily identify the films I now understand as collectively falling under a *giallo* umbrella as even being Italian—they were just ubiquitously "foreign," not Australian, not American, but sort of generically "European." More immediately, however, they were unified in my mind through the sensory experience of watching them; these films grabbed me by the throat and wouldn't let go, regardless—or perhaps precisely because—of how little orthodox "sense" they made. I was dazzled, provoked, and in a burgeoning critical way, fundamentally *activated*. I had been effectively radicalized not just merely by cinema, but by *cinema as art*. Simon Schama's following words in this sense scream loudly in my ear when I reflect upon my early experience of being seduced by *gialli*:

> The power of art is the power of unsettling surprise. Even when it seems imitative, art doesn't so much duplicate the familiarity of the seen world as replace it with a reality all of its own. Its mission, beyond the delivery of beauty is the disruption of the banal. Its operational procedure involves the retinal processing of information, but then throws a switch and generates an alternative kind of vision: a dramatized kind of seeing.[7]

As I will argue throughout this book, it is this power of art that not just permeates some of the most compelling and memorable *giallo* films, but in some of its most significant cases, effectively forms its central driving engine.

With their veneer of unabashed Eurosleaze, the Italian *giallo* film is revered in the hearts of horror film fans around the world. From Dario Argento's *The Bird with the Crystal Plumage* (*L'uccello dalle piume di cristallo*, 1970), *Four Flies on Grey Velvet* (*4 mosche di velluto grigio*, 1971), *Deep Red*, and *Tenebrae* (1982), to Mario Bava's *The Girl Who Knew Too Much* (*La ragazza che sapeva troppo*, 1963) and *Blood and Black Lace* (*Sei donne per l'assassino*, 1964), *gialli* are drenched with a lush perversity that circles almost ritualistically around spectacles of sex and death. And, as this book will explore, a perhaps surprising number of films in this category share a fascination with art, artistic representation and the creative impulse itself manifesting in a variety of ways.

As both a horror film fan, critic and academic, the *gialli* that have captivated me the most all share an interest on some level with the intersection of horror and art. Whether it's the gruesome mural of Saint

Sebastian that lies at the heart of Pupi Avati's *The House with Laughing Windows* (*La Casa dalle finestre che ridono*, 1976) or the conscious evocation of Francis Bacon and Salvador Dalí in Lucio Fulci's *A Lizard in a Woman's Skin* (*Una lucertola con la pelle di donna, 1971*), many of these films offer just as forceful and rigorous an interrogation of the status of art itself as the more highbrow "arthouse" cinema so often championed for its art historical engagement.

For cult movie fans, film critics and cinema academics alike, the *giallo* film is predominantly considered an auteurist domain, where films by the subgenre's big names—Mario and Lamberto Bava, Lucio Fulci, Aldo Lado, Sergio Martino, Umberto Lenzi, Luciano Ercoli, and Argento himself—have tended to garner the most attention. Translating literally to "yellow," *giallo* refers to the yellow covers of pulp crime novels released by publisher Mondadori during the late 1920s, placing the origins of *giallo* in the work of authors like Edgar Wallace and Agatha Christie. When moved to the screen, they take the form of what have since their '60s and '70s heyday become privileged objects of fascination and affection for cult audiences due in large part to their broadly defining consolidation of sex, horror and a near unrelenting dedication to a particularly excessive film style. *Giallo* cinema has little interest in naturalism and nuance; its obsessions—across many of its most intriguing films, as I argue across this book—lie in the nature, volatility and potential for a dark, perverse beauty within art itself. When we think of *gialli*, we think of their stereotypical iconography—the black leather gloves and the switchblade—even though not all films in the category feature them. As I will argue throughout this book, however, an engagement with art as a broader concept underscores a great many of these films in ways that have been largely unexplored.

My area of attention is not intended to be in combat with the more dominant critical modes that currently permeate *giallo* studies. Rather, this book hopes to fold elements of these into its consideration of how the broader category of "art" permeates *gialli*; how these films often engage with, explore, critique and at times even deconstruct the entire notion of creativity, artistic production and the art object itself. The widespread intertextuality that appears across the category—in particular reference to its engagement with painting, but also the other arts such as photography, fashion, theater, literature, sculpture and filmmaking itself—is a curious feature that permeates some of the greatest *gialli* ever produced.

While some of these case studies are certainly better known than others, all the films explored in this book are marked by a shared reflexivity regarding their *own* status as art: they explore, exploit and often simultaneously critique the very nature of art itself. "Great art has dreadful manners," Schama wrote. "Merciless and wily, the greatest paintings grab you in a headlock, rough up your composure and then proceed in short order to rearrange your sense of reality."[8] Whether the descriptor "great art" applies to *gialli* is up to you to decide for yourself, but what's less debatable is that at its best these films do *precisely* what Schama describes here. *Giallo* is art cinema with exquisitely dreadful manners.

ONE

Art, Cinema, Horror, Excess

"By the very fact that it is expressed both in space and in time," renowned French film critic Jean Mitry once wrote, "the cinema is connected to the arts which preceded it."[1] The point seems simple enough, but—far too often considered as manifesting in a vacuum dominated by notions of photographic and moving image technology rather than culture more broadly—it's been easy to narrow the pre-history of cinema down to the magic lantern, the zoetrope, the praxinoscope, the zoopraxiscope and the like, with references sometimes reaching back to Plato's allegory of the cave[2] for the truly adventurous. But there is a fascinating interdisciplinary arena where film and art history have collided with impressive results, sharing Mitry's broader historicization of cinema as part of the arts as a wider category. As Steven Allen and Laura Hubner noted, the visual arts and cinema have long influenced each other,[3] while Steven Jacobs emphasized early associations between the Lumiere brothers' films and to impressionism, their work in turn influencing modernist painters.[4]

Homing in on the use of recognizable works of art in film, in her foundational book *Cinema and Painting: How Art Is Used in Film* (1996), Angela Dalle Vacche broadly seeks to encourage film studies and art history to mutually engage, because in her words, "the advent of cinema has forever changed the meaning of the word 'art' and the meaning of the word 'history.'"[5] At stake here is what might be most easily conceived as long-established tensions between high and low culture, which Dalle Vacche notes significantly risks losing what cinema can offer art history. Cinema, she argues, blurs the lines between highbrow and pop culture, which makes cinema uniquely able "to challenge not just painting in isolation but rather the whole system of the arts, thus disclosing the possibility of new configurations, hierarchies, alliances and hostilities."[6] There are therefore two ways to approach the opportunities that the intersection of art and film offer, predicated on assumptions that "either film is plagued by a cultural inferiority complex and therefore obsessively cites other art forms, or it is self-confident enough to move beyond this state of dependency and arrive at the point where it can teach something new to art historians."[7]

As I will argue throughout this book, *gialli* are curiously positioned in relation to these supposed binaries. There is, on one hand, an undeniable excess to the use of art in many of these films (and in their style more broadly) that verges almost on glut, and are guilty on more than one occasion of brazenly using art in an attempt to elevate sex-and-violence heavy exploitation films to the level of something a little more highbrow. Importantly, this does not run in opposition to Mikel Koven's claim that as a form of vernacular cinema, "a traditional aesthetic consideration of the *giallo* alongside high-art filmmakers as Fellini, Bertolucci and Antonioni cannot work."[8] While he states emphatically, "the *giallo* is not high art,"[9] this is different to denying that the aspirations and references *to* high art are contained within these films. Rather, as I demonstrate throughout this book, some filmmakers have *engaged* with varying degrees of success with high art in this vernacular form. Which leads us to Dalle Vacche's second point; taking particular note of her choice of wording, there is in the very act itself of incorporating a known work of art in a film a kind of transgressive pleasure, which is the precise terrain of *giallo* cinema itself. "While some may feel that the film does not belong in the history of art, the fact is that filmmakers often use paintings to shape or enrich the meaning of their works," she says. "Thus the history of art is in film, even though, by evoking high art and creativity, rather than technology and mass culture, painting for the cinema constitutes a forbidden object of desire."[10]

While the relationship between painting and film has received some critical attention, it is marked predominantly by a preference for more highbrow, arthouse examples. Relevant to our interests, Dalle Vacche's book has a whole chapter on horror, comparing the F.W. Murnau's *Nosferatu: A Symphony of Horror* (1922) to German Romantic artist Caspar David Friedrich's paintings such as *The Monk by the Sea* (1809–10) and *The Cross in the Mountains* (1807–1808). Dalle Vacche concludes that these works are both "an accurate product of its time and, at the same time, an elusive statement about a whole epoch."[11] In her book *Incorporating Images: Film and the Rival Arts* (1995), Brigitte Peucker at first indicates a notable disinterest in popular horror, reducing slashers alongside "the pornographic film ... and the snuff movie" as nothing more than "marginal" texts.[12] Dominated by somewhat conservative taste hierarchies, then, Peucker in this book at least is clearly far more comfortable elevating her critical focus to more highbrow material such as those with the auteurist stamp of approval in her consideration of films by directors such as Éric Rohmer, Alfred Hitchcock, Rainer Werner Fassbinder, Peter Greenaway and Derek Jarman.[13]

There were 12 years between this earlier book and Peucker's later *The Material Image: Art and the Real in Film* (2007), where her anti-horror bias appears to have adjusted to reflect a broader postmodern embrace of lowbrow forms, resulting in a reference to George A. Romero's *Day of the Dead*[14] and even featuring a dedicated focus on Tobe Hooper's *The Texas Chain Saw Massacre* (1974) and his 1986 sequel, *The Texas Chainsaw Massacre 2*.[15] But while Peucker openly acknowledges the influence of Carol J. Clover's *Men Women and Chain Saws: Gender in the Modern Horror Film* (1992) in the creation of a critical environment where "no special dispensation should be required to take Hooper's film seriously,"[16] one gets the feeling she's still a little out of her comfort zone when branching out into non-sanctioned horror. In almost all other regards, she clings safely to the mainstream instead, turning her attention to films like *The Silence of the Lambs* (Jonathan Demme, 1991), *Hannibal* (Ridley Scott, 2001), *Red Dragon* (Brett Ratner, 2002) and (again) the films of Alfred Hitchcock.

This shift in Peucker's work—however tentative—reflects broader shifts within screen studies that occurred in the period between the release of her two books. The publication of Jeffrey Sconce's foundational essay "Trashing the Academy: Taste, Excess, and an Emerging Politics of Cinematic Style" in the same year *Incorporating Images* was published is worthy of note. Expanding upon Bourdieu's work on the political significance of taste, Sconce articulates a "gradual emergence of a growing and increasingly articulate cinematic subculture, one organized around what are the most critically disreputable films in cinematic history."[17] Sconce defines this category as "paracinema," which "includes entries from such seemingly disparate subgenres as 'badfilm,' splatterpunk, 'mondo' films, sword and sandal epics, Elvis flicks, government hygiene films, Japanese monster movies, beach-party musicals, and just about every other historical manifestation of exploitation cinema from juvenile delinquency documentaries to softcore pornography."[18] For Sconce, paracinema is "a particular reading protocol," less a generic categorization than "a counter-aesthetic turned subcultural sensibility devoted to all matter of cultural detritus."[19] Paracinema thus assigns value to films which have fallen well beyond the purview of supposed "legitimate film culture."[20]

In regard to the shift in Peucker's shifting focus (and visible comfort levels) in her art historical interrogation of horror cinema lies a manifestation of the very challenge that Sconce claimed paracinema issues to the field of screen studies more broadly:

> The study of trash cinema suggests a struggle over the task of cinema scholarship as a whole, especially in terms of defining the relationship between aesthetics and cultural criticism. Whether attacking traditional cultural markets and intellectual institutions as a fan, or attempting to bridge the two worlds as a student, the paracinematic audience presents in its often explicit opposition to the agendas of the academy a dispute over how to approach the cinema as much as a conflict over what cinema to approach.[21]

It is in this spirit that the following exploration of *giallo* has a far greater ambitions than merely "rescuing" supposedly trash texts by attempting to ascribe to them some kind of highbrow credibility. Rather, I argue that Italian *giallo* cinema (and horror in general) has *always* held the capacity for this type of analysis. When studied attentively, the case studies in this book demonstrate a highly developed and perhaps surprisingly complex visual and art historical dynamic at work throughout many of these films, both famous and lesser known examples alike.

Art Historians Go to the Movies

While significant figures, Peucker and Dalle Vacche are by no means the only important scholars who have worked at the interdisciplinary intersection of art history and screen studies. Even before the twentieth century, writers were drawing parallels between art and cinema, such as father of socialist realism himself Maxim Gorky in Russia. In 1896—the same year that Gorky wrote of cinema and art—an unidentified British art critic drew parallels (with somewhat unflattering intentions) between cinema and the Pre-Raphaelites.[22] Just as Ian Christie noted that many key works of early cinema were inspired by or simply directly reproduced famous works of art,[23] Lynda Nead suggests that many films of this period "seem to have had an ongoing fascination with the processes of art, images of the artist, and the setting of the studio," concluding that "film both perpetuates and parodies the myth of artistic creativity."[24] It does this because "at times the sole purpose of film seems to be to ridicule the figure of the artist and to demythologize the processes of artistic creativity,"[25] while at others it "appears committed to capturing and sustaining the alchemic myth, revealing and concealing the processes of artistic genius."[26] These are factors that come to the fore in my discussion of the figure of the painters in *gialli* in Part Three in regards to films including *A Quiet Place in the Country* (*Un tranquillo posto di campagna*, Elio Petri, 1968), *The Red Headed Corpse* (*La rossa dalla pelle che scott*a, Renzo Russo, 1972), and *Blood Delirium* (*Delirio de sangue*, Sergio Bergonzelli, 1988).

Early film critics and even artists themselves voiced strong ideas on the relationship between art and cinema, painting especially. Both Marcel Gromaire and Fernand Léger wrote about their feelings about cinema and how it related to art and creativity. For Gromaire, cinema was marked by its kinetic aspects, noting it "is an essentially modern art because it is mobile and restless," adding "thanks to the cinema, I saw a rose blossom. It was an extremely beautiful sight that our film producers ought to think deeply about."[27] In 1925, Léger discussed the role of cinema in the broader scheme of painting especially, noting "the future of cinema as painting lies in the attention it will draw to objects, to fragments, or to purely fantastic or imaginative inventions."[28] For Léger, cinema thus has the potential to "become the gigantic microscope of things never before seen or experienced," offering a significantly different creative potential much closer to artistic abstraction than what he saw at the time was an effective waste of a good artistic medium; "subject, literature and sentimentality are all negative qualities which weigh down the current cinema," positioning it closer to theater rather than the visual arts.[29] The latter for Léger is unambiguously where cinema's potential lies, wrapped up in its inherent nature as a moving image medium; "true cinema involves the image of the object which is totally unfamiliar to our eyes and which is in itself moving."[30]

Some years later, co-founder of *Cahiers du cinéma* André Bazin published two early essays in the influential French film magazine: "About Van Gogh. Space in Painting and Cinema" (published April 15, 1949) and "Painting Through a Keyhole" (published January 4, 1952).[31] In 1959, he reworked the later in another version called simply "Painting and Cinema."[32] Reflecting on the nature of the picture frame itself, Bazin notes how it provides a tangible border between the work of art and the world of beyond it, allowing for art to be contained, with no physical opportunity for representation and reality to blur; the borderless painting destabilizes the controlled space of the artwork itself. For Bazin, film works in a significantly different manner because "the outer edges of the screen are not, as the technical jargon would seem to imply, the frame of the film image. They are the edges of a piece of masking that shows only a portion of reality."[33] So while on one hand, while "the picture frame polarizes space inwards," in the case of cinema "what the screen shows us seems to be part of something prolonged indefinitely into the universe. A frame is centripetal, the screen centrifugal."[34] Consequently, "thanks to the cinema and to the psychological properties of the screen, what is symbolic and abstract takes on the solid reality of a piece of ore."[35] Rather than being in tension with other artforms, then, Bazin argues that "the cinema not only far from compromising or destroying the true nature of another art, is, on the contrary, in the process of saving it, of bringing it to general attention."[36]

In the years since, a range of critical work further examining and expanding this earlier criticism has been steadily produced, often focusing on specific aspects, cultural contexts or artforms. These include (but are not limited to) Dudley Andrews' 1997 edited collection *The Image in Dispute: Art and Cinema in the Age of Photography* that focuses on the place of images in both the nineteenth and twentieth centuries across still photography, cinema and video.[37] Region-specific books such as Linda C. Ehrlich and David Desser's 1994 edited collection *Cinematic Landscapes: Observations on the Visual Arts and Cinema of China and Japan*[38] are worthy of note, as is John A. Walker's book *Art and Artists on Screen* where—with particular relevance to the subject of interest of this book—he states, "works of art appearing on cinema and television screens are ... 'representations of representations.'"[39] As noted in Chapter Seven, portraiture in film has also been addressed, as in Steven Jacobs and Lisa Colpaert's *The Dark Galleries: A Museum Guide to Painted Portraits in Film Noir, Gothic Melodrama, and Ghost Stories of the 1940s and 1950s.*[40]

Susan Felleman's *Art and the Cinematic Imagination* (2006) combines strong art historical and screen studies perspectives and has thus been a major addition to this particular field. For Felleman, "When a film undertakes the representation of 'art' as a theme or engages with an artwork as motif it is, whatever else it is doing, also more or less openly and more or less knowingly entering into a contemplation of its own nature and at some level positing its own unwritten theory of cinema as art."[41] She continues, "Narrative films, then, can reveal much about their individual and collective undertaking and their sense of their own and their medium's origins through the incorporation or figuration of art."[42] As I will elaborate further in the many case studies that make up the bulk of this book, this sense of knowingness is fundamental not just to films that employ art as a central theme or motif, as Felleman notes, but in *gialli* to a point where it could be considered a broad signature of what are perhaps a surprisingly high number of films in the category.

Returning to the relationship between horror, cinema, and art more specifically, however, David Soren's now long out-of-print 1977 book *The Rise and Fall of the Horror Film: An Art Historical Approach to Fantasy Cinema* offers a particularly fascinating exploration of the intersection of these three areas, as demonstrated in its very title. Perhaps marking the tonal norm in scholarly writing at the time it was written—not too far, perhaps, from certain areas in the academy today, or simply just evidence of generational get-off-my-lawnism—Soren's book is framed very much as a requiem for horror which (except for some notable and frankly surprising exceptions) he broadly considers a genre in decline. He begins his books with almost undisguised despair as he shares an anecdote on seeing *Carrie* in a Missouri cinema in 1976:

> What a sad state of affairs it was when a fine director such as Brian De Palma could produce such senseless stomach-churning violence ... has the horror film become nothing more than a genre used to titillate and then brutalize the emotions? How did this all come to pass?⁴³

Similarly rejecting William Friedkin's *The Exorcist* (1973) as nothing more than "bed-shaking putrescence-spitting nonsense,"⁴⁴ he suggests that what unites the far superior horror films of yore (and the few worthy of his admiration at the time of the book's publication) is an awareness of their connection to art history more broadly. Soren's book then is fundamentally issued as a warning, stating on the first page no less that it is "essential that future filmmakers and critics realize the tremendous debt that the horror film owes to the history of art."⁴⁵

Without necessarily joining in with Soren's "kids these days" festival of pessimism, he makes a good basic point, both for filmmakers and critics alike. Horror cinema has an extraordinarily long and dense connection to art history (and *giallo* provides a bite-size area of deeper analysis to demonstrate precisely this point). Intriguingly, without even using the word *"giallo,"* Soren himself seems to agree. Despite his undisguised disillusionment with films like *Carrie* and *The Exorcist*, Soren is on the frontlines of the Dario Argento cheer squad, exclaiming, "in this

Director Dario Argento attends the press conference at the 21st International Moscow Film Festival, July 26, 1999 (Denis Makarenko, Shutterstock.com).

world of disgusting cinema," Argento is nothing less than an "authentic poet ... of violence" and "the real genius of paranoia."[46] Long before writers like Alan Jones or Maitland McDonagh became significant critical voices renowned for banging the drum for Argento's work, it seems a slightly irritable art historian in Missouri was already publishing the kind of praise that a decade later would permeate English-language cult film and horror zines, books and magazines. Says Soren:

> Argento's world is plunging into the abyss, full of evil and madness.... Unlike contemporary directors of violent films, Argento uses his camera and visual surroundings to give a total universe of fear. The camera restlessly prowls, jumps and dates like a diabolic menace loosed in the darkness of the city, constantly watching us.[47]

Crucial to the broader arguments of both Soren's book and mine here, he draws a distinct line between art historical influences and the mechanics of Argento's craft, noting that in *Four Flies on Grey Velvet* (*4 mosche di velluto grigio*, 1971) in particular, "Like Munch, Argento has learned not just to film violence but to use psychic acoustics to frighten and upset us."[48] As I will examine throughout this book, the broader engagement with art history by Argento's fellow *giallo* filmmakers is demonstrably much deeper than has been broadly been acknowledged.

Art and Horror Cinema

Horror films love art. Horror filmmakers love art. Think of that most almost clichéd basic haunted house scenario where the cut-out eyes of a painting act as peepholes, where real, seemingly disembodied eyes shift back-and-forth ominously from behind the artwork. A classic of the Old Dark House trope, this motif is far from rare across horror, so ubiquitous as to become as much a comedy reference point as much as anything intended to be genuinely scary. From *Scooby Doo* to Elliott Nugent's *The Cat and the Canary* from 1939, Samuel Gallu's *Theatre of Death* from 1967 with Christopher Lee to films like Del Tenney's *The Curse of the Living Corpse* (1964) or Fred Walton's 1986 slasher *April Fools' Day*, the portrait-with-the-moving eyes is surely as much a part of horror as Dracula turning into a bat or a hungry zombie slurring "brainssssss."

In literature we only need to look at short stories like Nikolai Gogol's "The Portrait" (1835), Edgar Allan Poe's "The Oval Portrait" (1842), H.P. Lovecraft's "Pickman's Model" (1927), or Sheridan Le Fanu's 1839 novel "Strange Event in the Life of Schalcken the Painter" to find pre-cinematic instances of the intersection of art and horror. Early cinema shared this fascination, as demonstrated in examples such as famous French filmmaker Abel Gance's now sadly lost *The Mask of Horror* (*Le masque d'horreur*, 1912),[49] *Genuine* (Robert Wiene, 1929) or Richard Oswald's *Unheimliche Gestichten* (1919) starring horror icon Conrad Veidt, which Oswald later remade again in 1932. It's an understatement to say that a fascination with art and artists (paintings especially) have permeated horror film history, with even the merest scratching of the surface revealing titles such as Roger Corman's *A Bucket of Blood* (1959), *Color Me Blood Red* (Herschell Gordon Lewis, 1965), Jack Hill and Stephanie Rothman's *Blood Bath* (1966), *Messiah of Evil* (Willard Huyck and Gloria Katz, 1973), George Barry's *Death Bed: The Bed That Eats* (1977) Abel Ferrara's *Driller Killer* (1979), and—one of the best of the category–Wendy Toye's segment "The Picture" in the 1955 British anthology *Three Cases of Murder* (whose other segments include one directed by an uncredited Orson Welles). While I will speak to this broader tendency more specifically in my Conclusion, it is worth noting that the utilization of artworks to create a sense of unease or unsettling disorientation is, notably, hardly unique to horror either; just think of the famous portraits that are so pivotal to Otto Preminger's *Laura* (1944) and Alfred Hitchcock's *Vertigo* (1958), or to William Dieterle's classic supernatural romance *Portrait of Jennie* (1948).

The collision of art and the supernatural is not film specific—as its very title indicates, it formed the basis for Rod Serling's television series *Night Gallery* (1969–1973)—and it is a notably global phenomenon. While again far too many examples exist to provide an exhaustive list, to give an indication of the scope we may wish to consider the Czech film *The Portrait* (*Podobizna*, Jirí Slavícek, 1948), *Zirneklis* (Vasili Mass, 1992) from Latvia, *Kadaicha* (James Bogle, 1988) from Australia, Mexican examples such as *Mary, Mary, Bloody Mary* (Juan López Moctezuma, 1975) and *One Minute Before Death* (Rogelio A. González, 1972), and from Japan, films including but not limited to *Guinea Pig: Mermaid in a Manhole* (Hideshi Hino, 1988), *Sweet Home* (Kiyoshi Kurosawa, 1989) and *Tomie: Re-birth* (Takashi Shimizu, 2001). More recent are films such as *The Devil's Candy* (Sean Byrne, 2015), *The Conjuring 2* (James Wan, 2016), *The Love Witch* (Anna Biller, 2016), *Velvet Buzzsaw* (Dan Gilroy, 2019), and *Bliss* (Joe Begos, 2019). Adam Egypt Mortimer's *Daniel Isn't Real* (2019) literally repaints a small detail onto the "Hell" panel of Hieronymus Bosch's iconic triptych *The Garden of Earthly Delights* (1490–1510), while Pieter Bruegel the Elder's macabre painting *The Triumph of Death* (1562) is an important reference point in *It Comes at Night* (Trey Edward Shults, 2017).

This of course doesn't take into account horror films that were more broadly influenced by great works of art; amongst many examples we discover that aspects of Andy Muschietti's *It* (2017) were inspired by his childhood fears of the work of Amedeo Modigliani,[50] William Hogarth's work was a direct influence on Mark Robson's Val Lewton-produced *Bedlam* (1946), William Friedkin's *The Exorcist* pays homage to René Magritte's *The Empire of Lights* (1953–1954), the house in Alfred Hitchcock's *Psycho* (1960) was inspired in its design by Edward Hopper's *House by the Railroad* (1925), the famous mask from the *Scream* franchise was a direct reference to Edvard Munch's *The Scream* (1893), and Robert Eggers has noted that the works of Francisco Goya were "definitely a touchstone" for his debut feature film *The Witch* (2015).[51] Guillermo Del Toro too has frequently discussed the influence of Goya on his films,[52] while critics have made their own art historical connections between certain horror films and specific artworks; David Soren has suggested that Munch's *Evening on Karl Johan Street* (1892) was a direct influence on the character design of Cesar in Robert Wiene's *The Cabinet of Dr. Caligari* (1920)[53]—in fact, he notes the influence of Munch on German cinema more generally.[54] Christopher Frayling has noted not just an art historical influence on the poster design for classical horror, but that it's legacy can be felt across the genre more broadly. Be it Goya's influence on Jack Pierce's iconic make-up design for Boris Karloff in James Whale's *Frankenstein* (1931), Arnold Böcklin's painting *Isle of the Dead* (1880–1901) on the design of Skull Island in *King Kong* (Merian C. Cooper and Ernest B. Schoedsack, 1933) to the pervasive influence of artists such as Edvard Munch and Caspar David Friedrich, for Frayling, the influence of Northern European art from the eighteenth and nineteenth centuries was largely "carried by émigré production designers and art directors."[55] In the case of surrealism, Adam Lowenstein has argued that a range of "horror-associated directors"—from David Cronenberg to Dario Argento, Jan Švankmajer to Marina de Van, David Lynch to Arturo Ripstein—have "made major contributions to the horror-surrealism imaginary, no matter what their stated loyalty toward or distance from the original surrealists may be."[56] Despite the broad lack of critical interrogation, argues Lowenstein, surrealism and horror cinema are notably interconnected, sharing "a long history of mutual admiration and reciprocal interest."[57]

There is obviously a key title missing from this overview thus far. Oscar Wilde's famous Gothic novel *The Picture of Dorian Gray* was first published in 1890, shocking audiences and critics at the time[58] and being made—and remade and remade again—across cinema history. The first film adaptation was the Danish film *Dorian Grays Portræt* (Axel Strøm, 1910), followed by a seemingly never-ending stream of various screen reimaginings under Wilde's original title (or shortenings of it) including those by Phillips Smalley in 1913, Eugene Moore in 1915, Vsevolod Meyerhold and Mikhail Doronin in 1916, Richard Oswald in 1917, Alfréd Deésy in 1918, Albert Lewin in 1945, two separate works by Charles Jarrott and Paul Bogart (both in 1961), Glen Jordan in 1973, John Gorrie in 1976, Pierre Boutron in 1977, David Rosenbaum in 2004, Duncan Roy in 2006, Jon Cunningham in 2007, Jonathan Courtemanche in 2009, and Oliver Parker in 2009, with Tony Maylam's *The Sins of Dorian Gray* in 1983 and Allan A. Goldstein's *Pact with the Devil* in 2004. Some of the more intriguing variations include Ulrike Ottinger's *The Image of Dorian Gray in the Yellow Press* (*Dorian Gray im Spiegel der Boulevardpresse*, 1984) and more adult-oriented fare such as Jesús Franco's *Doriana Gray* (1976) and Armand Western's *Take Off* (1978). Massimo Dallamano also adapted *Dorian Gray* in 1970, one of the many films that director made which featured paintings in significant ways alongside *The Night Child* (*Il medaglione insanguinato*, 1975) and *Venus in Furs* (*Venere in pelliccia*, 1969). Dallamano was no stranger to *giallo* either, with films such as *What Have They Done to Solange?* (*Cosa Avete Fatto a Solange?*, 1971) *and What Have They Done to Your Daughters?* (*La polizia chiede aiuto*, 1974).

But the influence of *The Picture Dorian Gray* on the haunted painting trope on horror cinema cannot be undervalued. Wilde's story follows its

Oscar Wilde, by Napoleon Sarony (1821–1896), New York, 1882. Albumen silver print (open access, Metropolitan Museum of Art, www.metmuseum.org, Gilman Collection).

The many faces of actor Helmut Berger, in the title role of Dorian Gray (*Il dio chiamato Dorian*, Massimo Dallamano, 1970).

eponymous protagonist, who has the portrait of the title painted by an artist called Basil Hallward who is overwhelmed by Gray's physical attractiveness. Through the artist, Dorian enters the indulgent, opulent art scene where beauty and sensory experience are privileged. Faced with the reality that the beauty that has bought him such attention is necessarily fleeting due to the reality of aging, he sells his soul so that it is the painting instead of he that will show the wear of time. The aging of the portrait accelerates with Dorian's increasingly immoral behavior but watching his portrait age is traumatic in itself for the ageless young man. Failing to return the portrait to its original beauty, he attempts to destroy the painting, inadvertently killing himself while the representation of him in the painting returns to the age Dorian was when it was originally painted.

While it certainly didn't invent the "haunted painting" trope, when it comes to a broader exploration of the relationship between art history and horror cinema as we move towards *giallo*, the importance of *The Picture of Dorian Gray* is fundamental. As Suzanne Raitt so eloquently notes, what is essential to Wilde's tale (and, arguably, the many films that it inspired) is how it ties artistic representation to the mortality of the physical body. "The picture substitutes for Dorian's mortal body so that the biology of aging is expressed not in the man but in the image," she says. "The immortality of art—its arrest of time and change—is transferred to the flesh that in normal circumstances would droop and wither as the body made its inexorable way toward death."[59] *The Picture of Dorian Gray* speaks of a range of fears surrounding the body and the supernatural; from the natural process of aging itself and the horror that provokes in someone as vain as Dorian, through to its shocking ending, where an act of violence against the painting results in an act of fatal violence against the person inflicting it. The work of art is less a mirror, then, as a portal where Dorian's own mortality and propensity to aging can be physically influenced, despite the absence of any explanation of how this is possible, disobeying as it does the natural order of things.

That violence and the artistic impulse may intersect forms the subject of Thomas de Quincey's famous 1827 essay "On Murder Considered as One of the Fine Arts,"[60] a satirical text supposedly delivered in a fictional public speech that had an enormous influence on writers spanning from GK Chesterton to George Orwell.[61] In the case of horror and art more broadly, as Matthew Collings pithily observed, "modern art is full of screams," citing everything from Munch's *The Scream*, "Francis Bacon's screaming popes [and] the screaming horse in Picasso's *Guernica*."[62] For Gillian McIver, art history is simply riddled with scenes of horror, her most fascinating analysis focusing on body horror especially which in relation to the ubiquity of graphic violence in *giallo* is of particular relevance. From the various paintings of the beheaded John the Baptist such as Italian Renaissance painter Andrea Solari's *Salome with the Head of Saint John the Baptist* (1507–1509) and paintings including Artemisia Gentileschi's *Judith Slaying Holofernes* (c. 1620) and Caravaggio's *The Sacrifice of Isaac* (1603), there is no lack of violence and horror in Italian art. In Western art more broadly, we need look only towards crucifixion scenes by artists such as German Renaissance painter Matthias Grünewald for evidence of this,[63] but a fascination with body horror also dominates "the bleeding dead game and slabs of meat of sixteenth- and seventeenth-century Flemish still life, and the highly symbolic skulls in *vanitas* paintings."[64] Crucially, for McIver "In both cases, the pictures were meant to remind the viewer of their own mortality, and that all the things of the earthly world are ultimately in vain."[65] She continues, "Only God separates us from the butchered pheasant. In the same way, body horror films also remind us of our own vulnerability of the flesh."[66] McIver's connecting body horror from an art historical perspective to contemporary horror film is a useful one for my focus on the hardly gore-shy *giallo* film:

> Body horror is based on deep-seated fear of the disfigurement and despoliation of the living body, and of the decomposition of the dead body. It reminds us of our mortality, frailty and vulnerability.... Body horror in art and cinema is based on the visual representation of this violence toward the body; to varying degrees, the shock in witnessing the desecration of the living or the dead.[67]

In the case of contemporary horror cinema, we need look no further than Henry S. Miller's *Animorph* (2007) for a succinct demonstration of precisely this. Starring Willem Dafoe as a police detective struggling with significant personal issues, he is drawn into a murder investigation surrounding horrendous crimes committed by an art history obsessed killer. Creating elaborately staged scenarios where his victims are placed to create macabre artworks, through camera obscura projection and anamorphic techniques (the latter from where the film gets its title) the final moments reveal a shocking *tableau vivant* of Francis Bacon's 1953 painting *Study after Velázquez's Portrait of Pope Innocent X*. This same artwork will be discussed further in Chapter Four in my discussion of Lucio Fulci's *Lizard in a Woman's Skin* (*Una lucertola con la pelle di donna*, 1971).

As *Animorph* and many of the horror films mentioned previously indicate, we can see precisely how reflexivity comes into play when horror films (indeed, any films) include recognizable works of art. For Susan Fellemen:

> Mainstream—that is feature-length, commercial, narrative—films that foreground art, as well as most that background it, can induce a rather curious tension, as the reflexive presence of art threatens the seductive flow of the fictional world within the film with a spasm of viewer self-consciousness. This is why we refer to such works as reflexive: it is as though a mirror has been held up to the beholder. The work of art *en abyme* (shown in depth) reminds the viewer that she is viewing.[68]

As Leon Hunt observed in 1992, the world of the *giallo* film is "intensely modern/postmodern,"[69] and there is something distinctly modernist and postmodernist[70] to this mode of artistic reflexivity. As Robert Stam has noted, reflexivity is "a key term in both modernism and postmodernism," in the former because "modernist artists challenge the taken-for-granted solidity of the world."[71] The way that texts can relate to other texts has been of critical interest as early as Aristotle,[72] and today is broadly understood through the term "intertextuality."[73] Coined by Julia Kristeva in 1969 through her encounters with the work of Mikhail Bakhtin,[74] the term is now often broadly employed beyond Kristeva's original specific theoretical framework.[75] For Mieke Bal, "intertextuality refers to the readymade quality of signs, that quality that the maker of images finds in earlier images produced by a culture." Positioning it in a broader art historical context, Bal notes "the concept may seem close to that of iconographic precedent,"[76] but she notes significant distinctions but "iconography seems to be nothing other than the examination of the reuse of earlier forms, patterns, figures."[77] The difference, she states, is crucial; "intertextuality—the specific quotation that is also the object of iconography is ... a particular instance of the more general practice of interdiscursivity, the mixture of various different visual and discursive modes."[78]

Using this critical background to turn more closely towards art and *giallo* cinema, Marcia Landy's focus on intertextuality in relation to the work of Dario Argento is of interest:

> Through the uses of art forms such as children's songs, poems and paintings (*Profondo rosso*, *La sindrome di Stendhal* and *Non ho sonno*), opera (*Opera* and *Il fantasma dell'opera/The Phantom of the Opera*), dance (*Suspiria* and *Non ho sonno*), literature (*Tenebrae*), architecture (the Three Mothers trilogy of *Suspiria*, *Inferno* and *La terza madre*), and endlessly manufactured dream landscapes, Argento's films explore the horrific through invoking the cinematic as a medium that has the potential to engulf other media, even television.[79]

She continues:

> Intertextual references animate the images of perverse sexuality and extreme violence, and disrupt any sense of continuous internal space, interrupting the flow of the narrative reminiscent of Buñuellian optics that are unstable and threatening. The viewer moves between surface and depth, works of classical and popular art that lose their shapes, their borders, the boundaries between the real and the imaginary, the subjective and objective, and, like the characters, becomes prey to the terrors of a constantly altering modern and visible world.[80]

These intertextual references to art as a broader field are not just specific to Argento but, as I will argue throughout this book, are a defining feature of what may be perhaps a surprising number of *gialli*.

Horror Vacui: Gialli *and the Love of Excess*

If the aesthetic regime that dominates *giallo* film can be described by any one single word, surely it is surely that of excess. In relation to Dario Argento's work specifically, McDonagh has suggested that

> ...the seductiveness of these films lies ultimately in the realm of their excess: the spatial and temporal warping, the curious disjunction between soundtrack and image ... the violently saturated colour palette, the obsessive examination of surfaces ... the full panoply of non-narrative detail that generates the overwhelming sense of weirdness evoked by Argento's work.[81]

This "weirdness" and excess, I would suggest, bleeds across *gialli* well beyond Argento's filmography. Speaking of *gialli* more broadly, Stephen Thrower has noted their "baroque extremes, frequently bordering on the ridiculous,"[82] while Barry Forshaw identifies a predominant sense of "delirious visual invention."[83] Even beyond the stylistic excesses, as Kannas notes even the lives of the characters that riddle *gialli* are marked by a sense of too-much-ness, "stacked with all the accoutrements of modernity and privilege" that collectively "deliver a sense of vacuous excess."[84] In her pioneering work on cinematic excess, Kristin Thompson argues that excess lies in opposition to meaning; excess is, in short, the "flab" that lies outside the real "meat" of the text. Cinematic excess are those elements which "are not contained by its unifying forces"[85]; excess disrupts and distracts from narrative logic and the coherence of a film as a whole. Crucially, from this perspective, excess pulls the audience out of the story-world and "defamiliarizes"[86] viewers. That which we are assumed to accept as a logical and coherent part of the film as a whole is through cinematic excess rendered incongruous, disorienting, or sometimes just outright weird.

But in the case of *gialli*, excess is often (although not always) what lures fans to these in the first place; its audacious disregard for what in more mainstream or classical films is the sanctity of plot and character. We're here for the glitter, the razzle-dazzle, as transgressive and as dirty as it can get. Homing in on the centrality of the set piece, Koven suggests they "structure the *giallo* as a cinematic poem, keying the spectator to interpret this free indirect subject with particular intensity."[87] He continues, "Within these set pieces we are continually distracted by their material construction.... But perhaps that is the point of them in the first place."[88] Reflecting on Pier Paolo Pasolini's influential essay "The Cinema of Poetry" (1965),[89] Koven notes that "for Pasolini, when stylistic liberties rupture the narrative prose and we are asked instead to contemplate the formal means of the image's construction, and when that rupture derives from a character's subjectivity thereby fusing the character's subjectivity with the mechanical reproduction of the camera itself, we are invited, if not *required*, to question the very poetics that are presented to us" (italics in original).[90] For Koven, it is the very excesses of *giallo* that align it with Pasolini's notion of the "cinema of poetry."[91] Stepping away from rigid definitions linked to an inflexible checklist of iconographic mise-en-scène, then—the switchblade, the black leather gloves, etcetera—I very much understand and recognize *gialli* as a distinct kind of cinematic mood poem marked by a particularly excessive display of core fascinations such as paranoia, insanity, sexual transgression, duplicity and doubling, riddles, and a kind of corrupted psychological insularity and internalized chaos that often marks the innocent as much (if not more) than the guilty. The ambivalence that permeates *gialli* in terms of the orthodox centrality of plot, character, etcetera, is one of the ways that they display what Koven has suggested is a broader "ambivalence to modernity."[92]

When Ian Olney notes that in *giallo* cinema "story often takes a backseat to style,"[93] in the case of many films he is frankly being polite. Forshaw nails this with his observation that often in these films, "what mostly serves for plotting is a tortuous stitching together of disparate narrative elements to provide integument for the blood-drenched set pieces."[94] But, as he suggests, this is perhaps a glass-half-full or glass-half-empty scenario; "if ... quality writing is in shorter supply ... the exuberant staging, sanguinary inventiveness and constant visual flourishes provide more than sufficient frissons."[95] This is the precise kind of excess *giallo* films not just offer but extend as their primary drawcard, and the reflexive referencing of art, artworks and artistic production that permeates the category—while at times certainly feeding into plot, characterization and/or narrative—are first and foremost there to add to the ubiquitous over-the-top, in-your-face glut of style that marks *gialli* at their best. Returning to Sconce's "Trashing the Academy" essay, he offers an alternative way of conceiving excess in relation to *gialli* and other paracinematic texts. For Sconce, "paracinema hinges on an aesthetic of excess, and ... this paracinematic interest in excess represents an explicitly political challenge to reigning aesthete discourses in the academy."[96] While at its best, aesthetic excess in more highbrow, culturally sanctioned films might bring an impression of "artistic bravado"[97] that complements the film as a unified whole, in paracinematic texts like *gialli* this excess sits in a notably distinct relationship to the film's diegesis. Instead, it is much closer to what Sconce suggests are the "profilmic and extratextual aspects of the filmic object itself."[98] None of these things are necessarily essential to the plot of a film, but are, as any *giallo* fan will tell you, essential to the experience of watching *gialli* and the pleasures they afford. Like paracinema more generally, these pleasures are spawned from "an excess that often manifests itself in a film's failure to conform to historically delimited codes of verisimilitude," bringing "attention to the text as a cultural and sociological document" and therefore collapsing "the boundaries of the diegesis into profilmic and extratextual realms."[99] For Sconce, this is fundamental to how the "reading protocols" of paracinema can be distinguished from those of traditional screen studies; rather than understanding excess in terms of themes and narrative, for instance, in *gialli*, what is of greater value is how "attention to excess seeks to push the viewer beyond the formal boundaries of the text."[100]

This all leads me towards a key art history term, that of *horror vacui*. Translating from Latin simply as the "fear of emptiness,"[101] it by no means has been quarantined to art history; in one if the earliest manifestations of the idea, for example, Aristotle used it in a more scientific context.[102] From an art and design perspective, *horror vacui* has been defined as "a tendency to favor filling blank spaces with objects and elements over leaving spaces blank or empty," pertaining to "a style of art and design that leaves no empty spaces."[103] It has also been positioned as diametrically opposed to minimalism,[104] and can thus, in this sense, be thought of instead as "maximalism," defined as a "more is more" approach.[105] Art historian E.H. Gombrich defines the term as "the urge which drives the decorator to go on filling any resultant void," yet in rather more positive language, he suggests rephrasing this notion as "*amor infiniti*, the love of the infinite,"[106] which speaks less of a lack of restraint as it does an embrace of the potential of creative space.

Across art history, there are a range of diverse works where *horror vacui* has been applied as a critical term. Often, these are not complimentary; a 1945 anonymous review of an Jackson Pollock exhibition that included *The Night Dancer* (1944) and *There Were Seven in Eight* (1943) leads to the accusation that "the artist suffers from a horror vacui; scarcely an inch of background is left vacant, and the total effect is labored rather than spontaneous."[107] Similarly, Erwin Panofsky accuses Titian's *Flaying of Marsyas* (1570–1576) of demonstrating "gratuitous brutality" where "no square inch is vacant."[108] The term has also been applied to the work or particular artworks by artists including Henri Rousseau,[109] Albrecht Dürer,[110] William Morris,[111] Gustav Klimt,[112] and Pieter Bruegel,[113] and, more recently, Willem de Kooning's,[114] Adolf Wölfli,[115] Thomas Hirschhorn,[116] and cartoonists such as Robert Crumb and S. Clay Wilson.[117] The term has even moved beyond the visual realm and been employed in critical writing about the work of British composer Brian Ferneyhough,[118] a central figure in the New Complexity movement which began in the 1980s.

As key figures in the underground comix movement, the inclusion of both Crumb and Wilson is useful in relation to the centrality of *horror vacui* to supposedly lowbrow art.[119] In terms of the lowbrow, exploitative assumptions about *gialli*, *horror vacui* proves a useful parallel to its particular mode of stylistic excess. Taste as a kind of crude glut is an association that spans well beyond cinema; as William Lidwell, Kritina Holden and Jill Butler observe, recent research on the reception of window marketing displays suggests "a general inverse relationship between *horror vacui* and value perception"; that is, "as *horror vacui* increases, perceived value decreases."[120] This, they suggest, can be seen amongst other things as a manifestation of the old "less is more" cliché.[121] In a key study on Australian exploitation cinema, Carol Laseur defined cinematic excess of this sort of paracinema as being defined by an intrinsic "moreness,"[122] a term that evokes distinct associations with *horror vacui* from this perspective. And, recalling Kristin Thompson's definition of cinematic excess as those elements that "are not contained by [a film's] ... unifying forces"[123]; this too finds significant parallels in Paul C. Castagno's suggestion that *horror vacui* divides "the image into separate nonintegrated parts; that is, each bunched group is isolated as a part rather than harmonized toward a unified whole."[124]

When it comes to horror specifically, Braxton Soderman's examination of horror videogames and *horror vacui* is useful in regard to how I utilize the term in relation to excess and *giallo* cinema. The "horror" of *horror vacui*, for Soderman, stems from "the terror of the void, of empty space ... the vacuum that would deny nature its plenitude."[125] In the context of aesthetics, it brings there is therefore something overwhelming, even suffocating, in its glut as it "marks the over-marking of visual space, excessive decoration that threatens to overwhelm what is being decorated, the stuffing of gaps and caesura with further representation because of the fear to let emptiness reside."[126] This can provoke the sensory experience of horror, as genre seeks to provoke responses such as "anxiety, repulsion, and the bristling and shivering of skin."[127] From the painstaking minutiae of the macabre interior design at the heart of Tobe Hooper's *The Texas Chain Saw Massacre* (1974) to the climactic orgy in Brian Yuzna's *Society* (1989) to the often-microscopic fascination with viscera that mark body horror cinema as a wider subgenre, there are surely many notable instances where this sensory experience of too-muchness, of overwhelming, suffocating excess, provokes a similar sensory response, resultant of, if you will, the *horror vacui* of horror itself.

As Lindsay Hallam has compellingly argued, this sensory aspect is the most immediate feature of *giallo*. "What is most striking about these films," she says, "is how they present these images of shocking violence in a way that is deeply felt by the spectator, evoking a strong bodily response."[128] Hallam continues, "The impact of these films is experienced immediately, before we subject them to intellectual analysis and place them within a framework where images are assigned political meaning."[129] In *giallo* cinema, while certainly not lacking in moments of excessive blood and guts, excessive nudity, etcetera, it is also just as much frequently marked by an excess of *style*. Through color, music, *mise-en-scène* and even performance styles, these films too are marked by a sense of too-muchness, an excess we can loosely align with this tradition of *horror vacui*. Riffing on this art historical term allows us to situate the often-brazen excesses of *giallo* film in a different way than film studies has traditionally suggested. Through paracinema and *horror vacui* we can rethink excess in *giallo* in a fundamental way, not in an attempt to elevate it from its often-assumed low brow status, but rather to open up further ways of thinking about *giallo* cinema and its representational encounters with painting, art, artists and artistic production more broadly.

Two

Giallo
Italy and Beyond

Despite its close association with a genre of Italian cinema that flourished in the late 1960s and 1970s, Mondadori's pulp literary *gialli* were first published in Milan in 1929. As Anne Billson points out in her essential 2013 article on these films, the origins of *giallo* can be traced in a manner similar to that of *film noir*, which found its origins in the French crime publishing imprint *Série Noire*.[1] With their eponymous yellow (*giallo*) covers, these cheap Mondadori paperbacks were often translations of popular English-language works by authors such as prolific British writer Edgar Wallace, whose work inspired Mario Camerini's 1934 film, simply titled *Giallo*. Adapted to the screen from a 1928 Wallace-penned play called *The Man Who Changed His Name*, Camerini's *Giallo* is not quite the kind of film we perhaps think of when we hear of its title today—for starters, it stands in striking contrast with Dario Argento's 2009 of the same name, where Adrien Brody tracks down a jaundiced serial killer whose medical condition gives his skin a yellow ("*giallo*") hue.

Camerini's *Giallo* follows Russian-Italian actor Assia Noris as the film's protagonist, Henriette. She is a bored, spoilt woman with an insatiable appetite for exactly these cheap crime novels. Swept off her feet by a handsome interloper, she is willingly seduced both romantically and by the idea that her excruciatingly dull husband Giorgio (Sandro Ruffini) is in fact a super-villain with a double life, laying low in Italy as he is a wanted man in Canada and now on the run. Unlike the tonal expectations we might bring to a film called *Giallo* today, Camerini's film is much closer to a screwball comedy with a crime twist than it is an excessive sex-and-violence fuelled murder mystery. But the film is a useful one to consider in relation to my fascination in this book on how *giallo* cinema builds major spectacles and set pieces around the relationship between art and reality, and the inclusion of artworks, artists and/or artistic production more broadly.

The film begins on a train at night as two unnamed lovers plan their escape from the woman's husband, who has briefly left them alone. They have only just met, but they are smitten, waxing lyrical about both their great mutual passion and the giant moon that shines above them as they strategize. As our entry point into the film, we have no reason to doubt the simplicity of the scenario, and on a very basic level, all the ingredients are here from which a wholly functional narrative can expand: there are sympathetic characters, there is a problem to solve, there is a goal to achieve. And it is precisely the ease with which we accept this as a viable "reality" in terms of the film's internal logic that Camerini is able to shatter it almost immediately. Without warning, a hand bursts through what we assumed was the "real" moon to reveal that it is in fact just a flimsy paper prop. This is a stage set, and the camera pulls back to reveal that we—and Henriette—have been watching a stage play in the theater of an opulent hotel. Wide-eyed and engrossed in the dramatic action, we too have unquestioningly accepted the verisimilitude of what is in fact a constructed work of art.

Koven identifies the "false opening" more generally as a distinctive feature of *giallo* poetics, which offer "an invitation to play the mystery game with these filmmakers."[2] While he offers the examples of Enzo Casterllari's *Cold Eyes of Fear* (*Gli occhi freddi della paura*, 1971) and Riccardo Freda's *Murder Obsession* (1981) as examples of this (a play in the former and a film scene rehearsal in the latter), as I shall discuss in closer detail later in regard to Lamberto Bava's *A Blade in the Dark* (*La casa con la scala nel buio*, 1983) and Mario Moroni's *Clap, You're Dead* (*Ciak si muore*, 1974), this false opening structure will find its way into many later *giallo* films specifically through the constructed-performance-suggested-as-real template. But for our purposes, there's more at play in Camerini's *Giallo* of interest than its opening alone. After a series of rather light-hearted twists and turns, Henriette reconciles with Giorgio, but only based on her belief that yes, he *does* have a secret exciting backstory that is far more exotic than the banality his day-to-day gardening routine might otherwise suggest. The film's ending verges on cute, bringing us back to Edgar Wallace and the cheap pulp paperbacks of the film's title; to maintain her excitement and interest levels in him, Giorgio reads *gialli* on the sly, reshaping their thrilling scenarios into supposedly real anecdotes from his past that he uses to entrance his young wife, thus guaranteeing both her romantic interest and marital fidelity. Again, supposed "reality" (or at least, how it is constructed within the film's diegesis) clashes with the concept of "art" (literature) with charming results.

While Camerini's *Giallo* is very far away indeed from the much darker, more stylistically excessive world of later *giallo* cinema, the way it playfully experiments with the borders between art and reality *does* find some curious later parallels. Think, perhaps, of Peter Strickland's 2012 neo-*giallo Berberian Sound Studio* which I will discuss further in Chapter Thirteen. While an altogether different cinematic experience, it too also deliberately manipulates the supposed lines between art and reality in its tale of an English sound engineer called Gilderoy (Toby Jones) whose unpleasant experiences working at the Italian film post production studio of that film's title find him descending into chaos. What this brief look at Camerini's *Giallo* suggests, then, is that ideas about art—expressed through the art form of cinema itself—have long been (and continue to be) entrenched in *giallo* cinema history.

More generally, the presence of and engagement with the visual arts in Italian horror films has not gone unnoticed. Roberto Curti has noted that haunted portraits and paintings in general were common in Italian Gothic horror movies of the 1950s and 60s,[3] in films such as *Terror in the Crypt* (*La cripta e l'incubo*, Camillo Mastrocinque, 1964),[4] *Mill of the Stone Women* (*Il mulino delle donne di pietra*, Giorgio Ferroni, 1960),[5] *Tomb of Torture* (*Metempsyco*, Antonio Boccaci, 1963)[6] and Mario Bava's *Kill, Baby ... Kill!* (*Operazione paura*, 1966),[7] and *Black Sunday* (*La maschera del demonio*, 1960).[8] Bava in particular loved a good painting—a fresco also sparks the action of Bava's haunting *Lisa and the Devil* (*Lisa e il diavolo*, 1973). Star of *Black Sunday* Barbara Steele is synonymous with Italian horror; director Riccardo Freda once said, "her eyes are metaphysical, impossible, like the eyes of a Chirico painting."[9] There is arguably something far deeper in the mindset of later *giallo* filmmakers that links them to visual art in particular. As Joseph Luzzi writes of Italian filmmakers such as Roberto Rossellini and Vittorio De Sica, that they "should be so deeply interconnected with the destinies of earlier art forms—and so concerned with the cinematic masterpieces that preceded them—is not surprising,"[10] precisely because of their very "Italianness." "The Italian nation has one of the most vaunted legacies in the visual arts, especially painting and sculpture, and has historically been one of the countries in Europe—indeed, the world—most open to experimenting with visual form."[11] He continues, "Italy's traditions in the iconography and religious painting of the Renaissance exerted a strong gravitational pull on the construction of the cinematic image."[12]

When it comes to Dario Argento, both James Gracey and

Horror imagery in Italian art I: Jacopo Ligozzi (1547–1627), *Allegory of Avarice*, 1590, oil on canvas, gift of Eric Seiler and Darcy Bradbury, and Edward A. and Karen S.W. Friedman, 1991 (open access, Metropolitan Museum of Art, www.metmuseum.org).

Horror imagery in Italian art II: Anonymous (Italian, Florentine, 15th century), *The Inferno according to Dante, after the Last Judgment fresco in the Campo Santo, Pisa*, ca. 1460–80, engraving, a later re-strike (possibly 19th century). Circle of Baccio Baldini (1436?–1487?); after Francesco Traini (active ca. 1321–45) (open access, Metropolitan Museum of Art www.metmuseum.org).

McDonagh have emphasized the centrality of horror iconography in Italian cultural history, positioning Italian horror and *giallo* film on a clear historical trajectory that continues this fascination. As McDonagh suggests;

> ...to grow up in Italy was to be surrounded by centuries of apocalyptic painting, sculpture, and literature, as close to hand as the local video store. European art museums contain grotesque depictions of the intemperate ecstasies and diabolically baroque agonies of the saints, which lurk alongside surreal paintings of the hell mouth, gaping jaws ready to gobble up sinners and deliver them to eternal perdition. A nondescript church might hold a sanctified vial of dried blood said to liquefy miraculously, or a glass box encasing a life-sized statue of a martyred saint with disarticulated limbs, anatomically correct to the bloody shoulder stumps.[13]

She continues;

> Italy has La Specola, the Florencian medical museum whose eerily lifelike wax anatomy models juxtapose flayed torsos and glistening viscera with serene, delicate faces that could belong to beatific saints; the macabre as art, easily and readily consumed by the European masses.[14]

Likewise for Gracey, "the great Italian Renaissance artists such as Michelangelo, Da Vinci and Caravaggio created baroque and majestic works of art celebrating the volatility of their heritage. The darkly romantic texts of Boccaccio and Dante revel in hellish descriptions of live burials and descents into Hell."[15] He continues, noting that in Italy "opera, too, is deeply passionate and contains violent outbursts and perverse love and death. The voyeuristic impulse to watch scenes of violence is thousands of years old."[16]

We can see this legacy where art and horror intersect in the family tree and personal career trajectories of a number of Italian filmmakers who made *gialli*. Mario Bava's father (and thus Lamberto Bava's grandfather) was a sculptor,[17] Dario Argento's father worked in the film industry and his mother was a photographer,[18] and (as discussed further in Chapter Four) Lucio Fulci was an art critic.[19] Michele Soavi's father was a renowned poet, novelist, critic and designer[20] who famously had his portrait painted by revered Swiss artist Alberto Giacometti in 1963.[21] Soavi's step-father was a painter, as is Soavi himself (one of his works appears in his 1991 horror film, *The Sect*, aka *La Setta*).[22] Mino Guerrini who directed the *giallo Murder by Appointment* (*Omicidio per appuntamento*, 1966) was a successful painter,[23] as is Francesco Barilli who directed the *gialli The Perfume of the Lady in Black* (*Il profumo della signora in nero*, 1974), discussed at length in Chapter Fifteen. "I'm not a director.... I'd rather see myself as a painter," Barilli said. "Being a painter, to me cinema is a succession of images."[24] Before further interrogating the intersection of art and *giallo* cinema, however, this chapter will turn its attention towards more fully articulating precisely what is meant by the latter. Let's start with those little yellow books.

Giallo *from Page to Screen*

We can see the overlap of art and *giallo* right back at the literary genre's formation. The first literary *giallo* was a translation of S.S. Van Dine's *The Strange Death of Mr. Benson*, published by Mondadori under the Italian-language title *La strana morte del signor Benson*.[25] The *nom de plume* for art critic Willard Huntington Wright, Van Dine was a name he adopted to pedal his hugely popular Philo Vance detective stories without damaging his reputation as a darling of New York's *avant garde* scene in the 1910s with his books such as *Modern Painting: Its Tendency and Meaning* (1915). Along with his other writings on art, this brought him to the attention of peers such as Georgia O'Keeffe and William Faulkner.[26] Long before the ubiquitous deceptive identities of cinematic *giallo* and its frequent overlap with a fascination in art and artistic production, it seems Van Dine was inadvertently well ahead of the curve in terms of the merger of art and *gialli*.

The famous yellow covers of pulp literary *gialli* stand in contrast to other color-coded strands in publishing; Mondadori also published a spy/thriller series *Segretissimo* ("Top Secret") from 1961 which had black covers, and had a popular romance series with blue covers, for example, and both Leon Hunt and Rolando Caputo have noted the influence of *fumetti neri* (or "black comics"[27]) on *gialli* also.[28] Perhaps adding to their mystique and sense of danger that would feed into the transgressive tone of its cinematic variation, *giallo* literature was banned during the Fascist regime in Italy due to Mussolini's fears it would corrupt what from his perspective were the more simple-minded Italians he understood as being attracted to such material.[29] Re-emerging in the years immediately after the war, while commonly associated with Italian-language translations of famous foreign crime writers (not just Wallace and Agatha Christie but writers such as the American Cornell Woolrich), a number of Italian authors also moved into the genre including Giorgio Scerbanenco and Leonardo Sciascia.[30]

Clearly the broader social and political climate of Italy during the rise in popularity and production of both literary and cinematic *giallo* is worthy of note. In the years preceding the explosion of the latter, Italy underwent a post-war economic boom period in the '50s and '60s which saw dramatic shifts in how Italian society viewed morality in particular. Described by Leon Hunt as a "renegotiation" of the country's cultural engagement with orthodox Catholic positions on morality,[31] the Second Vatican Council (1962–1965) was a moment of significant transformation for both Catholicism and Catholics themselves. As Marco Vanelli suggests, "for once in history, the Church was not only in step with the times, but even ahead of it in some areas."[32] Under Pope John XXIII, "the Church had encouraged reform and renewal initiatives among young Catholics during the Second Vatican Council."[33] It was here that the Pope announced amongst other things that the Church had to bring "the modern world into contact with the vivifying and perennial energies of the gospel."[34] Contraception and birth control was a hotly contested topic,[35] which we can see as feeding directly into representations of non-traditional Catholic attitudes towards sex and sexuality (particularly that of women) as typically depicted in *gialli*; to spell it out bluntly, it's hard to embrace sexual liberation when you have to worry about getting pregnant, so these factors were often the unspoken backdrop to the free-and-easy sexual lifestyle that marks so many of these films.

This cultural context was shaken even further by the *anni di piombo* ("years of lead") that lasted from the late '60s to the late '80s, which was marked by a series of radical acts of political terrorism by groups from across the ideological spectrum. In terms of the Years of Lead, *giallo* as a broader crime fiction phenomena, and terrorism specifically, Barbara Pezzotti argues that "thanks to the typical *topoi* of crime fiction—violence, victims and perpetrators—the *giallo* has been able to address the uneasy topic of the violence of the state and commemorate its victims,"[36] elsewhere noting that as "a powerful cultural response to moments of change and instability, the *giallo* fiction and film penetrate the interstices of history and interpret the past."[37] Alongside the popular *poliziottesco* (police procedural), Austin Fischer suggests that *gialli* "began to proliferate at the beginning of the 1970s, and then flourished during post-war Italy's most traumatic decade,"[38] and that both *giallo* and *poliziottesco* "commonly revolve around amplified levels of violence in contemporary Italian locales, and both invest in narratives that seek to solve or explain the causes of these irrational and perplexing acts."[39] Elsewhere, Seb Roberts has argued that

> ...the *giallo* was shrewdly perceptive in its projections of social anxieties during the most violent decade of Italy's postwar history. In transgression, the *giallo* saw thrilling possibility and dangerous disorder, and in hegemony, stability and suffocation. These films largely regarded the upheaval of modernity with ambivalence while nevertheless generating much of its diegetic tensions from the instability of social norms—particularly those surrounding gender. Trafficking in sleaze, shock, and slaughter, the *giallo* appeared to argue that the volatility of modern life necessarily produces death. However, this impression is but a first glance. A more

incisive examination of how the *giallo* presents transgression as a production of difference reveals a different understanding of social turmoil: as a generative force to be embraced.[40]

For Kat Ellinger, despite the seemingly "formulaic traits" of *gialli*, that "it was a highly experimental period in Italian film history" was a result of these broader social and cultural shifts:

> Aspects such as the lessening of censorship, commercial need, left-wing protests (following an explosive period in the Hot Autumn of 1969), working class disillusionment born from the exploitational side of the post-war economic miracle, the changing nature of gender roles, dirty politics, political violence and the breaking down of traditional values, all played a part in fuelling the giallo and crime thriller genres of the era.[41]

Gialli was not simply the result of these broader of cultural and social shifts and/or an inevitable by-product of literary *gialli*. Indeed, it simultaneously marks an important point in the history of Italian horror cinema. Russ Hunter has traced important precursors to the Italian horror genre back to the silent era, noting a number of key films including *L'Inferno* (Francesco Bertolini, Adolfo Padovan and Giuseppe de Liguoro, 1911), *Il cadavere di marmo* (Ugo de Simone, 1915), *Preferisco L'inferno!* (Eleuterio Rodolfi, 1916), *Malombra* (Carmine Gallone, 1917), and *Il mostro di Frankenstein* (Eugenio Testa, 1921).[42] Despite later films such as Alessandro Blasetti's *Dr. Jekyll and Mr. Hy*de-inspired *The Haller Case* (*Il Caso Haller*) in 1933, generalized histories of Italian horror mark its true formation in the films of Mario Bava and Riccardo Freda during the 1950s and 1960s. With *Black Sabbath* (1963) and *Black Sunday* (*La maschera del demonio*, 1960) especially, Bava was a central figure in the explosion of Italian horror that permeated the 1960s, 1970s and 1980s. But Freda is historically just as significant, if not more so; Bava co-directed and photographed two of Freda's films that are often considered the birthplace of Italian horror, *The Devil's Commandment* (*I vampiri*, 1957) and *Caltiki, The Immortal Monster* (*Caltiki, il mostro immortale*, 1959). Following in the footsteps of both Freda and Bava, there was a dramatic increase in the production of Italian horror films during in 1960 especially, with films such as Piero Regnoli's *The Playgirls and the Vampire* (*L'ultima preda del vampire*), Renato Polselli's *The Vampire and the Ballerina* (*L'amante del vampire*), Anton Giulio Majano's *Atom Age Vampire* (*Seddok, l'erede di Satana*) and Giorgio Ferroni's *Mill of the Stone Women* (*Il mulino delle donne di pietra*). In 1962, Freda released both *The Horrible Secret of Dr. Hichcock* (*L'orribile segreto del dottor Hichcock*) and *The Ghost* (*Lo sprettro*, 1963), alongside other key directors from this period including Antonio Marghereti with his two films from 1963 *The Castle of Terror* (*La danza macabre*) and *Horror Castle* (*La vergine di Norimberga*). Massimo Pulillo was another notable Italian horror filmmaker from this period, with *Bloody Pit of Horror* (*Il boia scarlatto*, 1965), and two films from 1966; *The Vengeance of Lady Morgan* (*La vendetta di Lady Morgan*) and *Terror Creatures from the Grave* (*Cinque tombe per un medium*).

A number of these filmmakers—Bava and Margheriti perhaps most famously—would make *gialli* also. From the late '40s, the market was a clear dominating factor in the production of not just horror films but other popular genre cycles such as peplum films and Mondo movies. As Stefano Baschiera and Russ Hunter have noted, "these production cycles tended to chime with whatever genre was performing well at both the domestic and international box office."[43] They continue, "it was a growing awareness of—and dependency upon—this market that would eventually lead Italian horror to the kind of onscreen excesses that would see it become exploitation cinema."[44] There were other notable influences that warrant acknowledgment on the boom period of the Italian *giallo* film (such as, for instance, the German *Krimi* film[45]), but in general terms, this is the broader scenario where, marked by their combination of the traditional *giallo* iconography of the disguised killer and the amateur detective figure, Koven dates the golden age of the "classic" *giallo* film from 1970 to 1975.[46]

Exploring Giallo *Cinema*

So now we have a loose map of how *giallo* came into being, what *precisely* is *giallo* cinema? On one hand, it is surely easy enough to define: inspired by pulp crime paperbacks with yellow covers? Check. Iconography like the switchblade and black leather glove? Check. Scads of sex and violence and dripping with stylistic excess? Check. And yet, as many critics have noted,[47] *gialli* in practice do not yield so readily to simple definitions. For Gino Moliterno, "the *giallo* is an extremely wide-ranging and permeable generic category that can include anything from the simple whodunit or police procedural to the psychological thriller and the horror and slasher film."[48] Kannas notes in her assessment of the term's usage that while in Italian it has become a broad shorthand for "all manner of crime, mystery and detection narrative," in English-language discourse it "connotes a smaller, if permeable, group of films which are profoundly indebted to Argento and Mario Bava's interpretations of the formula."[49]

While it is broadly agreed that Bava's *The Girl Who Knew Too Much* (*La ragazza che sapeva troppo*, 1962) was the first "real" *giallo* film with his later *Blood and Black Lace* (*Sei donne per l'assassino*, 1964) consolidating the category as it would soon become recognized, a number of precursors have been identified such as Giacomo Gentilomo's *Short Circuit* (*Cortocircuito*, 1943)[50] and *Obsession* (*Ossessione*, Luchino Visconti, 1943).[51] And yet, as Leon Hunt suggests, any attempt to cast an ultimate declaration on which precisely as the first "official" *giallo* film relies on locking the term down to something very solid to begin with, denying that the definition itself is in contention.[52] Yet regardless of where it began it was unarguably the blockbuster success of Argento's *The Bird with the Crystal Plumage* that saw the market veritably flooded with imitators eager to cash in on Argento's recipe.[53] Before this film, *gialli* were certainly not invisible, and a number of widely loved classics stem from this period (many of which will be discussed in this book), including, but not limited to, *Libido* (Ernesto Gastaldi and Vittorio Salerno, 1965), *Death Laid an Egg* (*La morte ha fatto l'uovo*, Giulio Questi, 1967) *Perversion Story* (*Una sull'altra*, Lucio Fulci, 1969), *The Sweet Body of Deborah* (*Il dolce corpo di Deborah*, Romolo Guerrieri, 1968), and *A Black Veil for Lisa* (*La morte non ha sesso*, Massimo Dallamano, 1968). But it is reasonable to say that the success of *The Bird with the Crystal Plumage* changed everything. In an extraordinary anecdote, cinematographer for Argento's *Suspiria*, *Tenebrae* and *Dracula 3D* (2012) Luciano Tovoli spoke of only knowing the director by reputation when he met him to discuss working on *Suspiria* but he knew the impact he had on audiences. Living in between two cinemas in Rome, he would watch audiences leaving one where *The Bird with the Crystal Plumage* had just played and rushing to the other cinema to see it again. Said Tovoli in a 2010 interview, "a director who provokes such brisk movement in a crowd should be a very good one!"[54] As McDonagh so succinctly noted, "Argento did not invent the *giallo*, but he helped define the form in all its stylish perversity."[55]

For those brave enough to attempt to solidify key features of *giallo* cinema, for the purposes of this book a number stand out for their deliberate efforts to allow some elasticity to their terms of classification. For Thrower, "the *giallo* crossbreeds the murder mystery with horror. It's a form where murder and intrigue, those staple features of popular drama, are taken to baroque extremes, frequently bordering on the ridiculous." He continues, "The general tone is one of moral decay and cynicism, with ever more convoluted plots emphasising morbid details in a Janus-faced world of paranoia and betrayal." For Thrower, "The horror ingredient comes from the *giallo*'s frankly perverse dwelling upon violence, and the voyeur in us is likely to be well served by a similarly blatant dose of sleazy sex."[56] For Philippe Met, it is marked by a virtual shopping list of key features:

Enigmatic childhood trauma flashbacks; the fetishistic ritual of black gloved hands getting ready for the kill; point-of-view shots of a faceless murderer wearing a shiny trench coat; the flash of a blade in the dark (be it a knife, a razor, a meat cleaver, or a hatchet); scantily clad "scream queens" being stalked and subjected to shocking and sadistic acts of violence; a morally decadent and sexually deviant upper-class milieu; an inept local police force and an eye witness as impotent amateur sleuth; a deleterious atmosphere of rampant suspicion; an abundance of red herrings and twist endings (that not too infrequently lapse into non sequiturs); a baroque or mannerist use of lighting and color.[57]

Even more simply, for Forshaw "eccentricity (of a self-conscious variety) is a hallmark of the genre."[58]

Forshaw's use of the word "genre," however, is somewhat of a Pandora's Box. Thus far, I have avoided referring to *giallo* cinema as a genre *per se*, as this has been the subject of much debate amongst critics and academics alike. Gary Needham's 2003 essay "Playing with Genre: Defining the Italian Giallo" is a key work, suggesting that "*giallo* in its cinematic form is that it appears to be less fixed as a genre than its written counterpart."[59] Instead, he opts for the alternative Italian concept *filone*, writing:

> ...the *giallo* is something different to that which is conventionally analysed as a genre. The Italians have the word *filone*, which is often used to refer to both genres and cycles as well as to currents and trends. This points to the limitations of genre theory built primarily on American film genres but also to the need for redefinition concerning how other popular film-producing nations understand and relate to their products. This introduction to the *giallo*, therefore, begins from the assumption that the *giallo* is not so much a genre, as its literary history might indicate, but a body of films that resists generic definition. In this respect it is unlike the Italian horror and *poliziotto* (police) genres yet, at the same time, the *giallo* can be understood as an object to be promoted, criticised, studied, etc.[60]

Needham proposes that "instead of defining the *giallo* in generic and historical terms, I would like to suggest that we understand it in a more 'discursive' fashion, as something constructed out of the various associations, networks, tensions and articulations of Italian cinema's textual and industrial specificity in the post-war period."[61] Consequently, *filone* has proven a useful alternate model for thinking through *giallo* in English-language scholarship.[62] For Koven, "perhaps, in some cases, what we think of as a film genre, like the *giallo*, may be a cluster of concurrent streamlets, veins, or traditions—*filone*,"[63] while for Kannas "conceptualizing the *giallo* as *filone* enables ... the flexibility to consider a wide range of films prone to consistent deviation from any established generic norm as nevertheless being part of the same discursive group."[64]

From this perspective, I hesitate to refer to *giallo* to a genre or sub-genre *per se* in reference to these very debates. And it is very much a subject of debate, as other critics have embraced the positioning of *giallo* in a generic context. In his 2013 book *Euro Horror: Classic European Horror Cinema in Contemporary American Culture*, for example, Ian Olney argues that *giallo* cinema *can* be conceived through a generic lens, and "that it is defined by its narrative debt to postwar Italian anti-detective fiction and by the characteristic way in which it uses formal devices to amplify the destabilizing, postmodern tendencies of this brand of fiction."[65] For Olney, "the *giallo* film possesses a strong generic identity," and it is through this that we are granted "a clearer picture of its relationship with horror cinema in general, as well as an explanation for its cult popularity among contemporary American viewers."[66] This is not America alone, as *giallo* film has grown as a broad object of cult fascination around the world. "Once a despised genre internationally," says Forshaw, "*gialli* have undergone a major critical re-assessment, with their visual stylishness and bizarre plotting now celebrated."[67] But, as Jamie Sexton has warned, there is still an aspect of irony to this supposed valorization.[68] And within cult fandom itself, despite writing in 2012, Brigid Cherry's observation that both a taste for and knowledge about European horror cinema more broadly "can be a signifier, particularly amongst male fans, of an elite position within the fan hierarchy which is used to subordinate other fans"[69] remains largely true today. Even just anecdotally there is still strong sense that the "boy's club" fandom mentality is still present, not just in terms of *giallo* specifically, but to horror in general. Which is, of course, nonsense; notable women film critics who have shown remarkable insight into *giallo* including (but certainly not limited to) Samm Deighan, Kat Ellinger, Kier-La Janisse, Virginie Sélavy, Rachael Nisbet, Alexia Kannas, Lindsay Hallam, Marcia Landy, and Maitland McDonagh, names which only begin to scratch the surface if we seek to demonstrate a strong, critically engaged audience of women for these films. Indeed, as McDonagh made this extraordinarily insightful observation in 2019 upon the endurance of *gialli* more broadly, underscoring that its relationship to gender difference—and who it "speaks" to—is *precisely* where its legacy lies; "They're about the way men and women do or don't connect; the social mores that shape people's lives and what it takes to say, 'just no; not doing that.'"[70] She continues, "The black-gloved killer who enforces the status quo with a knife isn't gone; he or she has just adapted. And that's why *gialli* still speak to us; they're not just retro kicks. They speak to the way we live now."[71]

Matters are further complicated by examining more closely the curious tension that *giallo* cinema sits in with traditional national cinema frameworks. Writes Kannas of her own experience in taking her first tentative steps towards studying *giallo* in an academic context:

> Because I had understood Italian horror first as Italian cinema, rather than "horror," the *giallo*'s near or total absence from key critical texts on Italian national cinema had surprised me as a university student. I soon came to realise that the "Italianess" of these films was marked by a sense of cultural illegitimacy. Unlike the canonised art cinema of directors like Fellini and Antonioni, *giallo* genre films were not seen as texts which make valuable contribution to discourses of Italian national cinema or identity. But the case of the *giallo* prompts us to question how the legitimacy of canonised Italian cinema has also determined the genre film's cultural value.[72]

While *gialli* are certainly linked closely to Italy in terms of both film and literature, as Koven notes, "the giallo was not entirely an independent phenomenon; these films were heavily influenced by, not to mention funded by and marketed to, international interests beyond Italy."[73] A number of key works on *giallo* cinema acknowledge these transnational cultural flows both into this unique kind of Italian cinema and the influence that it had on films produced (and still being produced) in other countries. As Baschiera and Hunter suggest, there is somewhat of a paradox because "so many of the characteristics most notably recognised as informing and defining Italian horror films—from the international casts, the use of directorial pen-names, the often non–Italian settings, the international funding arrangements, to the intended final market, etc.—challenge a clear sense of national identification."[74]

As tempting as it might be to position *giallo* as a hermetically sealed Italian cultural phenomenon, the reality of their production contexts speaks of a category that expanded far beyond national borders. For example, 68 of the 134 films listed in Adrian Luther Smith's *Blood and Black Lace* are international co-productions, and some of the subgenre's most well-known titles are international co-productions, the most famous of which perhaps include (but are certainly not limited to) *Lizard in a Woman's Skin* (*Una lucertola con la pelle di donna*, Lucio Fulci, 1971), *Paranoia* (*Orgasmo*, Umberto Lenzi, 1969), *Short Night of Glass Dolls* (*La Corte Notte Delle Bambole Di Vetro*, Aldo Lado, 1971), *So Sweet, So Perverse*, (*Cosi Dolce, Cosi Perversa*, Umberto Lenzi, 1969), and *Who Saw Her Die?* (*C'ha vista morire?* 1972, Aldo Lado). Many of the major works by Dario Argento were international co-productions, including his early "animal trilogy," *Cat O' Nine Tails* (*Il Gatto a Nove Code*, 1971), *Four Flies on Grey Velvet* (*Quattro Mosche di Velluto Grigio*, 1971), and *The Bird with the Crystal Plumage*.[75] For Baschiera and Hunter, then, "Somewhat perversely defining the 'Italian' in Italian horror is not a straightforward task."[76] They expand upon this, noting "A tendency towards more extreme, visceral content aside, there are few easily recognizable 'Italian features' in the films produced. So many of the characteristics most notably recognized as informing and defining Italian horror films ... challenge a clear sense of national identification."[77] As I explore further in this book, this has resulted in *gialli* being made in countries well beyond their assumed Italian origins, as we see today in neo-*giallo* in examples such as Belgium-based French filmmakers Hélène Cattet and Bruno Forzani with *Amer* (2009) and *The Strange Colour of Your Body's Tears* (*L'étrange couleur des larmes de ton corps*, 2013), Peter Strickland's *Berberian Sound Studio* and the 2014 Astron-6 film, *The Editor*.

As Austin Fisher observes, *gialli* are "self-consciously international,"[78] and this internationalism is rendered visible in many of the films

Top: J&B Whiskey as ubiquitous symbol of sophistication and internationalism in *All the Colors of the Dark* (*Tutti i colori del buio*, Sergio Martino, 1972); *bottom: The Case of the Scorpion's Tail* (*La coda dello scorpione*, Sergio Martino, 1971)

themselves, often set in non–Italian locales. There are far too many examples to list in full, but a random selection to illustrate the point includes the Australian-set *The Pyjama Girl Case* (*La ragazza dal pigiama giallo*, Flavio Mogherini, 1977), Riccardo Freda's *The Iguana with the Tongue of Fire* (*L'iguana dalla lingue difuoco*, 1971) which is set in Dublin, *Short Night of Glass Dolls* takes place in Prague (*La Corta notte delle bambole di vetro*, Aldo Lado, 1971), *The French Sex Murders* (*Casa d'appuntamento*, Ferdinando Merighi, 1972) set in Paris, *The Killer Is on the Phone* (*L'assassino ... è al telefono*, Alberto De Martino, 1972) is based in Bruges, while a number of *gialli* including *All the Colors of the Dark* (*Tutti i colori del buio*, Sergio Martino, 1972), *What Have You Done to Solange?* (*Cosa avete fatto a Solange?*, Massimo Dallamano, 1972), *Hatchet for the Honeymoon* (*Il rosso segno della follia*, Mario Bava, 1970) and *A Lizard in a Woman's Skin* are all set in London. Both *Seven Murders for Scotland Yard* (*Jack el destripador de Londres*, José Luis Madrid, 1971) and *The New York Ripper* (*Lo squartatore di New York*, Lucio Fulci, 1982) are relatively self-explanatory when it comes to this internationalizing tendency, and *Seven Deaths in a Cat's Eye* (*La morte negli occhi del gatto*, Antonio Margheriti, 1973) remains a personal favorite if only for a brief appearance of iconic French crooner Serge Gainsbourg as an investigator with an unconvincingly dubbed Scottish accent. The tendency towards protagonists who live a jet-set lifestyle underscores Needham's observation that these "characters don't seem fixed to a home or location; they are always (in) between different places."[79] This, he notes, allows not just exotic foreign advertising to litter the *mise-en-scène* of the *giallo* film, but also explains the iconic ubiquity of J&B whiskey,[80] a product whose presence in *giallo* cinema has become the subject of a "Where's Waldo" like treasure hunt for *giallo* fans in recent years. As Koven reveals, J&B were unaware of the use of the product in giallo cinema and thus was far from a product placement style marketing strategy. Consequently, the placement "was done willingly" and as such "has some specific connotation that the filmmakers ... wanted to convey."[81] He continues;

> The brand of whiskey a *giallo* character drinks, or at least has (prominently) in the house, like with the visual use of brand-name airliners, grounds the *giallo*, not only in an aura of sophistication, or at least *la dolce vita*, but in a consumerist reality that creates some connection with the audience's *liebenswelt*; even if they cannot afford to fly to London or drink highball cocktails, they at least recognize an assumed value of those signifiers.[82]

As Stefano Baschiera and Francesco Di Chiara note, "instead of 'hiding' the international involvement in the production of the films ... the *giallo* completely exploited the possibility offered by co-production agreements to shoot in suggestive international locations"[83] As such, "the *gialli* underplayed their national identity in favour of a more neutral 'international' one."[84] As Needham neatly summarizes, the ubiquity of "travel, tourism, exoticism, hybridity and foreignness" across *giallo* cinema therefore complicate more simplistic "concept[s] of a national film movement and a national identity."[85]

As mentioned earlier, Anglicized names were common. For example, Antonio Margheriti who directed *Seven Deaths in the Cat's Eye* was credited on that film under his pseudonym Anthony M. Dawson, Giuliano Carnimeo as Anthony Ascott for *The Case of the Bloody Iris* (*Perché quelle strane gocce di sangue sul corpo di Jennifer?*, 1972), Lamberto Bava as John Old, Jr., for *You'll Die at Midnight* (*Morirai a mezzanotte*, 1986), Mario Gariazzo as Ray Garrett for *Play Motel* (1979), and Gianni Matrucci as John Martucc for *Trhauma* (1980), et cetera. Similarly, a number of regular *giallo* actors also adopted English-language sounding screen names such as Ida Galli who was often credited as Evelyn Stewart, Nieves Navarro as Susan Scott, Renato Rossini as Howard Ross, and Jorge Hill Acosta y Lara as George Hilton. Aside from reducing what Koichi Iwabuchi has identified as the "cultural odor"[86] of *gialli* so as to not seem too exotic for audiences in foreign markets, this also had the simultaneous benefit somewhat ironically of making the movies more appealing to Italian audiences, suggesting they were watching something of a little more highbrow than a low-budget, locally-made genre film.[87] In practical terms, these co-productions brought in foreign money, and as such frequently necessitated the casting of internationally recognizable stars.[88] In the work of Dario Argento alone this tendency is easy to identify with the central casting of Tony Musante in *The Bird with the Crystal Plumage* (1970), Karl Malden in *The Cat o' Nine Tails* (*Il gatto a nove code*, 1971), Michael Brandon in *Four Flics on Grey Velvet* (*4 mosche di velluto grigio*, 1971), David Hemmings in *Deep Red* (1975), and John Saxon—who had previously starred in Mario Bava's *The Girl Who Knew Too Much*—also appeared Argento's *Tenebrae* (1982). There is a seemingly never-ending stream of other examples including Farley Granger in *Amuck!* (*Alla ricerca del piacere*, Silvio Amadio, 1972), *The Red Headed Corpse* (*La rossa dalla pelle che scotta*, Renzo Russo, 1972), *What Have They Done to Your Daughters?* (*La polizia chiede aiuto*, Massimo Dallamano, 1974), *So Sweet, So Dead* (*Rivelazioni di un maniaco sessuale al capo della squadra mobile*, Roberto Bianchi Montero, 1972), and the Gothic *giallo Something Creeping in The Dark* (*Qualcosa striscia nel buio*, Mario Colucc, 1971); Ray Milland in *The Pyjama Girl Case*; John Mills in *A Black Veil for Lisa* (*La morte non ha sesso*, Massimo Dallamano, 1968); Stanley Baker in A *Lizard in a Woman's Skin* (*Una lucertola con la pelle di donna*, Lucio Fulci, 1971); George Lazenby in *Who Saw Her Die?* (*Chi l'ha vista morire?*, 1972), and the many *gialli* of Carroll Baker, Mimsy Farmer, Suzy Kendall, and Barbara Bach. We only need look at the iconic British actor Barbara Steele who made her name with Italian horror films for evidence that there was already precedent for this approach in the Italian film industry more broadly, Francesco Di Chiara suggesting that "the success of Italian horror film was due at the same time to its compatibility with other, foreign genre products—they could fit in a double bill with an American International Pictures release, for instance."[89] As such, the success of the *giallo* film was not Italy-specific, with re-edited and dubbed versions being screened in grindhouses and drive-ins overseas.[90]

In terms of what inspired *giallo* cinematically, external influences have been broadly acknowledged, such as the aforementioned German *Krimi* film[91] and of course the films of Alfred Hitchcock.[92] The latter is visible from the outset in the English language title of Bava's ground-breaking *giallo The Girl Who Knew Too Much*, a conscious homage obviously to Hitchcock's *The Man Who Knew Too Much* (which he made originally in 1934, and again in Hollywood in 1956). In this tale, Fisher suggests "Bava plugs into a rich vein of transcultural borrowing in Italy, through which foreign narrative models offer a filter for the familiar locale."[93] Even the very story acknowledges this spirit of internationalism, he continues, "by presenting an American tourist with a cultural advantage over the Italian monster."[94] *The Girl Who Knew Too Much* was hardly a passion project for Bava, however. As Tim Lucas describes it in his exhaustive 2007 book *Mario Bava: All the Colors of the Dark*, the title and Hitchcock reference can be traced to a request by Sam Arkoff from American International Pictures (who made the film with Coronet Produzioni and Galatea) to effectively cash-in on the then in-vogue trend for "'Hitchockian' thrillers."[95] Lucas cites an anecdote from Luigi Cozzi who recalls that Bava was in the process of, in his words, "recovering from a nervous breakdown: I didn't feel like directing it, but I need the money, so I did it."[96] In his deep dive into the relationship between Hitchcock and *giallo* cinema, Philippe Met reveals that rather than merely following a trend Bava established with *The Girl Who Knew Too Much* almost on auto-pilot, a far more complex interrelation was at play. Recalling an oft-cited rumor that when Hitchcock saw Michelangelo Antonioni's *Blowup* (1966)—which would itself go on to directly influence Argento's *Deep Red*—the famous British director admitted that the Italians were "years ahead" of the work he was doing,[97] Met argues that "The specificity of *The Girl Who Knew Too Much* ... may be seen today as a swan song for the Anglo-Saxon whodunit archetype (both epitomized and popularized by Hitchcock) and a proto-giallo in the history of Italian genre cinema, thereby actuating a shift of paradigms."[98] From this perspective, Met suggests that "the Hitchcock touch might be situated somewhere between the superb craftsmanship of a Mario Bava, who would literally work wonders with bits and pieces (glass mattes, color gels, and sundry makeshift devices)" and what he identifies as "the operatic or grand guignol flourishes, at times verging on hysteria, of a Dario Argento."[99] The best *gialli*, Met suggest, might even be considered as manifesting "a definite streak of Italian 'baroquization' of Hitchcockian formalism."[100] So strong is this legacy of Hitchcock that Argento—broadly regarded as the master of the *giallo* category, if not at least its most famous international export—has long been granted the moniker "the Italian Hitchcock,"[101] a label he himself playfully acknowledges in his 2005 television movie, *Do You Like Hitchcock?*.

But rather than, as Sam Arkoff's recommendation to Bava suggests, merely seeking to profit from functioning in an increasingly global marketplace, there were also intrinsically Italian socio-political reasons why these films were both produced and flourished in Italy itself during this period. Koven unites this mode of urbane, cosmopolitan internationalism with stories fundamentally linked to violence, crime and deviancy which he argues reflect widespread tensions regarding the increasing presence of modernity in an Italy struggling to find an identity after World War II and its fallout; these films, in short, are a "vernacular" manifestation of anxieties around the broader social, cultural and political transformations that marked the period.[102] On this front, Koven does some impressive mathematics:

> Let us remind ourselves that these movies are thirty to forty years old now, made (predominantly) in the early 1970s. The characters are approximately in the thirties and forties, which means the characters would have been born between 1930 and 1950. If the past trauma these films' killers experienced was in childhood, or experienced by their parents, doing the math, we find they are traumas occurring during World War II under Mussolini's Fascist rule. The films' audiences are likely to be approximately the same age as the characters, so they either would have had early childhood memories of the war or been more than familiar with their parents experiences. Are these film reflecting more than the cultural explanation of 1970s Italian disassociation resulting from fascism, military defeat ... and postwar reconstruction?[103]

While critical positions on *gialli* are often similarly built on socio-political and/or industrial foundations, this does not necessarily imply a conscious intention on the part of the director. In his signature unrestrained style, for example, Lucio Fulci once stated bluntly that "social comment is always a mistake in a fantastic film. Our films have got nothing to do with all these films made by amateurs who cover up their shortcomings with social statements."[104] Alternatively, other Italian horror filmmakers have consciously started from explicitly ideological positions that have been largely missed; Dario Argento has noted, for example, that his 1985 supernatural *giallo Phenomena* was based on the premise "that, at the end of World War II, the Germans had won, not the English and the Americans, and that a new order had been established." He continues, calling it "a sinister order, in which people are reduced to nothing more than children, and teachers who behave as if in an S.S. camp."[105] As will be discussed further shortly, the films of Dario Argento—especially his *gialli*—are frequently set in the art world or amidst communities of practicing artists and creatives, signifying a contemporary lifestyle notably distinct from more traditional ways of living that manifests also in a range of *gialli* including *Who Saw Her Die?*, *Death Carries a Cane* (*Passi di danza su una lama di rasoio*, 1973), *Eye of the Labyrinth* (*L'occhio nel labirinto*, Mario Caiano, 1972) and a number of case studies in this book.

Like film more broadly, the presence of modern art in *gialli* often denotes modern living and an associated shift from tradition, such as in *Seven Blood Stained Orchids* (*Sette orchidee macchiate di rosso*, Umberto Lenzi, 1972), *Black Belly of the Tarantula* (*La tarantola dal ventre nero*, Paolo Cavara, 1971), and the Lichtenstein-esque comic-book art that adorns the kaleidoscopic disco scene in *The Sweet Body of Deborah* (*Il dolce corpo di Deborah*, Romolo Guerrieri, 1968). In *In the Folds of the Flesh* (*Nelle pieghe della carne*, Sergio Bergonzelli, 1970) canvases are even hung deliberately on dramatic angles to show a movement away from the orthodox artistic norms of yesteryear; there is just on a pictorial level a kind of rebellion against practices of yore (i.e., hanging pictures straight). Art ownership in *gialli* is an overt, often gaudy signifier of wealth, such as in *The Fifth Cord* (*Giornata nera per l'ariete*, Luigi Bazzoni, 1973), *The Iguana with the Tongue of Fire* (*L'iguana dalla lingua di fuoco*, Riccardo Freda, 1971) or the giant Warhol-like portraits in the home of one of the rich clients Carole Bouquet's protagonist Mystère visits in *Dagger Eyes* (Carlo Vanzina, 1983). Implicit in the wealth of her clientele is her value as a high-price sex worker; "Class has a price," she demurely tells a detective later in the film.

Warhol is a curious point of reference here. Identifying a significant relationship between Warhol's art practice and Walter Benjamin's foundational 1936 essay "The Work of Art in the Age of Mechanical Reproduction,"[106] Anna Pritchard suggests that in the face of Benjamin's argument that the ability for technology to reproduce art and thus deplete its aura and authenticity, "Warhol updates Benjamin in response to the society of the spectacle, mass media and commodity signs."[107] She continues, "While Benjamin focused on problematising the ideological discourse that produces 'aura' through reification of the original form, Warhol's work can be understood as emphasising the copy without the original."[108] It is fascinating to observe, then, how clearly *not* original works of art function in terms of *mise-en-scène* when they appear on walls in *giallo* film; for instance, copies of famous art nouveau works appear in Michele Soavi's *The Goodbye Kiss* (*Arrivederci amore, ciao*, 2006) and Luciano Ercoli's *Death Walks at Midnight* (*La morte accarezza a mezzanotte*, 1972)—Théophile Steinlen's *Le Chat Noir* and Alphonse Mucha's *Job* (both from 1896) respectively—implying that the characters in whose apartments they appear may not have the money and lifestyle to warrant original works of art, but that they still may have a taste for the exotic.

Class, art and the aura (or lack thereof) manifest in *gialli* in other ways. In *Oasis of Fear* (*Un posto ideale per uccidere*, Umberto Lenzi, 1971), for example, the glut of conservative, supposedly expensively framed "original" artworks that adorn the wealthy Barbara's (Irene Papas) home stand in strong contrast to the cheap photo booth softcore pornography made by her young, violent home invaders Ingrid (Ornella Muti) and Dick (Ray Lovelock). While they seem to hold the upper hand throughout the film, their relationship to the visual arts ultimately reflects their class position and in its final twist, both their and Barbara's relationship to power. Artistic practice can be professional as in *Phantom of Death* (*Un delitto poco comune*, Ruggero Deodato, 1988) or *A Blade in the Dark* (*La casa con la scala nel buio*, Lamberto Bava, 1983), and the many films set in the fashion industry going back to *Blood and Black Lace* can attest. Alternatively, artistic practice might indicate modern and flexible lifestyles (even lazy, indulgent ones) where such pursuits can be dedicated hobbies, or even time-fillers, such as in Jill (Edith Meloni) in Mario Bava's *Five Dolls for an August Moon* (*5 bambole per la luna d'agosto*, 1970), or Carroll Baker's amateur artists in both Umberto Lenzi's *gialli Knife of Ice* (*Il coltello di ghiaccio*, Umberto Lenzi, 1972) and *Orgasmo* (1969); "I paint for myself," her wealthy widow Kathryn says demurely in the later.

Amateurism is a key concept in *gialli*. As Koven notes, *The Girl Who Knew Too Much* introduced the *giallo* archetype of the amateur detective, "an innocent person, often a tourist [who] witnesses a brutal murder that appears to be the work of a serial killer."[109] This figure, he continues, is largely what separates *gialli* from the more traditional police procedural or other crime mysteries, because here "someone unconnected to professional detection takes up the central investigative

Amateur investigator Magda (Edwige Fenech) claims the iconography of the professional detective in *Strip Nude for Your Killer* (*Nude per l'assassino*, Andrea Bianchi, 1975).

role."[110] Significantly, the amateur detective figure is very often "an artist of some variety," because along with tourists and journalists, "all these types of people have sufficient time on their hands to travel about their respective cities investigating mysteries."[111] But if, as Koven notes citing films such as *The Bird with the Crystal Plumage*, *Deep Red*, *A Blade in the Dark* and *The House with Laughing Windows* (*La casa dalle finestre che ridono,* Pupi Avati, 1976*)*, that "sometimes a piece of art can hold the vital clue to uncovering the identity of the killer,"[112] I argue that the role of the amateur detective in terms of the spectator then is in many key instances expanded to incorporate that of the amateur art historian. Additionally, this is not merely in pursuit of uncovering the central answer to the mysteries that often very loosely structure these films but rather, as I demonstrate in so many of my primary case studies, the perhaps surprising thematic depths operate in tandem with the very excesses of visual spectacle that *gialli* afford. These films do not demand a rigorous background in art history any more than they demand a background in professional detection of its many protagonists; it is this sense of feeling our way through, immersing ourselves in the sights and sounds and drawing conclusions through our own methodologies, insights and instincts that adds to the pleasures of *giallo* cinema.

Turning now towards these case studies, it is worth noting that while I focus primarily on painting, other artforms are also explored, such as fashion design, photography, filmmaking, theater and performance, and, to a lesser degree, sculpture and literature. Yet while my focus is primarily on painting, this is not to underplay the significance of the other arts, including those that I do not discuss as fully. We do not need to look far to find famous examples of this extended engagement with the arts; Dario Argento's *Opera* (1987) for example is a key text where the very notion of art and spectatorship is placed under the microscope, inspired by the filmmakers own troubled attempt to bring Verdi's "Rigoletto" to the stage in Macerata's Sferisterio Theatre in 1985.[113] Indeed, the arts riddle *gialli*; in Maurizio Pradeaux's *Death Carries a Cane* (*Passi di danza su una lama di rasoio*, 1973), Nieves Navarro's Kitty is a sculptor, while Navarro's character Valentina in *Death Walks at Midnight* (*La morte accarezza a mezzanotte*, Luciano Ercoli, 1972) discovers that her boyfriend—sculptor Stefano (Peter Martell)—has been driven to murder in order to hide his smuggling of heroin in his artworks. Sculptures literally kill (or try to) in Argento's *Tenebrae* and *The Bird with the Crystal Plumage*, as well as *The Flower with the Petals of Steel* (*Il fiore dai petali d'acciaio*, Gianfranco Piccioli, 1972), while Michele Soavi's neo-*giallo* *The Goodbye Kiss* (*Arrivederci amore, ciao*, 2006) features Dutch artist Meike van Schijndel's controversial "Kisses" urinals designed in 2000 which reshape the ubiquitous public bathroom feature as open red lips. The couple at the heart of Duccio Tessari's *giallo Puzzle* (*L'uomo senza memoria*, 1974) met at the Guggenheim Gallery in New York City, while an art gallery is also a key location in the famous opening sequence of Brian De Palma's American *giallo Dressed to Kill* (1980). Architecture is crucial to Argento's films, particularly in *gialli* such as *Deep Red* and *Tenebrae* which utilize architect Pietro Fenoglio's Art Nouveau Villa Scott in Turin in the former and architect Saverio Busiri's brutalist Villa Ronconi in Rome in the latter. We find musicians everywhere from Argento's *Four Flies on Grey Velvet* and *Opera* to Ruggero Deodato's *Phantom of Death* (*Un delitto poco comune*, 1988), Sergio Martino's *Mozart is a Murderer* (*Mozart è un assassino*, 1999) and Lamberto Bava's *A Blade in the Dark*. Writers are not rare either; look, for starters, to *Amuck!* (*Alla ricerca del piacere*, Silvio Amadio, 1972), *Eyes Behind the Wall* (*L'occhio dietro la parete*, Giuliano Petrelli, 1977), and films already discussed, such as *Your Vice Is a Locked Room and Only I Have the Key* and *The Bird with the Crystal Plumage*. *Madness* (*Gli occhi dentro*, Bruno Mattei, 1992) and the Spanish *giallo Sexy Cat* (Julio Pérez Tabernero, 1973) are about comic book writers and artists. Dance features in varying degrees as a bodily spectacle across a range of *gialli* including *The Laughing Woman* (*Femina Ridens*, Schivazappa, 1969), *So Sweet ... So Perverse* (*Così dolce ... così perversa*, Umberto Lenzi, 1969), *Watch Me When I Kill* (*Il gatto dagli occhi di giada*, Antonio Bido, 1977), Lucio Fulci's *Perversion Story* (*Una sull'altra*, 1969), *The Sweet Body of Deborah* (*Il dolce corpo di Deborah*, Romolo Guerrieri, 1968), and *Murder Rock* (*Murderock—uccide a passo di danza*, 1984). While space considerations make it difficult to look at every single instance of an artist and artform in *gialli*, it is primarily through painting and then, briefly, through a few select additional case studies that I hope to demonstrate how pervasive a fascination with the arts as a broader category is across these films.

Famous Paintings

Three

Girls Asleep, Girls Afraid
Vermeer in The Forbidden Room
(Anima Persa, 1977)
and The Psychic
(Sette Note in Nero, 1977)

Turning now towards particular artforms and how they are utilized within *giallo* films, we begin with painting. In Parts One, Two and Three, I will explore how recognizable, famous paintings have been utilized in *gialli*, how paintings (including portraits and religious iconography) function as clues, and the representation of painters themselves. Echoing much of the previous critical writing on the intersection of art and film outlined in Chapter One, these case studies—and those later in the book—are aligned with a recognition that the inclusion of other artworks is often accompanied in many of these films by some degree of reflexivity that acknowledges a given text's own understanding of itself as a constructed work of art in its own right. In this way, *giallo* cinema adheres to Brigitte Peucker's claim that "film alludes to, absorbs, and undermines the discourses of the other arts in order to carve out a position for itself among them."[1] Whether a clichéd way of visually communicating the wealth of a particular character or working on a much deeper, more complex level that engages with what at times are the often microscopic details of a particular painting itself or its broader history, as we shall now discover there is a vast, diverse range of ways that *giallo* and painting intersect.

From the gigantic mural of Nicolas Poussin's *Midas and Bachchus* that adorns Rainer Werner Fassbinder's *The Bitter Tears of Petra von Kant* (*Die bitteren Tränen der Petra von Kant*, 1972) to the similarly dominating blow-up of Frans Hals' *The Banquet of the Officers of the St George Militia Company in 1616* that looms over the dining room in Peter Greenaway's *The Cook, the Thief, His Wife & Her Lover* (1989), while there is a demonstrable history of critical interest in the use of recognizable paintings by the great masters in art cinema, as we have previously seen less attention has been expended on the distinctly trashier terrain of horror cinema. And yet in the case of Italian *giallo* film especially, we are faced with an abundance of rich and often complex instances that surely rival their more highbrow counterparts for the conceptual density of how the deployment of these works intersect with other elements.

And often, it should be admitted, perhaps not so dense. Take, for example, the *tableau vivant*. Defined simply as "the static embodiment of well-known paintings by human actors,"[2] what was once a fun parlor game[3] spread in popularity from private homes to music halls around the turn of the twentieth century.[4] This popular form of entertainment spectacle thrilled audiences from all social strata not merely due to the physical demands it placed on its (often naked) performers and the technological display of lighting and other stage mechanics, but, as Daniel Wiegand suggests, much of their "attraction lay in their astonishing resemblance to real artworks and in their potential to play on visual perception."[5] Perhaps unsurprisingly considering the historical specificity of this phenomenon, it bled into early cinema, which mined the theatrical popularity of the *tableau vivant* and moved it under the camera's gaze. By doing so, for Wiegand "early films did not only harken back to already existing forms of optical illusion but tested out their own capacity to create images lingering in uncertainty,"[6] in that they were "indebted to a tradition of popular images in which the sudden discovery that visual objects may be different from what they seem."[7] Yet rather than being a mere historical curio, Steven Jacobs has emphasized how the *tableau vivant* in film contains both modernist *and* postmodernist tendencies. "On the one hand, reference to tableaux vivants in films can be interpreted as part of a modernist tendency towards self-reflexivity," he says. But "because of their hybrid and heterogeneous nature, both cinema and tableaux vivants were difficult to reconcile with a modernist aesthetic of self-investigation based on the idea of the essence and purity of a specific medium," and as such "tableaux vivants are thus rather fitting as an artistic strategy answering to a post-modern aesthetic."[8]

From this perspective, in *giallo*—and in cinema more broadly—the reflexive play of the *tableau vivant* deliberately pulls the viewer out of the diegetic world of the film to suddenly (and often quite unexpectedly) allow them to find themselves instead jolted by a moment of meta-textual recognition. Here, the knowledge that what is playing out before us is understood as *knowingly* engaging with art, and thus consciously revealing its awareness that it itself is a creative construction. At times, there is immense power to this, as shall be discussed shortly in the case of a climactic *tableau vivant* of the *Pietà* in Dario Argento's *The Stendhal Syndrome* (*La Sindrome di Stendhal*, 1996). Other images can be less direct and more playful; for instance, while not necessarily a conscious decision on Mario Bava's part, the bagged corpses that increasingly pile up in the walk-in freezer in *Five Dolls for an August Moon* for me at least provoke associations with the "meat" genre that has permeated art history with examples ranging from Dutch mannerist Pieter Aertsen's *A Meat Stall with the Holy Family Giving Alms* (1551), Italian Baroque painter Annibale Carracci's *Butcher's Shop* (1583), Rembrandt's *Slaughtered Ox* (1655), and even Francis Bacon's *Figure with Meat* (1954). Whether deliberate or not, that image of a plastic-wrapped Edwige Fenech and friends dangling from meat hooks next to a side of beef implies a reference to this art historical tradition with more than a hint of macabre humor.

Just as playful is a fleeting *tableau vivant* in *Spasmo* that bear more than what must be coincidental similarities to *Gabrielle d'Estrées et une de ses sœurs* (c. 1954) by an unknown painter from the late Renaissance French Fontainebleau School. Purchased by the Louvre in 1934, its inclusion in one of the world's most famous art collections leads to a safe assumption that for Europeans especially it would be a familiar painting. A cheeky reference to the painting appears *Spasmo* where the supposedly "sane" sibling at the heart of the film's action is revealed to be far from; after protagonist Christian (Robert Hoffman) is exposed as the murderer of a number of women throughout the film, a phone call to his brother Fritz (Ivan Rassimov) informs us that the psychiatric condition that caused Christian's violence is hereditary. It is in this context that we discover the symbolic "murders" of the mannequins that punctuate the film were in fact committed by Fritz, not Christian. As Fritz grasps the reality of his deteriorating mental health, he enters a hidden chamber in his office where he has carefully placed mannequins in the same position as famous paintings, *tableau vivant* style. In one instance, a wigless mannequin is shown in a certain position, the depth of field suddenly shifting dramatically from the foreground to the background to reveal the mannequin is mimicking a painting hanging behind her on the wall. But it is the mannequin-staged *tableau vivant* of *Gabrielle d'Estrées et une de ses sœurs* that appears to interest Fritz the most, sending him into a stabbing frenzy as he attacks another nearby mannequin to demonstrate his psychosexual derangement. A broad cultural signifier for same-sex desire between women, while the painting appears in more savory fare such as Jeanne Crépeau's lesbian romantic comedy

Julie and Me (*Revoir Julie*, 1998), it is not too radical to suggest that in the case of *Spasmo* at least, Lenzi—never one to hold back on sensationalized depictions of same-sex sexual encounters between women as we see in *Eyeball* (*Gatti rossi in un labirinto di vetro*, 1975) *Orgasmo* (1969), and *So Sweet ... So Perverse* (*Così dolce ... così perversa*, 1969) for starters—is drawing a broad line between the reference to the iconic painting and the supposedly comparable sexual "deviation" of Fritz himself. But Lenzi is hardly alone on this front; as we'll see shortly in our examination of Fulci's *A Lizard in a Woman's Skin*, representations of so-called "deviant" lesbians were not in short supply on the *giallo* front. That film too, as we shall discover, also engages with the *tableau vivant* tradition in one of its many excessively delirious dream sequences.

Moving away from *tableaux vivants*, we can see more explicit encounters with recognizable works of famous art in *giallo* cinema. Think, perhaps, of the Mondrian-esque painting on the wall behind the piano of blind composer Peter Oliver (Anthony Steffen) in *Seven Shawls of Yellow Silk* or the Miro-like painting that hangs above Kitty Wildenbrück's (Barbara Bouchet) bed in *The Red Queen Kills Seven Times* (*La dama rossa uccide sette volte*, Emilio Miraglia, 1972), discussed further in Chapter Seven. There's the Rubens art fraud that lies at the heart of Mario Sabatini's *Delitto d'autore* (1974), while there are references to Italian renaissance painter Pietro Perugino in *Torso* (*I corpi presentano tracce di violenza carnale*, Sergio Martino, 1973) and Rococo painter Giovanni Battista Tiepolo in *A Quiet Place in the Country* (*Un tranquillo posto di campagna*, Elio Petri, 1968), both of which will be discussed further elsewhere in this book. In *Amuck!* (*Alla ricerca del piacere*, Silvio Amadio, 1972), Farley Granger's character Richard gloats to Barbara Bouchet's Greta when he has purchased a work by Italian Renaissance artist Lorenzo Lotto that he has long desired. "Lorenzo Lotto, Artist. Born in Venice in the year 1480," he begins lecturing her. "...And died in the year of?" she interrupts. Sternly, he replies, "Nonsense! A true artist never dies. He's immortal!" And of that most iconic blank, fabric mask so synonymous with Mario Bava's *Blood and Black Lace* (*Sei donne per l'assassino*, 1964), McDonagh has suggested it "recalls Belgian painter René Magritte's eerie portrait of surreally swathed lovers"[9] in his 1928 painting *The Lovers I*. As I note in Chapter Fourteen, this painting is even more directly referred to in a *tableau vivant* in fellow *giallo* filmmaker Michele Soavi's zombie romantic comedy *Cemetery Man* (*Dellamore Dellamore*, 1994).

This art historical legacy can be felt through the poetics of contemporary filmmakers who have experimented with *giallo* traditions in their own works. The first two films by Hélène Cattet and Bruno Forzani *Amer*

(2009) and *The Strange Colour of Your Body's Tears* (2013) have positioned them as what Christoph Huber has rightly identified as the "foremost practitioners of what is termed neo-*giallo*."[10] While striking films in their own right, as has been widely acknowledged these two films do not merely just complement each other, but are also in active dialogue in terms of the gendering of both genre and the gaze itself.[11] As Michael Sicinski notes of the woman-centered *Amer*, "the most prominent image is an extreme close-up of a pair of eyes" which "are looking, attempting to possess the gaze, usurping the film's third-person perspective in favour of a direct first-person point of view."[12] But, he adds,

> Looking is never merely instrumental in *Amer*. It is always soaked through with anxiety and desire, and this is the result of accumulated tension, the moment of vision acting like the firing of a gun, pressure having been built up from all of the previous moments when vision and desire had been thwarted or deranged.[13]

Shifting in *The Strange Colour of Your Body's Tears* to a male protagonist centered film, as Dan (Klaus Tange) searches for his missing wife Edwige in the labyrinthine Art Nouveau building where they live, the building itself becomes emphatically gendered, physically materializing Dan's sexual anxieties, where Anton Bitel notes its "holes and cracks, hidden recesses and secret passageways, and entrances (sometimes locked, sometimes open) offer an architectural blueprint for the female anatomy."[14] My particular interest in painting intersects with precisely these psychosexual/architectural fascinations active within the film in regards to one of the first of the film's dizzying, sensorially provocative flashbacks as Dan moves through the building, ostensibly searching for clues as to the whereabouts of his wife in specific reference to a painting on a ceiling inspired by Alfons Mucha's lithograph *La danse* (1898).

As Dan begins his search for Edwige, he encounters a mysterious neighbor in the hope she may be able to provide him with clues. Instead, the woman recalls through flashbacks the circumstances surrounding the disappearance of her own husband, Paul. Cutting to a flashback, strange sensual groans of an unseen woman's voice can be heard as Paul and his wife have passionless, perfunctory sex. At night, the unsleeping Paul lies awake, transfixed by the Mucha-like figure painted on the wall above him. Surrounded by similar works, Paul is haunted by this largely aural abstracted feminine presence, which he attempts to gain mastery over by sexually dominating his complicit wife. But when the strange sensual groans they hear become a scream, Paul aggressively stops his wife from calling the police and searches for answers within the walls himself. Becoming increasingly obsessed, he ties his wife to the bed, drugging her so he can pursue his increasingly obsessive sexual fascination unhindered. Drilling a hole into the head of the figure painted above their bed inspired by *La danse*, when Paul inserts his finger, he is surprised to see that it comes out covered in blood. When his wife awakens, it is Paul himself who peers down at her through the hole in the painting's head, trapped in the ceiling himself. In an extraordinary sequence, his wife runs a stethoscope across the woman's figure painted on the ceiling in an attempt to detect Paul's presence, and is terrified when the sound of his voice and the location of the heartbeat do not match up spatially. It is in this moment of terror that a drop of blood falls on her from above; "I wiped off the drop of blood and I approached the hole," she tells Dan, "I saw an eye staring at me, filled with hatred, madness, fear." But before she can tell him more, a piercing scream interrupts her sentence as we return to the flashback, a close-up image of a wide-open eye and a wide-open mouth mirroring the strange portal between different sensorial (and sensual realms) that Paul created when he drilled a hole in the painting. At the end of her story, she expels Dan from her apartment without explanation, leaving him more confused than when he arrived in search of his missing wife.

While a cursory look at Mucha's work might suggest that old, art historical objectifying-woman-as-sexualized-subject cliché, the background to his rise to fame speaks of a very different relation to gender and power. Aligned very much with the gender fluidity that marks Cattet and Forzani's own filmography and experiments with *giallo* traditions more broadly, the *femininity* of Mucha's design work does not translate to a controlling male artistic gaze. With a career spectacularly launched when he was granted the opportunity to create the poster art for Sarah Bernhardt's 1895 play *Gismonda* at the Théâtre de la Renaissance in Paris, he was beholden to Bernhardt not just for his own personal success, but the sudden explosion in popularity of Art Nouveau. As Joseph Nechvatal has noted, "Art Nouveau had until then been the province of a small avant-garde coterie, but now fallaciously dubbed 'le Style Mucha' it suddenly had a vast new audience, and Mucha, via Bernhardt, became a celebrity in his own right, overnight."[15] Via this explicit reference to Mucha, this particular scene in *The Strange Colour of Your Body's Tears* therefore underscores the complexity of the gendered gaze—particularly that which culminates at the intersection of violence and sexual desire—in ways far beyond simplistic notions of subject/object, male/female. In keeping with the broader spirit of ambivalence that marks *giallo* cinema historically as noted by Koven and others, Cattet and Forzani discover a poetry active within the very slipperiness of such categories, here through an engagement with art history itself.

Shifting away from neo-*gialli*, Part One will take a similarly close look at the use of recognizable works of art and artists in precisely the kinds of films that have inspired contemporary filmmakers like Cattet and Forzani, emphasizing how each example employs these references in a variety of ways that enrich the text in ways that may not be immediately recognizable for all viewers. And yet in many cases, while all of these works are all quite famous, for those unfamiliar with them the film does not necessarily exclude those viewers from the broader pleasures of the film or the joy of the spectacles they provide. At their most basic, unrecognized level, they can still also communicate simple characteristics such as implying a broader impression of wealth and sophistication. To begin with, we turn to the works of Dutch master Johannes Vermeer in two *gialli*; Dino Risi's *The Forbidden Room* and Lucio Fulci's *The Psychic*.

A key figure amongst *commedia all'italiana* filmmakers,[16] Dino Risi may be less readily known to cult film fans for his *giallo*-aligned work than for comedy classics such as *Scent of a Woman* (*Profumo di donna*, 1974), famously remade in Hollywood by Martin Brest in 1992 in the Al Pacino-fronted film of the same name. But as a dark twisted mystery with a healthy dose of horror tropes and outrageous psychosexual twists (co-written by Risi and *Deep Red*'s co-writer Bernardino Zapponi, no less) Risi's 1977 film *The Forbidden Room* is a comfortable fit for the *giallo* label.[17] Also known as *Lost Souls*, *The Forbidden Room* is based on Giovanni Arpino's 1966 novel *Un'anima persa* and stars Catherine Deneuve as Elisa Stolz, the anxious aunt who hosts her nephew Tino (Danilo Mattei) who comes to stay with her and his Uncle Fabio (Vittorio Gassman) in Venice where he is to attend art school. Aside from the creepy, decrepit Gothic villa in which they live, Tino is given further cause for alarm at Fabio's increasingly peculiar and hostile behavior towards both himself and his aunt. With the assistance of his new friend Lucia (Anicée Alvina) who is a model at the art school, Tino investigates the strange goings-on and discovers not only is the crazed man in the attic Tino believes to be his uncle's brother in fact Fabio himself, but the little girl Beba of whom he finds maudlin, nostalgic traces throughout the house was in fact Elisa herself when she was younger. These are things that belonged to her as a child, not just memorialized but sexually fetishized by the pedophilic Fabio who announces with the shock revelation of Elisa dressed as a young child; "I loved her when she was a child, when she was innocent. Because youth is innocent. I wanted to make her stay young forever. But everything decays, gets spoiled. She grew up. Changed, and killed my little girl. The little girl I loved."

Frozen in time, the life of sexual and psychological abuse Elisa has experienced have stunted her development, rendering her an adult

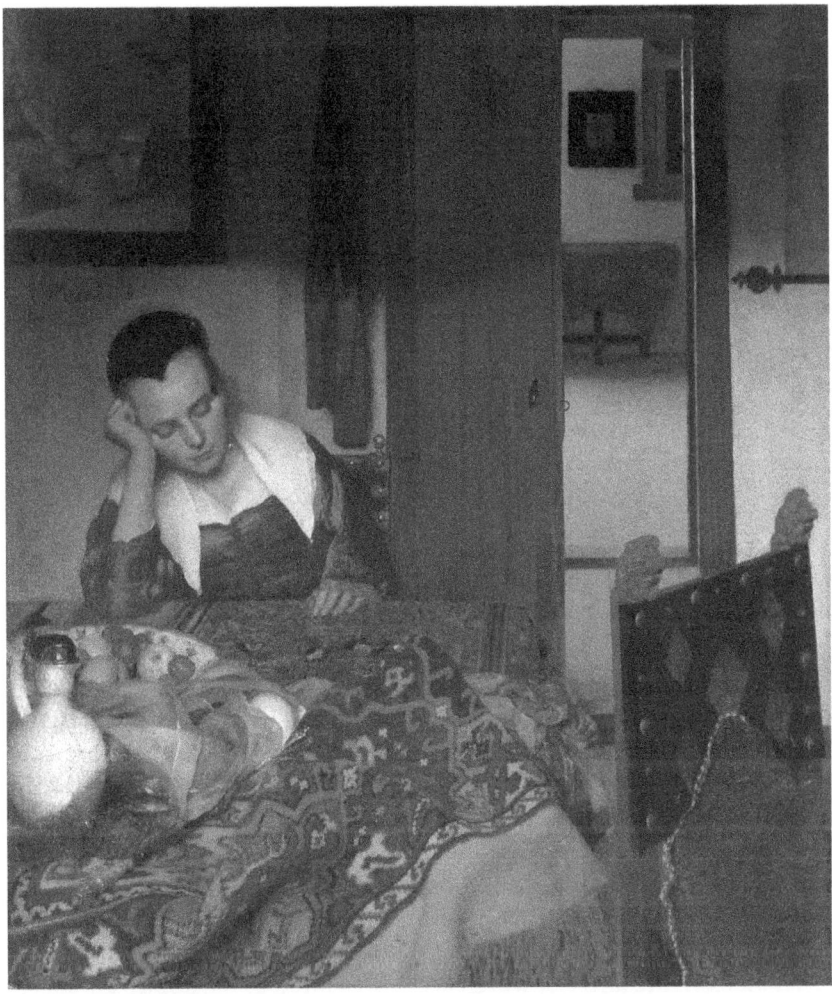

Johannes Vermeer (1632–1675), *A Maid Asleep*, ca. 1656–57, oil on canvas (open access, Metropolitan Museum of Art, www.metmuseum.org).

woman wearing a little girl's clothes in order to keep the perverse fantasies of a pedophile alive. That a symbolic suspension of femininity lies at the heart of film is, however, foreshadowed much earlier in the film, beyond the story of Elisa, Fabio and their distinctly problematic relationship. In a seemingly throwaway scene, Tino sits in an art history lecture, listening to a charmingly crabby and suitably eccentric teacher point out the similarities of a detail of bowl of fruit in Vermeer's *A Girl Asleep* (1657, also known as *A Maid Asleep*) and French post-impressionist Paul Cézanne *Apples and Oranges* (1900). Dismissing a discussion of the "virtues and beauty" of Vermeer's painting for another occasion, it is the parallel with the Cezanne that sparks his ire and upon which he hopes to cast the attention of his students, whom he clearly holds in some derision: "What did modern artists invent? Nothing!." In response to the unhappy responses by his students, he continues; "what contemporary painters do has already been done already by the old masters. But their paintings do so much more in addition. Get the idea, fools?."

There are echoes here, albeit more bluntly put, of a short but significant speech delivered by Adolfo Celi's Serafin early in Aldo Lado's *Who Saw Her Die?* (*Chi l'ha vista morire?*, 1972):

> I was just wondering how the artist today protests that his work has no ties with past tradition. But that's very wrong. Artists essentially are the mirrors of their age, as Rembrandt was, and Monet. And since we are aware that history repeats itself, is it not obvious that the same themes will recur in art, the same modes of expression? The artist there is merely to report; he does not create.

While Serafin is perhaps somewhat less of a provocative crank in this scene than the art lecturer in Risi's film, both speeches indicate an engagement with highbrow culture in a supposedly lowbrow form, and as such there is perhaps evidence of a kind of reflexive trolling regarding the sometimes lazy repetition that marks genre filmmaking itself; as Koven has noted, "Italian popular cinema, particularly horror cinema, is highly derivative."[18] But of more immediate interest is the sheer physical centrality of the Vermeer painting and the way it dominates the scene in terms of its *mise-en-scène*. The subject of much debate in art history in terms of its ultimate meaning,[19] Madlyn Millner Kahr notes that the specific pose of the sleeping figure has endured since Ancient Roman art.[20] Closely studying the objects around the sleeping figure, Millner Kahr suggests that she "personifies Sloth, the vice that opens the gate to all other vices,"[21] the latter of which are represented in the apples and pearl earrings (references to Aphrodite and sexuality). Similarly, the wine glass and jug on the table suggests to Millner Kahr not only the possibility of "intemperance, gluttony, and lechery," but leads her to speculate more directly if "the sleeping young woman is drunk."[22] It is, she concludes, a moral tale; "let us be alert to avoid the snares of sensual pleasures. All worldly satisfactions are but vanity. The freedom of our will makes each of us responsible for renouncing the earthly in favor of divine truth."[23]

Somewhat more in synch with Risi's deployment of painting, however, is Martha Hollander's observation that Vermeer's work here "is full of contradictions." For Hollander, it visually "combines sensuous richness with near illegibility," noting in support of her claim that "the elements are warmly colored and patterned but difficult to make out." Significantly, she suggests that "thematically, it offers an assemblage of erotic imagery in an otherwise meditative tone,"[24] tensions which are not unrelated to *The Forbidden Room*. Risi's film is marked by a sense of disjunctures, not merely in terms of its mystery narrative but how Tino struggles to make sense of his environment as a young man—a representative of the present day—in an archaic, oppressive house that he (and we) discover is governed by a horrendous secret that keeps perpetrator and victim locked in an unsustainable relationship governed by the transgressive sexual identity Fabio forces on Elisa, attempting to suspend her in time itself. As Edward Snow asks of this painting in his discussion of sexuality in Vermeer's painting, "has something taken leave, does it approach, or is it already *there* in some uncanny way?"[25] (italics in original). In wording that has particular pertinence to *The Forbidden Room*, Snow writes of multiple rooms we see in the painting that they "seem to contain ghostly presences; successive thresholds feel charged. Objects, light effects, space itself create a kind of phantasmagoria and take on the quality of things vivid and alive inside the mind."[26]

The enigmas of the painting that lies at the center of Tino's art lecture thus bleed into the film itself as a whole, not just diegetically in terms of Elisa's situation as the "sleeping" girl trapped in stasis—an unmoving, unchanging figure of oppressed femininity in a moving picture—but more deeply about how this temporal incongruity leaves an extraordinary impression upon the viewer at the film's conclusion. I would argue this lies beyond the traditional expected impact of a twist reveal, and that one does not need to know the interpretive enigma of this particular painting in an art historical sense to comprehend on some level that there is *something* important about this giant, privileged image of a sleeping girl. We do not need to know Vermeer to know that, as Snow puts it, "whatever haunts the girl asleep thus haunts us as well. It is not clear whose mind is at work in this painting, creating phantoms of feeling, vectors and precipitates of desire."[27] Ultimately, then, just as the reflexive emphasis on art—and this particular work of art—in this scene draws us out of the diegesis even for just a moment (highlighted by the memorable dialogue of the irritable lecturer about art and originality), so Snow observes that in the painting itself, "across the once firm barrier between viewer and subject there is a strange osmosis of imaginative states."[28]

Lucio Fulci's supernatural *giallo The Psychic* engaged even more centrally with the Dutch artist. While more rigid definitions of *giallo* might exclude films such as Mario Bava's *Kill, Baby … Kill* (*Operazione paura*, 1966) and *Hatchet for the Honeymoon* (*Il rosso segno della follia*,

1970), *Short Night of Glass Dolls* (*La corta notte delle bambole di vetro*, Aldo Lado, 1971), *Feast of Satan* (*Las amantes del diablo*, José María Elorrieta, 1971), *All the Colors of the Dark* (*Tutti i colori del buio*, Sergio Martino, 1972), *The Killer Reserved Nine Seats* (*L'Assassino ha riservato nove Paltrone*, Giuseppe Bennati, 1974), Mario Siciliano's *Evil Eye* (*Malocchio*, Mario Siciliano, 1975), *The Spider Labyrinth* (*Il nido del ragno*, Gianfranco Giagni, 1988) and Dario Argento's *Phenomen*a (1985),

The Love Letter, Johannes Vermeer, Dutch painting, oil on canvas, 1669–1670. From a dim room in the foreground, a woman playing a lute is interrupted to receive a letter from her maid servant (Everett–Art, Shutterstock.com).

by virtue of their inclusion of supernatural elements, Koven borrows a term from Kim Newman and calls these *"giallo-fantastico."*[29] Although not particularly abundant in number, these movies "embrac[e] ... the strong connection between the *giallo* and the horror film" as they "offer a more supernatural element."[30]

In 1971, a waiter stole Vermeer's painting *The Love Letter* (1669–1670) straight off the walls of Brussels' Fine Arts Museum, where it had been on loan from the Amsterdam's Rijksmuseum. This is renowned as one of the most audacious art heists of the 1970s, a reputation not lessened by the 200 million Belgian francs that were demanded as ransom, to be sent to Bengali refugees.[31] Rolled up and snugly hidden under the thief's bed, while the painting was eventually returned, these less-than-ideal conditions of its storage were far from those of the archive with which the work had previously been located, causing almost irreparable damage to one of Vermeer's most canonical artworks.[32] For better or for worse, this made *The Love Letter* front page news, and thus a familiar painting in the imaginations of the European public during this period for all the wrong reasons.

Ten years later, Lucio Fulci featured this painting centrally in *The Psychic*. Vermeer might lack the heavy metal morbidity of Caravaggio or the sensorial immersiveness of Peter Paul Rubens, painters who might more immediately come to mind as obvious points of comparison with Fulci's *gialli* and horror movies more generally. Vermeer is somehow a little too *nice* for Fulci; there's something so domestic, even tame, that doesn't feel like it quite gels. When we think of Fulci, many of us think not just of his *gialli* but of his gruesome horror films like *The Beyond* (*E tu vivrai nel terrore—L'aldilà*, 1981), *Zombie* (1979) and *City of the Living Dead* (*Paura nella città dei morti viventi*, 1980).

Taught at film school by Michelangelo Antonioni and beginning his film career as a documentary filmmaker,[33] Fulci had worked across numerous film genres before arriving at *gialli*; comedies, westerns, science fiction films and the like. Finding success with his Franco Franchi and Ciccio Ingrassia comedies, Thrower has noted that by the late '60s Fulci "had settled into a rut," and *gialli* gave him exciting new creative terrain to shift his focus.[34] Perhaps lagging only slightly behind Dario Argento for fame and notoriety in terms of internationally recognized Italian horror directors, if there is one single point where these two filmmakers most diverge, it is arguably that color is to Argento what light is to Fulci. From this perspective, parallels between Fulci and Vermeer begin to emerge, the latter revered as nothing less than "the painter of light" himself, to quote Giuseppe Ungaretti.[35] As artists, both Fulci and Vermeer relied on light perhaps more than any other element to create their own signature individual creative visions. When Martin Pops called the light in *The Love Letter* "dry and hard,"[36] for example, he could just as easily been talking about Fulci's use of light in *The Psychic*.

Despite the temptation to dismiss Vermeer's *The Love Letter* in *The Psychic* as a disposable highbrow reference, nothing could be further from the truth. Even Thrower, who acknowledges the presence of the work, does not perhaps give full credit to its centrality to the film as a whole when he notes that "a glancing cue from a painting by Vermeer suggests an appreciation of the Dutch painter's uncanny ability to accumulate hints and insinuations within the most apparently ordered of canvasses."[37] There is, however, arguably much, much more going on here. One of the most critically discussed feature of Vermeer's work in art history discourse has centered around his particular compositional "paintings within a painting"[38] style; paintings often appear on the walls of the scenes he paints, forming mini internalized painting-worlds that themselves have been laboriously studied by art historians in search of interpretive enlightenment. Fulci takes Vermeer's frame-within-a-frame structure and makes it his own in *The Psychic*, both in terms of how he carefully constructs the film as a visual work and, more broadly, in terms of the thematics of Vermeer's famous painting itself.

Like many *gialli*, *The Psychic* does not boast a particularly complex narrative nor rely on sophisticated characterizations, and its more supernatural qualities complement its traditional *giallo* elements nicely. *The Psychic* opens as an unidentified woman dies by suicide by hurling herself off the famous white cliffs of Dover (shown in Fulci's characteristic gruesome detail). Her young daughter Virginia in Florence has a psychic vision, instantly understanding what has happened to her mother by visualizing it in her mind. Although opening with a visceral bang, by Fulci's horror standards *The Psychic* is comparatively low-key in its representation of violence, and, for that matter, sex. Jumping ahead in time, we meet the adult Virginia (Jennifer O'Neill), who repeats a similar drive to that of her mother that opened the film, but the tone is now different. She is happy and smiling as she drives to the airport where her husband Francesco (Gianni Garko) will depart on a trip. Typifying the bourgeois jet-set lifestyle that permeates so many *gialli*, we understand almost immediately upon meeting Virginia that she is rich, sophisticated and world-wise. Yet as she leaves her husband, we discover things are not as perfect as they first appeared, another psychic vision presenting Virginia with a series of seemingly disconnected images that she will spend much of the film's remaining time trying to decipher; a broken mirror, a room with a red lamp, a red light flashing on a black screen, a limping man, a cigarette, the bloody face of a dead woman, a magazine cover, a black-and-white print of Vermeer's *The Love Letter*, and, from a significantly first-person perspective, a brick wall being constructed. The last element of her "vision" is not visual but aural, the iconic seven notes of the film's Italian title, *Sette Note in Nero* ("seven notes in black"), from a score written by long-time Fulci collaborator and renowned Italian film composer Fabio Frizzi.[39]

Not wholly unlike Hideo Nakata's *Ring* (*Ringu*, 1998) almost twenty years later, the narrative structure of the film seeks effectively to unpack each aspect of the montage of seemingly random images that constructs Virginia's vision. As each piece of the puzzle is solved, the story progresses to the next image, and the next. But the solutions at first arise less from an investigative spirit than they are premonitions of things to come—while we might recognize this as the audience, it takes Virginia a little longer to cotton on. Initially shaken by her vision and annoyed by the patronizing dismissal by her ex-boyfriend, parapsychologist Luca (Marc Porel), Virginia decides that in an act of self-care she will stay in one of her wealthy husband's many uninhabited mansions to renovate it "as a surprise." But upon entering a room in this building randomly, Virginia is shocked when she recognizes the same red lamp from as her vision. Driven to "solve" the rest of her vision, she starts digging into the walls of the room itself, finding to her great horror a hidden skeleton. These are the remains of Francesco's ex-lover, and he is soon arrested; with the stakes now dramatically heightened, Virginia's investigations (with Luca's help) start to uncover further truths, despite Francesco's often aggressive rejection of her psychic abilities.

Which brings us back to *The Love Letter*. As their enquiries take them to an art gallery, there is a dramatic shift in compositional style as Virginia and Luca are suddenly flattened, represented on-screen as solid black silhouettes that contrast sharply against ornate backgrounds. This is the context where Virginia sees the Vermeer painting; if there is any suspicion that the painting and its inclusion are random, empty indulgences on Fulci's part, they rapidly evaporate in the face of the sheer longevity he privileges precious screen time on it as his camera lingers on the title plate: he wants us to know *precisely* what this painting is. The Vermeer leads Virginia and Luca to the last of the main characters to enter the film, an ex-policeman called Emilio Rospini (Gabriele Ferzetti) who was involved in the original investigation when the painting was stolen some years earlier. Sound familiar? Fulci is making a direct reference to the highly publicized real-life theft of this exact painting in a clear metatextual reference. Rospini walks with a limp, yet another element of her original vision that now makes sense to Virginia. That he is so privileged in her vision leads her to suspect that Rospini is somehow involved with Francesco's past crimes, so she goes to his house to confront him.

Through a painstakingly constructed series of shots, this is where the logic behind Fulci's conscious privileging of *The Love Letter* begins to be revealed. As Virginia sits in a room waiting for Rospini, with almost surgical precision Fulci carefully restages in three separate shots his own version of Vermeer's "picture within a picture" composition. Here, picture frames, mirrors and other diegetic internal "frames" litter the *mise-en-scène*. Realizing what the audience has already deduced, Luca clicks that Virginia's visions are predictions of things to come, not flashbacks to things that have happened. Despite believing she has proven her husband's innocence and that he did not murder the girl in the wall, Virginia is still unsettled and grows increasingly desperate in her search for the truth behind her vision (this indicates—as does her clear romantic connection with Luca—that her driving mission to solve the riddle of her vision may have been less concerned with proving her husband's innocence as she protested, and more closely aligned with the inquisitive drive of the *giallo* film's amateur detective figure). With the discovery of the dead body of a woman Virginia believed could assist in unpacking further aspects of her vision, she is finally convinced that Luca is right about her visions being a premonition. Despite the woman's death, through information in her vision Virginia locates the evidence in question. Finding an envelope that contains the answers she seeks, before she can open it she is chased by the ominous Rospini, managing to escape to return the presumed safety of the mansion.

When Rospini's back is injured during his pursuit of Virginia and he is unable to continue, it seems that all that is now required is a quick dénouement and all will fall into place. But Fulci has something far more complex in mind that will return us in a more abstract way to *The Love Letter*. Virginia returns to the mansion, patiently waiting for Francesco's return. She takes the letter and places it on a sideboard, still without reading it. But as Francesco walks towards her, she notes he too has a limp; it was he—and not Rospini—who was the menacing, limping presence in her vision. But her recognition of this error of judgment comes too late; seeing the letter, Francesco assumes Virginia has read it and that she now knows the truth which (for our benefit) is spelled out by Rospini from his hospital bed: the young woman buried behind the wall worked with Rospini and Francesco to steal the Vermeer painting, Francesco murdering her. He lies to Rospini and tells him the young woman had stolen the painting, keeping it for himself and reaping the rewards. Believing Virginia now to be a threat, Francesco decides to murder her too and it is only in the final moments that her visions are explained; in the spirit of Edgar Allan Poe's *The Black Cat* (1845),[40] he bashes Virginia on the head and places her in the wall cavity, leaving her helpless as he bricks her inside.

Luca and the police arrive, but it is too late and Francesco appears to have succeeded, eradicating any evidence that Virginia was ever there. This is where we must start looking closely, as it is only in these final moments that *The Psychic* transcends what might be considered a standard color-by-numbers *giallo* ending. Here is what we see: a large dresser stands in front of the wall where Virginia has been buried. We do not see her again, and we do not know if she is alive or dead; the film is unequivocally ambivalent about this question. But just Luca exits the room, Virginia's watch alarm—those iconic "seven notes" of the film's Italian title—go off. The compositional brutality of what happens in many ways is far more disturbing and upsetting in its sheer ambivalence than showing Virginia's body; be it dead or alive, at least we would know what had happened to our central protagonist. Virginia is thus both present and absent, a frame within a frame, both in the room and not in the room. The significance of the wall cavity was foreshadowed in *The Love Letter* itself; as has been noted , this is significantly Vermeer's only painting with a fireplace in it.[41] We want Luca to be the rescuer, but we simply do not know if there's anyone even left to rescue. As he walks towards the dresser, he once again is converted from a human to a flat black shape, this time a shadowy moving figure that adds only further to the conclusion's overwhelming sense of bleak, existential dread.

The camera follows the moving shadow's trajectory towards the dresser that disguises the damaged wall behind which Virginia has been buried. With the soundtrack of Virginia's simple watch alarm, the final shot divided into two, a solid black block on the left and a brown, wood-paneled block on the right. Compositionally, this simple image speaks in a profound, disturbing way back through time and art history to *The Love Letter*. To be clear, the semantics of this visual match show how Fulci has effectively removed the central "action' segment of Vermeer's paintings, of his frames-within-frames. Fulci has "cut out" Virginia, following a logic suggested in Vermeer's paintings that indicate a modular quality of movable spaces. In this way, the two paintings behind the standing and seated figure in Vermeer's work are not the only internal ruptures as we step back and look at what surrounds them. When we consider how they are framed, *The Love Letter* functions almost as a triptych. In reference then to the Vermeer painting that he privileges in the film then, Fulci has not only this central "panel," but he has also destroyed all decorative or ornamental traces from the already plainer side panels: there are no maps, no curtains, just a wedge of black and a wedge of brown.

There is therefore a kind of pictorial violence in this image, even if we can't see Virginia and have no final answers as to what has happened to her. That violence is intrinsically linked to the composition of Vermeer's *The Love Letter*; not only because Virginia has been deleted from the image, but also, in a more sophisticated way, how the film as a whole has been so tightly aligned with her perspective, a perspective which we are now denied. This is a deliberate act of aesthetic subversion on Fulci's part that appears fundamentally linked to Vermeer's painting. Transcending the Fulci/Vermeer relationship, however, a third artist comes into play when we look—*really look*—at that final dual-tone shot: American abstract expressionist Mark Rothko, particular his painting *Black on Grey* (1969/70). If Rothko's painting is placed on its side, the conceptual leap across art history that Fulci made at *The Psychic*'s conclusion becomes apparent. While there are a good three hundred years between Vermeer's *The Love Letter* and Rothko's *Black on Grey*, Fulci collapses that gap in 20 seconds of language-less film. It is a door slamming shut, with women jammed in the middle.

These last moments of Fulci's film then are about more than just painting. Like *Girl Asleep* that is used to such powerful effect in *The Forbidden Room*, debate has raged over this Vermeer work also. R.H. Wilenski's interpretation, for instance, suggests that the image of the women in the room that makes up the center "panel" of *The Love Letter* is actually a reflection in a mirror[42]; if we look at it from a certain perspective, this makes sense. However as Anthony Bailey notes, whether it is or not a mirror ultimately has no impact that either way, "it is an unsettling picture ... we almost feel that we are looking into a perspective box ... which gives us a sense of gazing through a keyhole into a Dutch house 240 years ago."[43] There is a strange defamiliarizing sensation here built into how Vermeer reworked his signature frame-within-a-frame composition, most notably in the fact that *The Love Letter* is the only painting he ever did where a "scene is constructed beyond an open door."[44] Aside from adding a suffocating, abstract sense to the scene that takes us away from the action at the center of the painting, at the same time—and with particular relevance to *The Psychic*—this uncharacteristic composition effectively compresses the two figures at the center of the picture even further into an already confined space. Considering *The Love Letter* alongside Vermeer's *A Lady Writing a Letter with Her Maid* (1670–1671), Martin Pops' suggestion that that "Vermeer's enclosed women merge into their environments"[45] holds chilling echoes for the fate of Virginia in *The Psychic*. Fulci takes notion of "enclosed women merge[d] into their environments" to its literal extreme. Buried in the walls themselves *à la* Edgar Allan Poe, the brutality of Virginia's fate feels like the outside panels of Vermeer's *The Love Letter* closing in on the scene of women inside, hurling us across time and space into the abyss; the wholly abstracted realm of Mark Rothko.

The result—for both the viewer and Virginia herself—is a shared sensorial experience of suffocation. The final impact of this conclusion pivots on an association between this physical sensation of suffocation, claustrophobia, or being "shut off" or "closed in," just like we see in *The Love Letter*. This, I would argue, is an evocative art historical instance of Adam Lowenstein's "return of history through the gut"[46] of which the horror film is so uniquely capable, so eloquently identified in his 2005 book *Shocking Representation: Historical Trauma, National Cinema, and the Modern Horror Film*. Just as Rothko slams the frame closed upon Vermeer's already enclosed women, so too does Fulci to Virginia. Regardless of her supernatural gift, she is powerless in a constructed patriarchal universe.

There is a parallel, perhaps, in how Virginia can be understood as being trapped in art as much as behind a wall with the ending of Fulci's zombie masterpiece *The Beyond* (*E tu vivrai nel terrore! L'aldilà*, 1981) where Wheeler Winston Dixon notes; "Frozen in space and time, the camera pulls back to show the viewer that [David] Warbeck and [Kristy] MacColl['s characters] have become part of the painting, entombed forever in darkness, death, and decay."[47] Like *The Psychic*, a painting—albeit this time one painted by one of the film's characters (Schweick, played by Antoine Saint-John) is just as central to Fulci's narrative, thematic and aesthetic universe, if not more so. There is something fundamentally corporeal about Schweick's powerful painting in *The Beyond*; it not only can make those who gaze upon it bleed, but it bleeds itself. As we will now see further in *A Lizard in a Woman's Skin*, Fulci engaged with famous paintings in other *gialli* also.

Four

Swan Guts and Screaming Popes
*Salvador Dalí, Francis Bacon and
A Lizard in a Woman's Skin
(Una lucertola con la pelle di donna,
Lucio Fulci, 1971)*

Any suggestion that Fulci's inclusion of this specific Vermeer painting in *The Psychic* might be purely coincidental—that its selection was random and thrown in for a bit of highfalutin razzle dazzle—falls away instantaneously when one realizes just how entrenched he was in his previous career as an art critic. Fulci did not dabble and was far from a hobbyist. In a fascinating article at *Film Comment* that examines the intersection of Fulci's broader *oeuvre* and post-war Italian painting, Chris Shields notes that aside from working as an art critic for the Rome newspapers *Il Messaggero* and *Gazzetta delle Arti*, Fulci was also a member of the *Gruppo Arte Sociale* or the "Social Art Group," which included both critics and artists such as Renzo Vespignani.[1] Looking at Fulci's more overt body horror in films such as *The Beyond*, Shields thus suggests that a line can be drawn between Fulci and the early impasto paintings of postmodern Italian artist Mario Schifano. For Shields, "both impasto painting and the gore film can 'pass' for strictly representational art, but what makes them unique is their overwhelming concern with material."[2] He continues, "the impasto technique itself, which entails layering paint on a canvas so thickly that it can appear to be emerging from the canvas, resembles the effects of movie carnage, which can seem to flow off the screen."[3] From this perspective, Shields considers that "Fulci's work has more to do with the visceral manipulation of materials favored by post-war Italian painters than it does with the narrative fantasies of his predecessors (Mario Bava) and contemporaries (Dario Argento)."[4]

Just as Shields has noted that the apartment walls of the New York family at the heart of Fulci's *Manhattan Baby* (1982) are covered in Schifano's paintings, so too many years earlier we can find similarly familiar art hanging on the residence of the central protagonist of his 1971 *giallo*, *A Lizard in a Woman's Skin*. While I focus on three particular works that hang in Carol Hammond's (played by Florinda Bolkan) apartment—variations of a backdrop Salvador Dalí painted for the 1939 ballet *Bacchanale*, and versions of two works by Francis Bacon, *Pope II* (1951) and *Man in Blue V* (1954)—art references are not hard to find in *A Lizard in a Woman's Skin* more broadly. Although not shown close up or for any particularly long length of time, for instance, Carol's apartment includes amongst other paintings another Bacon reference, a variation of *Study for Portrait II (After the Life Mask of William Blake)* (1955).

And it is not just in Carol's apartment where art looms in a significant manner; for example, the Aubrey Beardsley prints that hang on the wall of Carol's murdered neighbor's wall underscore the victim's drug-fuelled bohemian party-girl lifestyle. As Elizabeth A. Fleming notes, Beardsley's work went through somewhat of a popular renaissance in the '60s an early '70s when it was adopted as a countercultural motif for young people linked to the precise kind of LSD-heavy hippy culture that Jenny (Penny Brown) and Hubert (Mike Kennedy)—the stoned, unseeing "witnesses" to the murder—typified.[5] That one of these prints in the film—*The Dancer's Reward, for Salomé by Oscar Wilde* (1907)—features a violent woman admiring her handiwork is not lost on the plot dynamics of the film (and the murder scene in question), the film's surprise twist being the revelation that the neighbor was killed by Carol herself. Likewise, that her neighbor's name is Julia Durer (played by *giallo* regular Anita Strindberg) is surely more than a coincidental reference to German Renaissance printmaker Albrecht Dürer, a key figure in the history of grotesque art. Another *giallo* regular Ely Galleani who plays Carol's step-daughter Joan also has her own more direct run-in with art and violence when she finds Jenny in an abandoned building executing her own version of Niki de Saint Phalle's famous action paintings, the *Tirs* series made during the '60s and '70s which she famously made by shooting her canvas. In the Fulci revision of the work, Penny instead throws paint-dipped palette knives at the canvas as she mockingly menaces Jenny in what appears to be an attempt to thwart the young woman's investigation.

Set in London, *A Lizard in a Woman's Skin* is narratively at least built around the mystery of Julie Durer's murder. Carol's sexually-loaded nightmares about her neighbor's death appear to come true when Julie's body is discovered, leading investigators Inspector Corvin (acclaimed

Welsh actor Stanley Baker) and Sergeant Brandon (Alberto de Mendoza) to initially suspect the psychologically delicate Carol of the crime despite the fact that Carol's father Edmond (Leo Genn)—and we, the audience—are encouraged to believe that she is the victim of that old *giallo* staple gaslighting, and that someone else is responsible for the murder. The twist in this sense is not a twist at all; Carol was in fact never mentally ill, and the dreams were concoctions to fool her psychiatrist whose commitment to psychoanalysis led him to *only* understand the symbolic, and not literal, nature of the dreams Carol had described to him. While both *The Psychic* and *A Lizard in a Woman's Skin* are built around abstracted psychological vignettes that stem from its two women protagonist's psyches—a dream in the latter, a psychic vision in the former—what they both share is Fulci's ambivalence to how these supposed puzzles can be easily solved. Human nature, he suggests, is far too messy to allow such an easy explanation.

A Lizard in a Woman's Skin begins with a deliriously unrestrained dream sequence that typifies Fulci at the top of his game; sex and psychological distress fearlessly intersect in a kaleidoscopic set piece accompanied by a psychedelic score by Ennio Morricone. Beginning with abstracted blobs of red pulsing on a black screen while the white credits roll, what at first begins as a standard train journey soon turns into something much different. It's an old train with wood paneled interiors, and a near-orgasmically distraught Carol pushes her way through the crowd until the train corridor changes into a long white corridor, and the demographic of the throng of people also changes; younger, wilder, less clothed and distinctly horny. Becoming increasingly dizzier, Carol falls in a breath-taking slow motion shot through abstracted black space, landing before the red velvet bed of a leering, seductive Durer. Despite her attempt to escape, Carol cannot, and a slow-motion sex scene follows, Fulci clearly unrushed in his desire to milk the erotic spectacle for all it's worth. Close-ups of Bolkan's face convert her earlier groans of disorientation into ones that are clearly sexual in nature, cutting back to "reality" as she orgasms, waking up in her own bed. Pulling back, the camera reveals her naked body writhing underneath white sheets and carefully shows that her bed is framed by a simple gold-colored bedframe.

Even before his work is introduced to the film, then, the function of this bedframe foreshadows Francis Bacon whose paintings are often marked by these kinds of three dimensional spaces. Described as evoking suggestions of a "glass-box torture chamber,"[6] and his tendency towards "barely visible cubic or elliptic cage[s] around the figures depicted to create his dramatic compositions"[7] from the 1930s onwards,

Four—Swan Guts and Screaming Popes

this simple bedframe allows a visual match to be made with a Bacon painting that will be soon introduced into the film. Recalling the "space-frames" that were so popular in Cubism, as Andrew Stewart MacKay suggests, by using this device Bacon's "sitter is a caged creature whose potential for horror and violence is contained and distanced and whose desire for succour or deliverance is denied."[8] This is, importantly, the space within which the non-dreaming Carol is first introduced; even if we've not seen the film before and never heard of Francis Bacon, we have concrete indications of Carol's psychological reality only five minutes in. Waking alone in her bed-prison, Carol is trapped—and ultimately doomed—by her sexuality.

Cutting to the next shot, we can still see the bed frame, but the bed itself is empty. Instead, our eye is drawn to a dramatic painting that hangs above Carol's bed, a framed version of Dalí's *Bacchanale*. While not identifying the painting as a Dalí reference, Michael Sevastakis in his book *Giallo Cinema and Its Folktale Roots: A Critical Study of 10 Films* (2016) demonstrates precisely the ease with which Fulci can communicate thematic strands through artworks, even if those works are not identified by the audience as specific to any particular artist. Says Sevastakis:

> The painting of a large swan on the back wall functions as a feminine symbol, a link to the unknown—from the erotic to the sublime, from the mysteries of life to those of death. These peculiarities are associated with the women's erotic relationship, Julia's murder, the mystery surrounding her death and the person responsible for it. The swan's sensual connotations are found in Greek mythology where Zeus, in the form of a swan, rapes Leda as she sleeps. In this dream Julia supplants Zeus by raping Carol, the new Leda, but it is Carol who has instigated the affair possibly because of strained conjugal relations with Frank who is seeing another woman.[9]

While Sevastakis is correct in noting the significance of the swan and its associations with Greek legend, there's two problems with this reading. Firstly, there is no evidence that Carol was *raped* by Julia; rape is very different to a woman who is clearly uncomfortable with her sexuality being involved a *consensual* sexual encounter, which this appears very much to be. As we discover, Carol's discomfort with her sexuality has as much to do with class as it does sexual identity; she deeply fears how it will impact her bourgeois lifestyle once Julia begins to blackmail her, threatening to tell her conservative father that her daughter is a lesbian. So intense is Carol's desire to maintain her social position that she turns to murder and deception. Secondly—as discussed further shortly in relation to a dream sequence where Dalí and Bacon's artwork feature centrally—according to the film's own pictorial logic, the swan is not aligned with Carol, but rather Fulci draws a direct connection between the swan and Carol's soon-to-be-murdered stepdaughter Joan, that latter of whom will display an open wound on her stomach in Carol's later dream, just like the swan in the painting.

The emphasis on the myth of Leda and the Swan is crucial when considering *Bacchanale* in the context of Dalí's own broader work as an artist. Swans were somewhat of a fascination for the famous surrealist, who would in 1949 reimagine the myth through a painting of his wife Gala in *Leda Atomica*, but, as the title alone suggests, also featured heavily as a visual motif in his 1937 painting *Swans Reflecting Elephants*. In light of these two other works, Fulci's specific choice of *Bacchanale* warrants further reflection; surely if he was simply trying to reference Leda and the Swan, either of these other (more famous) works might have been just as suitable, if not more so? Or, alternatively, if he simply wanted a Dalí painting with an aspect of visceral horror to it to experiment with in the forthcoming dream sequence, he could have just as easily chosen *The Bleeding Roses* (1930) or *The Face of War* (1941)? When we dig deeper, considering Fulci's background as an art critic we can recognize that the selection of *Bacchanale* was no whim.

In 1934, Dalí played with the idea of making a film about composer Richard Wagner, King Ludwig II of Bavaria and writer Leopold Ritter von Sacher-Masoch (the latter from whom the term "masochism" derives). While the film never eventuated, the three figures appeared in Dalí's 1939 ballet *Bacchanale* which premiered in New York City on November 9, 1939, which featured the giant swan painting as its backdrop. Focused primarily on the Bavarian king, the ballet homed in on Ludwig's psychological delicacy, and in words that have more than a passing relevance to Carol, Fèlix Fanés writes of the ballet that "Ludwig II [was] the mad king of Bavaria ... the devotee of extravagant luxury, the Romantic dreamer, the repressed homosexual" whose "plan for a 'decorative' monarchy coincided with the profound transformations taking place during the final third of the nineteenth century; industrialization, the decline of absolute power, and social egalitarianism."[10] While bourgeois excess and repressed queer desire may be the most obvious threads that tie Ludwig to Carol, this question of broader social transformation is not to be overlooked; as the film takes great pains to reveal, Carol is miserable and stuck in an out-of-date conservative rut that does not provide her with the space to express her true desires. She finds that space in the progressive, drug-fuelled party scene of London's so-called "swinging sixties," amongst Julia and her world of hippy artists. Stuck in this liminal space between past and future, Carol's fear leads her to violent action in order to maintain the very status quo that has repressed her.

Moving to the rest of the apartment that she shares with her husband Frank (Jean Sorel), it is here that the Bacon works are revealed. Above their dining room table hangs a version of Bacon's 1951 painting *Pope II*, part of his so-called "screaming popes" series, the most famous of which is no doubt *Study after Velázquez's Portrait of Pope Innocent X* which he painted the same year. Bacon reworked his own vision of the famous portrait by the fifteenth century Spanish baroque painter

A Lizard in a Woman's Skin (*Una lucertola con la pelle di donna*, 1971), Florinda Bolkan (front) and Leo Genn (courtesy Everett Collection, Alamy Stock Photo).

Diego Velázquez from the late '40s to the mid '60s in a series of paintings which effectively behead original pontiff and replace it instead with faces inspired by the screaming nurse from Sergei Eisenstein's early Soviet masterpiece, *Battleship Potemkin* (1925). This interest in cinema is no coincidence, Bacon once stating that "I would have been a film director if I hadn't been a painter."[11] While the influence of the Salvador Dalí and Luis Buñuel collaboration *The Andalusian Dog* (*Un Chien Andalou*, 1929) has been widely acknowledged to have influenced Fulci's penchant for eyeball violence,[12] in the most general terms it is not hard to see why Fulci would have been drawn to Bacon as well. Think, for example, of Gillian McIver's claim that "Francis Bacon's whole body of work could be considered an exercise in painting body horror,"[13] or Matthew Collings's description of Bacon which could apply just as easily to many of Fulci's *gialli* and horror movies: "existential horror, revulsion, loneliness, alienation are his overriding themes, treated with a hallucinatory, distorted realism that derive in part from the influence of film and photography, in part from an uncompromisingly bleak attitude to the modern human condition."[14]

Bacon's "screaming popes" not only undermine the all-knowing authority of the religious figure and replace it with something far more existential, but in terms of Bacon's homosexuality—and, for that matter, Carol's—they function as symbolically constructed prisons of oppression for desires that falls beyond that which are deemed acceptable by the Roman Catholic church. That Fulci turned specifically to *Pope II* of all of the "screaming popes" suggests something about its framing struck him as important; unlike many of the other paintings in the series, this one is seen from a perspective that is less intimate, and thus reveals more of the frame-cube around the enclosed figure. This, in terms of the centrality of Carol's sexuality in *A Lizard in a Woman's Skin*, is crucial, as it allows a more direct visual match to be made between her bed (the site where her sexuality has isolated her) and Bacon's famous boxes.

If this question of sexuality is raised through Fulci's inclusion of *Pope II* in the Hammond's dining room, it becomes even clearer by the privileged placement of a version of his 1954 painting *Man in Blue V* in the living room. Again, like Dalí's *Bacchanale* and Bacon's *Pope II*, for viewers not familiar with these works or their contexts, Fulci does not exclude them from the central pleasures the film affords; some background eye candy at best that, like paintings in so many *gialli*, act as a simple cipher to suggest wealth and sophistication. But *Man in Blue V* allows a direct continuation of a queer reading of the use of Bacon's work in *A Lizard in a Woman's Skin* that both enriches the film and continues to underscore just how deeply Fulci engaged with art history through his previous career as an art critic.

Bacon painted the seven works that make up the *Man in Blue* series in 1954 while he was staying at the Imperial Hotel in Oxfordshire in England where he became fascinated by a man he saw drinking every night at the bar. While it is unclear what Bacon's relationship to this man was, what is apparent is that he caught Bacon's eye, inspiring a number of works with an inescapably dark, ominous tone. While biographical readings of art tend to over-simplify and undervalue given works, these paintings are rarely discussed without a reference to the challenges Bacon himself was facing during this period; as a gay man living in a country where homosexuality was illegal, he is widely believed to have been experiencing abuse at the hands of his alcoholic lover, Peter Lacy. Although more low-key in content than the famous "screaming popes" series, this series too shares Bacon's fascination with "extremely lonely and tormented figures [who] find themselves isolated and trapped within themselves in a well-defined space."[15]

Like *Pope II*, *Man in Blue V* finds us in comparison to the other paintings in the series at a notable distance to the figure, who is so far away in spatial terms that he almost melts into his oppressive environment. We can see faint details of vertical lines behind him, again reminiscent of the prison-bar like encasements that entrap Bacon's myriad popes. His suit and tie acknowledge a recognition that the mysterious man in the bar understood that he was in public space and thus a figure potentially under scrutiny, an awareness that dominates Carol also. As an ex art critic, it is fair to assume Fulci surely would have been aware of the story behind not just Bacon's work in general, but the circumstances surrounding this particular series. Before Julia's murdered body is discovered, Carol has another dream where two of these paintings—Dalí's *Bacchanal* and Bacon's *Pope II* intersect in a *tableau vivant* riddled nightmare. The sequence begins again on the same train, but this time everyone is young, naked and sexed up from the outset. Carol rushes through the crowd again in slow motion, the dark tone set again by Morricone's chaotic score as it is the confrontational imagery. Cutting from the train, we can identify her family and close associates (despite being heavily made up to mirror the faces in Bacon's painting), re-enacting Bacon's pope paintings and shown from what we assume is Carol's first-person perspective. Shot on disorienting angles, the camera pans wildly across a row of "popes" as the music taking an even more dramatic, discordant tone when the most recognizable of the group— Joan—is shown not just in a silent scream but, as the camera pans down, to be nursing a gaping stomach wound, holding her entrails in her hands.

It is from this image that Fulci makes a direct link to Dalí's *Bacchanal* as, in a close-up of the viscera, the background turns to fog where the screaming, wildly flapping swan emerges moving towards the camera, it too marked by a gaping open space in its abdomen, mirroring Joan's injuries. Cutting to an ornate courtyard at a country estate—Carol's family home, perhaps—Fulci makes the link to Dalí even more explicit, as the shadows of the swans wings appear moving across the ground, mirroring the flying wings at the end of the iconic dream sequence Dalí famously designed for Alfred Hitchcock's *Spellbound* (1945),[16] chasing a moving figure we can perhaps assume to be Carol herself. Taking yet another dramatic shift, the nightmare now returns to Julia's bedroom where Carol sees herself stab her lover to death in graphic close-up.

Unlike *Spellbound*, which seeks to consolidate the authority of the psychoanalyst, *A Lizard in a Woman's Skin* does the opposite. As noted previously, Carol's confession is fundamentally misinterpreted by her psychiatrist from the outset by his inability to interpret her dreams beyond the level of the symbolic. As he tells her when she explains this dream to him;

> You killed Julia Durer; by killing Julia, you killed a part of yourself. The part attracted to degradation, vice. The conflict has been resolved by an act of violence. A firm decision, all of which shows we're dealing exclusively with a liberating dream. Even the outer appearances—the paintings surrounding you in your house—have a specific meaning of liberation.

On all counts, this supposed male expert on female neurosis has failed spectacularly; this a *literal* murder that Carol is recounting (carefully laying the foundations for her long-game defense to present herself as the perfect cliché of a neurotic, anxious woman). And, as we have just seen in a close look at these specific paintings that feature in her nightmare, their meanings relate to anything *but* liberation for Carol. The queer elements of the paintings themselves combine with the fact for closeted Carol, her home is a prison, demonstrated nowhere more symbolically than the Bacon-like pope-prison of her bed itself.

These paintings are art historically coded in numerous ways to not only denote entrapment, repression, suffering and pain, but—as recovering art critic Fulci could reasonably be expected to know—they are also marked historically by associations with queer artists or subjects. For Koven, *A Lizard in a Woman's Skin* typifies the *giallo* tendency towards ambivalence because "the sexual repression of the characters is framed against grand Victorian architecture, reflecting that on one hand the Victorian age built grand churches and the Royal Albert Hall ... but also was responsible for the stereotype of the cold, unemotional 'stiff-upper-lip,' sexually frustrated English."[17] While it might be tempting to dismiss the film's association between Carol's sexuality as homophobic—something fundamentally monstrous and corrupt[18]—I think there's something far more ambivalent at play. Most immediately, based on Bolkan's status at the time as a publicly out lesbian alone,[19] such a simple reading becomes less easy a fit. Instead—as perhaps nowhere more clear than the split screen sequences early in the film that show the happy, carefree party goers at Durer's house and the uptight, near-silent formality of the Hammond household—*A Lizard in a Woman's Skin* is as much (if not more) an assault on the hypocrisy of the upper class as it is a homophobic rendering of monstrous lesbianism. This question of class has been identified as a notable tension across *giallo* cinema more broadly, Leon Hunt suggesting they generally take place in a space "which suggests a wealth, an haute bourgeois world,"[20] while Joseph E. Dwyer notes that "essentially this is a cycle of films about rich or well off people who act in brash, selfish ways, and usually pay for it in some gruesome manner."[21] Yet while I argue that Carol is driven more by these sort of class anxieties and a fear of losing both her financial stability and her place in "proper" society if her status as a lesbian was revealed, that is not to bestow a necessarily "progressive" title on *giallo* regarding the representation of same-sex attracted women across the board; as I note later in my analysis of *The Killer Reserved Nine Seats* (*L'assassino ha riservato nove poltrone*, Giuseppe Bennati, 1974) alone, that would be disingenuous at best, and outright offensive at worst. And it is certainly difficult to deny that Fulci himself had any hesitations in utilizing of the spectacle of girl-on-girl sexual activity to provide a bit of salacious excitement to this movie or others in his filmography. As impressive as his art historical engagement may be in films such as this and *The Psychic*, he never lets us forget that he is, first and foremost, an exploitation master.[22]

Five

The Medusa's Warning
The Stendhal Syndrome
(La Sindrome di Stendhal, Dario Argento, 1996)

Just as Lucio Fulci once famously declared "violence is Italian art,"[1] so too horror and the arts are almost synonymous in the films of Dario Argento, perhaps even more so than Fulci. Time and time and time again, if art doesn't kill or menace such as the clarinet in *Sleepless* (*Non ho sonno*, 2001) or ominously pointy sculptures in both *The Bird with the Crystal Plumage* and *Tenebrae*, then it often plays a central role in either plot, tone or both across his filmography in the shape of murals, galleries or museums, paintings, or other works of art or artists themselves, including *Four Flies on Grey Velvet*, *Deep Red*, *Opera* (1987), and the *Three Mothers* trilogy.[2] But surely Argento's engagement with art as both a central spectacle and a thematic core manifest nowhere more aggressively than in his 1996 film *The Stendhal Syndrome*, which merges the rape-revenge trope with *giallo* to unforgettable effect.[3]

In a fascinating interview with Travis Crawford promoting the film upon its release, Argento makes explicit his relationship to great art, and precisely how he identifies in the force of its impact the source of horror. Said Argento:

> I remembered years ago—many years ago—I had read a book by Freud, that also had to do with the evil that is in the art, or at least great art. It is something like ... an infection that comes at you from the art, this was also something that interested me greatly. Because when you see great art, you can see how it can have that dangerous power, that emotional effect on someone. You can see that kind of power in the works of Rembrandt ... Caravaggio, Bosch.[4]

He continued:

> I think any great work of art has to have that sort of impact on someone—these are very disturbing works, in that there is something almost sinister in their power

over us. It's not like just looking at some … pretty landscape that you would put up on your wall, and think "Oh, isn't this nice and pretty." Great works of art are not like that—there is always something deeper, more profound when it has that kind of effect on a person.[5]

Considered an artist very much himself, Argento has been compared to both writers[6] and painters.[7] Argento has been direct about the influence of painting on his work, telling McDonagh "I'm very influenced by certain painters, surrealists like Magritte and Delavaux, for example … and of course, Hieronymus Bosch made a profound impression on me."[8] For some, the inclusion of art is a mere autobiographical quirk on Argento's part; Ronny Swennson, for instance, suggests that the reason so many of his films pivot both narratively and aesthetically around works of art is simply because his mother was a photographer.[9] While it is true that an early exposure to visual culture more broadly planted a seed of interest in the young Argento that would permeate his later work as a filmmaker, there is however perhaps more to it than that. In an interview where he discussed *The Stendhal Syndrome*, Argento talked about how heavily he was influenced as a child and adolescent "not only painting, but also architecture, sculpture, and works of art in general,"[10] even noting that he himself experienced something close to the Stendhal Syndrome himself while visiting the Pantheon in Athens.[11]

As will be discussed further shortly, questions surrounding the fallibility of memory and perception permeate Argento's work, most immediately visible in *Suspiria*, *Deep Red* and *The Bird with the Crystal Plumage* where a work of art that holds the secret to the mystery needs to be perceived "correctly" in order for it to be solved (both *Deep Red* and *The Bird with the Crystal Plumage* will be discussed further in the next chapter). Representation is complicated terrain in Argento's work, frequently hinging on a protagonist's battle to correctly interpret signs, and a keen interest in the ambiguity of visual representation runs throughout his directorial work; his sophomore feature, the *giallo Cat O' Nine Tails* (*Il gatto a nove code*, 1971), even featured a blind protagonist, played by Karl Malden. Describing himself as "obsessed with memory," Argento has noted in relation to both of these films specifically how "it is greatly influenced by our personality, by our culture, and by our environment."[12] Questions of "what did they *really* see?" are the narrative and thematic engines of these films, and as L. Andrew Cooper suggests, this "problem of looking, of the desire to see, is central to all of Argento's films" which results in an ultimate scenario where his "films challenge a viewer's accepted ideas about film spectatorship, meaning, storytelling, and genre."[13]

Combining elements from *gialli* with the rape-revenge formula,

Asia Argento and Dario Argento attend the 'La Terza Madre' photocall during the 2nd Rome Film Festival, October 24, 2007 (Denis Makarenko, Shutterstock.com).

surely nowhere is this challenge more aggressive than in *The Stendhal Syndrome*. One need only recall controversies surrounding films such as *I Spit on Your Grave* (Meir Zarch, 1976) and *Baise-Moi* (Virginie Despentes and Coralie Trinh-Thi, 2000) to highlight just how ethically explosive the rape-revenge category is, often dismissed as fundamentally regressive, exploitative and misogynistic. Yet there is a notable body of work from feminist film critics reconsidering this blanket dismissal of rape-revenge film,[14] largely spawned from Carol J. Clover's suggestion in her foundational 1992 book *Men, Women and Chain Saws: Gender in the Modern Horror Film* that these films in fact grant particular insight into the representation of gendered bodies in film. Questions of sexual violence, gender politics and representation have also been explored in art history, with Diane Wolfthal's extraordinary 1999 book *Images of Rape: The "Heroic" Tradition and Its Alternatives* compellingly arguing that contradictory representations of sexual violence co-existed in art long before the advent of the moving image.

Looking closer at rape-revenge films, we find that upon a detailed inspection they are difficult to dismiss as a collective whole and instead actively resist reductive classification. Yet as I have discussed elsewhere at length,[15] although the rape-revenge category is perhaps surprisingly diverse in cultural contexts, budgets and production values, intended audiences and (most of all) ideological treatment of violence against women, at their most basic level the majority of these films at least do rely on some kind of melodramatic tension between victim/villain, right/wrong good/evil, and female/male. As the name itself indicates, these films hinge at their most fundamental level of some kind of intersection of rape and revenge, and while their variations can play out in myriad ways in terms of a given film's political and/or moral agenda, these factors remain fundamentally central. The result is, as *The Stendhal Syndrome* perhaps demonstrates better than any other rape-revenge film ever made, the potential for some thoughtful, challenging and important cinema, even though many of the more famous films in the category might be considered anything but.

What Argento does in *The Stendhal Syndrome* is as simple as it is radical: he has made a rape-revenge film that explores the representation of sexual violence throughout art history itself, placing that history in a doomed conversation with his protagonist, Detective Anna Manni (played by his daughter, Asia Argento). While investigating serial killer Alfredo Grossi (Thomas Kretschmann), a lead takes Anna to Florence where she attempts to track Alfredo at the famous Uffizi Gallery. Distracted by the famous works of art in the gallery's collection, however, she is overwhelmed by the psychologically documented sensation called the "Stendhal Syndrome" where the sheer force of the great masters finds her hallucinating and, eventually, collapsing, unable to distinguish the worlds in the paintings themselves and her reality. Seeing her weakness, Alfredo realizes he can use this to his advantage and sets his sights on Anna as his new plaything. Breaking into her hotel room, he violently rapes her, leaving the deeply traumatized woman in a cat-and-mouse game which it appears she eventually wins when she hurls him into a river. Yet the murders do not stop; the film's climax reveals that Alfredo's continued harassment of Anna has resulted in her having taken on his persona, so thoroughly psychologically destroyed was she by his attacks.

Through a privileging of a number of famous works of Renaissance and Baroque art, the opening sequence in the Uffizi Gallery is central in constructing the kind of representational violence that is central to Argento's "meta" critique of any work of art—including film—that seeks to represent sexual violence. To riff on René Magritte's painting *The Treachery of Images* (1929), what we see in this film is *not* rape: what we are seeing is instead a *representation* of rape, and as Argento seeks to examine throughout the film, that is not the same thing, and can never be. *The Stendhal Syndrome* reveals how his fictional rape victim (it is perhaps not accurate, sadly, to call her a survivor) has been "framed" by art history itself, imprisoned by a number of representational templates that have dominated the representation of rape throughout the history of visual culture. This relates not only to art history, but to film history and social history also. Anna finds herself unable to escape the many go-to alternatives she sees as viable ways of conceiving her own identity post rape: avenging tomboy, professional investigator, *femme fatale*, and deranged murderer. This is further complicated by the fact that Anna is played by the director's daughter Asia, and that she herself is a rape survivor, revealed during the explosive allegations against producer Harvey Weinstein in 2017.[16] To complicate matters further, later allegations of sexual abuse were levelled against Asia herself by the actor who starred in her directorial effort, *The Heart is Deceitful Amongst All Things* (2004). Through all of these factors, we struggle to "see" Anna for herself; she is many things at once, but the most precious thing she loses is her *own* sense of identity.

As such, Anna collapses under the pressure of her "job" as a representational figure, an artistic invention made to carry the weight of rape itself. In this context, the revenge she does on a surface level successfully achieve against Alfredo is hollow and unsatisfying, for both Anna herself *and* the audience. But while Anna is effectively doomed to failure, Argento succeeds only too well in simultaneously collapsing and revealing the fundamental contradictions that lie at the heart of representing rape in the "bigger picture" of the history of visual culture itself. Through his highly sophisticated engagement with specific famous artworks, Argento exposes precisely how some things simply cannot be represented well enough to denote their true impact. At the same time, in the context of a rape-revenge film itself he reveals exactly *why* this equation is futile; there's a sharp reflexivity at play, not only in relation to itself broadly as a creative artifact, but *specifically* as a rape-revenge film. In short, *The Stendhal Syndrome* is ultimately

Actress Asia Argento speaks about her sexual abuse by Harvey Weinstein at The Women's March on Rome, January 20, 2018 (Anthony Ricci, Shutterstock.com).

therefore not *about* rape as much as it is about the fraught terrain of trying to *represent* rape.

From this perspective, then, we can conceive *The Stendhal Syndrome* playing out across three different representational planes or symbolic "canvases," each of which we can "read" in varying degrees in response to their conceptual opacity. The first of these are the subject of this section of the book as a whole; the paintings Anna sees at the Uffizi herself. The second conceptual "canvas" is her own body, which at one point she literally paints on but we see her attempt to transform through re-inscription in a range of different ways throughout the film; through costume, wig and make-up, for example, for her transformation into a Veronica Lake–styled *femme fatale*. And lastly but most importantly of these is the movie *The Stendhal Syndrome* itself which, through its representations of sexual violence on screen throughout the film, reveals both the impact of "showing" such constructions of gendered violence while simultaneously examining the dangers of *mis*representation. Actively rejecting the melodramatic victim/villain model upon which rape-revenge films are often predicated, Argento collapses the entire moral universe that the representation of rape in film so often implies in on itself. The result is chaos, despair, and for Anna, a total obliteration of identity.

The Stendhal Syndrome is a psychological condition identified by Italian Professor Graziella Magherini who wrote a book on the same name,[17] which has been summarized in English by Vivian Sobchack as pertaining to

> …a temporary set of symptoms that feature disorientation, panic, heart palpitations, loss of identity, fear and dizziness, and beset certain foreign tourists in cities like Florence and Venice where centuries of intensely vivid art and architecture overwhelm them and destabilize both the grounded space on which they stand and their temporal mooring to the present.[10]

It is in this sense that the very title of Argento's film flags a scenario where the person who experience Stendhal Syndrome[19] is diagnosed with what in clinical terms is a failure on the part of the person who suffers the condition to be able to "correctly" interpret signs; the lines between what is real and what is art blur so dramatically that it results not only in psychological, but sometimes even physical symptoms. Thus, even before the film begins Argento reveals a fascination with the violence of artistic representation and the chaos it can produce to the individual and their grasp on reality. For Colette Balmain, *The Stendhal Syndrome* therefore allows Argento to employ "the analogy between painting and cinema to provide his most extensive, and at times difficult, mediation on the nature of violence and the possibility of its transference."[20]

Returning to the beginning of the film, the opening scenes at the Uffizi Gallery utilize the famous space and the works contained within it to hammer in these associations in from the very outset. This is a physical space where crowds flock on a daily basis to experience first-hand the sensation of being in the "real" world and encountering the symbolic, weighty presence of great art; we see Anna fight her way through these very crowds before she even enters the building, scenes which are almost indistinguishable from the day-to-day business of the real gallery. The gallery space here demands the art spectator—in this case, Anna—finds a way to allow their realities (which we can identify as the diegesis of the film in our example) to co-exist with the representational worlds depicted in these paintings. The difficulty to make the distinction between art, film and gallery space is emphasized in the opening credits, however, even before the action begins as famous works of art by iconic painters—Warhol, Picasso, Rembrandt, Modigliani—scroll down the screen, the film-space itself becoming a gallery of sorts and thus collapsing the boundaries between art and the "real" in a way that will only be exaggerated once the film's action begins. So close is this to the opening credit sequence of Elio Petri's *A Quiet Day in the Country*—discussed in Chapter Eleven—that it is difficult not to read it as a conscious reference.

When it comes to looking more closely at the paintings Anna sees at the Uffizi that trigger her first bout of the Stendhal Syndrome, it states the obvious that Argento was clearly restricted to works held in that gallery's collection, but as we shall see shortly in the case of Rembrandt's *The Night Watch* (1642), he certainly found creative ways to incorporate other works. Her presence in the gallery is a trap, as we later discover, following a lead she received via an anonymous phone call that ended up being Alfredo with his voice disguised as a woman's. The first painting Anna encounters in the Uffizi is Paolo Uccello's *Niccolò da Mauruzi da Tolentino at the Battle of San Romano* (1438–1440) which provokes her first hallucination. Looking at a scene depicting horses in battle, the corresponding sounds are woven onto Ennio Morricone's ominous soundtrack, implying an intense aural hallucination. We see this pattern continue to form as she gazes at to Sandro Botticelli's *Birth of Venus* (1482–1485) where again, through the soundtrack, we are led to understand that the boundaries between art and Anna's reality are beginning to collapse. This time, the sound of wind accompanying a close-up image of the Zephyr's dramatic exhalation.

But in terms of the art historical representation of sexual violence, it is the next painting she encounters that begins to move us towards the territory that holds Argento's interest, Botticelli's *Primavera* (1482).

Paolo Uccello's *Niccolò da Mauruzi da Tolentino at the Battle of San Romano* (1438–1440), on view in Uffizi Gallery, Florence, 2016. Uffizi is one of the oldest museums in Europe, dating to 1560 (vvoe, Shutterstock.com).

We first see this painting from Anna's perspective through a first-person camera shot which allows Argento to visually indicate the shift of her attention as her eyes move across the canvas. But as much as she sees details in the famous work itself, she too sees herself reflected in the glass protecting it. Significantly she sees her own reflection appear on the glass right underneath the three Charites that figure on the left-hand side of the painting. Turning her attention to the figure of Flora, she then turns significantly towards Zephyrus and Chloris, the importance of whom is notable from an art historical perspective in regard to representations of rape. Based on Ovid's famous interpretation of this myth, as art historian Diane Wolfthal notes, what is depicted here recalls when "the west wind Zephyrus tried to seize the nymph Chloris, married her, and then transformed her into Flora, whom Botticelli depicts to the left of Chloris."[21]

For Wolfthal, *Primavera* is an important part of a tradition of paintings depicting so-called "heroic" rape imagery that celebrate marriage. She describes the painting as "typical of 'heroic' rape imagery" because "it depicts neither overt violence nor sexual intercourse."[22] Again, Anna's reflection is shown superimposed on this detail, the significance of Zephyrus's actions so integral to the film and the impact it has on Anna

Sandro Botticelli's *Primavera* (1482), Uffizi Gallery, Botticelli Hall, 2016 (vvoe, shutterstock.com).

that a detail of him reflected on her face forms the central imagery of the film's promotional poster. If, as the film suggests, Chloris's transformation into Flora is a cause for celebration as has been the traditional way it has been understood in art history, the way it is configured in Argento's movie presents it as anything but. Incapable of distinguishing between her own identity (reflection) on the work, Anna makes this confusion palpable as she touches the glass, trying to locate a tangible border. In doing so, that she sets off a literal alarm also functions as a figurative one; in these moments before she is raped, the film makes it clear through languageless action that there are real dangers and threats that exist within the collapse of artistic representation and reality.

Continuing these concerns and the increasing sense of looming menace, she next approaches Caravaggio's *Medusa* (1597), the merger of soundtrack with recognizable sounds increasingly blurring as Morricone's soundtrack issues a trumpeting sound when the painting is shown, partially suggestive of the Medusa's scream and again, seeming to issue a warning sound to Anna against an impending attack as much as trying to frighten her. Recalling the rape of Medusa by Poseidon, Linda Badley suggests that this very mythological embodiment of "rape victim as monster" is immediately relevant to Anna and her multiple (and futile) transformations throughout the film post-rape.[23]

Ultimately configured as monstrous forces, both Anna and the Medusa find themselves trapped within representational frameworks; the former within the confines of a feature film, the latter on Caravaggio's circular painted shield. This entrapment denotes a fundamental absence of power at the hands of male artists, their power significantly reduced by the representational apparatus that defines them. As Argento shrewdly implies, there is a direct parallel between questions of autonomy and identity in terms of rape itself.

The suggestion that the Medusa is an ally rather than a foe to Anna has precedent in feminist theory; while Freud has reduced the figure's significant to the crude psychoanalytic equation "to decapitate = to castrate,"[24] Hélène Cixous's response in her 1975 essay "The Laugh of the Medusa" seeks instead to radically shift the politics of the figure, locating her as a starting point to present her feminist writing strategy *écriture feminine*. For Cixous, "the power of the female gorgon as an image to revive women's writing ... [through] a language women do not borrow from men but create themselves" allows women the potential to write "by 'emplacing' their bodies into inscriptions."[25] For Cixous, the monstrosity of the Medusa is therefore in the eye of the beholder; "You only have to look at the Medusa straight on to see her. And she's not deadly. She's beautiful and she's laughing."[26] In this context, if Anna seems confronted by her encounter with the Medusa (the drama of which is hardly lessened thanks to Morricone's dramatic musical blasts), it is because she must ask herself questions: is this mythological figure, so maligned throughout history, an ally from the sisterhood foreshadowing approaching threats? With particular relevance to Anna not just in the Uffizi where she experiences the Stendhal Syndrome but in the film itself as a whole, for Louis Marin the Medusa "is simultaneously inside the represented space and outside the space of representation."[27] From Marin and Cixous perspectives, then, Anna's overwhelming encounter with the Medusa is less from the traditionally perceived threat of castration, turning to stone, etcetera, but rather that she on some level senses the threat and understands what is being communicated here, one mythological figure to (in cult film terms at least) another.

Anna's terror is not a response to the threat of the Medusa, but rather to the threat that the Medusa—one of art history's most famously vilified rape victims—is warning her off. This is not merely in terms of what lies ahead in her encounters with Alfredo, but the implication that Anna too may find herself captured within the exact same spatial-temporal representational apparatus that has so effectively trapped the Medusa, forever caught within Marin's contradictory binaries of being condemned to exist both within and beyond representation itself. As we soon learn, it is far closer to this than the traditional symbol of threat that the Medusa signifies in this instance. What will happen to Anna by the film's conclusion and, even here, her increasing difficulty to distinguish reality from artistic representation that has even seen her own image literally merge with the rape scenario in *Primavera* recall Marin's vision of "a Medusa who petrifies herself by looking at her image in the shield's mirroring eye," where she is "neither flesh nor stone; still flesh, already stone."[28] Anna is paralyzed by her own reflection; seeing herself in art, being incapable of pulling herself out of it. This leaves her dangerously exposed to Alfredo, thus denoting what is effectively the beginning of the end for her.

Consequently, even before Anna encounters the final artwork in the Uffizi that both casts her into the most all-consuming of her hallucinations thus far but also marks hers literal collapse, the famous artworks that she has encountered and her response to them have already revealed many things, if not to Anna herself then certainly to us. As an artist himself—the director of *The Stendhal Syndrome*, the very film we are watching—Argento is demanding an acknowledgment that artistic representations can be deceitful, their boundaries undefined. That both the Medusa and Anna find no alternative beyond monstrous femininity suggests that rape traps women in representational prisons which, try as they may, they cannot escape. When the truth of Anna's murder spree comes to light at the end of the film, she literally collapses—carried by her male colleagues in what can only be understood as a conscious re-enactment of the Pieta where the Virgin Mary cradles the dead body of her crucified son—under the weight of her own symbolic significance, a weight that crushes her own sense of identity. Like Christ, she is a martyr; in Argento's film, the pay-off for Anna's sacrifice is that we as audiences learn to *look at artistic representation differently*.

The final painting Anna approaches in the Uffizi is Pieter Bruegel's *Landscape of the Fall of Icarus* (1558), which marks not only her final collapse under the building pressure of the Stendhal Syndrome, but also introduces Alfredo as a key player as he rushes to her after she faints, feigning to assist her. Again, through close-ups on specific details on the painting, the cinematography implies a first-person perspective and that what we are seeing is a manifestation of where Anna's attention is focused at that moment on the canvas. Seeing Icarus's legs on the surface of the water as he falls underneath, Anna is suddenly immersed in an intense hallucination where she herself is sinking, knocking herself unconscious on the ocean floor (and fainting in the gallery) before being memorably resuscitated by a giant fish, which also brings her around in the Uffizi. This sensation of drowning, notes Badley, "suggests the suffocating entrapment of the female subject within the conventions of the painterly (and by extension, cinematic) frame."[29]

While the traditional reading of the painting and the myth it is based on reduces it to a warning against foolhardy aspirations,[30] in the context of this scene what appears to be more significant is just how easily the detail is missed (Argento had shown a previous interest in Bruegel in a painting central to the mystery of *The Bird with the Crystal Plumage*, as discussed in the following chapter). In typical Bruegel style, this is just one of many sites of action in his painting, and indeed it takes some effort upon studying the painting to even identify at first where Icarus is. Rather than the grand spectacle the myth implies, then, the tragedy of Icarus is reduced to something far more banal and insignificant, echoing the ways that the rape of Medusa and Chloris, for instance, has effectively been written out of art history as events of any particular gravity. These unseen, unacknowledged tragedies are difficult to not align with the treatment of those who have experienced sexual violence; so often ignored, undermined or accused of fabrication, Anna is one in a long line of women both on and off screen for whom broader attitudes towards rape and sexual violence have culminated in what often feels like a no-win scenario.

Leaving the gallery, Anna has one more encounter with a famous artwork before she is assaulted; a framed print of Rembrandt's *The Night Watch* that hangs in her hotel room, as previously mentioned. Just as the Bruegel-like print effectively functions as a kind of wormhole in *The Bird with the Crystal Plumage*, so too *The Night Watch* transports Anna in a similar way; looking at the painting, the experience of almost falling into it find her sucked through space and time to Rome where, at a crime scene, her status as a detective in the Anti-Rape Squad is confirmed, outlining the circumstances that have led her to Florence in the first place. As Balmain eloquently notes;

> Rembrandt's *Night Watch* becomes a door inscribing rhizomatic links between Florence (the present) and Rome (the past), through which Anna passes from one time to another and from one space to the next. This signals both a spatial and temporal disjunction, which is central to the breakdown of epistemological systems of knowledge, as past and present inhabit the same painterly, hallucinatory and cinematic frame.[31]

So while, as noted, Argento was restricted somewhat by the paintings he could use in the Uffizi sequence by the galleries collection holdings, here no such pressure applies. So why *The Night Watch*? Again, our answers lie in where Anna turns her attention when she looks at the painting, the close-up detail shown by the camera indicating what features of the painting have attracter her eye. As she is overwhelmed by the Rembrandt, it is the famous "girl in gold" that captures her attention, a notable moment in the film as a whole because it is the first and only time in the movie that her experience of the Stendhal Syndrome brings her pleasure. Bathed in a warm, golden light, she smiles when she hallucinates the girl's voice as it announces victory.

For Rembrandt, her golden clothing, the drinking horn and the regiment's emblematic chicken claws are purely symbolic in function: according to E. Haverkamp-Begemann, she embodies the company as a whole, and "it is for that reason Rembrandt awarded [her] ... a central place in the composition."[32] Like Anna, the golden girl too is consistently surrounded by men throughout the film, another point of identification for Anna that perhaps brings her joy through the euphoria of Rembrandt's figure. A "golden girl" in her chosen profession until the vicious attack we see soon after the Rembrandt hallucination changes the trajectory of her career and life more broadly, like "the golden girl" in the painting Anna too is trapped by the expectations of gendered representation. Anna's status as a representation have sapped her identity and autonomy; as Argento noted in an interview with Travis Crawford, "these works of art, like any great artwork ... take a lot out of a person."[33]

While these are the primary encounters with famous artworks in *The Stendhal Syndrome*, as noted previously Argento does not end his engagement with the broader conceptual terrain of artistic representation and the violence inherent to it there. An attempt at art therapy sees Anna turn from the canvas to her own body, painting on it in a literal attempt to change how she is represented. And, as noted, her various transformations—tomboy, *femme fatale*—likewise see her attempt to adopt new, culturally sanctioned personae that dominate the representation of women who have experienced rape trauma. But she cannot paint herself out of the film; no matter how hard she tries, the four sides of the screen-frame keep her eternally trapped in a historically defined representational apparatus, one that has dominated painting as much as cinema.

Clues, Presence and Painting

Six

Misreading Clues

Dario Argento's The Bird with the Crystal Plumage *(*L'uccello dalle piume di cristallo, *1970)
and* Deep Red *(*Profondo rosso, *1975)*

When they appear in cinema, paintings can tell us things. In the case of *giallo*, as we have seen in our first selection of case studies, recognizable paintings by artists including Vermeer, Bacon, Dalí, Bruegel, Botticelli and Caravaggio have been employed by filmmakers such as Dario Argento, Lucio Fulci and Dino Risi not only as part of a film's plot but to simultaneously act as visual spectacles. Turning away from canonical works by famous artists, however, as we now discover paintings can be employed in a range of alternate ways in *gialli* that do not rely as much on art historical references to specific paintings in a way many of these previous films have when it comes to understanding how these famous works function as clues. Instead, they use paintings created for the film specifically to harness the spectacular and narrative potential that exists solely (or, in some curious examples, bleed back into art history) within the diegetic world of a particular movie itself.

Sometimes, these paintings exist less as clues as they do sites for almost feverishly excessive spectacle, such as that involved in the gruesome death of British artist Kathy Adams in *Seven Blood Stained Orchids* (*Sette orchidee macchiate di rosso*, Umberto Lenzi, 1972). During a graphic murder vignette that occurs in that film's opening fifteen minutes, one of the many paintings in her apartment—a portrait—has bloody eyes painted on it by the black gloved killer, who after murdering her leaves her staring at the murals on her ceiling. Any doubt that these kinds of vignettes are somewhat ambivalently offered (perhaps even somewhat mockingly) as works of art in themselves is promptly put to bed with Kathy's murder in this film at least, the head of her murdered corpse surrounded by a picture frame as paint drips onto her body from open paint cans that are positioned above her. Murder here—as it is across *giallo* cinema more generally and echoing the title of the Thomas de Quincey essay discussed in Chapter One—is considered an art form.

Inspector Tellini (Giancarlo Giannini) discovers a painting turned around to face the wall which captures his attention and leads him to deduce it is a clue in Paolo Cavara's *The Black Belly of the Tarantula* (*La tarantola dal ventre nero*, 1971). In *Fatal Frames* (*Fotogrammi mortali*, Al Festa, 1996)—discussed further in Chapter Thirteen—Wendy Williams (played by beloved American B-film scream queen Linnea Quigley) discovers a gruesome painting in the house of the mysterious Countess Alessandra Mirafiori (Alida Valli). Painted by an artist called Bassani, the painting, considered a haunted or cursed artwork from within the film text, was supposedly stolen during World War II after the artist hung himself in prison after murdering his wife. One rumor surrounding Bassani's work is that he even used the "jelly" (the blood and other viscera) of his many victims as paint.[1] That the Countess is played by Alida Valli recalls her other art-centric horror films such as Dario Argento's *Suspiria* and, less well known perhaps, *Eye in the Labyrinth* (*L'occhio nel labirinto*, Mario Caiano, 1972). Playing a character called Gerda, Valli runs a bacchanalian artist colony that appears to be little more than a hotbed of vice and murder. Drawn to the seaside villa after the disappearance of her psychiatrist boyfriend, Julie (Rosemary Dexter) believes Gerda and her tenants are involved in his murder, with a strange painting depicting a man being murdered outside the premise only adding to her suspicions. In true *giallo* style, however, it's all a red herring; yes, her boyfriend has been murdered, but it was in fact Julie herself who committed the crime. Suffering from severe mental health issues, she killed him after he left her as his interest in her was purely professional (he saw her as little more than "a toy to take apart").

Turning now to more focused case studies, through portraits, murals, religious frescos and other kinds of paintings, a range of films including *Deep Red* and *The Bird with the Crystal Plumage* (both directed by Dario Argento), *The Red Queen Kills Seven Times* (*La dama rossa uccide sette volte*, Emilio Miraglia, 1972), *Your Vice Is a Locked Room and Only I Have the Key* (*Il tuo vizio è una stanza chiusa e solo io ne ho la chiave*, Sergio Martino, 1972) and *The House with Laughing Windows* (*La casa dalle finestre che ridono*, Pupi Avati, 1976), this section considers more closely how paintings in *giallo* function as enigmatic—and often visually excessive—clues. While *The Stendhal Syndrome* is perhaps the most explicit Dario Argento has been regarding his interest in the great masters and the thematics of art as a broader concept, many of the fascinations that underscored his engagement with art history in that film were visible in these earlier works. While this chapter will explore the function of painting specifically within *The Bird with the Crystal Plumage* and *Deep Red*, this wider domain of art, creative production, artists and the art world itself are significant to both of these early *gialli*. Both films concern male foreign artists living in Italy. Both men witness crimes they find themselves incapable of factually describing, misreading key elements to misrepresent their understanding of events, and thus leaving the killers in each respective film free to continue killing. Both are attractive to women, yet hopeless, impotent investigators incapable of recognizing a clue when they see it, let alone interpreting it correctly. By doing so, their failures place both themselves—and the women they are close to—in life-threatening danger.

Argento made his debut feature *The Bird with the Crystal Plumage* when he was 29 years old[2] after working for many years in the industry, including as a screenwriter where he most famously worked on Sergio Leone's classic spaghetti western *Once Upon a Time in the West* (*C'era una volta il West*) in 1968. *The Bird with the Crystal Plumage* follows an American writer called Sam Dalmas (Tony Musante) who, while walking home one night from a museum in Rome where his friend Carlo Dover (Renato Romano)—an ornithology professor—works, witnesses a man and a woman struggling in a glass-fronted art gallery. Opening one set of glass doors, Sam finds himself unable to get through the second set and is thus trapped and unable to get out on either side. When the police finally arrive, the man has escaped and the police rush to the aid of the injured, blood covered woman we learn is Monica Ranieri (Eva Renzi). Only vaguely able to describe the male figure who escaped, the police—lead by Inspector Morosini (Enrico Maria Salerno)—suspect her husband Alberto (Umberto Raho) may be involved, their concerns growing as they fear this attack is linked to three recent murders of young women. Morosini also has doubts about the American witness and holds his passport when he learns Sam and his girlfriend Julia (Suzy Kendall) plan to leave shortly for the United States.

The attitude of the police shifts, however, when Julia and Sam themselves are harassed, and while they are under police protection, the murders continue. When Carlo finally identifies the mysterious sound on a threatening phone call Julia and Sam have received as coming from the rare Siberian *Hornitus Nevalis* (a fictional bird supposedly famous for its white, glass-looking feathers of the film's title), Sam is able to trace the location the call was made to the Ranieri's apartment. Interrupting a struggle between Monica and Alberto, the latter falls out of a window, confessing to all the murders before his death. This, it is soon discovered, is a false confession, and Alberto only took the responsibility for the crimes to protect Monica, the true culprit. With this revelation, the penny drops for amateur detective Sam. It was not Alberto trying to kill Monica that he saw at the gallery that night, but the opposite; there was a struggle for the knife as Alberto tried to pull it out of Monica's hands. Traumatized by a violent assault that happened when she was younger, the already fragile Monica was hurled into violent psychosis when she saw a painting inspired by her attack for sale in a shop window.

As previously noted, like many of Argento's films including *The Stendhal Syndrome*, both *The Bird with the Crystal Plumage* and *Deep Red* engage with art in a range of ways. In the case of *The Bird with the Crystal Plumage*, for instance, so central is the art gallery to even the most cursory of plot summaries that it is almost impossible to describe the story without mentioning it. Describing the filming and composition of the scene in an interview with Alan Jones, Argento has said "the art gallery sequence was shot three times in all because I wanted it to be very geometric. I never expected audiences to guess the twist because I put the girl in white and the man in black—an amazingly simple way of distracting attention away from the truth."[3] More easily overlooked, however, is what happens *before* we reach this space. Accompanying Carlo, Sam visits the museum where his friend works to apparently pick up a paycheck for a book he has worked on as a writer. Approaching the office, as they chat the walls of the museum are lined with glass display cases, full of specimens that more often than not have been preserved via taxidermy. Moving to his own display case between the two sliding glass doors, Sam too becomes a subject of study—*our* study.

A still of the painting from *The Bird with the Crystal Plumage* (*L'uccello dalle piume di cristallo*, Dario Argento, 1970).

Just as the film itself hinges upon his struggle to perceive what happened with Monica and Alberto, we too find ourselves in a similar struggle as we attempt to comprehend what has happened to Sam himself; after all, we witness the same attempted murder scene he does, and like our protagonist, many of us too will fail to correctly interpret the scene unless we have guessed the twist ending. That Sam himself is being displayed is echoed in Lucas Balbo's description of the location as "an art gallery-aquarium,"[4] but he is notably not quite in the gallery itself when his plot- and theme-propelling misreading occurs. Rather, he is in a liminal space—not quite in the gallery, but not quite in the world. He is, in this way, stuck between art and reality; a rich metatextual acknowledgment for the popular form of *giallo* more generally, stranded in a state of confused hysteria between art and realism, not quite one or the other.

But let's turn specifically to the painting. When the identity of one of the murder victims leads Sam to the collectibles store where the young woman worked, it is through a conversation with the shop's flirtatious, unnamed owner (played by stalwart German actor Werner Peters) that Sam learns that the victim's last transaction was to sell a painting described as "strange, naïve yet macabre at the same time." Using the store owner's clearly sexual interest in him to his advantage, Sam convinces the man to let him borrow a black and white photograph of the painting which he takes home and pins to his and Julia's wall, convinced that it is an important clue. Upon seeing it, Julia has an intense and instantly negative reaction, finding it not just distasteful but actively frightening. The reproduction has power over Sam, too; as he stares deeply at it, foreshadowing the portal-like qualities of Rembrandt's *The Night Watch* in *The Stendhal Syndrome*, the camera moves slowly towards the print as if pulled by a magnet, the image suddenly becoming color as we realize we are looking at the original as the camera zooms back to show us in the domain of the killer who stares just as intently at the painting.

Realizing (eventually) that the best way to decipher the possible significance of the painting is to track down the artist, Sam contacts the man at the store who originally gave him the print. This leads him to the village of Aviano just outside of Rome where he meets the eccentric artist Berto Consalvi (played by German character actor Mario Adorf). Gaining entry to the eccentric recluse's boarded-up home by telling him he wants to purchase a painting, Consalvi allows him entry in the hope of making some money. Gently approaching the question of the painting in question, after explaining that he no longer paints such "crap" anymore ("I'm going through a mystical period," he explains. "I only paint mystical things ... because I feel mystical"), he tells Sam the story: inspired by real events that took place a decade earlier, he says "a maniac got hold of a girl I knew, tried to cut her up, just stopped him in time. Put him in an asylum for life." While this may suggest it is the man in the asylum represented in the painting who is responsible for the murders, as we discover it is the woman herself. As a smug psychiatrist rushes to explain in a hasty denouement at the film's conclusion as Sam and Julia board a plane to get the hell out of Rome, when Monica saw the painting in the store window it triggered a psychotic episode where she didn't identify with the victim in the painting (based on herself), but the perpetrator.

In Consalvi's home-studio, however, Sam rapidly loses his grip on the bigger picture when it is revealed in one of the film's most gruesomely comic sequences that the feral art-hermit has just fed his guest a big fat plate of steaming hot cat stew. Rushing to a phone to call Julia to tell her he is incapable of getting back to Rome that evening, he offhandedly tells her he learned nothing from the artist during his visit, where in fact he learned the secret at the core of the very mystery he is trying to solve. This is not the first time the painting's centrality is dismissed by Sam; just like he failed to correctly interpret the events in the art gallery and mistook the perpetrator for the victim, so too despite his intuition that the painting itself was somehow important, when Julia casually suggests earlier in the film "maybe the woman was the first victim," he dismisses it without thinking. In retrospect, however, Julia was right: not the first victim of the film's killer, sure, but the killer *herself* was the first victim in the series of crimes around which the film's mystery is built.

While not a famous painting in the same way that Argento would incorporate known works of art in *The Stendhal Syndrome* from Rembrandt, Botticelli, Caravaggio and Bruegel, as has been widely noted there are distinctive, conscious echoes in Consalvi's painting with Bruegel's 1565 painting *The Hunters in the Snow*. From this perspective, Consalvi's painting feels like it could almost be a detail taken from (but doesn't actually appear in) Bruegel's famous painting. Bruegel's painting was one of a series of six landscapes dedicated to depicting seasonal changes,[5] *The Hunters in the Snow* is particularly noteworthy for its widespread recognition as "a major milestone in the emergence of independent landscape" which importantly manifests "the expression of a personal and direct experience of nature, a portrayal of the harmony of human activities within the cycle of seasons."[6] For Michel Weemans, however, there is a dramatically different way of conceiving the painting when looking closely at its details in the context of the work of artists including Hieronymus Bosch, positioning the painting as part of a "series of works by Bruegel depicting a hidden or potential mouth of Hell."[7]

One doesn't need to have read Weemans' work, however, to grasp a sense of foreboding and something ominous bubbling under the surface in *The Hunters in the Snow*: there is surely something menacing even to the untrained eye in how the weapon-wielding men at the top of the hill with their flock of dogs look down on the distant, seemingly peaceful valley below, surrounded by the frames of blackened, leaf-less trees as birds circle the destination above the crowd they seem to be approaching. Effectively adding an element that does not appear in the original painting Argento—through the fictionalized Consalvi—makes the violence implicit in Bruegel's painting explicit, and then builds an entire film around it.

It is not too hard to find similar parallels with famous paintings in *Deep Red* either. Early in the film Argento includes what is clearly a carefully constructed *tableau vivant* of Edward Hopper's famous painting, *Nighthawks* (1942) which shows three customers—two men and a woman—sitting at a diner counter which a third man works behind. In her discussion of this reference, Alexia Kannas turns to critical histories of the work that identify its source of inspiration both as a specific diner on Greenwich Avenue in New York City, and Ernest Hemingway's 1927 short story *The Killers* of which Hopper was a great admirer (later adapted to the screen by in 1946 by Robert Siodmak with Ava Gardner and Burt Lancaster, and again in 1964 by Don Siegel with Lee Marvin and Angie Dickinson).[8] For Kannas;

> When Marc helps the drunken Carlo to his feet and walks him back to work, a shot of the Blue Bar reveals how Argento imports the sense of stillness manifest in Hopper's painting by the static and deliberate arrangement of customers sitting at the bar. His rather more theatrical rendering of the setting foregrounds the figures by sitting them in front of the bar, rather than behind it, but in this shot, as with Hopper's painting, the bar appears to have no entrance, encasing its customers behind the restaurant's glass window and shutting the viewer out. Argento's allusion to Hopper's painting also enables him to revisit the architectural scenario from *The Bird with the Crystal Plumage* in which Sam Dalmas witnesses the murder through the art gallery window.[9]

In terms of *Deep Red* specifically, Kannas adds that "as a study of the reflections made possible by the use of fluorescent lighting in the diner, *Nighthawks* mirrors *Deep Red*'s broader fascination with the way reflective surfaces work to generate further instances of doubling."[10]

While these notions of doubling permeate the film in a variety of ways, most overt is the centrality of a literal mirror to the plot itself, which holds the answer to the mystery at its core. Written by

Argento and Bernadino Zapponi and the first Argento filmed scored by prog-rock legends Goblin, the film begins as its opening credits are intercut with the primal scene that underscores the film; the supposed frivolity of a Christmas-time domestic scenario is subverted by a murder that appears in silhouette, accompanied by screams, concluding when a bloody knife that falls is picked up by a young child who stares at it in awe, mouth agape. Cutting to what appears to be the contemporary moment, British jazz pianist Marcus Daly (David Hemmings[11]) jams with his band in Rome, reminding them to loosen up, and that perfection is not always the ultimate goal for art. In another location, the medium Helga Ulmann (Macha Méril) is shaken during a public display of her psychic abilities when she senses the presence of a killer; "you have killed and you will kill again," she announces dramatically. Marc—who lives in the same building as Helga—talks to his drunk friend Carlo (Gabriele Lavia) in the public square below her apartment, when he witnesses Helga's murder. Rushing to her apartment, he walks anxiously towards the window where he saw her, discovering her body and seeing an escaping, shadowy figure in the streets below.

Like Sam, Marc is convinced that there is something important that he saw at the murder scene, but he cannot place it. Along with journalist Gianna Brezzi (Daria Nicolodi), Marc begins to investigate the murder, where an attempt on his own life leads him to an abandoned art deco mansion that he discovered through a folktale called *The House of the Screaming Child*, written by Amanda Righetti (Giuliana Calandra). She is murdered before Marc can speak to her about the story, which leads him to locate the house itself where he discovers a child's drawing of the murder scene shown at the film's beginning hidden underneath the plaster of the decayed building. Marc later returns to the house and, behind a wall, finds the decomposed remains of a body, but is knocked unconscious and the house set on fire. Rescued by Gianna, Marc finds another clue when Olga (Nicoletta Elmi)—child of the caretaker's daughter who admitted him to the property—has a drawing that she based on one she found in her school archives that resembled the mural Marc found in the house. Locating the original, he sees it was drawn by his friend Carlo as a child, and after Gianna is attacked, Carlo attempts to escape but is killed in the process. Believing the crime is solved, he returns to Helga's apartment to try and remember the thing that has been niggling at him, when he realizes that a painting he glimpsed at looked different because the first time he saw it, it also featured the reflection of the killer herself: Carlos' mother, Marta (Clara Calamai). Lying in wait, she attacks Marc with a meat cleaver and it is only when he attempts to escape that her long necklace gets stuck in the shaft of an old-fashioned, cage-like elevator and beheads her in a gruesome sequence[12] that he is finally safe, the film ending as he stares, shocked and silent, into a "deep red" pool of blood as the final credits roll.

Just as writer Sam was an amateur investigator haunted by something he saw at a crime scene that he cannot remember, so to with pianist Marc; in the former, it was that the person he believed to be the victim was in fact the perpetrator, while here, what Marc mentally processed as a painting was in fact the *reflection* of a painting with the killer standing in front of it. The revelation of the killer in both films therefore hinge directly on a failure by artists to "read" art. This is foreshadowed elsewhere in the film, when Marc discovers the hidden mural; while he scratches off enough of the plaster to see the figure of a terrifying adult with a gaping wound and a child seemingly victoriously lifting a bloodied knife above their head in front of a Christmas tree, after he leaves a chunk of plaster falls off the wall that reveals a third figure who—we realize at the end of the film—is the child's (Carlo) mother, Marta, the real killer. Assuming the version of the film being watched reveals Marta's face at the beginning of the film as Marc briefly passes her,[13] even though in retrospect we can spot Marta in the brief flash where she is shown, as Kannas notes "when Marc misrecognises the mirror's reflection as a painting, so do we: we may have seen Marta's face, but how could we have recognised it?" She continues, "As the tracking shot hurries past the temporary composition of white faces, it is close to impossible to register the features of a character we are yet to meet at this stage in the story."[14]

In retrospect, however, we register not just Marta but the painting itself. While McDonagh rightly identifies the works that litter Helga's hallway as "a veritable sea of Munchian faces, pale, ghastly and

Marc (David Hemmings) remembers seeing Marta (Clara Calamai) leaning near a painting in *Deep Red* (*Profondo Rosso*, Dario Argento, 1975).

anguished."[15] What we see, in fact, are paintings by Italian artist Francesco Bartoli,[16] inspired by the works of Italian surrealist painter and cat lover Enrico Colombotto Rosso[17]; of the intersection of the film's title and the artist's surname, Daniele Abbiati wrote in Italian for *Il Giornale*, "*da qui il titolo? Chissà...*"[18] ("Hence the title? Who knows"). Regarding the artist themselves, however, looking at the other paintings and drawings that clutter the walls of Helga's apartment, the dominant theme is not the supernatural but the grotesque, and the painting that Marta stands in front of is no exception. The presence of the grotesque permeates the scene, and as Marc does not know specifically what it is he is looking for, from the perspective of the amateur investigator and the amateur art historian alike, the details of the other works that we also glimpse in passing are in their own way just as revealing; one work in particular is marked by three ghoulish looking heads, all with their eyes blanked out, painted in solid ovals of white paint (a notable distinction from Rosso's portraiture, which is marked by a tendency towards painting subjects with their eyes closed). While not as central narratively as the painting at the heart of the mystery, from this perspective these other works are just as significant as they foreshadow the notion of blindness—of the inability to *see* properly—that lies at the heart of Marc's inability to solve the crime.

While there are acknowledged difficulties in reductively defining the term "grotesque" in a historical context,[19] Wilson Yates defines grotesque art as that "whose form and subject matter appear to be part of, while contradictory to, the natural, social, or personal worlds of which we are a part." He continues, "Its images most often embody distortions, exaggeration, a fusion of incompatible parts in such a fashion that it confronts us as strange and disordered, as a world turned upside down."[20] From this perspective, we can draw a direct line not merely between the artworks that adorn Helga's apartment as grotesque art, but, taking a step back, *Deep Red* itself can be considered to manifest these exact same features that can comfortably lead us to describing the film *itself* as grotesque art. *Deep Red* certainly wouldn't be the first horror film to be described as grotesque; in relation to Mikhail Bakhtin's work on the carnivalesque[21] alone there is a strong body of work in horror studies on the relationship between horror cinema and the grotesque.[22] But *Deep Red* is perhaps particularly noteworthy for how the traditions of grotesque art manifest through paintings themselves in a film whose revelations ultimately stem directly from a painting itself.

We see this too in other artworks in the film, such as Carlo's hidden mural and his drawing in the school's archive; for those doubting the centrality of art to the film, it is worth emphasizing that the school itself is named after revered polymath Leonardo Da Vinci, particularly renowned for his painting. Unlike the paintings in Helga's apartment, there is no immediate visual connection to famous works of art in Carlo's art. Rather, the manic scrawls and simplistic figuration imply a degree of authenticity to what is clearly meant to be the drawings of a young, traumatized child. Intersecting in these works is the notion of grotesque art as outlined by Yates with what is configured as body horror, defined by Paul Wells as "the explicit display of the decay, dissolution and destruction of the body."[23]

From *Children of the Corn* (Fritz Kiersch, 1984) to *Sinister* (Scott Derrickson, 2013) children's drawings function both as clues and to create a disturbing effect is far from rare, but in the case of *gialli* specifically an interesting precursor to *Deep Red* can be seen three years earlier in Tonino Valerii's *My Dear Killer* (*Mio caro assassino*, 1972), which also similarly employs a mirror and the idea of reflections as another central clue, and engages with the fallibility of vision.[24] Unlike *Deep Red*, the drawing in *My Dear Killer* highlights a particular house and is not as centrally focused on figures that represent key characters, but certainly the areas of overlap are far more important than the deviations. In Sergio Martino's *Torso* (*I corpi presentano tracce di violenza carnale*, 1973), like *Deep Red* and *The Bird with the Crystal Plumage*, the incorrect reading of visual clues also plays a role, although not as centrally when Dani (Tina Aumont) confuses a red scarf with black print as worn by her admirer Stefano (Roberto Bisacco)—who she suspects is the killer—for a red scarf with black print, knowing she's seen someone wear the latter, a vital clue in the murders plaguing the film. I shall talk further about *Torso* shortly, but beforehand I will turn specifically to the use of traditional portraiture in another Martino film *Your Vice Is a Locked Room and Only I Have the Key* and Emilio Miraglia's *The Red Queen Kills Seven Times*.

Seven

Haunted Portraits

The Red Queen Kills Seven Times
(La dama rossa uccide sette volte,
Emilio Miraglia, 1972) and Your Vice Is
a Locked Room and Only I Have the Key
(Il tuo vizio è una stanza chiusa e solo io
ne ho la chiave, *Sergio Martino, 1972)*

In defining the key terms of her 2012 book *Portraiture and British Gothic Fiction: The Rise of Picture Identification 1764–1835*, Kamilla Elliott notes that picture identification in the context in which she deploys the term pertains to "a cultural use of portraiture," a kind of "intersemiotic practice that most commonly matches an embodied, presented face to a named, represented face to verify social identity."[1] While she notes this is a practice broadly continued today with photographs (she offers the useful example of passports and driving licenses to verify identity against a pictorial representation),[2] in the period that she is exploring in relation to her focus on Gothic fiction, she suggests it is a far more complex affair. Marked by a paradoxically "absent presence,"[3] when portraiture is transported into the Gothic text, Elliott argues, questions of class come to the fore. The flip side of this "absent presence" is a "present absence" which reflects the aspirations of upward mobility of the middle-classes. As such, in Gothic fiction "aristocratic portraiture ... works to remythologize picture identification and co-opt if for bourgeois ascendancy."[4] For Elliot, "gothic fiction is the mother ship of literary picture identification—no other literary period or genre is so pervasively, didactically and obsessively concerned with it,"[5] and I would argue this continues through the Gothic traditions from its literary peak into horror cinema, including *gialli*.

A fascination with portraits is not specific to horror, and the influence of Alfred Hitchcock on *gialli* is significant here. So riddled is Hitchcock's filmography with looming portraits of varying centrality to plot and spectacle that Michael Walker identifies them as a key motif identifiable across the director's *oeuvre*, visible in films including *The Lodger* (1927), *The Manxman* (1929), *Secret Agent* (1936), *Young and Innocent* (1937), *Rebecca* (1940), *Suspicion* (1941), *The Paradine Case* (1947), *Stage Fright* (1950), *Vertigo* (1958), and even *Psycho* (1960), the latter in regards to a fleeting glimpse we are granted of a portrait hanging above Mother Bates's bed which Walker suggests is a portrait of the character herself when she was younger.[6] In his brief overview of the use of portraits in Hitchcock's films, Walker suggests four ways that portraiture is utilized in film. Firstly, it articulates the authority of a parent figure. Secondly, it may indicate the strength of family traditions. It may, alternatively, mark the identity of someone who has died, or may represent the desire of the part of the individual who looks at the painting.

Top: *The Night Evelyn Came Out of the Grave* (*La notte che Evelyn uscì dalla tomba*, Emilio Miraglia, 1971). Bottom: *The Red Queen Kills Seven Times* (*La dama rossa uccide sette volte*, Emilio Miraglia, 1972).

Steven Jacobs and Lisa Colpaert also examine the use of portraiture in *The Dark Galleries: A Museum Guide to Painted Portraits in Film Noir, Gothic Melodrama, and Ghost Stories of the 1940s and 1950s*. Highlighting the ubiquity of portraits in films during this era, their book is presented as a catalog for a fictional exhibition, examining each portrait they have "curated" with a focus on subjects including class, desire and our often complex relationship with death and absence.[7]

We can see examples of these and other variations across a number of *gialli*. For example, desire, a memorial for a loved one passed and the parent-as-authority-figure model all combine in *Your Vice Is a Locked Room and Only I Have the Key*, a film which shall be discussed in-depth further shortly. The desire model is further complicated in both Antonio Margheriti's *Seven Deaths in the Cats Eye* and Umberto Lenzi's *Spasmo*, for example. In the former, painter and musician Lord

Top: Your Vice Is a Locked Room and Only I Have the Key (*Il tuo vizio è una stanza chiusa e solo io ne ho la chiave*, **Sergio Martino, 1972**). *Bottom: Seven Deaths in the Cat's Eye* (*La morte negli occhi del gatto*, **Antonio Margheriti, 1973**).

James MacGrieff (Hiram Keller) tells Corringa (Jane Birkin) when she discovers a nude painting of Suzanna the French teacher (Doris Kunstmann) that Suzanna was hired to seduce him in the hopes of pulling him out of what the family perceived as his madness ("I paint a little bit of everything," he tells Corringa, "the sacred and the profane"). Portraits riddle this film more broadly, from disguising hidden corridors to a portrait of James's baby sister herself that adorns the dining room whom he was said to have murdered as an infant. In *Spasmo*, despite his growing romance with Barbara (Suzy Kendall), Christian (Robert Hoffman) seeks safety at his ex-girlfriend Xenia's (Maria Pia Conte) studio-home, where she is working on a portrait of him, dedicating herself to it despite his effectively dumping her for another woman. When it is revealed at the end of the film that Christian is a killer, it is shown in flashback that after murdering Xenia, he splashes red paint on the portrait. In another Lenzi film, *Orgasmo*, desire works in complex ways in relation to a semi-nude self-portrait by wealthy protagonist Kathryn West (Carroll Baker). While at first it plays a key part in her seduction by Peter (Lou Castel) who tells her "you have a very unusual belly button, just like the Botticelli *Venus*," when joined by his lover Eva (Colette Descombes)—who he tells Kathryn is his sister—it is revealed that Kathryn is the victim of a sadistic home invasion planned by her greedy Uncle Brian (Tino Carraro). As the drama unfolds and the reality of her situation is revealed, the portrait looks down upon the increasing chaos as a witness of sorts. Elsewhere, when wealthy, conservative relatives visit, Kathryn takes down the painting and replaces it with less scandalous fare, the self-portrait thus not only linked to desire but also shame. Desire is more clear-cut when it comes to the faded portrait of Wanda that Franco Nero's character Leonardo discovers in *A Quiet Place in the Country* (*Un tranquillo posto di campagna*, Elio Petri, 1968), while the family tradition model is essential to a portrait-clue in *The Killer Reserved Nine Seats* (*L'assassino ha riservato nove poltrone*, Giuseppe Bennati, 1974). As shall be discussed shortly, this family tradition model also is central to the portrait that haunts the protagonists of *The Red Queen Kills Seven Times*.

Rather than Walker's more rigid model, then, in *giallo* cinema a more elastic approach to the function of portraiture may be of use, with a particular emphasis on their uncanny, often haunting status as Elliott's "absent presences." In Susan Felleman's examination of the use of portraits in Hollywood cinema of the 1940s, she too looks towards Hitchcock's *Rebecca* and *Suspicion*, Preminger's *Laura* and Lang's *The Woman in the Window* as well as his later noir *Scarlet Street* (1945). Across films such as these, Felleman notes that portraits "threaten the viewer with awareness of the magic of the mimetic and narrative devices employed by the film itself to engage him or her."[8] As such, there is an inherent "danger in a number of movies in which the portrait assumes a more direct role and is incorporated into narratives whose realism is strained by, if not abandoned to, psychological or supernatural treatment of mortal desire."[9] Ultimately, Felleman considers portraits in these films to hold to hold at their heart a fundamental quality of morbidity, either "as an explicit theme or an implicit subtext." She continues, "in these films portraiture plays a distinct role in imbuing the characters' identity, anxiety, longing and desire with a morbid sensibility."[10] Certainly this applies to *gialli* as much as to Hollywood cinema of the period she discusses. Along with the films that form the primary case studies of this chapter—*The Red Queen Kills Seven Times* and *Your Vice Is a Locked Room and Only I Have the Key*—all of the films mentioned above share these same fascinations, cast as they are in the ever-present long shadows of death itself.

The Red Queen Kills Seven Times begins as two young sisters—blonde Kitty and brunette Evelyn Wildenbrück—fight over Kitty's doll. Evelyn, it appears, has a long history of tormenting Kitty, and as she runs away laughing with her sister's precious toy, they arrive inside an opulent castle in Germany where their ailing grandfather Tobias Wildenbrück (Rudolf Schündler) sits in a grand hall near a large, strange portrait. Fascinated by the generically "ye olde" painting of two women—a blonde having stabbed a brunette with a dagger, the latter bleeding from her throat—Tobias tells them its history:

> Many years ago, those two women lived in this very castle. They were sisters like you. The legend goes that they hated each other from childhood, when the Black Queen resigned herself to enduring her sister's evil pranks and maliciousness in silence and waited for the right moment to take her revenge. When they grew up, the Red Queen fell in love with a man, and the Black Queen finally took her revenge and murdered her sister while she slept. She stabbed her seven times with that dagger in the picture. Now the legend says that a year after her death, the Red Queen came back to life. She murdered six innocent people and the seventh was the Black Queen. At peace with herself again, it is said she returned to her grave forever, but the same thing happened a hundred years later. And a hundred years after that, always, always in this castle, and always involving two sisters, every hundred years.

While both girls are awestruck by the story, it is the malicious Evelyn on whom it clearly has the most immediate impact. Identifying with the stabbed brunette woman with the red cape, she says "I'm the Red Queen, and Kitty's the Black Queen!," before taking Kitty's doll and stabbing it in an almost feral fit of explosive violence. Horrified, Tobias demands that the painting be taken away and destroyed immediately.

Leaping ahead in time to the film's contemporary moment, it is now

100 years since the last Red Queen-related blood bath. Via flashback we discover that the adult Kitty (Barbara Bouchet) has accidentally killed Evelyn in one of the many assaults she endured at her sister's hands during the time that elapsed since we met them as children. With her older sister Franziska (Marina Malfatti) and Franziska's husband Herbert (Nino Korda), they hide the body and tell everyone—including the now very old Tobias—that Evelyn has gone to the United States. When Tobias dies of a heart attack triggered by the shock of seeing someone in his bedroom that he identifies as Evelyn, a red-cloaked, dark-haired figure runs cackling into the night, and a series of vicious murders begins that seem to be a manifestation of the Red Queen curse. Although Kitty's lover and boss Martin (Ugo Pagliai) is a suspect at first, it is revealed that Evelyn in fact survived her fight with Kitty and that it was Franziska who killed her, hatching a plan to inherit Tobias's fortune without having to share it. Knowing Tobias's secret—that Evelyn was in fact not Kitty's sister, but a young girl he swapped the biological sibling with when they were very young in hopes of thwarting the curse—Franziska located the real sister, who goes by the name Rosemary Müller (Pia Giancaro). Franziska told Rosemary about her real identity and got her a job at the fashion company where Martin and Kitty worked, plying her with drugs to convince her that fulfilling the curse was her destiny. It was therefore Rosemary—controlled by Franziska—who was responsible for the killings. At the end of the film, despite almost succeeding in killing Kitty, Franziska herself is killed, just as Rosemary was earlier after attempting to tell Kitty the truth.

The Red Queen Kills Seven Times was Miraglia's second *giallo* after the more Gothic-leaning *The Night Evelyn Came Out of the Grave* (*La notte che Evelyn uscì dalla tomba*) the year before. Like *The Red Queen Kills Seven Times*, *The Night Evelyn Came Out of the Grave* also made significant use of a portrait that haunted its main protagonist, although not as narratively central perhaps as it is in the later film. Here, the memory of the eponymous Evelyn looms large in the memory of her widow, the deranged, sexually sadistic Alan (Anthony Steffan) who has just been released from a psychiatric institution. Haunted by memories of his wife's infidelity before her death, he plays out his sexually-loaded revenge about his dead wife on a series of similarly red-headed young women he deceptively lures to his S&M dungeon. On the advice of his cousin and the heir to his vast fortune George (Enzo Tarascio), Alan decides to spend some time in London, where—wanting to break his addiction to red heads—he decides to marry blonde Gladys (Marina Malfatti). Upon returning with his new wife to his country estate, however, Alan's grasp on reality slides further as Gladys convinces him

Evelyn is in fact still alive and faked her death so she could escape with her lover. A number of murders follow and after the disappearance and apparent resurrection of Evelyn's corpse (hence the "risen from the grave" in the film's title) Alan loses control of his fortune when he loses his sanity and is institutionalized. This allows George to inherit Alan's fortune, and it is revealed that George and Gladys were lovers whose entire plan was to push Alan over the edge to gain his money. But Gladys herself has been fooled when it is revealed that one of the women we assume Alan had killed—a sex worker called Susan (Erika Blanc)—is in fact in cahoots with George and had set Gladys up as well. Susan is stabbed to death by Gladys, who herself is dying having drunk strychnine-filled champagne given to her by George. Adding a further twist, the final moments of the film reveal that Alan had in fact feigned his mental collapse to frame George, who is arrested by waiting police.

Aside from its notably ambivalent ending when it comes to the fact that Alan's own violence against women remains unpunished, *The Night Evelyn Came Out of the Grave* ultimately uses the portrait of Evelyn—the object of Alan's sadistic desire—as somewhat of a red (headed) herring. As the film's title suggests, she is very much the dominant absent presence in the film, and as typified by Alan's taste for other redheaded women to play out his sadistic, sexually violent revenge fantasies, Evelyn's presence is marked by a seemingly endless array of doubles. This becomes most overt near Alan's supposed final psychological collapse, where the blonde Gladys sits in front of the portrait of Evelyn wearing a red wig, clearly intending to push Alan over the edge. Hair color too plays a role in *The Red Queen Kills Seven Times;* blonde Kitty as a supposed double for the Black Queen and brunette Evelyn (another Evelyn marked by her absence) as the Red Queen of the title. While the portrait in this later *giallo* functions as a trigger in the sense that its presence sparks the narrative action of the film, it is more closely aligned with the family curse trope in that it materially represents the historical patterns that have so long cursed the Wildenbrück family.

While these two portraits are the dominant motifs that unify *The Night Evelyn Came Out of the Grave* and *The Red Queen Kills Seven Times*, that both films are also marked by quite nasty moments of sexual violence is also significant. In *The Red Queen Kills Seven Times*, Kitty is being blackmailed by Evelyn's ex-boyfriend Peter (Fabrizio Moresco), a drug dealer we later find out has been working with Franziska and supplying Rosemary with the drugs that made her susceptible to the suggestion that as Kitty's real sister, she was destined to become the murderous Red Queen of the family legend. After one of the film's strongest and most stylist vignettes—a nightmare where Kitty imagines herself being stabbed to death by the Red Queen herself—Kitty is raped by Peter in her living room, leaving her traumatized and pushing her closer to the brink of insanity.

In an extraordinary critical close analysis, Robert Mahoney considers this rape scene and the nightmare preceding it in relation to the art that adorns Kitty's home. Firstly, above Kitty's bed in both the nightmare and in her "real" bedroom is a piece described by Mahoney as "Miro-like,"[11] and there is no doubt whatsoever that this painting is very deliberately evoking conscious associations with Spanish proto-surrealist Joan Miró. But as Mahoney notes, the significance of this particular painting does not end there; this is no simple reference-for-reference sake. Rather, the precise composition of how Kitty is positioned in relation to the Red Queen mirrors the shapes within the famous portrait of the Red and Black Queen that dominates the film in what Mahoney notes is "quite good like-equals-like visual rhyming."[12] Continuing his analysis, Mahoney suggests that "to make the connection between the picture over the bed as a kind of abstract script of the legend picture," the ghostly, transparent dream-figure of Evelyn "steps out of the comparison space between the picture and the legend picture to bring the legend to life in her dream while she is lying in her bed."[13] Turning to the rape scene that follows this nightmare, Mahoney finds further evidence of the importance of paintings in the film in reference to an abstract work that hangs in Kitty's living room. While not as recognizably riffing on a particular artist in the same manner as the "Miro-like" one in her bedroom, this painting—a red/brown background with an abstract shape in the foreground constructed of three-dimensional looking brown and yellowish cubes with a large black arrow pointing at the structure from above—is still just as significant. That arrow, for Mahoney, and its particular positioning within the frame is crucial as it points downwards to the very area Kitty (now realizing she is under real threat of sexual violence from Peter) seeks to protect; that arrow, for Mahoney, "suggests the man's thoughts as it points decidedly downward to her black panties, and guides him to what he wants."[14]

Although rarely (but not always) little more than a sleazy excuse for depicting sexually victimized women as a titillating spectacle, rape is far from rare in *gialli*. In *Your Vice Is a Locked Room and Only I Have the Key*, the depravity of Oliviero (Luigi Pistilli) is made clear through an extraordinary parade of disgusting behaviors; after sexually humiliating his Black maid Brenda (Angela La Vorgna) who also is forced to endure abuse framed in explicitly racist and sexual terms, he rapes his apparently long-suffering wife—the film's protagonist Irinia (Anita Strindberg)—when she visits him after another public humiliation wearing a dress worn by his deceased mother in a portrait the film privileges from the film's opening moments. It is in this way that we meet two of the film's three central characters; opening with a quick shot of the dilapidated mansion from at night from outside, then cutting to a close-up of a black cat, the film turns to the portrait of Esther, Oliviero's beloved late mother, with whom he is clearly obsessed. Entertaining a large group of hippies from a nearby camping ground, Oliviero performs for them at the same time he gets lost in the image of his mother; "You deserve to be compared to Mary Stuart. No one else ever had such two diverse claims to fame; one as a murderess, the other as a martyr." Turning to his guests, he tells them, "She was a lady; a real aristocrat."

Recalling Kamilia Elliott's emphasis on the use of portraiture in Gothic literature, Ellinger has highlighted the Gothic aspects of Martino's films, noting how it blends aspects of the latter into the giallo formula. For Ellinger, "the film revels in Gothic concepts such as the moralistic decay inherent in the aristocracy, crumbling houses, decadent, libertine deviant behavior ... perversity, domestic violence and psychosexual themes."[15] Filmed at Villa Lugli in Teolo in northern Italy (also the location for *A Quiet Place in the Country*,[16] discussed in Chapter Eleven), *Your Vice Is a Locked Room and Only I Have the Key* begins by introducing Oliviero as a one-time successful writer who has been unable to write for many years, dominating his home with domestic violence, rape and his alcoholic mood swings. When a young woman—an ex-student—who works at a local bookshop that Oliviero was having an affair with is murdered, the police look to him as a potential suspect and tell him and Irinia not to leave town. Indulging in a moment of self-love as she wears the forbidden dress as Oliviero looks on, Brenda too is violently murdered, again apparently by Oliviero although we do not see the killer's face. Demanding Irinia help him hide her body, they bury her beneath a wall in their cellar. Things are further complicated with the arrival of Oliviero's sexually liberated, flirtatious niece Floriana (Edwige Fenech), the film's third central character. She seduces first Irinia and then Oliviero, as well as beginning a relationship with a young dirt bike rider from the nearby town. Encouraged by Floriana to kill Oliviero to end his abuse and violence, Oliviero has similar ideas and plans to dispose of Irinia. Discovering his plot, a terrified Irinia stabs him to death as he sits drunk and passed out at his typewriter. Turning to blackmail, Floriana demands Irinia give her Esther's jewels as payment for her silence, and having done so the two women bury Oliviero in the wall with Brenda's corpse before Floriana leaves. The film's final twist, however, reveals that Irinia had planned all of it with her lover Walter (Ivan Rassimov), who had helped her with the earlier murders that were implied to have been committed by Oliviero. Irinia successfully gaslighted the drunken Oliviero into thinking he was the killer, pushing him towards insanity. Walter kills Floriana and returns the jewels to Irinia, but she double crosses him too and pushes him off a cliff. Seemingly accomplished her mission of disposing of her husband (as well his mother before the film began, too, who she also gleefully confesses to murdering) and getting the valuable jewels back from Floriana, it appears Irinia has succeeded until the police arrive investigating a report of animal cruelty. Having stabbed the beloved black cat Olivero inherited from his mother (named Satan, no less[17]), Irinia's hatred of the feline is her undoing. Loosely adapted from Edgar Allan Poe's short story "The Black Cat" (1843), like that story too the bodies in the cellar are revealed by the sound of a wailing cat.

Although never a character in the film as such, the portrait of Esther wearing a Tudor-style gown dominates over much the action that takes place. A famous actress with many lovers, the historical costume worn in Esther's portrait belies the fact that she lived more recently. That it is not a portrait more specific to her contemporary moment is a significant decision as it implies a much grander sense of import and her power as a haunting presence over her son. At one point it is suggested Esther and Oliviero had a sexual relationship, this incestuous bond only adding further to the construction of Oliverio as a morally corrupt figure. If he is capable of having sex with his mother, it is implied his transgressions would surely not stop at murder. Bar the cat torture, the fact that our sympathies are largely with the beaten, sexually abused and extremely fragile Irinia is largely where the impact of the film's surprise revelation lies, but as Kier-La Janisse shrewdly observes in her analysis of her analysis of the film, there is something much more at stake here; "The Italian horror film, the giallo in particular, often features female neurosis as an adjunct to the husband's moral deficiency and/or mental illness, which is often a catalyst for the wife's own mental disturbance."[18]

Esther's portrait acts as both an omnipresent sexual/maternal presence over Oliviero and a witness to Irinia's actions, the severity of which Esther is aware of long before we the audience are. Positioned high up on the wall and effectively looking down on her son and the inhabitants of her household, the expression on her face implied an element of amused judgment. In the portrait, Satan the cat sits on her lap, and the cat's crucial role in the film's action therefore casts him almost as a representative stand-in for Esther herself. He torments Irinia by killing her white doves, and in return, Irinia stabs him in the eye viciously with a pair of scissors. Irinia has a genuine fear of the cat that appears to stem far beyond pedestrian ailurophobia; on some level, she recognizes the association between the cat and Esther, and the intensity of her fear appears at times to be a response to what in the film is presented as the enormous symbolic presence of Esther herself, despite no longer being alive. Satan's power to move between different symbolic spaces— between the painting where he appears to bring Esther's very presence into the real world to torment his owner's killer—is made literal in the film's conclusion, where his cries from behind the wall (beyond the grave, if you like) are ultimately what reveal Irinia's guilt and seal her fate.

Your Vice Is a Locked Room and Only I Have the Key was not the only time Sergio Martino engaged with paintings in his films. In *Torso* (*I corpi presentano tracce di violenza carnale*) the following year, Suzy Kendall plays Jane, an American art student studying at a university in Perugia. When a balaclava wearing serial killer begins to run amok on campus, the girls flee with a group of other young women to an isolated villa in Tagliacozzo owned by the uncle of Jane's friend Dani (Tina Aumont). But they are not safe here either, and all the girls are viciously murdered except for Jane. When the killer's identity is finally revealed, Jane is shocked to discover that it is her art history lecturer Franz (John Richardson), with whom she had tentatively begun to develop a romantic connection after they debated the aesthetics and cultural value of renaissance painter Pietro Perugino (an artist most famous for being Raphael's art teacher). The film begins with a quite lengthy speech from Franz in the context of an art history lecture on the failures of Perugino:

> This Saint Sebastian is in effect a Hellenistic statue set against a magnificent Da Vinci-esque scenery. His suffering, in fact, doesn't move us. Note how Perugino, that humble peasant, transformed the peasants from his origin into saints and Madonna's. And see how he manages to transform this tragedy of pain into a near lyrical indifference. Perugino was keen to paint blood and so his tears are like drops of dew on the eye. His scenes rarely exude and air of drama. This is true of his St. Sebastian in Stockholm and the one in the Louvre. Everything is bathed in an almost supernatural elegance. Here, the figure transcends all human experience. In his very own way, Perugino absorbed the lessons of the great Piero della Francesca, only then to decline, in his later years into a sort of convoluted and provincial formalism that decidedly undermines the power and originality of his early work.

Confronting Franz after class, Jane argues that "in the Saint Sebastian in the Louvre, you completely ignore the intensely spiritual aspect of the figure. Why, its practically overflowing with holiness." In reply, Franz reminds her that Perugino was virtually an atheist. A classmate—and a soon-to-be murder suspect, Stefano (Roberto Bisacco)—complains about Perugino's squeamishness and refusal to show blood, evidence he suggests of his bourgeois nature. Dani answers curtly, "he was a painter, not a butcher." Later in the film, a police investigator shows a close up of bloodied evidence on an overhead projector for the class as he begs anyone with information on the murder to come forward. "What you see on the screen is not a product of expressionist art," he says. "What you have here are fragments of cloth found under the fingernails of one of your companions who was barbarously murdered just one week ago." While the relationship between art and violence clearly fascinated Martino as well as directors including Argento, Fulci, Riso, Miraglia and others, then, this question of art and violence with specific relation to the figure of Saint Sebastian also lies at the heart of Pupi Avati's *The House with Laughing Windows*, which we will now examine further.

Eight

Paint Death Clearly

Saint Sebastian and The House with Laughing Windows *(*La casa dalle finestre che ridono, *Pupi Avati, 1976)*

Eschewing the urban locales so synonymous with *giallo* cinema and aligned with rural variants like films such as *Don't Torture a Ducking* (*Non si sevizia un paperino*, Lucio Fulci, 1972),[1] Pupi Avati's *The House with Laughing Windows* (*La Casa dalle finestre che ridono*, 1976) does not offer much in the way of traditional *giallo* iconography such as black leather gloves and switchblades. But what it lacks in readily identifiable motifs it makes up for in a near suffocating overabundance of atmosphere, paranoia and twisted histories coming back to haunt the present through vignettes marked by hyper-stylized violence. Perhaps even more than Argento's famous animal trilogy (*The Bird with the Crystal Plumage, Four Flies on Grey Velvet* and *Cat O' Nine Tails*), *The House with Laughing Windows* hinges upon a systematic process of defamiliarization taken to its most perverse extreme. While most often associated with Russian Formalism,[2] in *gialli* defamiliarization adheres less stringently to formalist (or neoformalist) conceptions, and far closer to Carlo Ginzburg's approach that involves not just "making things strange," but more consciously towards riddle-solving as a methodological template. "In order to *see* things," Ginzburg writes, "we must first of all look at them as if they had no meaning, as if they were a riddle."[3]

The titles of the films in Argento's animal trilogy make this explicit: they propose *riddles*, implying questions that demand answers. Avati's title works in a similar way, and thus its enigmas begin before the film even starts. While this is notable of Avati's *giallo*, it is not specific to it; just as we can ask how precisely can a house have

Amateur detective and art restorer Stefano (Lino Capolicchio) uncovers the horrors of the Saint Sebastian fresco in *The House with Laughing Windows* (*La casa dalle finestre che ridono*, Pupi Avati, 1976).

laughing windows, so too we might wonder how a bird have crystal plumage? What *exactly* is the strange vice of Mrs. Wardh? Precisely *why* are there strange drops of blood on Jennifer's body? While the overstuffed poetics of *giallo* film titles are one of its signature excesses ("as baroque and preposterous as the films themselves," as Anne Billson cannily notes[4]), the functional value of the inherent riddling of many of these names places the audience in a mode of abstracted detection before the films even begin. We seek clues to help us answer these title-riddles before a crime has been committed, and the questions they provoke are marked through their preference for hyperbolic, excessive poetics over logic or clarity.

The opening sequence of *The House with Laughing Windows* demonstrates how powerful even the simplest of visual riddles can be in this context. Sepia toned shots accompany a discordant tinkling piano as a series of bizarre shapes are revealed—closer to abstract paintings at first rather than the human figure, which is what they are soon revealed to be. What we are looking at, we soon realize, is a man being tortured. The disorienting camera angles are further abstracted by the footage being shown in slow motion, thus presenting a series of images we must "solve" to be able to identify it for what it is: an extreme vision of human suffering. The riddle of the film's title is only further complicated in these opening moments as we ask ourselves; what are we *actually* watching? And what do the strange poetics of the words we hear spoken in the voiceover mean, and why is this man suffering so? Because over this sequence—which feels more like Kenneth Anger than it does *giallo* masters like Argento, Martino, Lenzi, or Fulci—a mechanical-sounding male voice recites the following:

> The colours ... my colours
> They pour out of my veins
> They're sweet ... my colours
> Sweet ... they're sweet like the Autumn
> They're hot like blood
> They're smooth like Syphilis
> And they run, they run into the eyes of the people
> Carrying the infection to them all
> My colours, my colours
> They're inside my arm, my colours
> *Mio Deus*
> Far, far away my colours go
> They go far away
> They can go far away,
> But you have to die for them
> Open yourself inside
> *Oh Deus Signor*
> Purify
> Away, away
> Away with everything
> Purity, purity
> Is all my colours
> All my colours
> *Hijo de puta*
> Yes, here it goes...
> *Meus Deus*
> Here it goes, I feel he's dying
> Yes, he is dying
> Purify, purify[5]

As this last line is recited, the camera pulls back and reveals the body of a young man, slashed and torn, hanging from his arms in front of what we soon learn is a painted landscape backdrop. Through this imagery, we are instantly thrust into the visceral heart of a *tableau vivant* of Saint Sebastian's martyrdom, an enduring subject that has fascinated painters and sculptors in particular throughout art history and—as we saw in the opening scene of *Torso* alone—one whose transgressive violence has been referenced by more than one *giallo* filmmaker. With the centrality of Saint Sebastian to *The House with the Laughing Windows* now established, Avati's depiction of the iconic figure establishes a set of thematic binaries that will run throughout the film between the archaic and the modern, the pure and the dangerous, the local and the stranger, and the abstracted and the real. What to our eye at first appear as merely random shapes morph quickly into not just an identifiable human figure experiencing extreme violence, but through its association with Saint Sebastian, that figure is revealed almost instantly to manifest at the intersection of art history and theology, a near simultaneous iconographic reference point.

The film's amateur detective is an art conservator called Stefano (Lino Capolicchio) who is hired by Solmi (Bob Tonelli), the mayor of a village in the Valli di Comacchio region of in the Po Delta regional park to restore an unfinished fresco of Saint Sebastian in the local church. Originally painted by local artist Buono Legnani (Tonino Corazzari), he died by suicide before its completion, and Solmi is hopeful that restoring the work will boost the local economy by becoming a tourist attraction. Stefano is told that Legnani "suffered from a dark soul," and is described as the "painter of agonies." Almost immediately upon his arrival, Stefano begins to receive a series of threatening anonymous telephone, insisting he does not touch the fresco and suggesting that he leave Valli di Comacchio immediately. Warned of unusual things happening in the village by his anxious, seemingly paranoid friend Antonio (Giulio Pizzirani), Stefano is unable to find out anything more specific because Antonio is soon killed. Thrown out of the town's only hotel without a convincing explanation, Stefano relocates to the decaying villa of a paraplegic woman (Pina Borione), following a recommendation from the village's priest (Eugene Walter). With his lover, the young schoolteacher Francesca (Francesca Marciano) who has also recently moved to the community, Stefano begins to investigate Legnani's background and learns through the town drunk Coppola (Gianni Cavina) of the artist's two sisters. As Stefano discovers, the artist died by suicide when by setting himself on fire in front of his sisters and was assumed to have died, although his body was never found.

Unpacking the gruesome reality behind the troubled painter's artistic practice, Stefano is shocked to discover that Legnani would paint actual torture scenes that were staged before him by his sisters who would murder and maim models as he painted. Thus, Stefano concludes, the two women shown in the church's Saint Sebastian fresco that he uncovers during his restoration work are in fact portraits of Legnani's sadistic, vicious sisters. Not only this, but the sisters are apparently still alive, continuing their killings in the name of art and continuing their brother's legacy. Locating Legnani's home—a building with giant smiling mouths covering its windows, hence the film's titles—Coppola shows Stefano a mass grave where the sisters' victims have been buried. Deciding to flee the dangerous village with Francesca, before they can leave she is raped and murdered by the creepy young church hand Lidio (Pietro Brambilla), and Stefano discovers her body hanging from the ceiling in a hidden room in the paraplegic's home where he has been staying. With her body carefully positioned, we realize Francesca is hanging in front of the same background that the body we saw in the opening sequence of the film was also positioned. With his pleas for help ignored by the police, Stefano returns to the attic to find his hostess is not paraplegic at all, but one of the dreaded Legnani sisters herself, cackling wildly as she and her sister (whose face we cannot see) kill Lidio, himself hung from the ceiling hook, Saint Sebastian style. In the denouement, his hostess tells Stefano of the power of violent ritual in art, revealing to him that they had preserved their brother's remains so as to continue their "creative" relationship with him. After being stabbed, Stefano manages to flee and when turned away from the townsfolk, he has nowhere to go but to the church itself. It is here that he discovers that the priest is in fact not only a woman, but the other Legnani sister in male drag. Peeling off her clerical robes, she reveals a breast, and as the film ends the sound of the two sisters laughing combines with the sound of approaching police sirens.

It is, in the light of this synopsis alone, an understatement to say that the figure of Saint Sebastian is central to *The House with the Laughing Windows*; not only in relation to the story of the two sisters who appear in the village church's mural and their painter brother, but in the film's reflexive critique of the idea that there are culturally sanctioned, acceptable modes of the artistic representation of violence while in other contexts—*gialli* itself, perhaps—it is considered far less noble. For Koven, there is at play a broader critique on what was then a very real moral panic surrounding snuff film which was largely triggered by the scandal surrounding Michael and Roberta Findlay's *Snuff* (1976) which was promoted as an authentic snuff movie. For Koven, "the timing of Avati's film coincides with the appearance of *Snuff* in 1976, so the echoes may be intentional."[6] He continues, "By changing the artistic medium from filmmaking to painting (specifically fresco painting), Avati seems to be suggesting that regardless of the presumed contemporary nature of these snuff stories, they are—anachronistically—as old as Italy's artistic traditions."[7]

While certainly true, this risks underplaying the significance of the Saint Sebastian figure specifically to the film itself. As Valentina Liepa has argued, the meaning and representational trends surrounding particular images have shifted over time, dependent on cultural influences and the nuances of an individual artist's creative vision. Saint Sebastian was a very popular figure for medieval and Renaissance artists, the early medieval period being the moment when a predominant version of his story came to the fore: according to this legend, he was born in the Roman town of Narbonna and studied in Milan before moving to Rome where his courage and good character brought him to the attention of emperor Diocletian. Appointed as head of the Imperial Guard, Sebastian's secret status as a Christian was revealed when he tried to save fellow Christians from a death sentence. Unsettled that Sebastian's the young soldier make Christianity look attractive to others as he sought to convert them to his faith, Diocletian sentenced Sebastian to death where he was—as is depicted throughout art history—tied to a tree and shot with arrows on January 20 in the year 354. Left for dead, he was healed by Saint Irene and despite her suggestions that he flee, Sebastian returned to Diocletian to argue for the sanctity of human life. Fearing it was a ghost who had appeared before him, Diocletian again condemned Sebastian to death—he was more cautious in seeking confirmation this time—and Sebastian was beaten to death and thrown into a water-shoot. He was buried by St Lucia near Via Apia, the same site that Pope St Damascus built the Basilica of San Sebastiano in 367.[8]

Saint Sebastian was considered a protector against the threat of plague during the Middle Ages which no doubt added to his popularity as a subject in medieval art, but as Liepa adds, as the story of his being shot with arrows when tied to a tree required him being naked, it allowed Renaissance artists an opportunity to paint nudes while still appearing devout.[9] As typified by the representation of the figure in *The House with Laughing Windows*, Saint Sebastian is synonymous with this first attempted execution scene and throughout art history (although peaking in the fifteenth century), as Liepa notes, "he is usually depicted as a naked young man tied to a tree or a column and pierced with arrows," where "his figure usually stands against the background of a scene of Rome as viewed from Palatine Hill—the supposed place of his martyrdom."[10]

The first image we see that evokes associations with Saint Sebastian are in the opening sequence itself, later mirrored in the specific positioning of both Francesca and Lidio's bodies in the attic of one of the Legnani sisters. What we see is both arms are forcibly held above the head, as typical of works including Guido Reni's painting *St. Sebastian* (1615–16), and Martin Schongauer's fifteenth century engraving *Saint Sebastian*. When we first see the fresco in the church, however, while similar, the position of the Saint Sebastian figure is slightly different. Here, the figures hands are tied behind his back, closer in composition to Early Renaissance artist Andrea Mantegna's *St. Sebastian* (1480), reproduced elsewhere in other works such as Guido Reni's *Saint Sebastian* (1625), Perugino's *Saint Sebastian* (1495), Antonello da Messina's

Martin Schongauer (1435/50–1491), *Saint Sebastian*, ca. 1435–1491, engraving, Harris Brisbane Dick Fund, 1951 (open access, Metropolitan Museum of Art, www.metmuseum.org).

St. Sebastian (1477–79), and Albrecht Dürer's 1499 engraving *Saint Sebastian Bound to the Column.*

But it is Stefano's discovery of the two monstrous women who stand by Sebastian's side as he continues his restoration work that shows an important shift in the art historical references the film is making. Based most commonly on the role Saint Irene played in Saint Sebastian's story, the introduction of women to the scene is not new, and the particular composition in the film's fresco with a woman on each side has art

Albrecht Dürer (1471–1528), *Saint Sebastian Bound to the Column*, ca. 1499, engraving, bequest of Grace M. Pugh, 1985 (open access, Metropolitan Museum of Art, New York www.metmuseum.org).

historical precedent; see, for example, Vicente López Y Portaña's *Saint Sebastian Tended by Saint Irene* (1795–1800), or Dirck van Baburen's *St Sebastian Attended by St Irene and Her Maid* (1615).

In conversation after Antonio's funeral, the priest tells Stefano upon the revelation of the two additional figures in the painting that he is concerned that "the killers of Saint Sebastian seem to be enjoying it. Perhaps too much. What do you think?" In reply, Stefano tells him "I think we have the wrong idea. The painter did not have the intention of depicting the agony of the Saint. Everybody says the artist is a sensitive genius, but all he does is paint death ... of a human, without compassion." The fresco in Avati's film therefore turns its attentions towards these women, effectively blurring the lines between what have in art history been broadly configured in theological terms as helper-women and harmer-archers. Yet with their malign and sadistic expressions, Lengani's sisters in the fresco are shown as effectively trapping the Saint Sebastian in the center of the image. By doing this, Legnani blurs the morally opposed roles of the archers and the Holy Women where we see the actions of the latter wholly subverted in the scenario as Legnani depicts it. There is little doubt that the artist's sadistic sisters are sticking the daggers *into* Saint Sebastian, rather than what we know of Saint Irene and her helpers when they saved his life by pulling arrows out. Thus in effect, Avati—through Legnani—has subverted through defamiliarization not just the visual iconography of Saint Sebastian but the legend itself; rather than a scenario where good women nurse a wrongly-prosecuted good man back to life, we have a far more blasphemous reimagining where we are asked another riddle almost sacrilegious in nature. Based purely on the visual information we have in the paintings alone, was Saint Irene pulling the arrows out, or sticking them in?

When we look closely at paintings such as Jusepe de Ribera's *Saint Sebastian Tended by the Holy Women* (1621), we can see when taken only on their own merits how this question can arise: it is quite literally an act of faith to assume that the women are nursing him by removing the arrows rather than torturing him in a manner much closer to the actions of the Legnani sisters. Of course, this is not to suggest a grand religious conspiracy where Saint Irene was in fact a deranged torturer, but rather that when separated from the legend of Saint Sebastian, the visual information provided in purely pictorial terms is ambiguous. Avati takes this ambiguity and builds an entire mystery around it, adding a hefty dose of the perverse excesses of *gialli* to his recipe. Implying as it does a strong degree of ambivalence around the canon of Catholic saints and associated legends more broadly, Avati's film therefore reveals just how elastic the boundaries of *gialli* can be, even when consciously stepping away from its more stereotypical iconography.

While this certainly manifests most directly through the mystery built around Legnani and the Saint Sebastian mural, the paranoia and violence that results from this amateur investigator's delving into the mystery also relies on what is coded within the film as a monstrous, deceptive transgression of assumed gender norms. There are two key images that seek to collapse these assumptions; firstly, a self-portrait we see of Legnani with his head painted onto the body of a reclining nude

Saint Sebastian Tended by the Holy Women, painting by Jose de Ribera (1591–1652), on view at Bilbao Fine Arts Museum, 2017 (Naeblys, Shutterstock.com).

woman, and the final twist revelation that the priest is not only a woman, but is one of Legnani's sisters. From a contemporary perspective this may be far too easy to dismiss as a bigoted, conservative phobia against queer identities, but the casting of American author Eugene Walter specifically as the unnamed priest is important. Not only does Walter's presence consciously evoke his previous role as Mother Superior in Federico Fellini's *Juliet of the Spirits* (1965), but his camp personae—*The New York Times* described him in 2001 as "Truman Capote without the fame"[11]—perhaps further amplifies more contemporary understandings of Saint Sebastian as a queer icon.[12] As Richard Dyer notes, that there is "gender confusion aplenty in the film before the final twist" is of no small relevance to the close relationship of this gender-blurring with the clergy itself, "which itself plays upon the curious position of priests in Italy, fathers who by definition are not fathers."[13]

If Avati's film demonstrates some ambivalence to art historical representations of Saint Sebastian and its associated legends, then the film's conclusion is no less ambivalent. While Koven suggests that at the film's conclusion that the killers "manage to get away with their crimes,"[14] we *do* hear sirens and car doors slamming. But we have seen Solmi call the police after Stefano—stabbed and bleeding—is shunned by the townsfolk when he seeks help, so there is an implication that the police have been called not to protect Stefano and capture the sisters, but rather simply to clean up yet another Legnani sister bloodbath. There are echoes of wartime complicity with the Nazis, a theme that runs throughout the film, where authority, conspiracy and moral ambiguity runs rife; the townsfolk appear to silently accept the Legnani family's crimes so as not to provoke their ire. But rather than offering a concrete conclusion, the ending itself only presents more ambiguities: as Dyer asks, "will Stefano be believed? And even if he is, will anyone wish to dislodge the archaic hold of family and church?"[15] There are echoes of earlier riddles: are the arrows being pushed in, or taken out? How can a house have laughing windows? Just as it began, then, the film concludes with only more riddles. It is this ambiguity that allows Avati to underscore the meaning of that opening poem by addressing the politics of representation that dominate the film itself and the representation of violence more broadly: can death ever be painted as clearly as the reality it purports to represent?

PAINTERS

Nine

A Portrait of an Artist as a Mad Drunk

The Red Headed Corpse
(La rossa dalla pelle che scotta,
Renzo Russo, 1972)

More often than not in *giallo* film, where there are artists, there's trouble. Think of those we've met in this book so far alone. There's *Spasmo*, where not only is Christian's ex-girlfriend a painter, but he and his new squeeze Barbara hide out in the seaside tower of a painter friend of Barbara's after Christian mistakenly believes he has killed a man. Then there's the failed writer Oliviero in *Your Vice Is a Locked Room and Only I Have the Key*, a racist rapist, possibly a killer, and definite scumbag. There's Anna in *The Stendhal Syndrome* who turns to art to try and get a grip on her spiraling mental health. Marc in *Deep Red* is a musician, Sam in *Four Flies on Grey Velvet* is a writer, Tino in *The Forbidden Room* and Jane in *Torso* are art students, and the characters in *A Lizard in a Woman's Skin* and *The Red Queen Kills Seven Times* live in spaces dominated by paintings that will have a significant, violent impact on their lives. Moving beyond the films we've looked at so far, there are simply too many examples to list. Murders often overlap with communities of creative practitioners in a range of films including *Eye of the Labyrinth*, *The Crimes of the Black Cat*, *Death Walks at Midnight* (*La morte accarezza a mezzanotte*, Luciano Ercoli, 1972), *Death Carries a Cane* (*Passi di danza su una lama di rasoio*, Maurizio Pradeaux, 1973), *Murder Rock* (*Murderock—uccide a passo di danza*, Lucio Fulci, 1984), almost of all Argento's *gialli*, and many, many others. In the case of painters alone, beyond the case studies I look at in this section of the book we find artist Jill (Edith Meloni) in Mario Bava's *Five Dolls for an August Moon* who married for money, her painting a symbol of her lazy, indulgent lifestyle.

Nine—A Portrait of an Artist as a Mad Drunk   131

Doomed sleazebag Russell (Howard) in *The Killer Reserved Nine Seats* (*L'assassino ha riservato nove poltrone*, Giuseppe Bennatim 1974) needs birthday boy Patrick (Chris Avram) desperately as he's the only customer he has for his art, but Russell is still regardless quite happy to be sleeping with Patrick's fiancée Kim (Janet Agren) on the side. Carroll Baker's characters Kathryn in *Orgasmo* and Martha in *Knife of Ice*, both seemingly nice women who dabble in painting, turn out to be much more than we bargained for.

As Susan Felleman argues, "the representation of art in film tends to allegorize the medium as art, and the way in which the artist figures tends to constitute either a self-portrait or a kind of negative version thereof."[1] Certainly in *giallo*, this applies representations of artists and the worlds in which they inhabit; if they are not corrupt (or, at least, corruptible) themselves, then they are somehow flawed or indelibly linked to corrupt scenarios where murder, violence and other transgressions can flourish. Painters in *giallo* (and indeed, many artists in general) are curious figures to consider when reflecting on the "old artists' myths" as Doris Berger has identified them, where artists are "perceived as geniuses and society's outsiders who are only able to create 'great art' because of their special status."[2] In the three films I consider in this section—*The Red Headed Corpse* (*La rossa dalla pelle che scotta*, Renzo Russo, 1972), *Blood Delirium* (*Delirio di sangue*, Sergio Bergonzelli, 1988), and *A Quiet Place in the Country* (*Un tranquillo posto di campagna*, Elio Petri, 1968)—these assumptions are fleshed out in different ways in various degrees of success, both confirmed and simultaneously subverted in each film in different ways.

In the case of *The Red Headed Corpse*, Farley Granger's John Ward is very much one of "society's outsiders"—a reclusive weird drunk who lives on an isolated property and paints—but is hardly perceived as a genius by anybody's standards but his own, especially the gallerists who give him a pittance for his abstract paintings more out of sympathy than business prowess or art appreciation. Closer perhaps to Berto Consalvi in *The Bird with the Crystal Plumage*, John's "special status" renders him more a suspicious, dubious character rather than a genius, no matter how feebly both men cling to their visions of themselves as creative outsiders. And both are, unquestioningly, of interest to the audience less for their artistic abilities than for their failures; that Consalvi provides a vital clue in *The Bird with the Crystal Plumage* almost feels secondary to the revelation that he eats cats, and John's status as a demented alcoholic with a seriously bad attitude to women summarizes his primary character traits, the quality or value of his artwork fading to almost nothing in comparison.

Russo's *The Red Headed Corpse* is in practical ways a challenging film to provide a straightforward synopsis for. Partially, this is due to what is undeniably choppy editing and what may be objectively be described as a somewhat weak screenplay written by the director himself. There are, firstly, numerous edits of the film that have been released over many years under a variety of titles including *The Sensuous Doll* and *Sweet Spirits*, all featuring different levels of nudity, as well as a French version called *La Peau Qui Brule* which has hardcore inserts added to the sex scenes. Regardless, a basic scenario appears to run through most of these. As a Turkish-Italian co-production, *The Red Headed Corpse* is set in Istanbul and opens when a man reports his lover missing to police, saying that she was meant to meet him at the airport and they were to leave for Spain together. He voices concerns that the artist she lives with—Granger's John Ward—may have done something to her. Ward meantime meets a sex worker called Mala (Ivana Novak) in a bar who takes a liking to him, and when he shows no interest in a cash transaction, she suggests that they have sex anyway. When he mentions he is a painter, she excitedly offers to model for him. This suggestion has an immediate impact on him for reasons we are yet to understand.

Meeting a group of nomadic hippies in the woods near his home, a young man randomly gifts John with a beaten-up old shop mannequin and jokes that she is the perfect woman because she is unable to talk. At first John rejects the gift, but on second thoughts he picks it up and takes it home with him. Clearly unstable, he at first half-jokingly begins to talk to the damaged mannequin whose facial features have been entirely destroyed, grabbing his paintbrush and telling her that he plans to restore her. Scraping some kind of putty-like substance off her back, he is surprised when the scrape of the knife causes the mannequin to bleed, leading him to discover that she is not a mannequin at all, but rather a friendly mute played by Krista Nell. With her unable to speak and dressed in John's clothes, their relationship at first—although clearly one based in his fractured imagination—is relatively healthy and warm. But when he finds himself attracted to her and forces her to wear the clothes of his ex-lover, the relationship changes. After they have sex, he looks at her face and finds she has morphed back into his ex-lover, played by cult European star Erika Blanc of *Kill, Baby ... Kill* (Mario Bava, *Operazione paura*, 1966) and *The Night Evelyn Came Out of the Grave* fame. What follows appears to be some kind of alcohol-induced psychotic flashback through this troubled relationship marked by his unstable personality and her promiscuity that ends with John stabbing her to death, her disappearance leading to the reported disappearance at the film's beginning.

Nine—A Portrait of an Artist as a Mad Drunk   133

All of this, it seems, was triggered by Mala's suggestion that she be John's model, as it was Blanc's character's decision to model for him that in his mind at least marked the beginning of their troubles. Struggling to sell his abstract paintings, a gallerist tells him that what the market wants is more commercial paintings of naked women. Horrified by such a suggestion, Blanc's character—credited only as "The Sensuous Doll" in relation to Nell's "The Subservient Doll"—demands he be realistic, and in modeling for him he is able to produce paintings that sell for much, much more than the work he was more passionate about ever did. But with the paintings also comes the opportunity for her to develop a growing stream of new lovers, including a wealthy client of John's who becomes infatuated with her after purchasing one of John's paintings. Driven to the edge at the discovery that she plans to leave for Spain with one of her lovers, John stabs her to death. When the police arrive, however, all they find is that he has buried a mannequin—a real woman's body is nowhere to be seen. At the film's conclusion, he is driven to a psychiatric institution and there is no lead whatsoever on the real woman's location ("if she existed at all," a police investigator adds somewhat cryptically).

While wax figures and mannequins permeate horror film history spanning back at least to *Waxworks* (*Das Wachsfigurenkabinett*, Paul Leni, 1924), *Mystery of the Wax Museum* (Michael Curtiz, 1933) and *Mad Love* (Karl Freund, 1935), mannequins in particular were employed in *giallo* to disturbing, uncanny effect in such famous examples as *Blood and Black Lace* and Bava's later *Hatchet for the Honeymoon* (*Il rosso segno della follia*, 1970), Lenzi's *Spasmo*, Piero Schivazappa's *The Laughing Woman* (*Femina Ridens*, 1969)—a film discussed in Chapter Fifteen—and the *giallo*-esque French/Italian co-production *The Night Caller* (*Peur sur la ville*, Henri Verneuil, 1975) with Jean-Paul Belmondo. As typified by *The Red Headed Corpse*, in reference to Vito Adriaensens's discussion on life-like sculptures more generally, he notes, "the confusion that occurs between the real and the ideal when a statue comes to life is not beneficial for the characters of the horror film."[3] This is, to put it mildly, true of John: with traumatic memories of a murder he (maybe) committed triggered by Mala's offer to model for him, it is his close engagement with the crumbling mannequin that push him over the edge as he regresses for the bulk of the film into a flashback that retraces the minutia of a mutually destructive relationship. As Adriaensens continues, "films thematizing statuary often play on the idea that it is possible to blur the line between sculpted matter and flesh, often transforming one into the other through trick cinematography, the presence of a doppelganger, or craftsmanship that is more than once equated with surgery."[4]

With a hint of Ovid's Pygmalion myth in the air, in *The Red Headed Corpse* we see the mannequin brought to life through not merely a trick of editing, but the "surgery" John performs with his palette knife. The image of the bleeding mannequin or wax figure is hardly new; we can go back at least to horror magnum opus *The Cremator* (*Spalovač mrtvol*, Juraj Herz, 1969) to, more recently, Peter Strickland's *In Fabric* (2018) with its menstruating store mannequin in one of that film's most unforgettable scenes. But in *The Red Headed Corpse*, it is precisely the moment that the mannequin "bleeds" that in John's damaged imagination at least, she comes to life.

Turning away from his blocky abstract paintings to portraits of his lover in various states of undress due to both pressure from his lover herself and the economic reality that the paintings he likes to do will not make money, there is an important shift in John's artistic output that transcends a mere "selling out" to gain commercial appeal. In an oft-cited observation in 1974, American sculptor and visual artist Lynda Beglis called Abstract Expressionism "a big macho game, a big, heroic, Abstract Expressionist, macho sexist game. It's all about territory.

The Red Headed Corpse (*La peau qui brule Rossa dalla pelle che scotta*, Renzo Russo, 1971) (Photo 12, Alamy Stock Photo).

How big?"⁵ While made two years before Beglis's observation, that the famous Abstract Expressionists—William de Koonig, Jackson Pollock, Mark Rothko, etcetera—were all men (despite there being an important stream of women working in the same field⁶) certainly aligns with John's vision of himself as an artist-as-outlaw figure, aligning in his mind at least with the myth of the artist as genius outsider noted previously. That he turns to painting what is effectively softcore pornography is therefore a complex move; while still "macho" in the sense that the work in theory at least seeks to dominate a sexualized woman subject within its male gaze, that it is his lover who so aggressively demands that he paints her undermines this simplistic reading of this shift in his work. He does not paint nudes of his lover to dominate her; rather, she demands that *he* paint nudes of *her* so she cannot just control him, but bask in the ego-boosting attention she seems aware that she will receive. It is arguably more about her vanity, then, than a scopophilic tendency in his artistic practice.

The casting of Granger in the role of John clearly seeks to garner international attention for the film by featuring a "big" Hollywood name in the lead role, but there is additional significance stemming from the fact that his fame lay primarily in his collaborations with Alfred Hitchcock. After appearing in Luchino Visconti's period melodrama *Senso* (1954) with Alida Valli, Granger would later star in a number of *gialli* including *Something Creeping in The Dark* (*Qualcosa striscia nel buio*, Mario Colucci, 1971), *Amuck!* (*Alla ricerca del piacere*, Silvio Amadio, 1972) and *So Sweet, So Dead* (*Rivelazioni di un maniaco sessuale al capo della squadra mobile*, Roberto Bianchi Montero, 1972). Like *Amuck!* (where he plays another corrupt artist, this time a writer), *The Red Headed Corpse* seems to deliberately riff on Granger's work with Hitchcock on both *Strangers on a Train* (1951) and *Rope* (1948) which, has been noted, both share a homosexual subtext to varying degrees.⁷ When transposed to *gialli*, this association with Granger's screen personae is somewhat crudely (and hardly progressively) used to boost the transgressiveness and potential "perversity" of the characters he now plays. While in both *Rope* and *Strangers on a Train*, Granger plays characters who if not wholly innocent then at least are somewhat sympathetic, in these *gialli*—playing corrupt artists—he is outright monstrous. Presenting the artist as a figure virtually synonymous with a transgressive, unhinged outsider, *The Red Headed Corpse* therefore positions the figure of the painter in a distinctly negative light. While not any less troubled, this proves a curious point of comparison in regard to the next two films I seek to discuss; Elio Petri's *A Quiet Day in the Country*, and Sergio Bergonzelli's *Blood Delirium*.

Ten

The Myth of the "Mad" Genius
Vincent Van Gogh and Blood Delirium *(Delirio di sangue,* Sergio Bergonzelli, 1988*)*

If *The Red Headed Corpse* focuses on the failed artist as flawed protagonist, Sergio Bergonzelli's supernatural *giallo Blood Delirium* engages more directly with the myth of the "mad" genius via explicit references to Vincent Van Gogh. Embracing traditional *giallo* elements such as mysterious doubles, paranoia, and a near-overwhelming stylistic excess and combining it with the *giallo-fantastico* or supernatural *giallo* model, *Blood Delirium* begins as young piano player Sybille (Brigitte Christensen) is visited by a ghostly presence, a woman's voice who tells her of the symbolic potency of two candle flames merging to form one. Elsewhere, Sybille's doppelgänger lies dying; Christine too is a piano player, also played by Christensen. Christine's distraught husband Charles Saint-Simon (John Phillip Law) frets melodramatically over her death bed as she tells him with her dying breath "I won't leave you." The mourning rituals surrounding her death, however, are less poetic; weeping over her body, he implores the dead Christine "you've taken my inspiration with you, why go on living?" Yet while his back is turned as he plays overwrought music in her honor on a nearby organ, his servant Hermann (Gordon Mitchell) has sex with her corpse, much to Charles's understandable horror.

Struck by an inability to paint now he lacks Christine's music as inspiration, he demands Hermann exhume her remains from which Charles cobbles together a macabre masked puppet made from her skeleton which he seats at the piano in the hope this will rekindle his creative passion. But—perhaps unsurprisingly—this plan does not work.

Drawn by some kind of mystical force to Charles's art exhibition, Sybille is struck by her similarity to Christine in his paintings and remembers the supernatural visitation earlier in the film. Convinced Sybille is Christine returned to him, Charles's initial invitation for her to stay with him eventually turns into a hostage situation as he and Hermann drug her and keeps her in a glass case wearing a wedding dress, incapable of fighting Hermann's now-demonstrable pattern for rape and sexual violence. Returning from London, Sybille's partner Gérard (Marco Di Stefano) finally locates her and rescues her, leaving Herman and Charles to suffer the vengeance of Christine's now furious ghost who crushes them under the paintings that hang on the wall and falling debris from Charles's opulent castle itself, her voice telling him "you can do no more evil, you cursed man."

Aside from Hermann's taste for rape and necrophilia and Charles's for abduction and grave robbing, what Christine is specifically referring to is where her deranged widow finally discovers his artistic inspiration. After raping and murdering a local woman called Yvonne (Lucia Prato), Charles is horrified by Hermann's behavior but nevertheless assists him by offering to dispose of the body which lies in the stables. When lifting her corpse, however, Charles is struck by instant, almost dizzying artistic inspiration; the specific color of paint that has eluded him and thus made it impossible to capture the philosophical essence he so desperately seeks in his painting is blood itself. Draining Yvonne—and, later, Sybille's friend Corinne (Olga Hardiman)—Charles finds himself thrust into a whirlwind of creativity, the film's climax building towards him painting what he believes will be his greatest work, a painting called *Blood Wedding*.

From Herschell Gordon Lewis's *Color Me Blood Red* (1965) to Dan Gilroy's *Velvet Buzzsaw* (2019), horror movies where mentally disturbed painters use blood to paint is certainly not specific to *Blood Delirium*.[1] Like these other films, Bergonzelli draws a concrete link between insanity, violence and creative practice, where the art itself has a literal body count. Yet *Blood Delirium* is the least shy of all of these films in its attempt to tether this trope to the broader myth of the artist as "mad" genius through its specific privileging of the figure of Vincent Van Gogh. Although there are other art historical references in the film (the organ that Charles plays on while Hermann rapes his dead wife's corpse is positioned under a giant print of Michelangelo's famous fresco *The Creation of Adam* [1508–1512], for example), Van Gogh is central to the film both thematically and narratively, in ways that frequently are not marked by any particular flair for subtlety. Hermann calls Charles "Maestro Van Gogh," for instance, supposedly as a joke, but one where neither he nor Charles appears to laugh. Van Gogh's self-portrait looms large in Charles's studio and is mentioned throughout the film, clearly deployed as a somewhat crude cipher for the "insane" artist trope that Charles himself very much adheres to. When the ghost of Christine destroys Charles studio, she openly mocks him by saying "So you think you're Van Gogh, hey?" before he is flung backwards and an invisible force slashes his ear in a direct reference to the artist famously cutting off part of his ear in an act of self-harm after a blow-out with fellow painter Paul Gauguin. After destroying his studio completely, the only painting Christine leaves hanging on the wall is Van Gogh's portrait as Charles implores her, "forgive me."

The use of Van Gogh as shorthand for "mad" genius has been a subject for much debate within art criticism for many years. In a key work on the topic, Griselda Pollock writes in her 1980 essay "Artists, Mythologies and Media—Genius, Madness and Art History" that "all aspects of VG's life story and the stylistic features of the work culminating in VG's self-mutilation and suicide has provided material to be reworked into a complex but familiar of the madness of the artist."[2] Asking "why do we need VG as a *mad* genius?," Pollock proposes "the notion of madness and art which produce the category 'mad genius' have little to do with clinical pathology or definitions of sanity," but rather—with particular relevance to *gialli*—they "circle around categories of difference, otherness, excess."[3] The "mad" artist thus provides the

One of Vincent van Gogh's many self-portraits, a figure who haunts the protagonist in *Blood Delirium* (*Delirio di sangue*, Sergio Bergonzelli, 1988). *Self-Portrait with a Straw Hat*, oil on canvas, 1887. Bequest of Miss Adelaide Milton de Groot, 1967 (open access, Metropolitan Museum of Art, www.metmuseum.org).

perfect template for the *giallo* outsider, marked as they are by the "special and distinct modes of being which set the artist ineffably apart."[4]

The myth of the artist as "mad" genius that *Blood Delirium* links so explicitly to Vincent Van Gogh has a long history. As early as the Greek myth of Philoctetes and manifesting more recently in figures such as Sylvia Plath and Kurt Cobain,[5] the idea of suffering for one's art has been ubiquitous, and it is precisely this myth that *Blood Delirium* seeks to exploit. But here, the emotional suffering that Charles experiences is clearly incomparable to that of his and Hermann's victims, who Charles sees as necessary sacrifices for him to achieve his true creative potential. Importantly, the macabre direction that Charles's creative practice takes is foreshadowed earlier in the film at the art exhibition where he first meets Sybille. One guest—a critic or potential customer, perhaps—vaguely tells Charles that while they acknowledge the occult symbolism in the artist's work, they don't really understand what it all means. Regardless, the exhibition is packed and appears to be a rousing success; there is an implication, then, that artistic value in a commercial sense rises above actual content. Another patron notes in passing that not only does Charles believe in reincarnation, but that he *specifically* believes he is the reincarnation of Van Gogh himself.

This association merely adds further eerie mystique to Charles's already peculiar behavior, played in a genuinely jaw-dropping performance of such over-the-top, almost pantomime-levels of excess by John Phillip Law that it alone can be considered to offer the film's most immediate appeal. While *gialli* are not particularly renowned for naturalistic performances or complex characterizations, it is fair to say Law's Charles is, to opt for the vernacular, next level. Yet the inflation of the myth of the "mad" artist through the film's overt reliance on Van Gogh as a central motif in itself adds only further to the sense of abstract detachment that permeates the film. Even the most cursory knowledge of Van Gogh's life story presents a man whose life was very different to that of Charles Saint-Simon. Van Gogh was poor, Charles was rich. Van Gogh was a good painter and outside the packed exhibition, the film seems deliberately ambivalent about the objective quality of Charles's work; we see him in thrall of his own talent once he starts painting with blood, yes, but before this the works that dominate his studio are notable for their randomness. His style is not coherent nor consistent; he paints abstracts, portraits, landscapes. What is so remarkable about Charles's non-blood painting themselves is how thoroughly pedestrian they are. While no doubt the result of lackluster production design, Charles's milquetoast paintings reveal something fundamental about his character beyond the "mad" stereotype: his status as "genius" is a *performance*.

The Van Gogh connection is thus as much a branding strategy as anything else.

What this brings into question, then, is the very question of culpability. There is little evidence to suggest that Bergonzelli (who wrote the screenplay as well as directed the film) thought particularly deeply about this on a conscious level, but where perhaps the greatest significance of *Blood Delirium* lies is less in its at times pushy, even aggressive referencing to Van Gogh, but rather how the myth of the "mad" genius is used as a blanket excuse to explain (although of course not justify) the most heinous of crimes. At the heart of this lies not just Charles's behavior, but what in fact drives the film; the collaboration *between* Hermann and Charles. Despite being understandably horrified by the sight of Hermann raping his dead wife's corpse, what is less comprehensible is how this is ultimately just business as usual for Charles, who—despite never seeming to particularly like Hermann—not only accepts his servant's behavior and actively assists in covering it up, but even uses it to his advantage in his goal to attain victims to drain so he can use their blood for paint. From this perspective, *Blood Delirium* is less about Van Gogh *specifically* as it first appears. Rather, it extends—in ways I suspect are distinctly unintentional, but present nevertheless—towards a broader critique of how these exact kinds of myths that privilege and fetishize the artist and their outsider status can be dangerously internalized to justify fundamentally unjustifiable behavior.

Eleven

The Ghosts of Capitalism
Art, Labor and Exploitation in A Quiet Place in the Country (Un tranquillo posto di campagna, Elio Petri, 1968)

With an international reputation as an assertively political filmmaker, Elio Petri's *giallo A Quiet Place in the Country* (*Un tranquillo posto di campagna*, 1968) was not the only time he would experiment with popular genres. For example, in 1965 he released the classic dystopian science fiction film *The 10th Victim* (*La decima vittima*), an important entry into the "human game" subgenre marked by Richard Connell's 1924 short story *The Most Dangerous Game* and later cinematic additions including *Battle Royale* (*Batoru Rowaiaru*, Kinji Fukasaku, 2000) and the more recent blockbuster franchise *The Hunger Games* (2012–2015), based on the bestselling series of the same name by Suzanne Collins. Petri also later won the Oscar for Best Foreign Language Film for his quasi-*poliziotteschi Investigation of a Citizen Above Suspicion* (*Indagine su un cittadino al di sopra di ogni sospetto*) in 1971. So adaptable and successful was Petri at bringing his own defining trademark to a range of different genres that Franco Nero[1]—star of Petri's *A Quiet Place in the Country*—has described him as the "Italian Stanley Kubrick."[2]

Described as "a surrealist horror film that explores the ultimately elusive meaning of art,"[3] *A Quiet Place in the Country* is not merely about the "meaning" of art, but more specifically, about the exploitation and commodification of artists themselves. Beginning his career as a film critic for the Italian Communist newspaper *L'Unita*,[4] Petri brought a specifically leftist agenda to his relationship with cinema even before he started making own movies. While Petri would certainly make more overtly political films when it came to the exploitation of labor such as

Franco Nero and Vanessa Redgrave at the 61st Berlin Film Festival at Berlinale Palace, February 14, 2011 (Denis Makarenko, Shutterstock.com).

The Working Class Goes to Heaven (*La classe operaia va in paradiso*) in 1971, *A Quiet Place in the Country* similarly addresses the plight of a man pushed to the edge through the pressures put on him by his job. In *The Working Class Goes to Heaven*, it is factory worker Lulù (Gian Maria Volonté), while in *A Quiet Place in the Country* it is artist Leonardo Ferri (Nero).

Despite his success as an artist, Leonardo is in crisis. The film opens with a nightmare where he sits, tied with a white rope in a fetishistic, S&M manner to a chair wearing nothing but his underwear in the fashionably minimalist home he shares with his partner and agent Flavia (Vanessa Redgrave). Flavia enters the room with a range of frivolous household electronic devices—a knife sharpener, a television you can watch underwater, an electric shoe polisher—seductively listing these and other products, placing them around the silent, observant Leonardo who sits on a slightly raised platform behind her. While he has given nothing away, Flavia's combination of flagrant consumerism and flirtatious seduction send him into a violent frenzy, releasing him from the ropes as he picks up a freshly sharpened knife and pursues her downstairs where she showers. What begins as him trying to violently stab her is dramatically reversed when, saying patiently "It's a pity; we had everything. Almost everything," it is in fact Flavia that stabs him in the bathtub. Waking from his nightmare, their relationship at first appears to be not so troubled as his dream suggests as they joke about its contents. But moving around their home, it is equally full of indulgent symbols of their excessive wealth (an uncomfortable looking metal chair-sculpture, for example). On a subconscious level, Leonardo does not merely have clear issues in terms of his relationship with Flavia, but those issues are linked to money; despite the minimalist surfaces of their environment, in his mind it is stuffed with the meaningless clutter ostentatious wealth demands. For Fernando Gabriel Pagnoni Berns and Leonardo Acosta Lando, Flavia "is his lover, but also his link to the capitalist world that he so desperately wants to flee." In the eyes of her and those so enamored with Leonardo's youth and status as the current artist-of-the-moment, "Leonardo, from this capitalist perspective, is just another young artist to manage, not an individual personality."[5]

In this context, it is unsurprising Leonardo is suffering the painter's equivalent of writer's block. In a vibrant, kinetic scene, we see him at work in his studio. Nero optimizes his physical presence in this extraordinary montage with immersive effect as he dabs, smears, rolls and presses paints of different colors across a range of surfaces on planes both vertical and horizontal. Petri plays particular note to the minutia of Leonardo's labor; there are close-ups of this throughout the film, his hand squeezing watery, paint-stained sponges into a bucket that foreshadows the violence to come as the liquid it oozes is a bright, arterial red color. Pacing and unfocused, Leonardo watches a series of slides hoping for inspiration; again, violence and sexuality intersect through this quick montage of deformed breasts intercut with scenes of war and civil unrest. Increasing the sense of pressure and intensity to this sequence, despite being alone, Ennio Morricone's score combines the sound of a phone ringing into an incessant, pounding rhythm from which Leonardo cannot escape. This non stop phone ring only adds further to the sense of pressure that the artist is under.

Needing a break, Leonardo insists on leaving Milan to seek a change of pace in the titular quiet place in the country. For Berns and Lando, this is a distinct rejection of modernity itself, another hallucination before he leaves the city showing Milan "as a nightmarish space, a grey and dreary landscape where he sees himself being pushed along by wheelchair through the streets."[6] Despite having the opportunity to work in the mansion-home of one of his collectors, he is inexplicably attracted to a run-down, abandoned villa near Venice, drawn to it by what appears to be an apparition of Leonardo himself, his own ghostly yet joyful doppelganger. Although bewildered by Leonardo's decision, Flavia dismisses it as a quirk of the artistic temperament and agrees. But rather than rekindling his creative passion, Leonardo finds himself even further disconnected from his art practice and instead becomes increasingly fascinated with the story of a seventeen-year-old countess who used to live in the house called Wanda who died during an air raid during the war. Investigating her story and even visiting her frail, lonely mother, Leonardo's interest turns into a toxic sexual obsession which leads him to turn his violence against Flavia. Believing he has killed her, at the film's conclusion she has him committed to a psychiatric institution where she bribes a nurse to trade Leonardo's manically produced artworks for pornography and candy, keeping her business going.

That Flavia effectively replaces Leonardo in her life with a dog called Snoopy as revealed in the final moments is a strong indication of the way that the exploiter views the exploited; he may have been her lover, but their relationship was never equal, her sexual placation of the porn-obsessed artist just one of the ways Flavia sought to keep her "pet" happy in return for good (profitable) tricks. While the emphasis on pornography might at first suggest a gender political reading of the film adhering to a simplistic association with the misogynist male gaze of the pornography-consumer, this tends to fall apart somewhat in the face of the fact that not only is Flavia clearly the figure of economic control in the relationship, but that she herself was also a happy, willing and consenting consumer of pornography also. There is no evidence in the film, for example, that she only *pretended* to enjoy pornography to satisfy Leonardo; in a scene early in the film, their mutual pleasure derived from reading pornographic magazines appears to play a key role in their sexual intimacy. Sexual pleasure is a product to be consumed like everything else; it is yet another thing to be bought, and for the rich, you can buy a lot of it. Like the blenders and the knife sharpeners and the waterproof televisions and the electric shoe polishers in Leonardo's opening dream, pornography itself isn't necessarily demonized, but in this broader frenzy of consumerism it adds to the dehumanizing, nightmarish glut of products that riddle his sleep and has merged with his sexuality on a deep, unconscious level. He is a man haunted by capitalism and his own status as a producer; not an artist, but as a maker of just more *stuff to buy*.

If Leonardo can't paint, then, from this perspective it is not difficult to see why. In the face of this "swinging sixties" portrait of the artist as an exploitable commodity, that *A Quiet Place in the Country* finds its origins in a famous ghost story may come as somewhat of a surprise. Loosely based on Oliver Onions' 1911 short story *The Beckoning Fair One*—a favorite of literary luminaries of the caliber of H.P. Lovecraft, no less[7]—the original story follows Paul Oleron, a writer in his mid-40s who after years of scraping by is poised on the brink of success with the promising new novel he is currently working on, *Romilly*. Yet while working steadily on the manuscript, he finds himself compelled almost on a whim to pack up and move into new lodgings in an apartment in a decrepit, otherwise abandoned building in a lower-class part of town. Working hard on renovations that almost bankrupt him, he is transfixed with his new lodgings, yet unable to write. Alienated further when his friend of a decade Elise Bengough remains unmoved and clearly bewildered by his sudden relocation, she is further appalled when he tells her he plans to scrap all fifteen chapters of *Romilly* that had so impressed her and start writing the novel again from scratch. After a series of inexplicable accidents that befall her on her visits to Paul, Elise senses that the building itself does not want her there, and so begrudgingly—she is in love with Paul and had secretly hoped they would wed—visits less frequently. Slowly and mostly through aural visitations rather than visual ones, the increasingly isolated Paul realizes he is not alone in his lodgings, and christens his fellow inhabitant "The Beckoning Fair One" after an old song "she" plays to him through the sound of a dripping tap. Realizing "she" does not want Elise to visit and is in fact jealous, Paul retreats further into his apartment, besieged by paranoia and agoraphobia, and he eventually stops eating. The story ends when the police break down the door and find a bedridden, emaciated Paul and, elsewhere in the house, Elise's dead body.

While the film is certainly a loose reimagining of Onions' story, it is not hard to see how Petri and co-writer Luciano Vincenzoni[8] utilized the basic structure of *The Beckoning Fair One* and sculpted it into *A Quiet Day in the Country*. Unlike the myth of the "mad" artist that seeks to link "genius"—and, it is implied, productivity—with eccentricities of varying degrees of intensity, both *A Quiet Day in the Country* and *The Beckoning Fair One* mark the psychological decline of their protagonist-artists (a painter in the former, a writer in the latter) by their *inability* to create. The ghost story aspect that marks both Leonardo and Paul's romantic obsession also distinctly marks a fundamental shift in their creative focus: while each is clearly struggling psychologically before moving into the run-down homes central to each story, it is upon moving to their new domiciles that their passions shift from their work to the feminized presence they sense living with them. What Elise and Flavia share is, as Anthony J. Fonseca notes of the short story, "the possibility of a jealous female ghost who attempts to seduce the protagonist is juxtaposed against the psychological explanation—that his oversensitive nature and writerly imagination are causing him to succumb to mental illness."[9] That both Paul and Leonardo's rage shifts towards the *real* women in their lives is, however, driven by different reasons. Paul realizes Elise believes they have a future as husband and wife together and that idea repels him; he rejects *Romilly* when he realizes how much the title character of his half-finished novel disgusts him, based as it was subconsciously at least on Elise herself. But in *A Quiet Place in the Country*, the pressures of modernity, of commerce, of capitalism itself inherent to the reality of being a working artist are embodied by Flavia, his agent-lover.

There is therefore a mutual attraction and repulsion for Flavia that Leonardo cannot resolve, framed consciously by Petri in the context of a horror story (at one point, Leonardo even reads Edgar Allan Poe's *Tales of the Unexcepted* in the garden). In the earlier hallucination where he sees himself pushed through Milan in a wheelchair, it is Flavia who is his nurse. Throughout the film she refers to herself in a variety of ways as his mother; while clearly gendered roles in the context of the film, they are also ones that hinge on his incapacitation and reliance on her. His desire to escape this control manifests in his belief at the film's climax that he has in fact killed Flavia, and as Berns and Lando suggest, his "argument for killing her is that the ghost hates Flavia. But there is very little evidence that a spectre is actually haunting the house."[10] Referring to the broader notion that it is capitalism itself haunting Leonardo, they suggest instead that "Leonardo's many attempts (real or imaginary) to kill Flavia are a more direct reflection of the artist's desire for freedom from the constraints of the art market embodied in the countess, thus achieving true art."[11]

True art, it seems for Leonardo, can therefore only exist when untethered from an economic motive. "I like it here," Leonardo tells Flavia of his new home when she tentatively and only half-jokingly enquires about whom she suspects is another woman. "I've even stopped wanting to paint. Let the others paint. Children, old people, all of them. Give them what they need. Paints and canvas, free of charge, an hour a day." Near the end of the film, amongst his many delirious hallucinations this earlier idealist wish is brought to life in a field where a range of people stand working happily at easels in the sunshine as birds chirp merrily. But the idyllic scene is merged with the presence of soldiers, linked both specifically to the events surrounding Wanda's death during wartime, and, in this particular context, to the more broadly symbolic "militarization" of artistic practice that has seemingly done irreparable damage to Leonardo's mental health.

As Berns and Lando note, when Leonardo does finally find his ideal "quiet place in the country" where he is capable of returning to painting, it is a psychiatric institution. Here he attains a degree of invisibility, as "nobody sees him as anything more than a patient."[12] He is "mothered," but this time by strangers, rather than his lover-agent; his hair is brushed like that of a little boy, and—wholly infantilized—he sits obediently in the hope that good behavior will be rewarded. The irony is that it is only in this context "his art has achieved the highest degree of perfection."[13] It's a bitter ending; both Flavia and Leonardo ultimately get what they want (she, access to art she can buy cheap and sell at a high price, and he, peace and quiet to paint without the direct pressures of the art market weighing on him). But it is still transactional in nature; reducing his sexual fantasies to their most basic biological identifiers, that a (male) nurse bribes him with pornography and peanut brittle for his paintings that the nurse sneaks out of the institution to sell to the waiting Flavia. For Roberto Curti, then, despite finally achieving the isolation he so desperately craved while working in the city, he is now only able to find inspiration through commodified sexuality; "porn becomes the symbol of a society that reduces individual needs to consumer goods."[14]

While the content of Leonardo's paintings in this final moment have been critically noteworthy, further exploration of the particular *style* of his art may be worth exploring more deeply. While his initial work earlier in the film seems aligned with abstract expressionism,[15] the broader aesthetics and reference point in the film to the art world are more immediately suggestive of Pop Art. Expanding then from my earlier observations on the "macho" aspects of Abstract Expressionism, the move to Pop Art's overt association with consumer culture can therefore conceivably be understood in the case of Leonardo at least as a commercialization or commodification of the "macho" brand of masculinity that the casting of Franco Nero himself would imply. With his star persona even today still linked closely to his performance in the title role of Sergio Corbucci's iconic Spaghetti Western *Django* (1966)—a role Nero himself said he only accepted on the advice of Petri and his wife[16] Nero's very on-screen presence has been identified by Chris Nashawaty as "macho, drunken-swagger charisma."[17]

For artists themselves, the relationship between Abstract Expressionism and Pop Art has been the site of some contention. As artist David Charles Fox has suggested, "in many ways, Pop Art was a reaction to Abstract Expressionism. Rather than trying to create art that is a reflection of the medium, Pop Art typically used screen printing in order to mass produce its works."[18] But Croatian feminist artist Sanja Iveković sees it differently, emphasizing the shared gender landscape of both Pop Art and Abstract Expressionism; "pop art was not radically different from abstract expressionism: the content had changed but everything else stayed the same," she said. "Pop art seemed to be an almost exclusively male movement so it wasn't inspiring for me."[19] From this perspective, the definition of Leonardo's work seems almost beside the point; even from within the "boys club"—be it of Pop Art or Abstract Expressionism—there are gender-constructed pressures to conform, performative aspirations that Leonardo struggles with on the most basic level. In discussions with a random art buyer at a get-together Flavia has sprung on him unexpectedly, Leonardo finds himself unable to toe the line. "Your work is really the utter quintessence … to me, they express a deeply human crisis. A crisis that only the artist knows, naturally," his admirer gushes. Eschewing pleasantries, his retort comes simply; "the crisis of horse turd, actually."

While *A Quiet Place in the Country* homes in on Pop Art, it makes clear before the film even begins that it has its sights set on a much broader notion of the art industry than that of an art movement specific to the mid-twentieth century. Like Dario Argento almost thirty years later in *The Stendhal Syndrome*, Petri renders the opening credit sequence of his *giallo* akin to a gallery space also; while Argento's sequence of famous artworks across history scroll horizontally alongside the credits as Morricone's haunting soundtrack plays, Petri opts for a fast-cut edited sequence, again set to Morricone but this time the music is more discordant and disorienting. Intercut between the credits themselves and a reflexive inclusion of the very materiality of film itself (marking itself from the outset as a "made" piece in a way recalling Ingmar Bergman's *Persona* in 1966), Petri features details a number

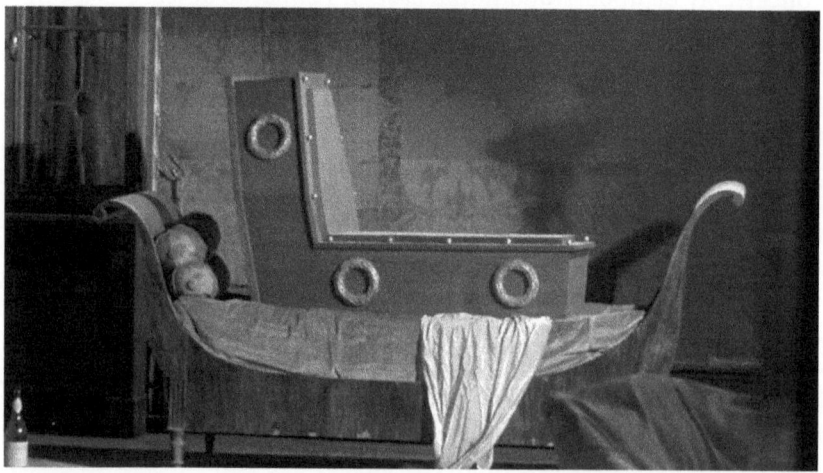

Leonardo (Franco Nero) perceives a woman in a vision that reconstructs René Magritte's *Perspective: Madame Récamier by David* (1951), in Elio Petri's *A Quiet Place in the Country* (*Un tranquillo posto di campagna*, 1968).

of famous artworks from across history: Rembrandt's *Slaughtered Ox* (1655), Jacques-Louis David's *Portrait of Madame Récamier* (1800), Ingres's *Grande Odalisque* (1814), an 1815 self-portrait of Goya, Delacroix's *The Death of Sardanapalus* (1827) and *Women of Algiers* (1833), Mondrian's *Composition in Color A* (1917), Picasso's *Portrait of Sylvette David* (1954), Francis Bacon's *Figure with Meat* (1954), as well as *Gabrielle d'Estrées et une de ses sœurs* (1594), discussed earlier in relation to Umberto Lenzi's *Spasmo* (1974). While the majority of these paintings foreshadow the film to come's fascination with sex, death or violence in some way, of all the works included most notable is the repeated image of René Magritte's reworking of David's *Portrait of Madame Récamier*, where he replaces the seated figure with a bent coffin seated on a similarly positioned lounge in his painting *Perspective: Madame Récamier by David* (1951). The "perspective" is the looming mortality that hangs over the young, beautiful woman in David's original painting; in regard to Leonardo, facing Wanda's still-living mother—aged, lonely and desperate—he cannot engage with her as human, nor even see her as such. Visually exchanging her in his mind with Magritte's seated coffin, he only sees the presence of death having replaced the immortality of Wanda's youthful sexuality as he has imagined it.

And yet the association between Leonardo's art and Pop Art *specifically* are far from incidental. In fact, the juxtaposition of the disparate artworks itself has a Pop Art quality to it, and even more directly, American pop artist Jim Dine is credited in the film as providing the artworks.[20] According to Larry Portis, Petri studied Dine's practice in detail, taken by what the filmmaker described as the "expressive rhythmic gestures"[21] of how artists work, which we see manifest in Nero's almost boisterous, almost aerobic physicality in the art-making sequences throughout the film. Filming Dine at work, Petri was struck by the realization "he always wanted to appropriate objects and insert them into his work; it was like a continual theft of reality in a constant attempt to express something. There was a terrible despair in this little film."[22] In summary, then, for Portis what Petri has produced is a film where "the disintegration of the artist's personality as his lack of creative inspiration, or should we say his inability to creatively channel his fantasies, leads to psychosis."[23] There is at stake, however, much, much more than just trotting out the good old fashioned myth artist as "mad" genius trope. Citing an interview with Jean A. Gili from 1974 he had translated,[24] Portis writes,

> Petri said of *A Quiet Place in the Country* that, ultimately, he was motivated to say something about art and the creative process in our processed world where, as Marx said a century and a half ago, every thing "melts into air." If, explained Petri,

Jean Auguste Dominique Ingres (1780–1867), *Odalisque in Grisaille*, oil on canvas, ca. 1824–34 (open access, Metropolitan Museum of Art, www.metmuseum.org).

the abstract expressionists and other "pop" artists may be seen as "avant-garde" and "modern," they are only expressing alienation differently from previous generations of artists. For him, the problem is that "the relationship between the painter and nature is still 'romantic,' it is still the 'return to nature,' to simplicity, to pure food, to what still makes humankind happy" (Gili 1974: 62–63). What the pop artists seemingly do not understand is that this romantic vision of nature is only a myth, that reality is quite different. Problems of alienation have always existed, but the society has changed and, consequently, the artistic expression of alienation has changed. Pop art, no matter its appeal to popular sensibilities, is the surface sign of profound anxieties that the mastery over (and the destruction of) nature has engendered in society and in the human psyche.[25]

Here and elsewhere in his filmography, Petri's broader politics and identification as a Marxist cannot be separated from *A Quiet Place in the Country* and its reflections on the art world, the artist, and creative practice itself. Reflecting on his work, in another interview Petri noted; "In my first film, *Il Assassino* (*The Martyr* [1961]), l was preoccupied with the question of psychological alienation. In my second film [*His Days Are Numbered, I giorni contati*, 1962], in spite of a strong existentialist accent, there was already a clear position taken against work."[26] He continued, "alienation was studied not as a psychological phenomenon, but as a social fact."[27] In relation to Marx's theory of alienation where social hierarchies and class distinctions lead to *Entfremdung* or estrangement, Petri adds that this theory permeates his filmography. "This is the basis of my work and in the last analysis it can be found in all my work,"[28] he continues. "As the movement of opposition to capitalism in both Europe and Italy in particular has gathered strength, the political character of my films has been enriched and strengthened In consequence."[29] In *A Quiet Place in the Country*, Petri deliberately complicates the myth of the "mad" artist; if the artist is mad, it is capitalism that made him so.

Other Art Forms

Twelve

Fashion and Photography

While so many of the defining features of *giallo* cinema can be traced to *Blood and Black Lace* (the switchblade, the gloves, the hat-and-overcoat-combo, the mask as well as the paranoias, sexual transgressions and range of deviancies from drug abuse to murder), just as significant is its fusion of spectacle with fashion and the fashion industry, a legacy that permeates a vast number of *gialli* from this point onwards. While we can perhaps trace this fashion-centric Eurothriller tradition at least back to Arne Mattson's Swedish pre–*Blood and Black Lace* films *The Lady in Black* (*Damen i svart*, 1958) and *The Mannequin in Red* (*Mannekäng i rött*, 1958), the latter of which Tim Lucas has called a "pre-*giallo* thriller" that had a direct influence on *Blood and Black Lace*.[1] And of course, from *Blood and Black Lace* onwards there are no lack of fashion references. We can see this in their titles alone; take, for instance, *A Black Veil for Lisa* (*La morte non ha sesso*, Massimo Dallamano, 1968), *Death Walks on High Heels* (*La morte cammina con i tacchi alti*, Luciano Ercoli, 1971), *A White Dress for Marialé* (*Un bianco vestito per Marialé*, Romano Scavolini, 1972), *The Pyjama Girl Case* (*La ragazza dal pigiama giallo*, Flavio Mogherini, 1978),[2] and *Fashion Crimes* (*La morte è di moda*, Bruno Gaburro, 1989). And as we see in titles such as *Nothing Underneath* (*Sotto il vestito niente*, Carlo Vanzina, 1985) and *Strip Nude for Your Killer* (*Nude per l'assassino*, Andrea Bianchi, 1975), states of undress and the removal of clothing are also offered as tantalizing sexual hooks for potential audiences.

In terms of plot, there are too many examples to list but even a cursory glance presents a number of examples where fashion accessories are central to a mystery; a cufflink in Sergio Martino's *The Case of the Scorpion's Tail* (*La coda dello scorpione*, 1971) and a scarf in his film *Torso*, and a necklace in both Argento's *Four Flies on Grey Velvet* and Sergio Pastore's *Seven Shawls of Yellow Silk* (*Sette scialli di seta gialla*, 1972). In terms of sheer spectacle, the visions of some of the wilder fashion moments across *gialli* are as burned into my memory as the slashed throats and night-time stalkings; think of the ominous cutting of Dagmar Lassander's pirate-style dress lacing during the attempted rape scene at the beginning of *The Forbidden Photos of a Lady Above Suspicion* (*Le foto proibite di una signora per bene*, Luciano Ercoli, 1970), the rippable, paper-like dresses at the center of the party sequence early in Sergio Martino's *The Strange Vice of Mrs. Wardh* (*Lo strano vizio della signora Wardh*, 1971), the festival of truly impressive eyewear in Luigi Bazzoni's *The Fifth Cord* (*Giornata nera per l'ariete*, 1971), Nieves Navarro's inexplicable tubular silver wig in *Death Walks at Midnight* (*La morte accarezza a mezzanotte*, Luciano Ercoli, 1972) or—a personal favorite—the equally bewildering, seemingly home-made Bee Gees t-shirt a random schoolgirl wears in Argento's supernatural *giallo Phenomena* (1985), made all the more mystifying because the costumes in that film were famously created by revered Italian fashion designer Giorgio Armani.[3] Argento would collaborate again with a famous fashion designer the following year when he directed "Action," a promotional TV special for Trussadi's casual wear line in 1986 where, amongst other things, he included the figure of the iconic *giallo* killer in black leather gloves prowling the catwalk, dragging a model off-stage in a body bag.[4]

Bava too would return to fashion again in his *gialli*, either using the industry as a backdrop for his tales of madness and murder such as in *Hatchett for a Honeymoon*, or using costume as the source of extraordinary spectacle, such as the iconic striptease routine by a sequins-and-gold-lamé clad Edwige Fenech in the opening moments of *Five Dolls for an August Moon*. It all goes back to *Blood and Black Lace*. Set in Rome at the Christian Haute Couture design house, Countess Christina Como (Eva Bartok) runs the business with her partner Max Morlan (Cameron Mitchell) after the death of the Countess's husband in an accident. The film begins as a model called Isabella (Francesca Ungaro) who works at the fashion house is brutally murdered; at first annoyed with her unprofessional absenteeism, Christina is horrified to discover Isabella's corpse hidden in a cupboard inside the building. With an investigation led by Inspector Sylveste (Thomas Reiner), it seems everyone involved with the business has something to hide. This includes not just Max himself but his employees, designer Caesar Lazar (Luciano Pigozzi) and the epileptic Marco (Massimo Righi), as well as a number of the model's boyfriends including cocaine dealer Frank Scalo (Dante DiPaolo) and the financially desperate Marquis Richard Morell

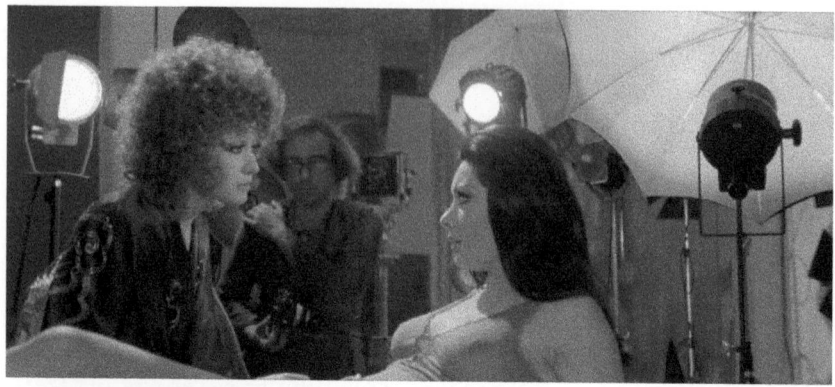

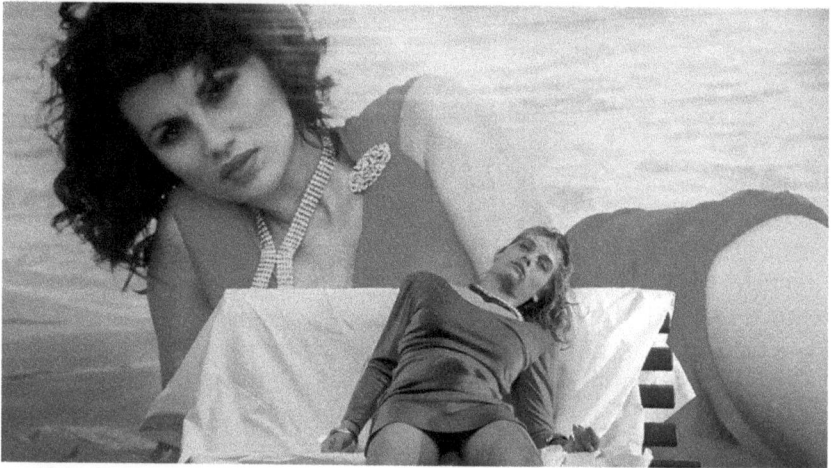

Top: Fashion and photography in *The Case of the Bloody Iris* (*Perché quelle strane gocce di sangue sul corpo di Jennifer?*, Giuliano Carnimeo, 1972). *Bottom:* Fashion and photography in *Delirium* (*Le foto di Gioia*, Lamberto Bava, 1987).

(Franco Ressel). With the discovery early in the film that Isabella kept a secret diary, paranoia runs high and results in the murder of a number of other models, almost all in visually spectacular horror vignettes including Nicole (Arianna Gorini) being gauged with a gruesome medieval looking gauntlet, Peggy (Mary Arden) tortured on a hot stove, Greta (Lea Krugher) suffocated underneath a pillow, and Tao-Li (Claude Dantes) in the film's famous bathtub sequence. While the police suspect a "sex maniac" is responsible for the crimes, it is revealed that the murders have been committed by Max and Christina themselves who were being blackmailed by Isabella. She knew that they had murdered Christina's late husband, and with their paranoia spiraling out of control, the murders piled up as they attempted to cover their tracks, ending in their own deaths.

While *Blood and Black Lace* would have an almost indescribable effect not just on *giallo* cinema but horror more generally, it is very much the way that Bava presents his material rather than the nuts-and-bolts narrative that marks its importance. The opening credits effectively brace the audience for the intensity of the sensory onslaught to come, both in terms of sound and vision. Alexia Kannas beautifully describes this sequence:

> This film's opening encapsulates so much of the *giallo* film's peculiar allure. The sequence's colour palette transports the viewer at once to the dark world of the stylized *giallo* mise-en-scène; there are beguiling compositions that bathe the character's faces in eerie washes of deep rose or moss green as they pose, mannequin-like, with actual mannequins of deep red velvet, wearing shiny black wigs. Bava uses the opening sequence vignette as a formal device to playfully introduce the forthcoming mystery's characters, but also to foreground the film's aggressive stylization from the moment it begins. Frozen in deliberate configurations of body and body-double, the characters and mannequins are positioned among the skeletal effigies of dressmaker's models in green, red and blue, or beneath the abstract glitter of an out-of-focus chandelier, lit in twinkling chartreuse.[5]

The film's aesthetics have led Rolando Caputo to draw parallels with Italian comic strip art, suggesting *Blood and Black Lace* was therefore "Bava's first attempt to introduce the *fumetto* style into his work" which "he was to master with remarkable results in his 1968 film *Diabolik* (*Danger: Diabolik*),"[6] and that additionally, "though much less extravagant, Bava's style here is in some ways comparable to the pop art, comic strip concoctions of the wonderful Japanese filmmaker Seijun Suzuki."[7] For Thrower, *Blood and Black Lace* is nothing less than "perhaps the most stunning Italian thriller of the 1960s"[8] which, although playing with tropes that had previously been established in the West German *Krimi* film, the turn from the black-and-white cinematography that dominated this genre towards "the Italian director's chillingly violent, colour-drenched delirium"[9] was largely the secret to its success. "Playing with the audience in a daringly avant-garde manner, Bava saturated the sets with garish, ominous colour lighting, cluttered the mise-en-scene with antique bric-a-brac and scanned across the mayhem with grandiose, unmotivated camera movements,"[10] says Thrower. "Even now it remains an incredible experience, possessing a unique mood; oppressive yet carnivalesque."[11] He continues, "When, for a couple of brief scenes, we see characters outdoors in daylight locations we feel disorientated; because the natural light of day has been usurped by a new dominion—of glowering reds, shimmering greens, arctic blues and jostling hordes of deep shadows."[12]

On the surface, the world of fashion appears at first to be a simple story device to put a lot of young women in close proximity in an opulent, affluent environment where there is an emphasis on their physical beauty. While this is true, there is perhaps more to *Blood and Black Lace*'s setting than first meets the eye. In their important work on the broadly overlooked critical overlap between fashion studies and horror studies, Gundrun D. Whitehead and Julia Petrov suggest that "dress in horror can be understood as the guise of society's norms and fears, displaced, symbolized, and condensed in horror as they might be in a dream."[13] They continue, "The fears inherent in horror are coded visibly through the dress of characters: foreignness, decadence (sexual and material), hegemony, anonymity, disability, criminality, aging and so on."[14] While they do not mention *Blood and Black Lace* specifically, the hyper-theatrical, color-drenched world of the film aligns almost aggressively with this dream-state of which they speak. The film's focus on the fashion industry puts the models very much lower down the food chain to their employees, and their jobs are linked to what Laura Mulvey has famously described as a "to-be-looked-at-ness."[15] This is relevant to the sexualized male gaze of which Mulvey so importantly wrote of classical Hollywood in her foundational essay "Visual Pleasure and Narrative Cinema" (1974), but this gaze is also important in terms of the fashion industry which deploys the sexualized gaze as a simultaneously commercial, commodifying one. This underscores a very brief but important shot early in the film where Christina walks from her office on the left to talk to her models in an open works space. Moving past a number of much less glamorous women wearing uniform-like pale blue dresses—one of whom is even mopping the floor—these women are positioned even *further* down the power structure than the models. Here we see very different kinds of women who we do not see much of again; less glamorous women who *aren't* to-be-looked-at, so much so that we almost don't notice them. These are working class women whose appearance and style of dress is notably different from both the models and Christina herself who, albeit briefly, therefore challenge the blanket assumption that unites women in the film with a professionalized to-be-looked-at-ness. This is not merely because they are not presented as the central gendered spectacle of the film—young beautiful women—but also because they represent that which the film otherwise seeks to repress; the reality of manual labor in the fashion industry. This shot is therefore an important one for Bava to include, and the point also applies more broadly perhaps to the character of the older servant Clarice (Harriet White Medin).

This relationship between power and dress reflects on the work of costume designers on the film itself. The bulk of the costumes were designed by Tina Grani, a long-time collaborator of Bava's who had worked with him on a number of films including *Black Sunday* (*La maschera del demonio*, 1960), *Erik the Conqueror* (*Gli invasori*, 1961), *The Girl Who Knew Too Much*, *Black Sabbath* (*I tre volti della paura*, 1963), and *Kill, Baby ... Kill!* (*Operazione paura*, 1966). She dressed all the women in the film except, notably, the film's lead actress Eva Bartok, whose famous black mourning outfit—a tight-fitting pencil-thin affair in black with a fishtail styled ruffle around the knees—which was designed by celebrated fashion designer Eleanora Garnett, the only film credit to her name.[16] Garnett's designs are held in fine art museums and other art collections around the world. Of course, the designs worn by the stream of disposable young models at the heart of the film are rendered significant in terms of spectacle for its ability to be removed as much as for how they look on their bodies. The sexualized nature of the murder vignettes spans from exposed décolletage and bared legs revealed underneath ripped garments to, in Tao-Li's case, being drowned in nothing but a white, translucent lacy bra. For Whitehead and Petrov, "dress in horror rarely involves outright nudity. Instead, the psychological tension comes from a fear of the disruption of boundaries—the social and physical categories we shore up against chaos."[17] Thus, in their status as high-cost consumer items to be sold to a wealthy elite, produced by working class labor, Bava deliberately indicates to us from the film's outset, the "violence" in the film against the young models is therefore two-fold; it is not merely a sexualized violence against beautiful young women by whom we are lead to believe is a "sex maniac," but there is a more symbolic violence by the destruction and transgression against valuable design commodities—the expensive dresses themselves.

While the centrality of the fashion industry and the spectacle of beautiful, fantastically dressed young women that it affords permeated *giallo* after *Blood and Black Lace*, later films often added another element to the formula, that of fashion photography. As Sevastakis has suggested, the photographic studio is so ubiquitous across these films that it can be fairly considered a *giallo* trope.[18] Regardless of the photographer's gender, the on-screen interplay between photographer and their subjects formalizes the relationship between the gazer and the gazed-upon, the former often acting as a surrogate for the viewers themselves to justify lengthy shots of women posed in frequently sexualized positions. As a technology of looking, photography riddles *giallo* cinema; on one hand because it not just permits but demands the activation of the scopophilic gaze from within the film's diegesis, but also because it is an artform itself, and thus continues the broader reflexivity

I have argued is significant across *gialli* that engage with art, either as a broader concept or in relation to specific practices such as painting.

Even beyond the context of fashion, photography, photographs and photographers pop up frequently in *giallo* cinema. Again, we need only look at some film titles to underscore this; while I will talk about Lamberto Bava's *Delirium* (*Le foto di Gioia*, 1987) more shortly, the eponymous snapshots in *The Forbidden Photos of a Lady Above Suspicion* refer to the pornographic photos Nieves Navarro's Dominique shows Dagmar Lassander's protagonist Minou, the latter keeping one in her handbag when she is shocked to see the man who has stalked and tormented her in one of the photographs. *Snapshot of a Crime* (*Istantanea per un delitto*, Ezio Alovisi, 1975) follows a man called Luca (Luis La Torre) who takes kinky photos of himself with his girlfriend Mirna (Erna Schurer) that, while seemingly consensual, imply he raped and strangled her. But when both the Mirna herself and the roll of go missing, Luca is blackmailed as part of a mystery that justifies the film's title. Photographers, photographs and darkrooms appear in many *gialli*, perhaps—like Argento's *Deep Red*[19]—inspired either directly or indirectly by Michelangelo Antonioni's *Blowup* from 1966 which centers on David Hemmings' photographer character Thomas and some mysterious photographs he took in a park. In terms of the gendered gaze, power is marked in Piero Schivazappa's *The Laughing Woman* (*Femina Ridens*, 1969) through who holds the camera; while I discuss this film further in Chapter Fifteen, it is worth noting that part of Dr. Sayer's (Philippe Leroy) strategies to dominate and humiliate Maria (Dagmar Lassander) include taking photographs of her as he tortures her. Later, after he has fallen in love with her, she takes what appear to be much less malign photographs as they frolic in the countryside. In the film's final moments, however, once her status as a feminist avenger has been revealed, the photographs she has taken of Sayer (and many of her other victims) are revealed as trophies that she places in a photo album. Here, the holder of the technological gaze (the camera) holds the power in a relationship that is constructed as a battle of the sexes.

Other *gialli* that include photographs or photographers include but are not limited to *Death Walks at Midnight*, *Death Carries a Cane* (*Passi di danza su una lama di rasoio*, Maurizio Pradeaux, 1973), *Autopsy* (*Macchie solari*, Armando Crispino, 1975), *Play Motel* (Mario Gariazzo, 1979), *The Red Light Girls* (*Prostituzione*, Rino Di Silvestro, 1974), *The Strange Vice of Mrs. Wardh* (*Lo strano vizio della Signora Wardh*, Sergio Martino, 1971), *So Sweet, So Dead* (*Rivelazioni di un maniaco sessuale al capo della squadra mobile*, Roberto Bianchi Montero, 1972), *The Black Belly of the Tarantula*, *The Dead Are Alive* (*L'etrusco uccide ancora*, Armando Crispino, 1972), *Eyeball* (*Gatti rossi in un labirinto di vetro*, Umberto Lenzi, 1975), *I due gattoni a nove code ... e mezza ad Amsterdam* (Osvaldo Civirani, 1972), *Police grope in the dark* (*La polizia brancola nel buio*, Helia Colombo, 1975) *Dagger Eyes* (*Mystère*, Carlo Vanzina, 1983), *The Killer Wore Gloves* (*La muerte llama a las 10*, Juan Bosch, 1974), *Il delitto di Via Monte Parioli* (Antonio Bonifacio, 1998), *A Taste for Fear* (*Pathos—Segreta inquietudine*, Piccio Raffanini, 1988), *Trhauma* (Gianni Martucci, 1980), *Calling All Police Cars* (*...a tutte le auto della polizia...*, Mario Caiano, 1975), and Argento's *Cat o' Nine Tails* (1971) and *Giallo* (2009), just for starters. The killer in Argento's *The Bird with the Crystal Plumage* takes photos of her intended victims while she stalks them, and the protagonist in his *Four Flies on Grey Velvet* is blackmailed with photos of an accident that make it look like he killed a man—taken, no less, by a creepy mask-wearing villain.

While an interest in gender politics certainly runs throughout many of the intersections of *giallo* and photography in the films noted above, when it comes to fashion photography specifically, like *Blood and Black Lace* the gendered spectacle of women and their "to-be-looked-at-ness" comes particularly to the fore. In Anandi Ramamurthy's overview of the subject, femininity and fashion photography became so synonymous from the 1930s onwards that the commodification of women that lies at the heart of the commercial artform necessarily seems to demand an analysis on the "constructions of gender and sexuality within these images."[20] We see this perhaps most neatly typified by a scene early in Andrea Bianchi's *Strip Nude for Your Killer* where a photographer from the Albatross Modelling Agency Carlo (Nino Castelnuovo) sees an attractive young woman called Lucia (Femi Benussi) wearing a skimpy bikini at a public swimming pool. "She's just the model I've been looking for!" he tells his male friends as he pursues her aggressively, taking photos of her without her permission as he follows her to the cafeteria. Using all the clichés of the sleazy fashion photographer and bragging of his high profile and work for *Vogue* and *Harper's Bazaar*, he is clearly used to namedropping his profession as an entry point for an attempted seduction. He has no problem manhandling her, luring her to a sauna with the promise of a new career in exchange for sexual favors. He is, frankly, a thoroughly revolting character; he tells her she's fat, he is sexually aggressive and does not take no for an answer, and if it wasn't for her interest in his promises of being able to help her career, there is no doubt their sexual encounter would be easily defined as non-consensual. Here, the sadistic male gaze is formalized through the professionalization of that gaze through the male fashion photographer's camera. This is contrasted with the professional work ethic of Edwige Fenech's

Magda, a woman photographer with whom Carlo soon begins a sexual relationship, and whose relationship to her models is notably different. But like many things in *gialli*, it is difficult to draw a clear distinction; like Carlo, the owner of the Albatross Modelling Agency Gisella (played by the mononymous Amanda) has no problem using her position of power and promises of future employment to pressure young women models into sexual relationships.

As Fenech's character suggests, fashion photographers in *gialli* are far from exclusively men; see, for example, Cléo Dupont (Anita Strindberg) in Sergio Martino's *The Case of the Scorpion's Tale* (*La coda dello scorpione*, 1971), Jane (Elsa Martinelli) in Lucio Fulci's *Perversion Story* (*Una sull'altra*, 1969), Faye Dunaway's title character in Irvin Kershner's 1978 American supernatural *giallo Eyes of Laura Mars*, and Barbara Bouchet's Kitty in *The Red Queen Kills Seven Times* (which, like *Strip Nude for Your Killer*, also features a motorbike as a central prop in a fashion photo shoot, no doubt seeking to amplify fetishized associations between motorbikes and masculine virility). Beyond the centrality of gender and the spectacle of (usually) women's bodies that dominates fashion sequences in *gialli*, it is also worth adding that much of the pleasure of these sequences for contemporary audiences at least comes from their "retro" quality[21]; they privilege styles not just in fashion at the time of production but in image-making styles and trends that are almost aggressively marked by their zeitgeist. At their most audacious, think perhaps of the amazing sequence in *The Case of the Bloody Iris* where Edwige Fenech poses next to a motorbike in painted-on "clothes," or the butterfly-pasties photoshoot in *Perversion Story*; the thrill of these sequences is, for audiences today, surely as much for their "retro" vibes as it is their sexuality. As John Ingledew has observed, this is very much part of the nature of fashion photography itself, as it "moves forward more quickly than other facets of photography, constantly seeking originality and impact."[22] If, as he notes, in fashion photography "yesterday's look is immediately forgotten,"[23] these sequences in *giallo* act as spectacular reminders of looks now framed only as often-kitsch historical reference points. For Rosetta Brookes, this means "fashion photography has traditionally been regarded as the lightweight end of photographic practice" because "its close relationship to an industry dependent on fast turnover makes the fashion photograph the transitory image par excellence."[24]

With Brookes's specific focus on the fashion photography of Helmut Newton, Deborah Turbeville and Guy Bourdin, the latter is a particularly important figure to acknowledge in relation to the specific intersection of fashion photography, sex and violence that marks many of these *gialli*, his work surely embodying Susan Sontag's famous observation that "there is an aggression implicit in every use of the camera."[25] Beginning his work for *Vogue* in 1955, it is not hard to see where the work of the famous French fashion photographer overlaps with *giallo*. His first shoot for *Vogue* showed the origins of this obsession of sex, death and glamor that would permeate his work, set it in a Paris meat market where an Audrey Hepburn-looking model in a veiled hat stands underneath a row of severed cow heads hanging from meat hooks above her. For Gaby Wood, "Guy Bourdin influenced a generation of photographers with sadistic images drawn from his own appetite for sexual perversion,"[26] while for Natalia Borecka, "like never before in fashion photography, women's body parts became things, to be enjoyed separately from the real person that they were attached to," which she concludes reflected an implied misogyny in the work of a figure Borecka describes as "needy, possessive and controlling man" (she even cites the death of two girlfriends by suicide as evidence of just how extreme his behavior towards women was).[27] "Perhaps," Borecka speculates, "it was these tragic events that provoked Bourdin's fascination with death in his images."[28]

Regardless of how directly we wish to draw a line between autobiography and art, there is little doubt that Bourdin's fashion photography shares with *giallo* the notion of murder as an artform that while articulated in the Thomas de Quincey essay discussed in Chapter One, in the case of *giallo* as Donna de Ville suggests, its origins can be traced to *Blood and Black Lace* and "Bava's tradition of the murder act as an artistic endeavor and the victim as *objet d'art*."[29] The association between fashion photography and *giallo* have specifically been acknowledged by Leon Hunt, who notes "In many ways Argento's murders perhaps more closely resemble ... fashion shots,"[30] looking specifically to Helmut Newton who he says "place[s] his elaborately coiffured models in scenarios which play on androgyny, fetishism (guns, panthers and orthopedic corsets), aggression, and punishment."[31] For Hunt, "while the violence inherent in these photographs is often condenses into their extreme objectification, some display a more overtly sadistic voyeurism."[32] Hunt therefore identifies in Argento's *gialli* that a "link is repeatedly made between 'high fashion' and 'high violence' as two affective mediations of sexual difference."[33] While this applies to the broader representation of glamorized dead women often shown as climactic tableaux to elaborately staged murder vignettes that mark *gialli* beyond Argento's work, in the context of films that involve fashion photography, the gruesome tableaux that mark the crime scenes in Lamberto Bava's *Delirium* are possibly the most excessive examples. Co-starring iconic French fashion model Capucine, the film restages *tableau vivant*-style in its opening moments a real photoshoot by legendary Italian fashion and celebrity photographer Angelo Frontoni. *Delirium* makes other direct links between fashion photography and murder as an art form even more explicit when a number of victims turn up in carefully staged crime scenes that the killer has photographed, their victims' bodies placed with great care in front of giant blown-up images of the eponymous magazine owner Gioia (Serena Grandi), with whom the killer is obsessed. Sevastakis has identified a continuation of Mulvey's notion of "to-be-looked-at-ness," noting that Gioia's "image in these stills, joined through wipes, has been coded for strong erotic impact in conventional exhibitionist fashion where women are marked for a powerful erotic impression signifying to-be-looked-at-ness." He continues, "The photos produce two results: they glorify the flesh, freezeframing it in a historical moment by preserving its transience, and secondly feed the models' narcissism through their self-gratification as erotic commodities."[34]

In *gialli* that privilege fashion photography purely as a spectacle, aside from the surface functionality of adding a bit of sexy, glamorous razzle dazzle—such as in Giuseppe Vari's *giallo/poliziotteschi* hybrid *Who Killed the Prosecutor and Why?* (*Terza ipotesi su un caso di perfetta strategia criminale*, 1972)—I would suggest that it demonstrates a specific example in cinema of Christine Moneera Laennec's claim that "fashion photography is in its own way a particularly revealing manifestation of popular culture, since it does not represent the reality of a given time and society—far from it—but an ideal image that society has of itself, and a reflection of its preoccupations and anxieties."[35] *Gialli* appear to present both the ideal—the glamorous beautiful woman, as either a sexual conquest and/or an aspirational goal—and simultaneously the "anxieties" that come with living up to those ideals bring with it; not just that success is fleeting, but that the site of that idealized image (the body itself) is vulnerable, disposable, *murderable*. The dreams the fashion model presents are shattered in many *giallo* by the fact that they are so often the subject of a killer's destructive intent, and we often see the trauma and anxiety that this brings these women, such as Fenech's Jennifer in *The Case of the Bloody Iris*.

Whether overtly sexualized or not, fashion photography sequences in *giallo* offer a fantasy that is destabilized by its status as a commodity whose construction as a "made" artifact we see very clearly through the exposed apparatus of the behind-the-scenes activity; the make-up artists, lights, and the photographer themselves. If, as Ingledew claims, "fashion photography is often about creating the illusion of perfection,"[36] through the legacy of Guy Bourdin, Mario Bava and the likes, we see this illusion not just subverted but actively undermined. To be clear, there is no doubt that there is an inescapably regressive titillating spectacle often at play in the representation of beautiful young women being graphically slaughtered. More often than not, this often leads critics to a notorious Dario Argento line quoted second-hand by Carol J. Clover in her foundational book *Men, Women and Chain Saws: Gender in the Modern Horror Film* (1992) from William Schoell's *Stay Out of the Shower* (1985), but which originally appeared in an interview with Alan Jones in *Cinefantastique* in 1983. "I like women, especially beautiful ones.... If they have a good face and figure, I would much prefer to watch them being murdered than an ugly girl or man," goes the section of the quote most frequently cited. But he continues, "I certainly don't have to justify myself to anyone about this. I don't care what anybody thinks or reads into it. I have had journalists walk out of interviews when I say what I feel about this subject."[37] While Clover includes the first part of this quote as a seemingly self-explanatory example of the misogyny of horror filmmakers—which, to be fair, it succeeds in doing pretty convincingly—it does perhaps somewhat disingenuously ignore the broader complexities of gender in Argento's films. In an interview with Élie Castiel, for example, he notes, "I think that in my films there's an equitable justice in victim selection. As many women as men are murdered. Moreover, women are often the ones who solve the mysteries."[38] In another interview with Alan Jones, Argento said "People who accuse me of favouring women to kill just haven't done the math. I'm for sexual equality when it comes to murder victims. When I imagine my movies I don't immediately lock on to men torturing women. Anybody who thinks that is having far more warped fantasies than I do!"[39] Landy supports this observation, arguing "an overview of Argento's filmmaking indicates that his murderers and victims are male and female, masculinised and feminised, and violence is inherent both as spectacle and more often as a means of investigating its existence, affects and effects."[40] This transcends Argento specifically; the complex gender politics of *giallo* cinema more broadly have been further developed by Michael Mackenzie, who has provides a useful taxonomy divided "into two distinct subcategories—'M-gialli,' focusing on male protagonists, and 'F-gialli,' focusing on their female counterparts—and examining the differing ways in which they negotiate the same anxieties about gender and modern sociocultural transformation, and the differing solutions (or lack thereof) that they propose."[41] Beyond this, as Argento notes, not only are many *giallo* killers women themselves,[42] but—borrowing Ian Olney's words from his analysis of Lucio Fulci's vicious *giallo The New York Ripper* (*Lo squartatore di New York*, 1982)—I would suggest that in many cases, whether consciously or not, some of these films at least potentially offer a feminist deconstructions of "the figure of the male killer and prompt the viewer to interrogate, in a performative act of spectatorship-as-drag, the sadistic male gaze."[43]

Dario Piana makes the potentially dormant feminist elements of some *gialli* even more explicit in his rape-revenge *giallo Too Beautiful to Die* (*Sotto il vestito niente II*, Dario Piana, 1988), the sequel to *Nothing Underneath* that was followed by a third film in 2011 called *The Last Fashion Show* (*Sotto il vestito niente—L'ultima sfilata*, Carlo Vanzina) co-starring a somewhat bewildered looking Richard E. Grant. This film is a useful example of how these more progressive aspects can often create an ambiguous, even contradictory, tension when they are positioned alongside clearly non-feminist elements, but as I have discussed elsewhere this is not typical of *giallo* cinema alone and permeates the broader rape-revenge category itself.[44] The opening credits run over a disembodied pair of plump, dark red lips that recall Salvador Dalí's *Mae West Lips Sofa* (1937). This reference is made clear as the credits end and we cut to a hyper-stylized fashion vignette, where three models sit on a replica of the sofa and another woman stands behind them. Stylistically referencing the iconic music video for Robert Palmer's hugely successful 1988 song "Simply Irresistible" that hit the music charts around the world about six months before Piana's film was released, in *Too Beautiful to Die* these models all have pale white faces, wear sunglasses and have their hair pulled back under black head scarves. They wear black low-cut trench coats with high leg-slits sit on a sofa. While framed as a high-fashion, music-video style vignette, the women remove their outer layers in a manner also clearly coded as softcore erotica, with slow-motion close-ups on their breasts, underwear, legs and patent leather high-heeled shoes. It is only when they are down to their lacy white lingerie that the women remove what we discover are masks, revealing their faces underneath; each woman is a different ethnicity, underscoring an exotic internationalization disguised by the ubiquitous whiteness of the masks. As the camera pulls back, the apparatus of a film shoot from within the film is revealed, and we have been watching the making of an advertisement. Focusing on Sylvia (Gioia Maria Scola), photographer David (François-Eric Gendron) tells her he would like to include her in a forthcoming music video for a song called "Blade."

In *Too Beautiful to Die*, however, the fashion industry is synonymous with sexual exploitation, and Alex (Giovanni Tamberi) from the modeling agency David uses is also effectively a pimp who supplies models to high-paying customers. Sending the naïve Sylvia to what she believes is a party with the three other models from the opening fashion shoot, when she resists the clients advances she is held down by the other girls while he rapes her, one of the women telling her "relax, he's a very important friend." Distraught, Sylvia flees after the assault as Alex shouts after her "Find yourself another agency, bitch, if anyone will take you. You're finished in this town." Sylvia fails to turn up for the "Blade" shoot and it is revealed she has died in a car crash after leaving the party. A number of murders are committed as David finds himself infatuated with a model who has newly arrived from New York, Melanie (Florence Guérin). Amongst a series of both elaborate murder vignettes as the three models involved in Sylvia's rape are killed one by one and glamorous fashion shoots set to pop music from bands like Huey Lewis and the News and Frankie Goes to Hollywood, it appears Melanie is there to avenge Sylvia's death, one of the model's suspecting they were sisters.

And yet, adhering to the *giallo* tradition of gender-swapping the assumed killer, it is revealed that the killer dressed as a woman was in fact David himself. He was Sylvia's secret lover, and she tried to break up with him because of his artistic arrogance; "I'm not insane, I'm a god ... who has the power of life and death over his creatures." Rushing to him after her assault, David killed Sylvia because she had been, in his mind, "soiled." *Too Beautiful to Die* is an overt instance of a *giallo* film where the scenes of violence are not just often merged with or shot like fashion photography scenarios, but where the violence-free fashion vignettes are offered just as determinedly as a source of pleasure for the audience to indulge in its visual excess. Like filmmaking itself, fashion photography as a collaborative form of commercial art has been widely acknowledged,[45] and in the next chapter I turn to filmmaking more specifically as an example of the reflexivity that runs throughout so many *giallo*. While not specific to *giallo*, these films-about-films continue to demonstrate just how strongly a fascination with art, artists and artistic production runs throughout so many of these movies.

Thirteen

Filmmaking

Although Christopher Ames was writing specifically about Hollywood cinema, when it comes to *giallo* films whose stories center around the art of filmmaking itself, the following observation from his 1997 book *Movies About Movies* is a useful one. For Ames,

> Film foregrounds its own mythology more insistently than do other media. This insistent foregrounding arises partly because movies are a twentieth-century mass medium: their status as a technological novelty is still in recent memory, and the discourses of magic, illusion and wonder still influence how the moviegoing experience is depicted and marketed.[1]

The captivating, illusionary nature of cinematic spectacle is hardly difficult to locate in the mainstream in more recent years in effect-heavy success stories including the seemingly never-ending onslaught of blockbuster superhero films and franchises such as *Star Wars*, *Harry Potter*, and *The Lord of the Rings*. At play is the legacy of what Tom Gunning has identified as the "cinema of attractions" which finds its origins in early cinema; it is, for Gunning, "an exhibitionist cinema ... that displays its visibility, [and is] willing to rupture a self-enclosed fictional world for a chance to solicit the attention of the spectator."[2] The emphasis on spectacular bodies in often extreme flights of intense emotion resultant of sensory experience (be it the result of violence or sex) and the stylistic excesses that so broadly mark *giallo* cinema lead us to the same place as Fernando Ramos Arenas, who has suggested that "the duality of narrative and spectacle ... situates the *giallo* in regions close to those of the cinema of attractions."[3]

Perhaps most famously, the nature of horror spectatorship as a spectacle in its own right manifests in *giallo* nowhere more iconically than in the famous image of Betty (Cristina Marsillach), an opera singer tormented by a serial killer in Dario Argento' *Opera* (1987) who forces her to watch his vicious crimes by sticking a row of needles underneath her eyes so she cannot close them. While, as its title suggests, the

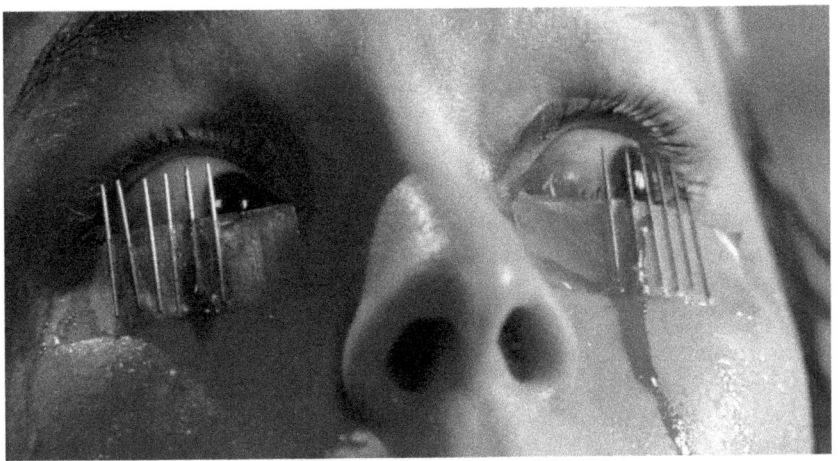

Horror and spectatorship in *Opera* (Dario Argento, 1987).

film is located in the opera world, that the director of the opera Marco (Ian Charleson) is an horror film director is worth of note not merely because it reflects Argento's own frustrated attempts to stage Verdi's "Rigoletto" in 1985,[4] but, as Sevastakis suggests, by having Marco as a "surrogate for Argento himself," Argento is simultaneously "deriding the viewer's voluntary suspension of disbelief, the film reviewer's search for a rational plot and motivation, and the censor's protests about cinematic violence."[5] Alternatively, Landy draws parallels between the killer and the horror film director himself; focusing on the needles taped below Christina's eyes, she notes that "the victim is threatened with blindness if she blinks and refuses to gaze at the murder being perpetrated before her eyes," and as such "this episode introduces the element of cruelty attributed to the killer, if not translated to the filmmaker."[6]

If the illusionary quality of *giallo* is amplified by its excesses, then much like the deployment of fashion photography within a given film's diegesis, so too *giallo* films about filmmaking denote a self-conscious awareness that they recognize their own status not just as artforms, but as illusion-making machines. This can be said for all films-about-films more generally, and this is a long tradition; "almost from the beginning of the film industry, its artistic productions have been associated with the glamour and luxury of those who make them,"[7] says Ames. "Some early critics worried that films that showed behind-the-scenes making of movies (and there are many from the silent days, including documentary short subjects) would spoil the illusionary magic of films, but this has not proved the case."[8] In the case of *giallo* cinema (and many horror films about movie-making more generally), there is a curious tension therefore between *extending* the illusionary nature of the movies themselves into a secondary "meta" diegesis where that fantasy is both corrupted (through violence or the threat of violence). And yet, as a fictional narrative based on spectacle and excess, the illusion is corrupted in the sense that it is no longer privileged as an unchallenged ideal. Rather, *gialli* present a world of deceit, paranoia and violence. Echoing tensions in films such as *Sunset Boulevard* (Billy Wilder, 1950), then, what is presented is simultaneously both an idealized illusion *and* a nightmarish delusion. "When movies about the movies reveal cinematic fakery or show, they generally put forward an alternate reality that contrasts with the illusion of the movies," says Ames. "But because the entire film inevitably is trapped in the cinematic realm for the viewing audience, the identification of a genuine 'truth...' becomes ironic or paradoxical."[9]

There are some thrilling moments across *giallo* cinema that bring this paradox to the fore, such as murders committed in cinemas themselves in *Who Saw Her Die?* (*Chi l'ha vista morire?*, Aldo Lado, 1972), *Closed Circuit* (*Circuito chiuso*, Giuliano Montaldo, 1978), and *The New York Ripper* (*Lo squartatore di New York*, Lucio Fulci, 1982). While this paradox more generally recalls the opening scene of Mario Camerini's 1934 film *Giallo* discussed in Chapter Two, it is also echoed—admittedly with a little less grace—in Mario Moroni's *Clap You're Dead* (*Ciak si muore*, 1974) which begins with a false opening in a manner that would be more famously restaged by Brian De Palma in his 1981 American *giallo Blow Out*. In both *Clap, You're Dead* and *Blow Out*, we do not know that the action we are watching is a horror movie being filmed, much as in *Giallo* we did not realize that we were watching a stage play. As Adrian Luther Smith says of the former, "The film itself is a very low budget, kitschy attempt to emulate, and at the same time parody, not only the *giallo* genre but the entire process of film production." He continues, "this cheeky little offering partly succeeds, especially during the first half when we witness the filmmakers constantly bickering, the actresses stripping off and the killer's murderous interventions."[10]

Clap, You're Dead opens with a car moving in slow motion through a car-wash, and it is only when the woman inside the car leaps out and shouts "how long do I have to stay like this to satisfy you sadists?" that we discover she is an actress talking to her film crew. The film's credits start and we see the car-wash sequence again only this time with the title of the movie we are watching (as opposed to the one being made within the film's diegesis) appear, along with its cast and crew, marking a further degree of reflexivity. This time, however, the actress we have previously seen in the car falls out dead; she has been murdered, and the police are called in. While much of the film is a pedestrian procedural, at its best *Clap You're Dead* functions as a bleakly comic satire that revels in its excessive depiction of the ugliness of making movies; little more than just a parade of people angrily screaming at each other, it is riddled with misogyny, bitterness, frustration and—of course—violence.

While not exactly overflowing with subtlety and artistry—it's hardly Federico Fellini's *8½* (1963) in terms of its treatment of the plight of the filmmaker-as-artist—*Clap, You're Dead* is most compelling when we are unable to distinguish between what on one hand is the film being made *within* the film, and what is the surrounding movie itself. A funeral we believe is for the murdered actress is revealed to be a scene that is being shot, pulling back to show the egotistical filmmaker character Benner (Antonio Pierfederici) sitting in his director's chair. Later, when we see a scene being shot where actress Mary (Thea Fleming) is being burned at the stake like Joan of Arc, our assumptions that this will be how she "really" dies are thwarted when she instead falls prey to a gloved assassin as she sits in her nearby trailer. With more of his cast being killed off, the police tell Benner to stop production, but with only one scene left, the director refuses. In a visually spectacular climax shot in Turin's beautiful Teatro Regio (also a key location for Dario Argento's 2009 film *Giallo*), the police pursue the killer who wears a distinctive *Diabolik*-style body stocking; the problem is, the all-male cast in the scene Benner is filming are dressed identically. In an amusing twist, it is revealed that the killer was the screenwriter of the film-within-the-film Ross (Carlo Enrici), bitter that Benner once again is in his mind was not doing justice to his screenplay. Pulling a knife on Benner, Ross exclaims "he made his name on destroying my work!."

A film director character takes on the role of the amateur detective in Al Festa's *giallo Fatal Frames* (*Fotogrammi mortali*, 1996). Alex Ritt (Rick Gianasi) is an American director who travels to Italy from America to work on a music video for Madonna-wannabe pop superstar Stefania Stella (a real pop star using her own name who was married in real life to *Fatal Frames*'s director Al Festa). Traumatized by the vicious murder of his wife back in the United States, a series of murders in Italy by a killer who films his murders echo the manner of how his wife was killed which lead investigators to suspect Alex. The film begins with all the stylistic elements of the Old Dark House film, shot in black-and-white and complete with ominous shadows as a wandering camera reveals an old man sitting in a room watching a what appears to be a pornographic snuff movie on an old projector where a woman is beaten and cut up. Echoing the primal scene at the beginning of *Deep Red*, a young boy whose identity we believe will later be revealed to be that of the killer enters the scene. The old man forces the child to watch the sexually violent film by holding him in a tight, aggressive embrace. This introduction—alongside that of *Clap, You're Dead* and even *Too Beautiful to Die* discussed in the last chapter—make literal Koven's observation that the *giallo* set piece is "a kind of minimovie, around which the plot of the film is constructed. These sequences are spectacles in themselves, much like the song and dance numbers in a Hollywood musical or the various sex acts in a pornographic feature."[11]

Moving to the film's then-contemporary moment, another familiar horror film trope is restaged, this time of a traditional *giallo* killer (disguised in a fedora hat, trenchcoat, and black leather gloves) who beheads a young woman in a night-time alley drenched in jewel-toned red and blue lighting. The killer films the murder on a hand-held video camera in black and white, recalling the film from the movie's opening scene. Witnessing the scene, Alex rushes to get the police but by the time they have returned the body has vanished. In a dramatic tonal shift, '90s Italo disco blasts as we see the stylish music video Alex is working on with Stefania, and it is hoped that while she is already a big star in Europe, with Alex's help this will be her breakthrough into the American market. Madonna is even later mentioned by name, with an observation that her blockbuster hit "Like a Virgin" was filmed in Venice, thus making Italy a natural choice for Alex's music video. Replicating the excessive visual style of the '90s pop music video, *Fatal Frames* is drenched with inexplicable zooms, random, dramatic camera angles, an active abuse of colored lights and lots of slow-motion softcore glamor scenes of Stefania herself. But alongside this is also a fetishization of both traditional *giallo* iconography such as the black leather gloves, and filmmaking technology itself in both the form of the old projector from the primal scene and more contemporary video technology itself as the killing spree continues and the murderer continues to film their work.

Stefania takes Alex to a party of at the home of Countess Alessandra Mirafiori (Alida Valli) who, as noted in Chapter Six, has a mysterious painting in her home that provides clues to the broader mystery. Suspicious of Alex and investigating parallels with his murdered wife, they contact a detective in the United States. Played by Donald Pleasance (who died while making the film, leading Festa to dedicate the film to him), the movie's intention to appeal to an American market through recognizable horror stars is further demonstrated by the additional casting of scream queen Linnea Quigley and Angus Scrimm from the first *Phantasm* films. The police make connections with the New York "video killer" which, after the hyper-stylized murders continue, lead to the deduction that it is Stefania herself who is the killer, having lived in

New York herself at one stage. But in the film's climax, an extraordinary sequence where the returned zombified corpses of all the victims reappear and—in a room filled with television sets—confront Alex himself and accuse him of the murders. Breaking down, he confesses; he killed his wife because she wanted to leave him, and the other murders were to cover up that crime. Revealing the misogyny that has underscored his crimes, he repeatedly states "you're all bitches." One of his victims in New York was in fact Stefania's sister, and all the murders in Italy were faked by Stefania in an attempt to push Alex over the edge and force him to confess.

The primal scene thus bookends the film; realizing that the child is in fact Alex himself, it locates the origins of both his violent misogyny and his interest in filmmaking at the very same moment. Again echoing *Deep Red*, the original primal scene is now replayed with extra information included; while far from distressed at being forced to watch the sexually explicit, violent film, the child laughs hysterically and points delightedly at the screen as he watches. The film concludes with the implication that Alex was simultaneously inspired to make film and become a sex killer because of this formative childhood experience. Within the diegetic framework of *Fatal Frames* itself, then, the "guilt" of the filmmaker in relation to representations of sexually-coded violence as a broader concept is clear; while there is certainly some leeway to discuss the success of the film's intentions, it does appear then that on some level Festa is attempting to engage with the same kind of reflexivity of directors such as Dario Argento. An obvious parallel, perhaps, is Argento's placement of himself within his films as the figure who wears the black leather gloves in close-ups during murder scenes.[12]

This reflexivity expands even further when we consider that Festa himself began his career directing music videos, working for filmmakers such as Bruno Mattei before turning towards *giallo*-styled horror films in the 1990s,[13] a period not renowned for its particularly prolific or high-quality *giallo* turnover. This sort of reflexivity is fundamental to movies-about-movies. As Ames argues, "cinematic self-reference, as in modernist and postmodernist literature, retains the power to undermine the realist illusion: it calls attention to the work as an artefact rather than unmediated experience." He continues, "When we are reminded that we are reading a novel or viewing a film, the realist frame is temporarily broken. But self-reference in film typically does something that self-referentiality in literature does not: it foregrounds the circumstances of artistic production and reception, the dynamics of industry and audience."[14] This is a useful starting point to think through Lamberto Bava's *A Blade in the Dark* (*La Casa con la Scala nel Buio*).

Initially developed as a made-for-television movie, Bava's determination to include high-level violence made a feature film a more viable option. Shot on location at producer and co-writer Dardano Sachetti's own home and using a small cast and crew,[15] the film follows a composer called Bruno (Andrea Occhipinti) who has been hired to write the soundtrack for a forthcoming horror film made by director Sandra (Anny Papa). Renting a modern, isolated home from Tony Rendin (Michele Soavi) so he can immerse himself in his work, the film recalls a similar strategy as *Clap, You're Dead* by showing the scene of a film which we have no way of recognizing as such, and thus interpret it as real. Showing a group of three children, two young boys bully a third, anxious one into retrieving a ball from the spooky basement of an abandoned house. Hesitating and terrified, the other boys mock him by somewhat unsubtly challenging his developing sense of masculinity, chanting "You're a female! You're a female!" in a cruel, sing-song voice, clearly traumatizing the child.

Returning to this sequence throughout the film as Sandra works on her movie, it is revealed that the scene was based on a story told to her in confidence by her friend, Linda. The previous tenant of the home in which Bruno now lives, it becomes increasingly clear that Linda is responsible for a series of murders marked this time less by the *giallo* killer's traditional, distinctive black leather gloves, but rather notably feminine handiwork—we see women's clothing in fleeting glances, painted nails, and high-heel shoes. Following De Palma's *Blow Out* by two years and Francis Ford Coppola's *The Conversation* (1974) by almost a decade, as the amateur detective in *A Blade in the Dark* Bruno's primary clue comes from a whispered conversation he accidentally records while working. Trying to decipher the strange events unfolding around him and attempting to grasp how they relate to Sandra's film, as Bruno gets closer to discovering the identity of the killer his own life and that of those around him are increasingly under threat. This culminates with the revelation of the killer: "Linda" was in fact Tony himself dressed as a woman, the implication that the "you're a female!" taunt from his childhood trauma skewed his gender identity and made him a killer.

While not exactly a particularly progressive conclusion on the gender politics front, the revelation that the killer is a transvestite lies in fascinating tension with Bava's clearly very conscious decision to make the director of his horror-movie-within-a-horror-movie a woman. This stands in notable opposition to the reality of Italian horror during this period, where women filmmakers were virtually unheard of (although more recently, we can look towards horror filmmakers such as Luna Gualano and Silvana Zancolò as bucking this tradition). So while the cross-dressing gender-blurring of Tony/Linda is difficult to frame in a positive light, it does stand in notable contrast with Sandra who, it must be added, appears throughout the film on numerous occasions herself in a kind of "male drag." While not configured as monstrous in the same way as that of Tony/Linda, Sandra's quirky fashion style is instead more reminiscent of screen idol Marlene Dietrich's penchant for cross-dressing[16] and of Diane Keaton's fashion style in *Annie Hall* (Woody Allen, 1977). This comparison between Tony and Sandra's cross-dressing is complicated further when Sandra's career choice itself is somewhat of a "transgression" of sorts itself in the broadly women-director-free zone of Italian horror filmmaking during its golden era. While not a killer like Tony, it is significant that Sandra herself is killed; punished, perhaps, for the precise professional transgression of being a woman daring to make a horror movie.

If reflexivity marks films such as *A Blade in the Dark*, *Fatal Frames* and *Clap, You're Dead*, then more recently Peter Strickland's neo-*giallo Berberian Sound Studio* (2012) made this even more explicit. Before even moving to the filmmaking narrative core of the film, the arts permeate *Berberian Sound Studio* in its very name; inspired by the real life Studio di Fonologia in Milan, founded in 1955 by Luciano Berio and Bruno Maderna, the film's title is a reference to the celebrated composer and mezzo-soprano Catherine Berberian who worked with both Berio (to whom she was married) and Maderna as well as *avant garde* icons such as Kurt Weill and John Cage.[17] The film follows sound engineer Gilderoy (Toby Jones) who has flown from his home in rural Britain to Milan to work at the Berberian Film Studio on a movie called *The Equestrian Vortex*. Specializing in documenting found sounds in natural environments, his background led Gilderoy to assume that this would be a movie about horses, and is shocked to find that it is in fact a gory horror film instead, a genre which he politely yet firmly voices some discomfort with subject-wise. Attempting to be as professional as he can in a difficult workplace environment where passive-aggressive and at times outright hostile colleagues shock his British sensibilities, he struggles to keep a stiff upper lip despite the increasing turmoil surrounding him. Very much a "mummy's boy," letters from home at first keep him centered, but bad news combines with his circumstances in a foreign country to seemingly push Gilderoy over the edge. Collapsing into kaleidoscopic, hallucinatory chaos, Gilderoy's switch from speaking English to Italian and a range of spectacular visual effects combine with an extraordinary experimental soundtrack by English band Broadcast make it impossible for us—let alone Gilderoy—to distinguish reality from deranged fantasy, as the horror-film-within-a-horror-film becomes the framing movie we are watching, *Berberian Sound Studio*, itself.

As Strickland noted in an interview upon the film's release, "genre is a starting point for me, that is my personal taste. I love to screw around with it. Of course, there were many *giallo* references, but it's more about people making *giallo*, rather than becoming so itself." He continued, "we pay lip service now and again in the way we use certain shots, certain zooms, but we wanted to depart from it too."[18] This "lip service" extends these effects, however, in the formation of what Basia Lewandowska Cummings describes as being *Berberian Sound Studio*'s status as a "meta-*giallo* audio-chiller"[19]; aside from the aggressive stylistic experimentation that marks the film and the narrative centrality of paranoia and omnipresent violence of an at-times particularly sexual nature, although the configuration of these elements lies well beyond what might be understood as historically-coded *giallo*, Strickland brings an even further degree of playfulness to this in his casting *giallo* regular Suzy Kendall of *Torso* and *The Bird with the Crystal Plumage* fames as what the credits list as "Special Guest Screamer." As Strickland said at the time, "I'm not interested in showing horror. But I am interested in the effects of it"[20]; by beginning with a horror-film-about-making-a-horror-film framework and then deliberately collapsing the boundaries that mark the two spaces by sensory provocation over orthodox narrative clarity, the very excesses of *giallo* cinema that inspired *Berberian Sound Studio* allowed Strickland to focus on precisely these effects. If, as Ames contends about movies about movies, that the "triumph of illusionary art lies in showing how the trick works and still making the trick work,"[21] then *Berberian Sound Studio*, *A Blade in the Dark*, *Fatal Frames* and *Cut, You're Dead* all reveal how precisely this has been attempted in a *giallo* context, with varying degrees of success.

FOURTEEN

Theater and Performance

Stages and theaters are far from rare in *gialli*. We can find them in films such as *The Forbidden Room*, *The Bloodsucker Leads the Dance* (*La sanguisuga conduce la danza*, Alfredo Rizzo, 1975), *You'll Die at Midnight* (*Morirai a mezzanotte*, Lamberto Bava, 1986), *The Killer Reserved Nine Seats* (*L'assassino ha riservato nove poltrone*, Giuseppe Bennati, 1974) to *The Killer is on the Phone* (*L'assassino ... è al telefono*, Alberto De Martino, 1972), *Stage Fright* (*Deliria*, Michel Soavi, 1987) and, as noted in the previous chapter, the use of Turin's Teatro Regio in both *Clap, You're Dead* and Dario Argento's *Giallo*. Theaters offer a perfect environment where the ubiquitous *giallo* fascination with duplicitous identities, deceptive performance and a reflexive acknowledgment of their own status as constructed works of art can play out. Argento's *gialli* especially show a particular proclivity for these spaces; in *Four Flies on Grey Velvet*, Roberto Tobias (Michael Brandon) is lured to an empty theater (his entrance marked by a series of red curtains being pulled back with dramatic flourishes) where he accidentally stabs a man, while an unknown figure in a mask takes photos of the incident and uses them to torment Roberto. In *Deep Red*, a red curtain is dramatically raised (just the one this time) as a camera shot from a disorienting, disembodied first-person camera position wanders into the theater where the psychic Helga demonstrates her mind-reading skills, putting her in distressingly intimate contact with that film's killer and triggering the action that follows.

Horror cinema more broadly hardly lacks examples of the stage and the world of the theater being used to reflexively denote an awareness of a given film's own textuality, underscoring its status as a constructed artifact. While partially the interest in the theater as the location of a murder mystery may be further evidence of Hitchcock's influence on *giallo* with his 1950 film *Stage Fright*, in the case of horror specifically it is certainly predated by Gaston Leroux's 1911 novel *The Phantom of the Opera* and its many screen adaptations (including one by Argento himself in 1998), as well as a range of horror movies including *The Last Performance* (Paul Fejos, 1929), *Theatre of Death* (Samuel Gallu, 1967), *Murders in the Rue Morgue* (Gordon Hessler, 1971), *The Flesh and Blood Show* (Pete Walker, 1972), *Theatre of Blood* (Douglas Hickox, 1973), *Bloodsucking Freaks* (Joel M. Reed, 1976), *Nightmares* (John D. Lamond, 1980), and *The Wizard of Gore* (Herschell Gordon Lewis, 1979; Jeremy Kasten, 2007). For André Loiselle, many horror films set in the theater world "emphasize the artifice of stage performance as both reflexive and constitutive of cinematic terror."[1] The effect of these films finds its origins in ancient theater where, "like Greek tragedy, horror cinema allows spectators to confront their deepest fears within the safe space of the auditorium."[2]

Where there's the theater there are often, although not always, actors, who in and of themselves are useful figures to play out the recurrent *giallo* themes of duplicity and deceptiveness; their professions, after all, are as performers whose job it is to pretend to be someone they are not. From this perspective, the figure of the actor therefore formalizes, professionalizes and thus in large part validates deceptive identities of a more malign nature, whose transgressions may fall across a spectrum from unfaithful spouses at one end, right through to killers at the other. Sometimes these non-professional performances are of a somewhat macabre joking nature, such as the false murder scene that opens Mario Bava's *Five Dolls for an August Moon* when Edwige Fenech's Marie is supposedly stabbed after giving it her all in that film's spectacular opening dance sequence. Sometimes these performances aim to deceive a character about their own nature; *The Forbidden Photos of a Lady Above Suspicion*, for instance, begins with Dagmar Lassander's protagonist Minou's internal narrative, revealed through voice-over. Extinguishing a cigarette she had been smoking in the bath in an ashtray housed in a soap holder, she says to herself; "I'm going to give up cigarettes today, and I'm going to stop drinking. And I am not going to take any more of those tranquilizers—anyway, they say it's bad for you to take them if you drink. That should make Peter happy!." Painfully insecure in her marriage, she coaches herself into be someone she is not in order to please her husband Peter (Pier Paolo Capponi), sensing that he does not really love as intensely as she loves him. But she doesn't stop smoking, she doesn't stop drinking, she keeps taking tranquilizers and—as it turns out—Peter is a sadistic murderer anyway who had not only killed others but hatched an elaborate scheme to drive Minou to suicide so he could cash in on the life insurance policy he had taken out without her knowledge. As she wanders aimlessly through her expensive vacation home, she passes a large artwork hanging on the wall made up of a series of blank three-dimensional mask-like shapes. Reflecting the multiple deceptive identities that populate the film—including her own, to some degree—this artwork is suggestive of the way that "blank" faces can be easily filled with qualities that may not be representative of the person who lies beneath the mask.

Alberto De Martino's *The Killer Is on the Phone* also focuses on deceptive identities, this time in the case of a character who is an actress.[3] Described by Samm Deighan at *Diabolique Magazine* as "one of the single most batshit *giallo* films in the history of the genre,"[4] there's a good chance she might be underrating it for what even by *giallo* standards are some impressive peculiarities. Eleanor (Anne Heywood) is a successful stage actress who blacks out on her return to Bruges where she lives after visiting London for work. She awakens with amnesia, triggered by seeing a man she does not recognize but we soon learn is a figurine-collecting, homophobic killer-for-hire called Ranko Drasovic (Telly Savalas). An American, he is in Belgium to assassinate an emissary from the United Nations who is involved in high-stakes oil negotiations between foreign powers. Losing the last five years of her memory, Eleanor has forgotten that her partner Peter (Roger Van Hool) had died in a car accident, and she fails to recognize her husband of the last three years, the theater critic George (Giorgio Piazza). Confused and

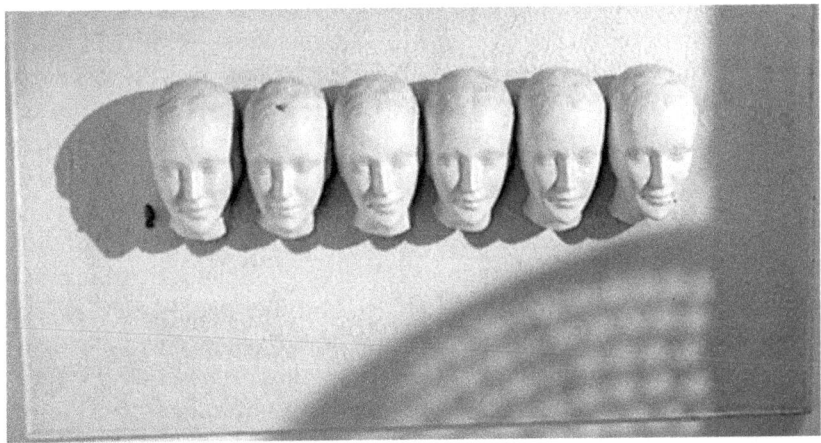

The centrality of duplicitous identities manifests in artwork in *The Forbidden Photos of a Lady Above Suspicion* (*Le foto proibite di una signora per bene*, Luciano Ercoli, 1970).

increasingly paranoid, Eleanor attempts to return to work, but although cast in the role of Lady Godiva, when on stage she instead delivers a monologue from William Shakespeare's *Macbeth*. As the past and present blur chaotically in her mind, she loses her starring role in the play to her sister Dorothy (Willeke van Ammelrooy), who Ranko kills in the theater dressing room; seeing her from behind the Lady Godiva style long wig, he believes he is killing Eleanor herself, who he has been stalking, neglected the job he had originally been sent to Bruges to perform. With George's help, Eleanor's memory returns as she recalls seeing Ranko murder Peter and faking the accident everyone assume killed him. Witnessing Ranko kill George, Eleanor flees to the deserted theater itself with Ranko in pursuit; immobilizing him under a fallen lighting rig that she drops on him, when attempting to shoot her in the dark he instead shoots through the ropes holding up a heavy solid safety curtain that falls and crushes him to death. Deducing who hired Ranko to kill Peter, Eleanor confronts Peter's wealthy sister Margaret (Rossella Falk) who owns the theater where Eleanor works. Demanding to know her motive for killing Peter and ultimately being responsible for the death of both Eleanor's sister Dorothy and husband George, the cold Margaret admits that she wanted Eleanor for herself. After kissing her,[5] Eleanor tells Margaret that her revenge will be watching Margaret grow old alone and unloved; after walking out, Eleanor hears a gunshot, implying that Margaret has died by suicide.

With the past and present blurring so chaotically and amnesia rendering Eleanor unable to recognize people around her for who they are, *The Killer Is on the Phone* engages in the volatility of identities in a variety of ways, all in the performance-based environment of the theater world. "I know it's fairly common to say a film is dreamlike when the proceedings really just don't make any sense," says Deighan, "but in the case of *The Killer is on the Phone*, Eleanor's experience with amnesia and a 'truth serum' blur the lines between past and present, fiction and reality, and it's often difficult to tell whether she is in the grip of fantasy and imagination, or whether she is remembering actual events."[6] Through her affliction with amnesia, there is something poignant that Eleanor's reputation as a great professional actress finds her unable to "play" the role of Eleanor herself. While perhaps not exactly narratively watertight, the most memorable elements of the film are those where not only Eleanor's past and present merge, but her memories of roles she played on stage in the past bleed into flashbacks she interprets as having happened in real-life. Of these, one of the film's most convincing red herrings follows a series of her memories about a passionate sexual affair she recalls having with her colleague Thomas (Osvaldo Ruggieri) that leads to a murder plot; she wears the same clothes that she wears in the supposedly "real life" segments of the film (a white trench coat and orange dress), and we are led to believe that the plan culminates in Eleanor being stabbed and her dramatically shooting her lover Thomas in his apartment. As the camera pulls back, however, we see that we are watching a stage performance. Again, as consciously as this section of the film deliberately attempts to collapse the lines between "reality" and "performance," it is not wholly believable; later she tells Thomas it was from an updated version of *Macbeth* they had performed together. Yet that this isn't particularly convincing adds even further to the disorienting subjectivity of Eleanor's experience; like Eleanor herself, the audience struggle to distinguish the past from the present, staged fiction from "realistic" truth.

Because Ranko's guilt is apparent from the outset, *The Killer Is on the Phone* is not so much a whodunnit but a why/howdunnit; the mystery concerns the circumstances surrounding Peter's death—and then Dorothy and George's—that led to Ranko killing them. Eleanor's job as an actress, then, problematizes the volatile nature of identity play in terms of how it relates to the truth; "you're all actors playing parts!" she says early in the film when she first sees George at her doctor's clinic, unable as she is to recognize her own husband. As contemporary horror director Jerome Sable has said, actors "essentially lie as they put on costumes and masks" and "are full of this pretending energy. It's a rife place for horror."[7] *The Killer Is on the Phone* is therefore far from the only film to make this connection between characters diegetically presented as actors themselves; see, for example, Richard Ciupka's *Curtains* (1983) and Andreas Marschall's *Masks* (2011), the latter of which also has a strong neo-*giallo* quality. But in *The Killer Is on the Phone*, it underscores the driving broader fascinations across *giallo* with duplicity, paranoia and identity-play, presented in a scenario that allows for an excess of cinematic style (excessive lighting, acting styles, etcetera).

In the supernatural *giallo The Killer Reserved Nine Seats*, the illusionary potential of the theater bleeds into ontological questions about at the heart of the mystery; is the man we are led to believe is probably the eponymous killer a real person or something more otherworldly? Despite its Gothic and supernatural elements, the film otherwise plays out as a typical proto-slasher body count *giallo*[8] as a group of people in an isolated area, unable to escape, are killed off one by one. The film begins as a group of family and friends arrive at an isolated theater that has not been used for a whole century. It belongs to the family Patrick (Chris Avram) who has been celebrating his birthday, the decision to move the party to the theater suggested by a mysterious stranger who joins their party, notable for his distinctive Nehru-style velvet jacket (played by Eduardo Filipone). As they approach the theater in their finery—denoting their wealth and privilege—the dark building and looming archways cast an expressionist shadow, prompting one character to glibly joke that "it looks like Dracula's summer home." As they enter the theater itself, however, they are struck by its beauty, and before too long secrets are slowly revealed about the private, hidden interrelations amongst the group including Patrick and his fiancé Kim (Janet Agren), Patrick's adult daughter Lynn (Paola Senatore) and her partner Duncan (Gaetano Russo), Patrick's ex-wife Vivian (Rosana Schiaffino) and her new husband Albert (Andrea Scotti), Kim's artist lover Russell (Howard Ross) who sells paintings to Patrick, as well as Patrick's lesbian sister Rebecca (Eva Czemerys) and her partner Doris (Lucretia Love).

From the outset, these complex relationships lay the foundations for a number of possible motives for the murders to come, beginning with an attempt on Patrick's life when a rope is cut by an unseen assailant and a heavy beam falls from above, almost killing the host. While this theater-focused *giallo* does not hinge around a formal stage performance as such at this stage at least, the bourgeois hypocrisy and pretense of the characters themselves provide the central performances within the film, as different "roles" are taken on by a number of duplicitous characters. This is made clear by Patrick himself, who pulls back the painted backdrop to reveal the backstage workings of the theater and declares dramatically to his "audience," "the actors are present and now the play can start." Discovering a costume room, aspiring actress Kim takes to the stage and performs the scene of Juliet's suicide from Shakespeare's *Romeo and Juliet*. The complexities within the original the play where the status of real and "pretend" death merge so dramatically (she dies by suicide believing Romeo is dead, unaware he has faked it) is playfully reimagined within *The Killer Reserved Nine Seats* in this scene as the moment Kim plunges the dagger into her heart—a key moment in Shakespeare's play—the killer stabs *her* to death from behind, unseen, with a second dagger at the same moment.

With Kim's death, the internal fracturing amongst the group becomes more vocal as their suspicions and rivalries are revealed. As these intensify, the group are killed off one by one by a figure wearing black gloves, a mask and a long black cape. The film's denouement reveals that it was Lynn who attempted to kill her own father in the theater, she and Duncan hoping to drive him mad so they can inherit his money. They succeed up the point that it is revealed the bulk of the murders were apparently committed by Patrick himself, but the supernatural elements of the film provide the final twist. Earlier in the film, Vivian discovers a portrait of a man called Lord Hamilton that is clearly dated

1708, the figure in the painting looking exactly like the stranger who had joined them that evening and lured them to the theater. Patrick—haunted by a family curse—shows his peers his own artistic evidence, a 500-year-old parchment that reveals a long tradition of the exact kind of killings that have plagued the group that evening. Explaining the curse, Patrick tells that every 100 years a group of people are killed in the theater—just as is happening to them—as the legacy of an ancestor who murdered a group of friends and family at a banquet on that same date years earlier. Attempting to flee the theater after killing Patrick and ready to inherit his money, Kim and Duncan face the supernatural presence as they frantically seek an exit via the family crypt in the basement. Here, the man in the Nehru jacket—a spirit of the long-deceased Lord Hamilton—tells them that the curse can only be broken once the taste for incest that has plagued the family stops. With Lynn and Patrick's inappropriate and often highly sexual canoodling shown throughout the film, it is clear this is not the generation where that behavior will cease. Screaming and terrified, Lynn and Duncan discover next to the graves of victims from centuries ago not only the recently killed Patrick's gravestone, but their own graves, too.

That the curse is punishment for incest in *The Killer Reserved Nine Seats* demonstrates what Loiselle has suggested is "one of the central functions of theatricality in the horror film: cinema relies on theatre's disciplinarian artificiality to expose horror's dual purpose as an entertaining spectacle of fearsome excess and an unflinchingly repressive morality tale."[9] As Loiselle wrote earlier, "cinematic tales of terror that acknowledge their theatrical antecedents ... do so in order to comment on a common tension in horror cinema between, on the one hand, overindulgence in sex, violence, and deception and, on the other hand, a ferocious compulsion to contain and punish such behaviour."[10] It is from this perspective that the film contains some fascinating moral contradictions. Aside from the overt incest plotline and the curse that punishes that particular transgression, there is no question that the film's most extreme violence is expended on the queer Rebecca in an objectively vicious sequence that seems an unfathomable escalation in its intensity when compared to the way other characters die. With her clothes ripped off and breasts exposed, although it is not shown on screen the positioning of the murderer and his victim strongly implies that Rebecca is stabbed repeatedly in the vagina, a rape-stabbing sequence of gruesome and frankly mindboggling offensive proportions. As if this is not enough, her body is then dragged over to a nearby board leaning against a wall where her hand is nailed to it, crucifixion style. If there are any doubts that this extreme "punishment" is because of her status as a lesbian, those doubts evaporate when her body is finally discovered by Duncan and Lynn later in the film—pulling back the stage curtain, Duncan accidentally reveals Doris and Rebecca's dead, naked bodies, carefully positioned in a sexually provocative tableau.

There is, to be clear, zero room to reframe the fate of Rebecca in *The Killer Reserved Nine Seats* as anything but undisguised, vicious homophobia that seeks to simultaneously "punish" the queer woman and simultaneously present the violence committed against her as a sadistic, scopophilic spectacle. At the same time, the film subconsciously offers a *very* useful example of how a single text can contain both progressive *and* regressive elements simultaneously; the feeble critical tendency to define the politics of a single film along a binary line of either/or often forbids an acknowledgment of the sometimes very challenging but always very interesting contradictions that can and do exist within the same text. Importantly, *The Killer Reserved Nine Seats* does not end with the supernatural entrapment of Lynn and Duncan Lynn's family's crypt. Instead, a brief coda returns upstairs to Valerie, who we believe Patrick had previously murdered. But he did not succeed, and she rises, shaken and injured, but is able to stand up and stumbles downstairs. Behind her, a door magically opens as if by an invisible hand, granting her escape and the film ends as she flees the building and, we assume, runs to safety. While an ensemble film with no main character as such, Vivian is certainly the most likeable and in functional terms provides key information about the overarching supernatural tale with her discovery of Lord Hamilton's portrait. Despite her having remarried and Patrick being engaged to money-grabbing, unfaithful Kim, there is clearly still a strong, affectionate bond between Vivian and Patrick, and the reasons for their separation are revealed the be the result of his learning of her background as a sex worker. Accepting and understanding of the choice the wealthy aristocrat made at the discover, Vivian is notably unashamed; it is part of her life, and while she did not willingly seek to share that information with him, as she points out there are some things that are considered forgivable transgressions and some things that are not.

What is so significant is that in the world of the film at least, Vivian considers lesbianism very much as the former, a socially acceptable "eccentricity." Yet according to the film's *own* moral logic, based on the genuinely shocking violence that befalls Rebecca especially, it is clearly *far* from acceptable or so easily dismissed. This contradiction—between who lives and who dies and Vivian's articulation of what is supposedly acceptable in high society and what is not—ultimately then can only really make sense if returning to the notion of the characters themselves all being "actors" in Lord Hamilton's human drama that he stages in the theater itself on the night of the centennial bloodbath. While Doris and Rebecca were out—there relationship was not hidden—they were, like almost all of the other characters in the film, neither faithful to each other, nor particularly likable or trustworthy in general. Vivian was the only character who was not deceptive; she accepted Patrick's reaction to the discovery of her life as a sex worker in the past and yet never apologized for it. She was not unfaithful, she was not greedy, and she was, at the end of it all, the only character amongst the group of partygoers who continuously told the truth. As the only "non-actor" amongst them in the sense that she was not presenting a deceptive identity during the runtime of the film, then, she was guaranteed her release and protected from the curse.

Michele Soavi's *Stage Fright* continues with a similar body count format, a film Ellinger has described as "a slasher/*giallo* hybrid, which draws the best parts from both sub-genres" that even references the earlier *The Killer Has Reserved Nine Seats*.[11] Echoing the false opening sequences in the style of both *Clap, You're Dead* and *A Blade in the Dark* discussed in the previous chapter, *Stage Fright* perhaps takes us back to 1934 Mario Camerini's *Giallo* by specifically locating its "fake" opening sequence in the context of a stage play. Based on the spectatorial tendency to normalize the hyper-stylized aesthetics of the *giallo* and accept them as diegetically-coded verisimilitude, *Stage Fright* begins where a woman who appears to be a sex worker is standing on the street in a

Theater as crime and performance space in *Stage Fright* (Deliria, Michele Soavi, 1987).

rough-looking neighborhood, quietly smoking and ignoring the propositions we hear off screen from a potential male client. It is only when she is pulled backwards into a darkened doorway and a human figure leaps out after strangling her wearing a large, ornate owl mask as a high-energy pop soundtrack starts do we realize we are watching something that, in terms of the film's own internal logic, is not intended to be presented as "reality," but rather a play we soon discover is called *The Night Owl*.[12] Dancing begins as a crowd circles the crime scene, and if we're not already convinced that we are watching a constructed, artificial work of art, the saxophone playing Marilyn Monroe look-alike in the iconic *Seven Year Itch* dress is surely enough to put any doubt to rest.[13] As the camera pulls back—like these earlier *gialli* with false openings—the apparatus of the theater is revealed in the shape of lights and other paraphernalia, as well as the presence of the director Peter (David Brandon) himself.

Although one of the crew working on *The Night Owl* describes it as an "intellectual musical," Peter is not shy about hiding his exploitative intent; what he initially conceives as a rape musical is quickly reimagined after an escaped serial killer from a nearby psychiatric institution kills one of his crew. Recognizing the commercial potential the added media attention can bring, he tells the press it was in fact an actress who was killed, and plans to re-name the owl-killer after the man known to have committed the murder at the start of the film. This is Irving Wallace (Clain Parker), an actor-turned-mass-murderer who had been institutionalized as he awaits trial for the butchering of sixteen people. With Peter locking his cast into the isolated theater where he insists they must rework the play according to his new vision, the idea is rapidly revealed to be a bad one as the killer is also inside the building and the key to the locked door has disappeared. With characters killed one by one in a series of gruesome murder vignettes, aligning closely with the slasher tradition of the Final Girl[14] is Alicia—the woman we saw in the very opening scene who is attacked by the killer owl during rehearsal—who seemingly brings the event to a close. Returning to the theater after the police and media attention have died down to retrieve her lost watch, however, she realizes there was one body missing in the police's final body count. With Wallace back to finish her off, she is saved at the last minute by the caretaker Willy (James Sampson), who shoots Wallace between the eyes.

Considering the film's titular stage stetting and killer Wallace's professional ambitions, Loiselle classifies *Stage Fright* as being typical of what he has identified as the "actor as psycho-without-psychology" trope of theatrical horror because of the little interest the film has in

Fourteen—Theater and Performance

giving the killer a motive.[15] Rather, Wallace is driven by a perverse reimagining of the notion of "performance" itself in his violent return to the stage, fulfilling an unexplored and unarticulated desire to "appear centre stage and indulge in a performance of sadistic carnage."[16] This indifference to Wallace's motivations for Loiselle marks a somewhat hollow victory as here, "the psycho-killer is but a poor player who slashes and slaughters his hour upon the stage, and then is heard no more."[17] But in keeping with the broader ambivalence of *gialli* more generally, it makes sense; immersed in the feverish stylistic excess where elaborately staged vignettes hinging around sex and violence reign supreme, Wallace's function is a purely perfunctory one. Says Loiselle:

> ...there is no explanation *whatsoever* as to why this fugitive from an insane asylum chooses to slaughter actors. And, in fact, there is only *one* reference to the fact that he is an actor gone mad: neither the cause of his madness nor the reason for his revenge is ever made clear. All this psycho-actor seems to want is to appear centre stage and indulge in a performance of sadistic carnage until the bloody spectacle has exhausted its Dionysian energy and returned to the stability of Apollonian death.[18] [italics in original]

This dismissal of Wallace wanting to "appear centre stage" as an unconvincing motive is undermined when positioned in the context of the governing regime of stylistic excess that marks *giallo* as a broader category. When Wallace does finally appear center stage it is done so quite literally as he sits amongst a tableau of the carefully positioned corpses of his victims; *this* was his motive, and he largely achieves it before finally being killed himself.[19] While recalling similar gruesome tableaux in earlier North American slasher films such as *Halloween* (John Carpenter, 1978) and *Happy Birthday to Me* (J. Lee Thompson, 1981), in terms of Soavi's own filmography he would later turn to the *tableau vivant* as in what is undeniably his magnum opus, the 1994 zombie comedy *Cemetery Man* (*Dellamorte Dellamore*). In one beautiful, macabre moment in an ossuary where he brings René Magritte's famous 1926 oil painting *The Lovers II* to life in a scene between Rupert Everett's Francesco Dellamorte and Anna Falchi's *femme fatale*, Soavi reminds us that artistic creation can be a reward unto itself, no matter how perversely he or Irving Wallace interpret that action.

FIFTEEN

Hybridity

Throughout this book, I have explored the ways that art—until now predominantly visual art, specifically painting—has been utilized across *giallo* cinema in a variety of ways that, while the function and utility of these elements is not static, at their most significant offer a reflexive meditation on their own status as constructed works of art in their own right. In this chapter I turn to two films that engage with the arts in a different ways that I am loosely conceiving as a kind of hybridization. From literature to illustration to sculpture to interior design and beyond, these films engage with "art" in a range of different ways, revealing an often complex and sophisticated interplay of reference and influence. Both *The Laughing Woman* (*Femina ridens*, Piero Schivazappa, 1969) and *The Perfume of the Lady in Black* (*Il profumo della signora in nero*, Francesco Barilli, 1974) stand out to me on a purely subjective level not just for how they engage with art as a broader category, but for their own striking status as art objects in and of themselves. While this can be said of many of the films in this book and these are certainly not the only *gialli* that weave together different kinds of art forms and artistic practices into single texts, I highlight these two films because the affective punch of each film lies not just in how they utilize artworks themselves, but how these different references so satisfyingly entwine and intersect in relation to both narrative, theme and each film's distinctive style.

The Laughing Woman follows wealthy philanthropist and sexual sadist Dr. Sayer (Philippe Leroy) who drugs and kidnaps journalist Maria (Dagmar Lassander) after the regular sex worker Gida (Lorenza Guerrieri) he sees each week fakes an illness and cancels their regularly scheduled appointment. As she is mentally, physically and sexually tortured, Sayer boasts to Maria about the women he has murdered and how his behavior is justified because it upholds his defining belief in the superiority of men over women. Trying desperately to keep herself mentally and physically afloat, Maria collapses under Sayer's continuing systematic abuse and attempts suicide by overdosing on pills. Deeply shaken when Maria almost dies, Sayer's bravado dissipates and he confesses that he in fact had never murdered anyone, and that outside of women that he had paid to participate in his twisted sadistic rituals, Maria was the first woman he had actually abducted. Finding himself falling in love with Maria as a fledgling traditional romantic relationship begins to develop, Sayer experiences a dramatic transformation. After a day frolicking in the sunshine happily together, however, he has a heart attack during sex. It is only now that the film's title begins to make sense; rather than an unsuspecting victim, Maria has been in control the entire time. Paying Gida off so Sayer would not have a woman to torture over the weekend, Maria made sure she was in the right place at the right time so he could not resist the opportunity to abduct her. Knowing the intimate details of Sayer's perverse sadistic rituals from Gida, she was able to not just prepare herself for his abuse, but was able to manipulate Sayer into falling in love with her. And, knowing of his obsession with his own virility and his past medical history, she planned the circumstances that would trigger his heart attack down to the smallest detail. After signing Gida's check and telling her the world is full of men like Sayer, we see Maria—if that even is her name—in her modern designer home in her "true" state; glamorously dressed for yoga, her butler brings her photographs she had taken of Sayer during their day of supposed happiness together. Putting it in a photo album of other men we assume she had likewise punished (if not to death like Sayer, then as in the case of a colleague of Sayer's with an eyepatch we see earlier in the film, then certainly towards ruin), with the camera lingering on a blank page we see that these are only just the beginning. There are more men out there like this out there, and Maria is ready to take them all on, just as she has Sayer.

Very much at the sexploitation end of the *giallo* spectrum, as is widely acknowledged in its sadomasochistic themes and astonishing visual style there are parallels between *The Laughing Woman* and the films of Radley Metzger, the latter's Audubon Films distributing Schivazappa's in the United States. Beyond Metzger, *The Laughing Woman* also contains echoes of Henri-Georges Clouzot's *Woman in Chains* (*La Prisonnière*, 1968) which was released the previous year, a film that no doubt was a significant influence on *giallo* filmmakers with its emphasis on transgressive sexuality, excessive film style and—not coincidentally—set in the Paris *avant garde* art scene. But while *The Laughing Woman*'s synopsis does not suggest through the occupations of its two central protagonists (a philanthropist and a journalist) any particular interest in the visual arts, Schivazappa makes this fascination central from the film's opening moments. As the film begins, we witness an extraordinary title credit sequence where we first see what appears to be Sayer's recurring nightmare: a large, brightly painted sculpture of a woman lying on her back where her vagina acts as a gaping black doorway. As he stands between her legs in a black, shadowy silhouette, the scale of the woman's body—marked by the vaginal abyss—looms large over the misogynist Sayer's psyche, as he watches a steady stream of men in suits lining up (some with flowers) to enter. Later in the film when he makes the decision to sexually surrender to Maria, he has a vision where he enters the gaping hole (surrounded by pointed white triangles symbolizing teeth and thus making his fear of vagina dentata overt), and nothing but a feeble skeleton exits, its body unable to support its skull which rolls off and falls on the ground between the sculpture's spread legs.

This symbolism might not be subtle, but it's undeniably effective. As the film's credits note, the sculpture was a reimagining of a famous installation artwork called *HON—en katedral* (*SHE—a cathedral*), a collaboration between Niki de Saint Phalle, Jean Tinguely and Per Olof Ultvedt, who are acknowledged in the film's credits. This work was installed at the Moderna Museet in Stockholm from June 4 to September 4, 1966, and remains one of the most influential exhibitions in the gallery's history.[1] Though the installation was destroyed upon the project's conclusion, a large amount of documentation has survived which in 2018 provided the basis for a retrospective exhibition at the Moderna Museet.[2] On the

Niki de Saint Phalle, Jean Tinguely and Per Olof Ultvedt's *HON–en katedral* (1966), reimagined in *The Laughing Woman* (*Femina Ridens*, Piero Schivazappa, 1969).

gallery's website for the exhibition, the description of the original work is evocative, to say the least:

> The exhibition "She—A Cathedral" consisted of a giant sculpture, a "cathedral" (23 m wide and 6 m tall) in the form of a pregnant woman lying on her back, which the audience could enter. Inside, visitors encountered an aquarium full of goldfish, a two-seated sofa for lovers, a bar, an exhibition with paintings, a small cinema that showed a Greta Garbo movie, a slide for kids, and many other surprises. At the apex of the belly was a peephole where visitors could stick their head out and have an overview of the entire exhibition space.

Nana sculpture by Niki de Saint Phalle, a French-American sculptor, painter and filmmaker. She was one of the few women artists widely known for monumental sculpture. Montreal, Canada, 2017 (meunierd, Shutterstock.com).

While the work is officially recognized as a collaboration between a woman and two male artists, feminist art historians have tended to agree that it was first and foremost a Saint Phalle work, a view which the artist herself also shared.³ The striking external design of *Hon* continues de Saint Phalle's "Nana" works which she began in 1964 and have become almost synonymous with her name as an artist, although her output was broad. According to the Moderna Museet website;

> The inspiration for these works came from her friend Clarice Rivers, who was pregnant at the time. The Nanas bear witness to Saint Phalle's belief in the divine nature of women and are frequently taken to represent a feminist perspective in her art.⁴

From this perspective, it is not hard to see why this famous work of 1960s European art would have appealed to Schivazappa for *The Laughing Woman*. Taking what was literally conceived as a place to honor women and motherhood, nothing could be considered more horrific to the misogynist Sayer, a man so crippled by his fears of emasculation that it has driven him well beyond the consensual terrain of kink culture and into something far uglier and vicious. In contemporary parlance, Sayer would be called an MRA, a Men's Rights Activist who sees women's sexuality and capacity for motherhood as an active threat to the virility and superiority of men. For him, de Saint Phalle's "Cathedral" for women is legitimately his worst nightmare, and we see that play out on screen; it is where he is lured in and spat out as a genderless skeleton, eaten alive not just by women's sexuality, but by women's art.

What neither Sayer nor the audience (on a first-time viewing, at least) recognize is that the intensity of women's power that he so fears *does* actually exist and is quite *explicitly* out to get him. But Maria does not usurp his delusions of masculine authority simply because he is a man, but because he is *specifically* a violent, abusive, sadistic misogynist. She is not a misandrist, but rather a feminist avenger, embodying the spirit of women's strength and power that lay at the heart of the second wave feminist movement that exploded during the 1960s and 1970s and that can be located as inspiring de Saint Phalle's Nana works (including *Hon*). But art transcends this central reference in *The Laughing Woman*; look carefully, for example, at the different artworks Schivazappa has hanging on both Sayer and Maria's walls. We see the former just before Sayer drugs her, where upon her enquiries as the nature of the unusual artworks, he answers "They were painted by a missionary. he paints the blow-ups of microscopic slides of various types of bacteria and protozoa; bubonic plague, leprosy, typhus, cholera, carbuncles, tetanus, diphtheria, rabies." For Sayer, then, whether it is his internalized corruption of de Saint Phalle's *Hon* or the artworks framed and hanging on his wall, art equals death; it is diseased and poses a threat. Compare this with the drawings we see in Maria's yoga room at the end of the film, however; shown in close up, we see a number of striking illustrations of giant naked women looming over cars, skyscrapers and bridges. What is interesting in Marie's artwork of choice is that it is not men that she shows as being submissive to women and their sexuality (and thus she cannot be seen as mirroring Sayer in her hatred of men), but rather it is *the symbols of patriarchy itself* that she has set in her sights as that which demands feminine and feminist control. Sayer seeks to destroy women themselves, whereas for Maria it is a broader system and those who embody its abuses of power that she seeks to avenge.

Like *The Perfume of the Lady in Black*, through its striking formal style and the gleeful excesses that mark its highly sexualized (and often violent, be it physically or emotionally) vignettes, *The Laughing Woman* also stands as a work of art in its own right through its incorporation of other artistic elements. As noted in its end credits, "the main decorative elements are a tribute to Claude Joubert, 'Plexus' and to Giuseppe Capogrossi," the latter an Italian painter whose artwork can be seen as a strong influence on the wallpaper design of Sayer's home, while the French magazine Plexus was at the cutting edge of design culture in Europe during this period (many of its covers designed by Claude Joubert). Beyond these specific design references, the broader status of *The Laughing Woman* as an art object in its own right thus recalls Rudolf Arnheim's observation in 1933 that "film resembles painting, music, literature and the dance" in that "it is a medium that may, but need not, be used to produce artistic results."[5] While not as well-known as the *gialli* of Dario Argento, Sergio Martino, Umberto Lenzi, Luci Fulci or the like, *The Perfume of the Lady in Black* certainly has its admirers, although the film's star Mimsy Farmer is not amongst them, rejecting it as "grotesque," a "cinematographic 'mongrel,'" and, more generally, opining that "the problem with these films is that the directors are not very ironic, they take themselves too seriously."[6] But not everyone has been harsh; Adrian Luther Smith praises both the film's craft, and—despite her feelings to the contrary—even Farmer herself, who he suggests "gives the performance of her career."[7] In relation to the broader concerns of this book, however, what captivates me so completely with this film is its artistic hybridity; the way that different art references, art forms and its own qualities as an art object intersect in such a fascinating manner. Barilli's past involvement with more highbrow "art house" cinema certainly suggests this is more than a coincidence. His relationship with brothers Giuseppe and Bernardo Bertolucci is well known, with Giuseppe even producing *The Perfume of the Lady in Black*. As for Bernardo, Benjamin Halligan has identified a number of both thematic and aesthetic parallels between their work, and in the case of *The Perfume of the Lady of Black* he notes it shares with Bernardo's *The Spider's Stratagem* (*La strategia del ragno*, 1970) a "secret or hidden personal history through the metaphor of the search for a deceased parent."[8]

The most immediate intertextual reference we find in Barilli's film lies within the title itself, a direct reference to Gaston Leroux's novel *The Perfume of the Lady in Black* (*La parfum de la dame en noir*, 1908). Secondly, however, the film is also consciously engages on a fundamental level with both Lewis Carroll's *Alice's Adventures in Wonderland* (1865) and *Through the Looking-Glass, and What Alice Found There* (1871), both in the form of iconographic references or direct quotation.[9] These literary allusions form the foundations upon which Barilli builds a primarily visual toolkit to subvert what in essence is suggested to be the overriding moral and ethical heart of the film; the punishment of a killer for her crimes. But as the cannibalism elements imply, the film seeks to destroy ("cannibalize," even) such obvious interpretations, and it does through not only through its literary references, but broader aesthetic regime.

The Perfume of the Lady in Black follows Farmer's scientist character Silvia Hacherman who is dedicated to her career almost to a fault, leaving her new boyfriend Roberto (Maurixio Bonuglia) feeling somewhat neglected. At a dinner party hosted by a professor friend called Andy (Jho Jenkins), Silvia finds herself suddenly in crisis as the strange conversations about human sacrifice and related ritual traditions seem to trigger a flood of repressed memories about her mother whose traumatic and unexplained death is complicated further by Silvia's less than idealized memories of the woman. Coming home after dinner and fighting with Roberto in the car, she sleeps for over twelve hours and awakens to find a framed photograph of a family portrait shown in the film's introduction shattered on her bedroom floor. As the distinction between reality and delusion begin to collapse, Silvia's mental health begins to suffer as she falls deeper and deeper into the abyss. Add to this a not-wholly explained cannibal conspiracy, and the revelation at the end of the film that it was Silvia herself who murdered her mother seems almost to be the least of her problems.

The tensions between *giallo* and cannibal film elements in *The Perfume of the Lady in Black* are thus only one of the binaries that the film mines to create its unique, disorienting effect. On one hand, the *giallo* boxes are more than adequately ticked with the bulk of its screen time dedicated to subjective experience of its protagonist, where paranoia, mental illness, guilt, sexual hang-ups and a deeply buried personal secret drive the core of the narrative. The parallel revelation of a mysterious cannibal cult obviously aligns it with a spate of cannibal films produced in Italy during this period; traced back at least to the "Mondo" shockumentaries of the early 1960s, this category includes movies made by a number of filmmakers who also made *gialli*, such as Ruggero Deodato's *Last Cannibal World* (*Ultimo mondo cannibal*, 1977) and *Cannibal Holocaust* (1980); Umberto Lenzi's *Deep River Savages* (*Il paese del sesso selvaggio*, 1972), *Eaten Alive!* (*Mangiati vivi!*, 1980) and *Cannibal Ferox* (1981); and Sergio Martino's *Slave of the Cannibal God* (*La montagna del dio cannibal*, 1978).[10]

Barilli is aligned with this category just as much as he riffs on his literary influences. Less orthodox adaptations as such, *The Perfume of the Lady in Black* employs elements of both the Leroux and Lewis texts without seeking to remake them as such. Although very different works, Leroux's *The Perfume of the Lady in Black* and Carroll's *Through the Looking-Glass, and What Alice Found There* share with Barilli a focus on themes such as physicality, vulnerability, and the instability of both logic and identity. On the surface at least, the appearance in of Silvia's mother (Renata Zamengo) dressed in black and putting on perfume appears to be the film's only direct connection to the title of Leroux's novel, but the associations run much deeper. While most famous perhaps for his novel *The Phantom of the Opera* (*Le fantôme de l'Opéra*, 1909), Leroux's *The Perfume of the Lady in Black* followed the blockbuster success of the first in his Joseph Rouletabille mystery series, *The Mystery of the Yellow Room* (*Le mystère de la chambre jaune*, 1908). Leroux's *The Perfume of the Lady in Black* is set at in a château on the French Riviera and follows newlyweds Mathilde and Robert who are being menaced by the series' villain, Mathilde's ex-husband Frederic Larson. When Larson is murdered, journalist and investigator Rouletabille is on the case, traveling to the château where he too—like Silvia—must deal with his own deeply repressed mommy issues.

Chapter Twelve of Leroux's book is called "The Impossible Body," and certainly this notion is an enduring fascination across much of Leroux's work. Most obviously perhaps, Erik in *The Phantom of the Opera* is at first believed to be a ghost who is haunting the Paris Opera, but throughout the tale his presence becomes more literal (and less "impossible"). Along with *The Mystery of the Yellow Room*, Leroux's *The Perfume of the Lady in Black* typifies the classic "locked room mystery," where a crime is "perpetrated in apparently sealed rooms or under other impossible conditions."[11] The central enigma within Leroux's *The Perfume of the Lady in Black* then hinges around how precisely Larson could have appeared in Mathilde and Robert's locked bedroom, an act described by one character as "mysterious and beyond human comprehension."[12] As Rouletabille notes, this "impossible body" is the source not only of a puzzling mystery but a source of real fear; "the dead Larson who leaves the room dead, without having entered it either dead or alive, terrifies me more than the live Larson!"[13] Just like Silvia in Barilli's *The Perfume of the Lady in Black*, then, Rouletabille too is haunted by seemingly "impossible bodies"; people who both *are* and *are not* there.

As Barilli will go to great lengths developing in his film's visual style and *mise-en-scène*, nothing in Silvia's world—people or things—are what they appear to be, including Silvia herself when it becomes clear that it was she herself who murdered her mother when she was a child. In Leroux's *The Perfume of the Lady in Black*, the protagonist is equally suspect. Ann C. Hall recalls a scene in this novel where Leroux himself appears as a "character" within the book itself when he buys a newspaper from a young Rouletabille; it is the generous tip given to the fictional character by the author himself that allows Rouletabille to start his own business and escape the life of poverty caused by his parents' abandoning him. For Hall, there is much more at stake than a cute cameo:

> In some ways, readers who equate Leroux with his novel are doing exactly what the novel teaches its readers to avoid, to assume that what we are being told is true, that the speaker and the author are one and the same, that they have our best interests at heart by presenting factual information. In this way, the "facts," though clearly fabricated, seduce us to "suspend disbelief" and judgement. But the novel's entire purpose is to encourage its readers to analyse, question, and become our own literary and life detectives.[14]

Like the novel from which it takes its name, Barilli's *The Perfume of the Lady in Black* also "seduces" its viewer in order to get us to "suspend disbelief." In many ways, there is little choice but to do so, as the "impossible bodies" that riddle the film do not permit much room for alternate modes of understanding until the truth of Silvia's crime (thus explaining the severity of her mental health issues) are fully revealed. If Leroux's novel seeks "to encourage its readers to analyse, question, and become our own literary and life detectives," Barilli's movie is less interested in the act of detection as it is a tantalizing—and often taunting—demand that we accept the fact that some mysteries (and bodies) will forever remain "impossible."

Of all the "impossible bodies" in Barilli's *The Perfume of the Lady in Black*, it is the apparent coming-to-life of John Tenniel's iconic illustrations of Alice from Carroll's beloved children's books in the shape of a small girl with long blonde hair. For Deighan, traces of Tenniel's Alice manifest elsewhere, particularly in Mario Bava's *Kill, Baby ... Kill!* and

Fifteen—Hybridity

Federico Fellini's "Toby Dammit" segment of the anthology film *Spirits of the Dead* (*Histoires extraordinaires* , 1968).[15] This multiplying of Alices across these films more broadly manifests within the Barilli's film through the division of Silvia herself; as Kier-La Janisse eloquently notes, the split of Silvia into "Big" and "Little" doubles is flagged rather explicitly by the Alice reference, a rather "unsubtle hint of doppelgänger

Ghosts of Lewis Carroll's Alice in Italian horror. Top: *Kill, Baby ... Kill!* (*Operazione paura*, Mario Bava, 1966). Bottom: From Federico Fellini's segment "Toby Dammit," in the anthology *Spirits of the Dead* (*Tre passi nel delirio*, 1968).

theory" at work.[16] Played by a young Lara Wendel who had previously starred as the kidnapped child at the heart of Tonino Valerii's 1972 *giallo My Dear Killer* (*Mio caro assassino*) discussed elsewhere in this book, Wendel would go on to appear in later *gialli* including Dario Argento's *Tenebrae* (1982) and Lamberto Bava's *You'll Die at Midnight* (*Morirai a mezzanotte*, 1986). This imagining of Tenniel's Alice drawings in the form of a flesh-and-bone child is important, as like Barilli's *The Perfume of the Lady in Black*, Carroll's Wonderland stories share Leroux's focus on this idea of impossible bodies. In fact, this Alice/Little Silvia figure is crucial not only to the visual spectacle of the film but much of its thematic parallels with Lewis; Silvia herself and her own "impossible body" appears to shrink and grow much like Alice's did down the famous rabbit hole. Through Alice, Lewis presents "a story where sense and non-sense of the body send her continuously back to the definition of her identity."[17] In a similar way, then, Silvia is forced to ask similar fundamental questions through the destabilizing of her *own* identity (Big Silvia! Little Silvia!) about not just her past, but the truth about herself and what she is and has been capable of doing. For Barilli himself, Alice represented a specific kind of madness that was closely aligned with the kind of story that he wanted to tell about Silvia and her experience:

> I've always liked *Alice in Wonderland*. I bought an edition with good drawings, the one you see in the film.... One day I thought what if she relates to Alice instead of Cinderella? Because Alice is pure madness. I used her a lot in this film. Once I read it, I saw the similarities and decided to use Alice. The character becomes Alice, she finds Alice in her. You don't need rationalizations when you make a film. You do things because you like them, sometimes it's automatic.... I was crazy about *Alice*, it was easy. She was perfect for that film, she was perfect in my mind. Alice is completely insane and surrounded by insane people.[18]

Mad worlds and mad people are what, for Barilli, unite Carroll's Alice stories and *The Perfume of the Lady in Black*. Silvia's experience then is not only of psychological disorientation, but also a physical one also; through the imagery of Tenniel's Alice, Barilli subverts the fantastic world of talking rabbits unable to make appointments, smiling cats and millinery-themed tea parties, and replaces it with an altogether much darker vision of rape, murder, and cannibalism.

As different as their circumstances may be, Alice and Silvia are caught in the homonymic trap of "sense" itself; as Kamilla Elliot notes of Carrol, he "plays on the distinctions between sense as semantic meaning and sense as in sensory perception, placing them in conflict with each other,"[19] which is in many ways is surely what Barilli does also. Both Alice in the novels and Silvia in the film are caught in a paradox where their survival depends on grasping the logic of

Fifteen—Hybridity

illogical environments, made nowhere more visible than their duality as "Big" and "Little" versions of themselves. But Barilli's engagement with Carroll extends beyond the visual depiction of Little Silvia and these broader themes, as both texts are focused on much broader scenarios where meaning itself is collapsed. From this perspective, Barilli's film perfectly reflects Elliot's description of Carroll's *Alice* which she describes as "self-consciously concerned with the representational capacities of verbal and pictorial signs, with dynamics between the aural and visual aspects inside individual signs, and with splits between form and content."[20] Alice and Silvia exist in worlds that are not what they appear to be. Filled with deceptive signs, while Alice can mark a clear distinction between the real and the fantastic, Silvia is incapable of identifying such boundaries.

But just as Alice's shift from one realm to another is marked by her famous tumble down the rabbit hole, it is feasibly possible to suggest the precise moment when Silvia's reality makes a similar shift. I would argue that the moment of transformation occurs far earlier in the film than the narrative itself might suggest, thus emphasizing Barilli's strong utilization of the pictorial over plot (as noted earlier in this book he is, after all, a painter himself). I contend that the only moment of stability, of factually evidenced "reality" we see in the context of the film's diegesis, is presented as photographic evidence, cleverly camouflaged, hidden in plain sight in a single still image that lasts almost a minute and a half. This is, of course, the vintage-styled family portrait in the film's opening credit sequence where we see the Alice-esque Little Silvia for the first time; significantly, we see Little Alice (based as she is so overtly on Tenniel's illustrations in her appearance) before we even meet Farmer's Big Silvia. While we may not register it on first watching the film, on subsequent viewings this potentially marks the "reality" from which everything else spirals away from. So if this is the "normal" and everything we see after it deviates from that point onwards—marked by the destruction of the nuclear family—what evidence is there in the film itself to suggest that the world in which we meet Farmer's adult Silvia is an abstracted fantasy realm?

It's all there, right in front of our eyes; it's in the art of the film itself in terms of its pictorial qualities and *mise-en-scène*, rather than the deceptive traps of the narrative itself. Stepping away from the story and actually looking at the film—closely—we discover just how excessive its emphasis on synthetic environments is, marked by the not-real or the almost-real. These artifices permeate the film on a fundamental level far too much to be merely hollow stylistic excess or mere coincidence. Excessive, yes, but there is a strategy behind this excess; like so many *gialli*, it's not style *over* substance, but style *is* the substance. For Deighan,

> Barilli's film becomes overwhelmed by images of artificial, contained nature as Silvia's madness encroaches: manicured public parks and sculpted fountains give way to a trip to the city zoo; she visits a taxidermy shop and her boyfriend's (Maurizio Bonuglia) flat is crowded with framed and preserved animals and insects. Flowers and plants choke the second half of the film; they are literally represented or appear as decoration, upholstery, and even as a tattoo on the hand of a psychic medium who allegedly communicates with Silvia's dead father.[21]

Let's work through a number of these and other specific examples in-depth. After the opening credits finish, for example, we see a boat floating on water. At first, there is no reason to believe that this is anything other than what it appears to be, but as the camera pulls back, we see it is a toy boat that a young child plays with in the fountain outside of Silvia's apartment building. Why? Why is this shot located in such a privileged position in the film? It is instantly clear, then, that things in this film are deceptive; they are not what they appear to be. In the scene where Silvia and Roberto attend the dinner party at Andy's home, his house is a faux-jungle, filled to the brim with plant-life that makes any distinction between inside and outside hard to readily identify. Roberto's bedroom is painted sky blue, where framed butterflies and a flock of stuff birds on a shelf that sits in front of it replicate a sky scene; it is simultaneously sky-*like* but not sky. The film is riddled with extraordinary, almost psychedelic floral wallpapers and murals, deliberately theatrical backdrops that again simultaneously indicate a design inspiration *from* the natural environments, while very much being anything but "natural" themselves.

Even some of the environments in the film that at first appear to be "natural" are, upon further reflection, far from. Consider, for example, the zoo, an important location in the film because it is here where Silvia not only reflects on her dead father, but also were she establishes her friendship with her sleazy elderly neighbor Signor Rossetti (Mario Scaccia), whom she will murder later in the film as she spirals further out of control. Yes, the zoo is a space where real animals live rather than representations of living animals such as we see in the stuffed birds and pinned-and-framed butterflies in Roberto's bedroom. But the entire concept of the zoo itself is that it is *not* a natural environment at all, but rather a contrived outdoor habitat that seeks to replicate their natural environment. This is, again, Wonderland-in-reverse: yet another banal replication of a real environment that works in opposition to Carroll's fantasia of familiar objects and figures granted new whimsical life.

Further subversions of Carroll's stories are visible in the use of mirrors throughout *The Perfume of the Lady in Black*, with Deighan noting Carroll's poem "Jaberwocky" that features in *Through the Looking-Glass, and What Alice Found There*. The poem provides curious parallels to the film: both are concerned with mirrors and reflections because "the poem can only be read when it is viewed in a mirror," says Deighan. "Its themes of violence and death are integral to Farmer's Silvia, who ultimately succumbs to them both throughout the film."[22]

At its most basic level, Barilli's film employs this metaphor to speak simultaneously of fractured identities and, in relation to Alice, alternate planes of reality. Leroux's notion of "impossible bodies" come back into play in the various "splits" we see in Silvia's own identity between Big Silvia, Little Silvia and her mother herself, whom she at one stage even dresses like. Long before Silvia's instability has become apparent, mirrors permeate the film's *mise-en-scène*. Her bedroom features a number of mirrors, and above her bed is a painting that is fundamental to the film; painted by Barilli himself, this was the first creative engagement he had with the story he sought to tell. "I need to draw. All directors draw, even non-painters," he explained.[23] "Drawing is necessary. ... cinema is drawing." On the significance of the painting itself, he said:

> I was born a painter in a family of painters so I am used to being visual. This visual aspect is important to me. So when I write I'm always drawing and I drew a woman lying on her back on a bed as someone might be with a mental disorder. A wall, a bed, a yellow sheet, which is suicide, and a woman's back. I painted this. It represents Mimsy and mother. I painted this oil painting in Rome and it's in Paris now.

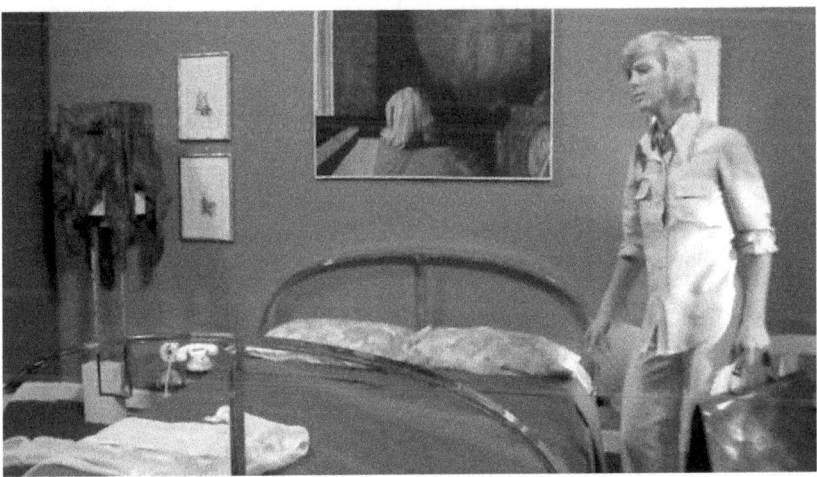

The painting that hangs in Silvia's (Mimsy Farmer) bedroom in *The Perfume of the Lady in Black* (*Il profumo della signora in nero*, Francesco Barilli, 1974).

> I really did paint it and based the film on it. The first thing Bertolucci saw was the painting. I told him this was the film. He asked if she ever turns around. She turns around!²⁴

On closer inspection, we can see the visual match between the painting that hangs in both Silvia and her mother's bedrooms and Silvia's own bedroom in terms of the use of color and composition which "reflects" the scene in which it is set; a green bed showing the back of a figure wearing the same shade that Silvia herself often wears.

Reflections manifest in more literal ways, also. The apparition of her dead mother's "impossible body" importantly appears in a mirror the first time Silvia sees her, acting like a sort of gateway or wormhole from one plane of existence into another, again echoing Carroll's *Through the Looking Glass*. Both of the film's sex scenes are shown in mirrors; the first when Roberto and Silvia have sex, and later when Silvia has a flashback to seeing her mother and her lover Nicola (Orazio Orland) in bed together, just before Nicola rises—naked—and, it is implied, sexually menaces the young child who hits back (in Silvia's memory of the scene, at least). Little Silvia and Big Silvia have their first encounter in the latter's apartment in front of a large mirror, effectively fracturing even further the already doubled/divided image of Silvia, converting two on-screen figures into four. Most disturbingly, Silvia's experience of being chased around her deserted childhood home by Nicola before he rapes her centers on his reflection being shown in a mirror during the assault. For Deighan, this is a kind of traumatic flashback to the suggestion of child sexual assault indicated earlier in the film, which leads to Little Silvia killing Big Silvia/Mother herself, so divided is her psyche;

> Silvia is unable to resolve this spectral force in her life. After goading her to visit the site of her assault as a child, an experience she is forced to brutally relive, Silvia's younger self ultimately pushes her off the roof, and they fall together to Silvia's death. In this sense, Barilli takes Carroll's Alice to her most monstrous extreme. Young Silvia represents a morbid rejection of sexual maturity and stands as a physical manifestation of feminine sexuality as horror—resulting in a radical reinterpretation of one of the classics of children's literature.²⁵

Unlike Leroux and Carroll where there is a status quo that has been disrupted but, eventually at least, holds the promise of a return to order, Barilli's multiple, complex system of mirrors complicate any hope of tidy binaries that make clear distinctions between the fantastic and the real, the visible and the invisible. In *The Perfume of the Lady in Black*, mirrors herald the presence of a potential threat to Silvia or at the very least mark the presence of something inexplicable. But their function is unstable and can produce different meanings from scene to scene, thus collapsing the binary of Carroll's Looking Glass Land between "here" and "there."

Silvia's body is therefore rendered an "impossible" *mise en abyme*. Unlike Alice, there is no one to explain the rules to her, no matter how nonsensical they may seem, and there is no Joseph Rouletabille to provide a tidy dénouement. This notion of *mise en abyme* takes its most literal form in one of the film's most breathtaking compositions during a session at Sylvia's neighbor Francesca's (Donna Jordan) apartment with the blind psychic Orchidea (Nike Arrighi). Traumatized by the suggestion that her repressed memories about her parent's deaths may come to the surface, Silvia's tenuous psychological state is brought to life through her environment, a dizzying, intense frenzy of excessive, overstimulating visuals rendered even more chaotic by the seemingly infinite reflections that are the result of the room's mirrors-facing-mirrors layout. Again, the wallpaper is a loud floral print, this not-garden rendered even more confrontational and befuddling by the frenzied of eternally reflected mirrors. These kinds of multiple, disorienting reflections appear elsewhere, too, such as a shot of Silvia's bedroom where a three-way mirror reflects not only the room itself, but the painting on the wall that reflects her bedroom. It is in this same mirror later in the film where Little Silvia and Big Silvia can both be seen, a third figure alluded to through Silvia's dressing as her own mother. Technically, there is only one person in the shot—Silvia—but pictorially Barilli renders the fracturing of her psyche literal by dividing her into multiple figures.

So what about the cannibals? In the documentary *Ritratto in nero* that appeared on the 2004 Raro Video home entertainment release of *The Perfume of the Lady in Black*, Barilli outlined how the final film was the result of the merger of two distinct projects: one was about a woman having a psychological collapse, the other a "black and white film about a cannibal cult in Geneva about rich guys with Rolls Royces going down to the city's underground and eating people."[26] Certainly it was not Barrili's first encounter with the cannibal film as he had earlier worked for a brief period on the screenplay of Umberto Lenzi's *Deep River Savages*. But as Barilli suggests, the union of these two separate projects made sense to him because the idea that "they (the cannibal cult) choose you, stalk you, abuse you, drive you mad and eat you was such a modern idea."[27] Whatever the intention, however, by design or luck, these two plotlines co-exist in a far more ambivalent manner in the film. Certainly it is apparent that Silvia is the subject of some kind of conspiracy early in the film when a strange man in a duck-print shirt follows her (his shirt yet another instance of a reference to the natural world that is only a synthetic representation of it). Elsewhere, it is also suggested that Andy, Roberto and even the doorman of the building where she lives are somehow involved in something ominous, even before the cannibal plot is revealed. This becomes clear when Silvia returns home from Francesca's apartment after her strange encounter with Orchidea. As they leave her at home, Andy, Orchidea and Signor Rosetti drive to a strange meeting in a deserted tunnel where they are welcomed by the man in the duck shirt. The next day, after Signore Rosetti has fed his cats a woman's finger (painted fingernail and all), it is revealed that Francesca has gone missing, and we assume her to be the owner of the digit that has since become cat food. Things do not become any less concerning in Silvia's apartment where—recalling the macabre kind of tableau previously discussed in Michel Soavi's *Stage Fright*—Silvia has seated the bodies of the three men she has murdered throughout the film (Signor Rosetti, Nicola and Roberto) around her dining room table, happily quoting Carroll's Alice in her own macabre rendition of the Mad Hatter's tea party.

Finally, with the suggestion that Silvia murdered her mother becoming more overt throughout the film, it is Little Silvia herself who murders Big Silvia by restaging the scene where Silvia as a child killed her own mother. It is now that the cannibal plot comes to the fore. Ritualistically repeating the previous sequence with Signore Rosetti, Orchida and Andy attending their previous meeting at the seemingly deserted tunnel, more "impossible bodies" appear; despite our having witnessed Silvia murdering them, Nicola, Signor Rosetti and Roberto are all in attendance to witness and participate in that evening's human sacrifice, this time of Silvia's own body as she is cut open and her innards devoured by the group. Clearly, this raises more questions than it answers, far from the tidy world of Leroux or even Carroll's conclusions—there is no status quo to return to, just incoherent, illogical death. So how can we conceptually position this deliberately illogical conclusion? Was the whole film a fantasy, a twisted, gruesome Wonderland with Silvia as its doomed, fractured Alice, and if so, whose corpse is lying on the table? Whose fantasy *is* this?

The final answer, it appears, is that no wholly unified reading of the conclusion is possible, which, for a film so determined to consistently collapse boundaries all the way through its run time, is exquisitely consistent if not exactly coherent in terms of traditional film narrative. Even the final actions in these last moments speak to chaos; while all the activities of the cannibal cult have spoken of carefully executed rituals and control, the gurney upon which Silvia's naked body is laid out upon is somewhere between a sacred altar and a dinner table. While the cannibal community at first move as a unified whole, once the feasting starts, their carefully controlled behavior collapses into pandemonium. This is not a case, in the anthropological sense, of reassimilating a transgressor back into the community through ritualized cannibalism. Instead, the order that dominates both the activity on screen and Barilli's careful composition collapses—greed takes over and it is every man (and woman) for themselves. There is no ritual, just people grabbing want they can and running away, scurrying like rats to feast on scraps in animalistic, paranoid solitude. Consumption therefore fractures the community, resulting in what feels less like an anthropological exploration of transgression and punishment than it does a less-than-subtle attack on capitalism itself.

Barilli's *The Perfume of the Lady in* Black is, then, ultimately the most "impossible body" of all. The seemingly superfluous cannibalism plotline is essential to the film precisely because of its incoherent excesses; it actively undermines its narrative and demands that the viewer engage with the pictorial, the intertextual and the literary references that permeate it instead.

Conclusion
Style Is the Substance

If there's one enduring phrase that has permeated negative criticism of *giallo* cinema it is the dismissal that it is style over substance.[1] As I have argued throughout this book, however, the very excesses of *giallo* cinema—in particular reference to a reflexive engagement with art, artists and artworks more generally (painting especially)—render this simple dismissal far more complex than the criticism might at first suggest. There is, I argue, meaning within the *horror-vacui*-like excesses of *giallo*; that meaning may not always be as thematically focused as I suggest it is in Argento's *The Bird with the Crystal Plumage*, *The Stendhal Syndrome* or *Deep Red* or Fulci's *A Lizard in a Woman's Skin* or *The Psychic*, but as I have argued throughout this book, the fascination with the arts—particularly the visual arts—deserves far greater consideration than it broadly has received.

In *giallo*, the style *is* the substance; this is where it packs its sensorial punch, how it captivates us in ways beyond the orthodox methods more traditional mystery-based films have programmed us to. These films demand we privilege the experience of our eyes, ears and other bodily sites of sensory registration over the intellect. Recalling the real-life phenomenon of the Stendhal Syndrome that inspired Argento's 1996 film of the same name, *giallo* films that engage with art do not just merely invite us to become amateur art historians as much as amateur detectives like so many of the protagonists that haunt the category, but they lure us in, pulling us into their own worlds-of-art themselves. So often drenched with sex and death as much as excessively saturated color and overwhelming soundtracks, the horror, the thrill, and the broader experience of these films is, at their best, fundamentally intoxicating.

As Nicholas Caruso has argued, when it comes to style over

substance, one need "look no further than the Italian *giallo* film for proof on how style sculpts the surrounding world and influences storytelling." This, he argues, is its legacy, as "style continues to shape modern horror and at its most effective, nurture subtlety in storytelling."[2] For filmmakers Hélène Cattet and Bruno Forzani, style over substance is built into the very foundations of their glorious 2013 neo-*gialli Amer* (2009) and *The Strange Colour of Your Body's Tears* (2013), as discussed in Chapter Three. Says Forzani of the 2013 film;

> ...we worked on the whodunnit structure and we had to deconstruct it. So it was like, how can we talk about something differently than just a detective interrogator who will tell a detective story. So we had the idea of the split screen—it's not just aesthetic, it's a way to talk about the guy and his relationship with the detective: is he a double? a reflection? Each time, we tried to work on each sequence to tell the story we want to tell—the story about the guy, not just the detective story. So we can cinematographically talk about our subject—because for me *Amer* was a story about paranoia, and this one a story about schizophrenia. And so, when I hear "style over substance," for me it's an archaic debate, because it is not an antagonism between the substance and style.[3]

For Forzani, "Style turns to substance, style is the substance, so...," Cattet adding, "...they complete each other."[4] As Virginie Sélavy has shrewdly observed, Cattet and Forzani utilize *giallo* as the raw materials for their more experimental approach to genre filmmaking, noting they "have developed a style in which they take elements of the *giallo* and use them to compose intensely sensual cinematic experiences."[5] Forzani rejects the term "homage," noting that they instead "reinterpret and re-use the *giallo* language to tell our story."[6] Cattet expands on this, stating "We use it as a tool, especially because there are strong iconographic elements whose meaning we can subvert."[7] For Peter Strickland—director of *Berberian Sound Studio*, discussed in Chapter Thirteen—his engagement with *giallo* is similarly experimental and based on the sensory provocation of the earlier films, claiming "for me, the attraction was the atmosphere, the music, the flamboyance; I just lapped it up."[8]

On one level, filmmakers such as these engage with *giallo* cinema through a spirit of remix culture, as demonstrated in the title of *The Strange Colour of Your Body's Tears* which Cattet and Forzani have said was the product of merging a number of *gialli* film titles including Sergio Martino's *All the Colors of the Dark* (1972) and *The Strange Vice of Mrs. Wardh* (1971) with Giuliano Carnimeo's *What Are Those Strange Drops of Blood on Jennifer's Body?* (1972).[9] But their relationship to these older films runs much deeper on a conceptual level, again configured around the status of the *giallo* film as an art object itself. As Forzani states,

> For me *Deep Red* is about [how] you have to blow up, you have to relearn to watch, an image, as the killer is in the image—and all what we are doing in *The Strange Colour*, it's about this concept: you can watch an image in different ways, and find different meaning for one image. I think it's the philosophy of *giallo*, in fact: you have to watch the image differently from the first look.[10]

As Cattet adds, "It's a game with the viewer, a game with the point-of-view."[11] It is precisely this image-game that permeates so many of the films that I explore in this book; *giallo* demands we engage with images (both art historical and cinematic) in new ways that often pull us well outside our comfort zone. From this perspective, the desire to seek the easy dismissal of "style of substance" perhaps naturally seems like a much easier, less demanding way out of playing precisely the "image-game" that Cattet identifies.

While films such as *Amer*, *The Strange Colour of Your Body's Tears* and *Berberian Sound Studio* may offer the most compelling and experimental engagements with the conceptual legacy of *giallo* cinema from this perspective, even beyond its oft-cited influence on North American slasher cinema[12] there is no lack of further evidence of the legacy of *gialli*. The arts riddle many neo-*gialli*, from the Astron-6 pastiche *The Editor* (2014), to Luciano Onetti's many love-letters to the category including *Deep Sleep* (*Sonno Profondo*, 2013), *Francesca* (2015), and, co-directed with Nicolás Onetti, *Abrakadabra* (2018). Joseph F. Parda's *5 Dead on the Crimson Canvas* (1996) makes its affection for the art historical fascinations that permeate *giallo* explicit in the title alone, and Yann Gonzalez's breathtaking queer neo-*giallo Knife+Heart* (*Un couteau dans le cœur*, 2018) again uses the world of filmmaking—this time pornography—as the site of its tale of sex and murder in a world drenched with sensory provocative stylistic excess. Moving into the mainstream, as has been noted previously the influence of *giallo* has been widely acknowledged in Hollywood movies such as Irvin Kershner's *Eyes of Laura Mars* (1978) and Brian De Palma's *Dressed to Kill* (1980), both of which continue the traditions of *giallo* cinema's fascination with fashion and photography in the case of the former, and the gallery space in the case of the latter. Perhaps the most recent neo-*giallo* success story is Nicolas Winding Refn's *The Neon Demon*, a film widely acknowledged as engaging with *giallo* which is perhaps most satisfyingly summarized by Donald Clarke as "equal parts Giallo *All About Eve* and butcher's-apron *A Star is Born*."[13] And in more general terms, it would be remiss not to mention the breathtaking cameo by *giallo* queen Edwige Fenech—as an art teacher, no less—in Eli Roth's *Hostel II* (2007).

But as I noted in Chapter One, a fascination with art, artists and the artistic process is far from specific to *gialli* alone and runs throughout horror more broadly. While *gialli* provide an effective case study to begin exploring this broader phenomenon more in-depth—an area of study I hope this book will pay at least a small part in promoting—to list all horror films made around the world since the advent of moving image culture that have engaged with painting alone would be impossible in the context of this brief conclusion. But adding to the many films identified previously, from David Bowie's film debut *The Image* (Michael Armstrong, 1969) to Ivan Reitman's *Ghostbusters II* (1989); John Carpenter's *In the Mouth of Madness* (1994) to the *Candyman* films (1992–1999), paintings are an enduring and captivating motif across horror cinema. Through these works and the many films discussed in this book, horror films that engage with art—painting in particular—bring to life with vibrant ferocity the words of Henry Fuseli, the artist of the terrifying 1781 oil painting said to have inspired Mary Shelley's *Frankenstein*. "Some enter the gates of art with golden keys, and take their seats with dignity among the demi-gods of fame," Fuseli wrote, while "some burst the doors and leap into a niche with savage power."[14] It is precisely this "savage power" within the divine excesses of horror in general—and *giallo* cinema specifically—that has rendered it such an enduring, influential and intoxicating site of fascination for its ever-growing legion of admirers, be they fans, critics or filmmakers themselves.

Chapter Notes

Introduction

1. Virginia Woolf, "The Movies and Reality," The New Republic, 4 August 1926, https://newrepublic.com/article/120389/movies-reality.
2. All film titles in this book will be referred to by their English-language release name first and Italian title second, if they are different. If a film does not have an English-language release title, I will refer to it only by its original Italian-language name.
3. In his fascinating essay on the shifts in distribution and consequent (sub)cultural value of *giallo* cinema in regards to its material modes of home entertainment distribution, Raiford Guins has noted that these sorts of tacky VHS covers were part of the 'package' of *giallo* consumption for a certain generation; "Like the videocassette covers crafted to target a supposedly nondiscerning audience, poor dubbing became synonymous with viewers' first experience of Italian horror on videocassette. Voices were often rerecorded to change accents and in certain cases dialogue was changed." See: Raiford Guins, "Blood and Black Gloves on Shiny Discs: New Media, Old Tastes, and the Remediation of Italian Horror Films in the United States," in *Horror International*, eds. Steven Jay Schneider and Tony Williams (Detroit: Wayne State University Press, 2005), 20.
4. Alexia Kannas, *Deep Red* (New York: Columbia University Press/Wallflower Press, 2017), 3.
5. See: *Defining Cult Movies: The Cultural Politics of Oppositional Tastes*, eds. Mark Jancovich, Antonio Lázaro Reboli, Julian Stringer and Andrew Willis (Manchester: Manchester University Press, 2003).
6. Pierre Bourdieu, *Distinction: A Social Critique of the Judgement of Taste* (Cambridge, MA: Harvard University Press, 1984), 6.
7. Simon Schama, *Power of Art* (London: BBC Books, 2006), 7.
8. *Ibid.*, 6.

Chapter One

1. Jean Mitry, *The Aesthetics and Psychology of the Cinema*, translated by Christopher King (London: The Athlone Press, 1998), 4.
2. The parallels between Plato's allegory of the cave and screen culture are far from opaque, and thus has often been discussed in media studies more broadly. See, for instance, John O'Neill's *Plato's Cave: Television and its Discontents* (Cresskill: Hampton Press, 2002) and Nathan Andersen's *Shadow Philosophy: Plato's Cave and Cinema* (Abingdon, UK: Routledge, 2014).
3. Steven Allen and Laura Hubner, "Introduction," in *Framing Film: Cinema and the Visual Arts*, eds. Steven Allen and Laura Hubner (Bristol: Intellect, 2012), 3.
4. Steven Jacobs, *Framing Pictures: Film and the Visual Arts* (Edinburgh, UK: Edinburgh University Press, 2011), ix.
5. Angela Dalle Vacche, *Cinema and Painting: How Art is Used in Film* (Austin: University of Texas Press, 1996), 2.
6. *Ibid.*, 3.

7. *Ibid.*
8. Mikel J. Koven, *La Dolce Morte: Vernacular Cinema and the Italian Giallo Film* (Lanham, MD: The Scarecrow Press, 2006), 16.
9. *Ibid.*
10. Angela Dalle Vacche, *Cinema and Painting: How Art is Used in Film*, 1.
11. *Ibid.*, 196.
12. Brigitte Peucker, *Incorporating Images: Film and the Rival Arts* (Princeton, NJ: Princeton Univerity Press, 1995), 166.
13. *Ibid.*
14. Brigitte Peucker, *The Material Image: Art and the Real in Film* (Palo Alto, CA: Stanford University Press, 2007), 164.
15. *Ibid.*, 177–182.
16. *Ibid.*, 177.
17. Jeffrey Sconce, "'Trashing' the Academy: Taste, Excess, and an Emerging Politics of Cinematic Style," *Screen*, 36.4 (1995): 372.
18. *Ibid.*
19. *Ibid.*
20. *Ibid.*
21. *Ibid.*, 380.
22. Ian Christie, "Painting and the Visual Arts," in *Encyclopedia of Early Cinema*, ed. Richard Abel (Abingdon, Oxfordshire, United Kingdom, Taylor & Francis Ltd., 2005), 695.
23. *Ibid.*
24. Lynda Nead, "The Artist's Studio: The Affair of Art and Film," in *Film, Art, New Media*, ed. Angela Dalle Vacche (Houndsmills: Palgrave Macmillan, 2012), 24.
25. *Ibid.*
26. *Ibid.*
27. Marcel Gromaire, "A Painter's Ideas About the Cinema," in *French Film Theory and Criticism: A History/Anthology, 1907–1939. Voume 1: 1907–1939*, ed. Richard Abel (Princeton, NJ: Princeton Univerity Press, 1988), 174.
28. Fernand Léger, "Painting and Cinema," in *French Film Theory and Criticism: A History/Anthology, 1907–1939. Voume 1: 1907–1939*, ed. Richard Abel (Princeton, NJ: Princeton University Press, 1988), 373.
29. *Ibid.*
30. *Ibid.*
31. Hervé Joubert-Laurencin, "André Bazin and 'Arts': The Reverse of a Theorem," *Film Criticism*, 39.1 (Fall, 2014): 82.
32. *Ibid.*, 84.
33. André Bazin, "Painting and Cinema," in *What Is Cinema? Essays* selected and translated by Hugh Gray (Berkeley: University of California Press, 1967), 166.
34. *Ibid.*
35. *Ibid.*, 168.
36. *Ibid.*
37. Dudley Andrew (ed), *The Image in Dispute: Art and Cinema in the Age of Photography* (Austin: University of Texas Press, 1997).
38. Linda C. Ehrlich and David Desser, *Cinematic Landscapes: Observations on the Visual Arts and Cinema of China and Japan* (Austin: University of Texas Press, 1994).
39. John A. Walker, *Art and Artists on Screen* (Manchester, UK: Manchester Univerity Press, 1993), 5.
40. Steven Jacobs and Lisa Colpaert, *The Dark Galleries: A Museum Guide to Painted Portraits in Film Noir, Gothic Melodrama, and Ghost Stories of the 1940s and 1950s* (Ghent: AraMER, 2013).
41. Susan Felleman, *Art and the Cinematic Imagination* (Austin: University of Texas Press, 2006), 2.
42. *Ibid.*, 2–3.
43. David Soren, *The Rise and Fall of the Horror Film: An Art Historical Approach to Fantasy Cinema* (Columbia: Lucas Brothers Publishing, 1977), i.
44. *Ibid.*, 58.
45. *Ibid.*, i.
46. *Ibid.*, 101.
47. *Ibid.*, 101.
48. *Ibid.*, 102. With only the briefest of exhibition windows before it was famously released officially on home entertainment in 2009, it is doubly impressive that it was this particular Argento film that was the one to woo Soren to Argento's craft. Roger Ebert also saw the film during this initial release but was not as impressed, See: "Four Flies on Grey Velvet," RogerEbert.com, 18 October 1972., https://www.rogerebert.com/reviews/four-flies-on-grey-velvet-1972.
49. While the film itself is lost, there is some remaining documentation including Gance's hand-written treatment and some images from the film. I write about this documentation at length in my book

Masks in Horror Cinema: Eyes Without Faces (Cardiff: University of Wales, 2019).

50. John Squires, "Muschietti Talks Paintings that Inspired Nightmarish New 'IT' Creature," *Bloody Disgusting*, 10 September 2017, https://bloody-disgusting.com/movie/3458110/muschietti-talks-paintings-inspired-nightmarish-new-creature/.

51. Kristofer Jenson, "Season of 'The Witch': A Q&A with Robert Eggers and Anya Taylor-Joy," *Newsweek*, 19 February 2016, https://www.newsweek.com/interview-robert-eggers-anya-taylor-joy-witch-movie-428681.

52. Gillian McIver, *Art History for Filmmakers: The Art of Visual Storytelling* (London: Bloomsbury, 2016), 144.

53. David Soren, op. cit., 14.

54. David Soren, op. cit., 9.

55. Christopher Frayling, "We Live in Gothic Times...," in *The Gothic Reader: A Critical Anthology*, ed. Martin Myrone, consultant ed. Christopher Frayling (London: Tate Publishing, 2006), 18.

56. Adam Lowenstein, "Horror's Otherness and Ethnographic Surrealism: The Case of The Shout," A Companion to the Horror Film, ed. Harry M. Benshoff (Somerset: John Wiley & Sons, Inc., 2014), 520.

57. *Ibid.*, 519.

58. "The furor was unsurprising: no work of mainstream English-language fiction had come so close to spelling out homosexual desire. The opening pages leave little doubt that Basil Hallward, the painter of Dorian's portrait, is in love with his subject. Once Dorian discovers his godlike powers, he carries out various heinous acts, including murder; but to the Victorian sensibility his most unspeakable deed would have been his corruption of a series of young men." Alex Ross, "How Oscar Wilde Painted Over 'Dorian Gray,'" *The New Yorker*, 1 August 2011, https://www.newyorker.com/magazine/2011/08/08/deceptive-picture.

59. Suzanne Raitt, "Immoral Science in The Picture of Dorian Gray," in *Strange Science: Investigating the Limits of Knowledge in the Victorian Age*, ed. Lara Karpenko and Shalyn Claggett (Ann Arbor: University of Michigan Press, 2017), 164.

60. Thomas de Quincey, "Thomas de Quincey," *Project Gutenberg*, 2004, https://www.gutenberg.org/files/10708/10708-8.txt.

61. Robert Morrison, "Introduction to On Murder by Thomas De Quincey" (Oxford: Oxford University Press, 2006), xxxvi.

62. Matthew Collings, *This Is Modern Art* (London: Weidenfeld & Nicolson, 1999), 76.

63. Gillian McIver, op. cit., 144.

64. *Ibid.*

65. *Ibid.*

66. *Ibid.*

67. *Ibid.*, 143.

68. Susan Felleman, op. cit., 3.

69. Leon Hunt, "A Sadistic Night At the Opera: Notes on the Italian Horror Film," *The Velvet Light Trap*, 30 (Fall 1992): 72.

70. For Stam, in the case of postmodernism—despite how contorted definitions of the term have become—"all its meanings carry an element of reflexivity." Robert Stam, *Reflexivity in Film and Literature: From Don Quixote to Jean-Luc Godard* (New York: Columbia University Press, 1992), xv.

71. *Ibid.*

72. Richard Bauman, *A World of Others' Words: Cross-cultural Perspectives on Intertextuality* (London: Wiley-Blackwell, 2007), 1.

73. *Ibid.*, 4.

74. Julia Kristeva, *Semeiotike: recherches pour une sémanalyse* (Paris: Editions du Seuil, 1969).

75. Judith Still and Michael Worton, "Introduction," in *Intertextuality: Theories and Practices*, eds. Judith Still and Michael Worton (Manchester, UK: Manchester Univerity Press, 1990), 1–2.

76. Mieke Bal, *Looking In: The Art of Viewing* (Amsterdam: G+B Arts, 2001), 68.

77. *Ibid.*, 68.

78. *Ibid.*, 272.

79. Marcia Landy, "The Argento Syndrome: Aesthetics of Horror," in *Italian Horror Cinema*, eds. Stefano Baschiera and Russ Hunter (Edinburgh University Press, 2016), 103.

80. *Ibid.*

81. Maitland McDonagh, *Broken Mirrors/Broken Minds: The Dark Dreams*

of Dario Argento (Minneapolis: University of Minnesota Press, 2010), 21.

82. Stephen Thrower, *Beyond Terror: The Films of Lucio Fulci* (Godalming: FAB Press, 2002), 63.

83. Barry Forshaw, "Giallo," in *Directory of World Cinema: Italy*, ed. Louis Bayman (Bristol: Intellect Books Ltd., 2011), 134.

84. Alexia Kannas, "No Place Like Home: The Late-Modern World of the Italian *giallo* Film," *Senses of Cinema*, 67 (July 2013), sensesofcinema.com/2013/uncategorized/no-place-like-home-the-late-modern-world-of-the-italian-giallo-film/.

85. Kristin Thompson, "The Concept of Cinematic Excess," in *Narrative, Apparatus, Ideology. A Film Theory Reader*, ed. Philip Rosen (New York: Columbia University Press, 1986), 131.

86. *Ibid.*, 134.

87. Mikel J. Koven, op. cit., 137.

88. Mikel J. Koven, op. cit., 137.

89. See: Pier Paolo Pasolini, "The Cinema of Poetry," in *Movies and Methods. Vol. 1*, ed. Bill Nichols (Berkeley: University of California Press, 1976), 542–558.

90. Mikel J. Koven, op. cit. 145.

91. Mikel J. Koven, op. cit. 146.

92. Mikel J. Koven, op. cit. 46.

93. Ian Olney, *Euro Horror: Classic European Horror Cinema in Contemporary American Culture* (Bloomington: Indiana University Press, 2013), 104.

94. Barry Forshaw, op. cit., 134.

95. *Ibid.*

96. Jeffrey Sconce, op. cit., 380.

97. Jeffrey Sconce, op. cit., 387.

98. *Ibid.*

99. *Ibid.*

100. *Ibid.*

101. William Lidwell, Kritina Holden, and Jill Butler, *Universal Principles of Design, Revised and Updated: 125 Ways to Enhance Usability, Influence Perception, Increase Appeal, Make Better Design Decisions and Teach Through Design* (Beverly: Rockport Publishers, 2010), 128.

102. Ludmila Makuchowska, *Scientific Discourse in John Donne's Eschatological Poetry* (Newcastle upon Tyne: Cambridge Scholars Press, 2014), iv.

103. William Lidwell, Kritina Holden, and Jill Butler, op. cit., 128.

104. *Ibid.*

105. See, for example; Otto Saumarez Smith, "Painstakingly Perfect and Utterly Peculiar—The Drawings of Jean-Jacques Lequeu," *Apollo Magazine*, 18 February 2019, https://www.apollo-magazine.com/jean-jacques-lequeu-drawing-petit-palais/; Julia Skelly, *Radical Decadence: Excess in Contemporary Feminist Textiles and Craft* (London: Bloomsbury, 2017), 102.

106. E.M. Gombrich, *The Sense of Order: The Study in the Psychology of Decorative Art* (Ithaca, NY: Cornell University Press, 1979), 80.

107. "The Passing Shows: Jackson Pollock," *Art News*, 44.4 (1 April 1945); 6.

108. Erwin Panofsky, *Problems in Titian: Mostly Iconographic* (New York University Press, 1969), 171.

109. Cornelia Stabenow, *Rousseau* (Cologne: Taschen, 2001), 75.

110. David Price, *Albrecht Dürer's Renaissance: Humanism, Reformation, and the Art of Faith* (Ann Arbor: The University of Michigan Press, 2003), 64.

111. John Hassard, Mihaela Kelemen and Julie Wolfram Cox, *Disorganization Theory: Explorations in Alternative Organizational Analysis* (London: Routledge, 2008), 99.

112. Zuzanna Stanska, "Gustav Klimt And His Love For Trees In Paintings," *Daily Art*, 9 October 2018, https://www.dailyartmagazine.com/gustav-klimt-trees-paintings/.

113. Brian T. Allen, "'Bruegel: The Hand of the Master' Makes Its Debut," National Review, 22 December 2018, https://www.nationalreview.com/2018/12/art-review-pieter-bruegel-vienna-showcase-a-success/#slide-1.

114. Barbara Hess, *Willem de Kooning, 1904–1997: Content as a Glimpse* (Cologne: Taschen, 2004), 79.

115. Claudia Betti and Teel Sale, *Drawing: A Contemporary Approach* (Belmont: Thomson Wadworth, 2008), 212.

116. David Joselit, "Truth or Dare: The Art of Witnessing," *ArtForum*, September 2011, https://www.artforum.com/print/201107/truth-or-dare-the-art-of-witnessing-28804.

117. William Lidwell, Kritina Holden and Jill Butler, op. cit., 128.

118. John Borstlap, *The Classical Revolution: Thoughts on New Music in the 21st Century* (Lanham: The Scarecrow Press Inc., 2013), 49.
119. Ricardo Martinez, "From Pop Surrealism to Lowbrow—Something Got Lost in Translation," *Widewalls*, 5 December 2015, https://www.widewalls.ch/pop-surrealism-lowbrow/.
120. William Lidwell, Kritina Holden and Jill Butler, op. cit., 128.
121. *Ibid.*
122. Carol Laseur, "Australian Exploitation Film: The Politics of Bad Taste," *Continuum*, 5:2 (1992), 370.
123. Kristin Thompson, op. cit., 131.
124. Paul C. Castagno, "The Mannerist Space in Early Commedia dell'Arte Iconography," in *Theatrical Spaces and Dramatic Places: The Reemergence of the Theatre Building in the Renaissance. Theatre Symposium; A Journal of the Southeastern Theatre Conference.* Volume 4 (Tuscaloosa: University of Alabama Press, 1996), 110.
125. Braxton Soderman, "'Don't Look ... or It Takes You': The Games of Horror Vacui," *Journal of Visual Culture*, 14.3 (2015), 312.
126. *Ibid.*
127. *Ibid.*
128. Lindsay Hallam, "Touching the Colour and Sound of Your Body's Tears: Affect and Homage in the Neo-Giallo," *16:9 Filmtisskrift*, 22 October 2017 www.16-9.dk/2017/10/touching-the-colour/.
129. *Ibid.*

Chapter Two

1. Anne Billson, "Violence, Mystery and Magic: How to Spot a Giallo Movie," *The Telegraph*, 14 October 2013, https://www.telegraph.co.uk/culture/film/10377468/Violence-mystery-and-magic-how-to-spot-a-giallo-movie.html.
2. Mikel J. Koven, op. cit., 152.
3. Roberto Curti, *Italian Gothic Horror Films, 1957–1969* (Jefferson, NC: McFarland, 2015), 130.
4. *Ibid.*
5. *Ibid.*, 52–3.
6. *Ibid.*, 96.
7. *Ibid.*, 164.
8. *Ibid.*, 45. Martyn Conterio discusses the use of portraiture at length in this film in his monograph dedicated to Bava's film, *Black Sunday* (Leighton Buzzard: Auteur, 2015).
9. David Del Valle, "When Sex and Death are Indissoluble: Riccardo Freda's *L'Orribile segreto del dottor Hichcock* (*The Horrible Secret of Dr Hichcock / Raptus*, 1962)," *Kinoeye: New Perspectives on European Film*, 3.12 (27 Oct 2003), http://www.kinoeye.org/03/12/delvalle12.php.
10. Joseph Luzzi, op. cit., 11.
11. Joseph Luzzi, op. cit., 11–12.
12. Joseph Luzzi, op. cit., 12.
13. Maitland McDonagh, *Broken Mirrors/Broken Minds*, op. cit., xii.
14. *Ibid.*
15. James Gracey, *Dario Argento* (Harpenden: Kamera Books, 2010), 19.
16. *Ibid.*, 19.
17. Louis Paul, *Italian Horror Film Directors* (Jefferson: McFalrand & Company, Inc., 2005), 67.
18. Ronny Swennson, "Tenebre," *Fantasy Film Memory*, 4/5 (1991): 41.
19. Luca Palmerini, "For Your Eyes Only: The Lucio Fulci Interview," *Giallo Pages*, 1 (Spring 1993): 35.
20. "Giorgio Soavi," *ADC Global* (no date) adcglobal.org/hall-of-fame/giorgio-soavi/.
21. "[GIORGIO SOAVI]," *Fondation Giacometti* (no date), https://www.fondation-giacometti.fr/en/database/163890/giorgio-soavi
22. Chas Balun and John Gullide, "Michele Soavi: Under the Influence," *Giallo Pages*, 1 (Spring 1993): 7.
23. Roberto Curti, op. cit., 169.
24. Roberto Curti, "Francesco Barilli Interview: Cinema Between Brush Strokes," *Offscreen*, 15.12 (December 2011), https://offscreen.com/view/francesco_barilli_interview
25. Danny Shipka, op. cit., 71.
26. "S. S. Van Dine," Wikipedia (no date), https://en.wikipedia.org/wiki/S._S._Van_Dine
27. Leon Hunt, "Kings of Terror, Geniuses of Crime: Giallo Cinema and Fumetti Neri," in Italian Horror Cinema, eds. Stefano Baschiera and Russ Hunter (Edinburgh University Press, 2016), 146.
28. See: *Ibid.*; Rolando Caputo, "Blood and Black Celluloid: Some Thoughts on

the Cinema of Mario Bava," *Metro*, 10 (1997): 58.

29. Gary Needham, "Playing with Genre: Defining the Italian giallo," *Fear Without Frontiers: Horror Cinema Across the Globe*, ed. Steven Jay Schneider (Godalming: FAB Press, 2003), 135.

30. Ian Olney, op. cit. 106.

31. Leon Hunt, "Burning Oil and Baby Oil: Bloody Pit of Horror," in *Alternative Europe: Eurotrash and Exploitation Cinema Since 1945*, ed. Ernest Mathjis and Xavier Mendik (London: Wallflower Press, 2004), 175.

32. Marco Vanelli, "Italian Cinema and Catholicism: From *Vigilanti cura* to Vatican II and Beyond," in *A Companion to Italian Cinema*, ed. Frank Burke (Malden: John Wiley & Sons, 2017), 117.

33. Stuart J. Hilwig, *Italy and 1968: Youthful Unrest and Democratic Culture* (Houndmills: Palgrave MacMillan, 2009), 78.

34. Quoted in Aline H. Kalbian, *Sexing the Church: Gender, Power, and Ethics in Contemporary Catholicism* (Bloomington: Indiana University Press, 2005), 58.

35. See: Alana Harris, "Introduction: The Summer of '68—Beyond the Secularization Thesis," in The Schism of '68: Catholicism, Contraception and Humanae Vitae in Europe, 1945–1975, ed. Alana Harris (Basingstoke: Palgrave Macmillan, 2018), 5; Aline H. Kalbian, op. cit., 58.

36. Barbara Pezzotti, *Investigating Italy's Past Through Historical Crime Fiction, Films, and TV Series: Murder in the Age of Chaos* (New York: Palgrave, 2016), 242.

37. *Ibid.*, 201.

38. Austin Fisher, "Political Memory in the Italian Hinterland: Locating the 'Rural Giallo,'" in *Italian Horror Cinema*, eds. Stefano Baschiera and Russ Hunter (Edinburgh, UK: Edinburgh University Press, 2016), 163.

39. *Ibid.*

40. Seb Roberts, "Strange Vices: Transgression and the Production of Difference in the *Giallo*," *Imagination: Journal of Cross-Cultural Image Studies*, 9.1 (29 October 2018), imaginations.glendon.yorku.ca/?p=10655.

41. Kat Ellinger, *All the Colours of Sergio Martino* (Shenley: Arrow Books, 2018), 13.

42. Russ Hunter, "Preferisco L'Inferno: Early Italian Horror Cinema," in *Italian Horror Cinema*, eds. Stefano Baschiera and Russ Hunter (Edinburgh: Edinburgh University Press, 2016), 17

43. Stefano Baschiera and Russ Hunter, "Introduction," in *Italian Horror Cinema*, eds. Stefano Baschiera and Russ Hunter (Edinburgh: Edinburgh University PRESS, 2016), 6.

44. *Ibid.*

45. "The krimi cycle ran from roughly 1959 to 1972, adapted mainly from the English mystery writer Edgar Wallace (and later, his son Bryan Edgar Wallace)," notes Leon Hunt, but "three things distinguish *Sei donne per l'assassino* from its German counterparts: its Rome setting (which is also different from the Roman Holiday-style Eternal City of *La ragazza che sapeva troppo*), its use of colour and its lurid sexualised violence." Leon Hunt (2016), op. cit., 157.

46. Mikel J. Koven, op. cit., 6–7.

47. See: Gino Moliterno, *The A to Z of Italian Cinema* (Lanham: The Scarecrow Press, Inc., 2009), 150; Peter Hutchings, "Bavaesque: The Making of Mario Bava as Italian Horror Auteur," in *Italian Horror Cinema*, eds. Stefano Baschiera and Russ Hunter (Edinburgh: Edinburgh University Press, 2016), 84; Gary Needham, op. cit., 144.

48. Gino Moliterno, op. cit., 150.

49. Alexia Kannas (*Deep Red*, 2017), op. cit., 102.

50. Adrian Luther Smith, *Blood & Black Lace: The Definitive Guide to Italian Sex and Horror Movies* (Liskeard: Stray Cat Publishing, 1999), n.p.

51. Mikel J. Koven, op. cit., 3.

52. Leon Hunt (2016), op. cit., 145.

53. Alexia Kannas (*Deep Red*, 2017), op. cit., 10.

54. Stanley Manders, "Terror in Technicolor," *American Cinematographer* (February 2010), 68–76.

55. Maitland McDonagh, *Broken Mirrors/Broken Minds*, op. cit., xxvii.

56. Stephen Thrower, op. cit., 63.

57. Philippe Met, "'Knowing Too Much' About Hitchcock: The Genesis of the Italian Giallo," in *After Hitchcock: Influence, Imitation, and Intertextuality*,

eds. David Boyd and R. Barton Palmer (Austin: University of Texas Press, 2006), 195.
58. Barry Forshaw, op. cit., 133.
59. Gary Needham, op. cit., 135
60. Ibid., 135–6.
61. Ibid., 137.
62. See, for example: Mikel J. Koven, op. cit.; Austin Fisher, op. cit.; Donato Totaro, "A Genealogy of Italian Popular Cinema: the Filone," *Offscreen*, 15.11 (November 2011), https://offscreen.com/view/genealogy_filone.
63. Mikel J. Koven, op. cit., 6.
64. Alexia Kannas, "All the Colours of the Dark: Film genre and the Italian giallo," *Journal of Italian Cinema & Media Studies*, 5.2 (2017): 173–190, 176.
65. Ian Olney, op. cit., 115.
66. Ibid., 106.
67. Barry Forshaw, op. cit., 133.
68. Jamie Sexton, "Creeping Decay: Cult Soundtracks, Residual Media, and Digital Technologies," New Review of Film and Television Studies, xiii (1), 12–30. Cited in Alexia Kannas (Deep Red), op. cit., 103.
69. Brigid Cherry, "Beyond Suspiria? The Place of European Horror Cinema in the Fan Canon," in *European Nightmares: Horror Cinema in Europe Since 1945*, eds. Patricia Allmer, Emily Brick, and David Huxley (London: Wallflower Press, 2012), 26–7.
70. Maitland McDonagh, "Strip Nude for Your Killer,," *Alliance of Women Film Journalists*, 11 July 2019, https://awfj.org/blog/2019/07/11/strip-nude-for-your-killer-review-by-maitland-mcdonagh/.
71. Ibid.
72. Alexia Kannas, *GIALLO! Genre, Modernity and Detection in Italian Horror Cinema* (Albany: State University of New York Press, Forthcoming).
73. Mikel J. Koven, op. cit., 5.
74. Stefano Baschiera and Russ Hunter, op. cit., 2.
75. Of his fascination with animals, Argento told Alan Jones in an interview; "I've always been fascinated by animals since my youth. Fish, insects, chimpanzees, dogs, snakes and horses—I can spend the whole day watching a cat just to try and understand what they are thinking. Animals' mental circuits intrigue me, which is why I adore working with them

and use them in my stories." Alan Jones, *Profondo Argento: The Man, The Myths and the Magic* (Godalming: FAB Press, 2004), 35.
76. Stefano Baschiera and Russ Hunter, op. cit., 2.
77. Ibid.
78. Austin Fisher, "Italian Popular Film Genres," in *A Companion to Italian Cinema*, ed. Frank Burke (Malden; John Wiley & Sons, 2017), 259.
79. Gary Needham, op. cit., 143.
80. Ibid.
81. Mikel J. Koven, op. cit., 49.
82. Mikel J. Koven, op. cit., 50.
83. Stefano Baschiera and Francesco Di Chiara, "Once Upon a Time in Italy: Transnational Features of Genre Production 1960s–1970s," *Film International*, 8.6 (2011), 34.
84. Ibid.
85. Gary Needham, op. cit., 143.
86. "Cultural odor" is a term famously defined by Koichi Iwabuchi "to focus on the way in which cultural features of a country of origin and images or ideas of its national, in most cases stereotyped, way of life are associated positively with a particular product in the consumption process." Koichi Iwabuchi, *Recentering Globalization: Popular Culture and Japanese Transnationalism* (Durham, NC: Duke University Press, 2002), 27.
87. Barry Forshaw, op. cit., 134.
88. Stephen Thrower, op. cit., 71.
89. Francesco Di Chiara, "Domestic Films Made for Export: Modes of Production in the 1960s Italian Horror Film," in *Italian Horror Cinema*, eds. Stefano Baschiera and Russ Hunter (Edinburgh: Edinburgh University Press, 2016), 30.
90. Ian Olney, op. cit., 104.
91. Antonio Bruschini and Stefano Piselli, *Giallo and Thrilling All'Italiana (1931–1983)* (Florence: Glittering Images, 2010), n.p.
92. Adam Lowenstein, "The Giallo/Slasher Landscape: Ecologia del delitto, Friday the 13th and Subtractive Spectatorship," in *Italian Horror Cinema*, eds. Stefano Baschiera and Russ Hunter (Edinburgh: Edinburgh University Press, 2016), 129.
93. Austin Fisher, "Italian Popular Film Genres," in *A Companion to Italian*

Cinema, ed. Frank Burke (Malden; John Wiley & Sons, Incorporated, 2017), 260.
    94. *Ibid.*
    95. Tim Lucas, *Mario Bava: All the Colors of the Dark* (Cincinnati: Video Watchdog, 2007), 449.
    96. *Ibid.*
    97. Philippe Met, op. cit., 198.
    98. *Ibid.*, 202.
    99. *Ibid.*, 207.
    100. *Ibid.*
    101. L. Andrew Cooper, *Dario Argento* (Urbana: University of Illinois Press, 2012), 24.
    102. Mikel J. Koven, op. cit., 45–59.
    103. *Ibid.*, 109.
    104. Luca Palmerini, op. cit. 37.
    105. John Martin, "Profondo Argento," *Giallo Pages*, 1 (Spring 1993): 5.
    106. Walter Benjamin, "The Work of Art in the Age of Mechanical Reproduction," Marxists.org, https://www.marxists.org/reference/subject/philosophy/works/ge/benjamin.htm.
    107. Anna Pritchard, "Envisaging the Possibilities for Art in the Age of Mechanical Reproduction, Consumer Culture and the Pervasiveness of the Media: Andy Warhol," *Deep South*, 6.3 (Spring 2000), https://www.otago.ac.nz/deepsouth/spring2000/pritchardone.html.
    108. *Ibid.*
    109. Mikel J. Koven, op. cit., 4.
    110. *Ibid.*, 85.
    111. *Ibid.*, 87.
    112. *Ibid.*, 90.
    113. Alan Jones (2004), op. cit., 159.

Chapter Three

    1. Brigitte Peucker (1995), op. cit., 55.
    2. Brigitte Peucker (2007), op. cit, 30.
    3. *Ibid.*
    4. Daniel Wiegand, "The Unsettling of Vision: Tableaux Vivants, Early Cinema, and Optical Illusions," in *The Image in Early Cinema: Form and Material*, eds. Scott Curtis, Philippe Gauthier, Tom Gunning and Joshua Yumibe (Bloomington: Indiana University Press, 2018), 29. As Wiegand notes, tableaux vivants can also restage famous sculptures.
    5. *Ibid.*
    6. *Ibid.*, 34.
    7. *Ibid.*
    8. Steven Jacobs, op. cit., 94.
    9. Maitland McDonagh, *Broken Mirrors/Broken Minds*, op. cit., 44.
    10. Christoph Huber, "A Language of Their Own: An Introduction to Hélène Cattet and Bruno Forzani," *Senses of Cinema*, 87 (June 2018) sensesofcinema.com/2018/split-screen-cattet-forzani/-introduction-to-helene-cattet-and-bruno-forzani/l.
    11. Anton Bitel, "The Gender(s) of Genre in Cattet and Forzani's Ambisexual Cinema," *Senses of Cinema*, 87 (June 2018) sensesofcinema.com/2018/split-screen-cattet-forzani/the-genders-of-genre-in-cattet-and-forzanis-ambisexual-cinema/l.
    12. Michael Sicinski, "The Gaze in Hélène Cattet and Bruno Forzani's *Amer* (2009)," *Senses of Cinema*, 87 (June 2018) sensesofcinema.com/2018/split-screen-cattet-forzani/the-gaze-in-helene-cattet-and-bruno-forzanis-amer-2009/l.
    13. *Ibid.*
    14. Anton Bitel (2018), op. cit.
    15. Joseph Nechvatal, "How Alphonse Mucha's Smoking Designs Made Art Nouveau," Hyperallergenic, 9 January 2019, https://hyperallergic.com/478909/-how-alphonse-muchas-smoking-designs-made-art-nouveau/.
    16. "Italian-styled" comedy named after Pietro Germi's *Divorce Italian Style* (*Divorzio all'italiana*, 1961) that flourished from the late 1950s to the late 1970s.
    17. See: Adrian Luther Smith, op. cit., 50.
    18. Mikel J. Koven, op. cit., 10.
    19. Martha Hollander, "Vermeer's Empty Room," *Raritan* 10 (Fall 1990): 1–17, accessed online via EBSCOhost, 16 June 2019.
    20. Madlyn Millner Kahr, "Vermeer's 'Girl Asleep': A Moral Emblem," *Metropolitan Museum Journal*, 6 (1972), 116.
    21. *Ibid.*, 127.
    22. *Ibid.*, 128.
    23. *Ibid.*, 131.
    24. Martha Hollander, op. cit.
    25. Edward Snow, *A Study of Vermeer* (Berkeley: University of California Press, 1994), 58.
    26. *Ibid.*
    27. *Ibid.*
    28. *Ibid.*

29. Mikel J. Koven, op. cit., 9.
30. Mikel J. Koven, op. cit., 15. Kat Ellinger has also added to this list *A Quiet Place in the Country* (Un tranquillo posto di campagna, Elio Petri, 1968)—discussed in Chapter Eleven—and, even more fascinatingly, Carrado Farina's *Baba Yaga* (1973) which I agree shares some aspects of the giallo tradition "although the latter is more of an erotic mystery-type thriller, than a straight up giallo film." *All the Colours of Sergio Martino*, op. cit., 22.
31. Simon Houpt, *Museum of the Missing: A History of Art Theft* (New York: Sterling Publishing Co., 2006), 95.
32. Anthony Bailey, *A View of Delft: Vermeer Then and Now* (London: Chatto & Windus, 2001), 236.
33. Louis Paul, op. cit. 94.
34. Stephen Thrower, op. cit., 63.
35. Giuseppe Ungaretti, "Preface," in Roberta D'Adda, *Vermeer* (New York: Rizzoli, 2005), 11.
36. Martin Pops, *Vermeer: Consciousness and the Chamber of Being* (Ann Arbor: University of Michigan Research Press, 1984), 96.
37. Stephen Thrower, op. cit., 103.
38. Ivan Gaskell, *Vermeer's Wager: Speculations on Art History, Theory and Art Museums* (London: Reaktion Books, 2000), 48.
39. Famously, this musical motif was later used by Quentin Tarantino in *Kill Bill Volume 1* (2003).
40. Fulci would focus more explicitly on Poe's *The Black Cat* in his 1981 horror film of the same name starring Patrick Magee, Mimsy Farmer and David Warbeck. The Poe story also influenced Sergio Martino's *Your Vice Is a Locked Room and Only I Have the Key* (*Il tuo vizio è una stanza chiusa e solo io ne ho la chiave*, 1972), a film discussed at length in Chapter Seven. *Two Evil Eyes* (1990)—a project directed by Dario Argento and George A. Romero—was also based on the works of Poe, Argento's segment again being yet another reimagining of "The Black Cat."
41. Philip Steadman, *Vermeer's Camera: Uncovering the Truth Behind the Masterpieces* (Oxford, Oxford University Press, 2001), 62.
42. Anthony Bailey, op. cit., 223–225.
43. Anthony Bailey, op. cit., 223.
44. Roberta D'Adda, *Vermeer* (New York, Rizzoli, 2005), 138.
45. Martin Pops, op. cit., 80.
46. Adam Lowenstein, *Shocking Representation: Historical Trauma, National Cinema, and the Modern Horror Film* (New York: Columbia University Press, 2005), 48.
47. Wheeler Winston Dixon, "Surrealism and Sudden Death in the Films of Lucio Fulci," *Film International*, 24 December 2012 filmint.nu/?p=6616. Not everyone is as passionately convinced the painting's presence is central as my or Dixon's reading, however; Donato Totaro instead suggests that it "foreshadows the (minimally) apocalyptic landscape which the two 'survivors' (Warbeck and MacColl) find themselves in at the end of the film." Donato Totaro "*The Beyond*: Lucio Fulci's Zombie Masterpiece," *Offscreen*, 1.2 (July 1997) https://offscreen.com/view/the_beyond.

Chapter Four

1. Chris Shields "Art/Form: Fulci's Brush with Death," *Film Comment*, 24 July 2017, https://www.filmcomment.com/blog/artform-fulcis-brush-death/.
2. *Ibid.*
3. *Ibid.*
4. *Ibid.*
5. Elizabeth A. Fleming, "Britain," *Encyclopedia of Interior Design*, ed. Joanna Banham (London, Routledge, 1997), 188.
6. "Figure With Meat" (1954)," Art Institute of Chicago, no date, https://www.artic.edu/artworks/4884/figure-with-meat.
7. "Francis Bacon: Invisible Rooms," *Tate*, 22 January 2016, https://www.tate.org.uk/press/press-releases/francis-bacon-invisible-rooms-0.
8. Andrew Stewart MacKay, "A Five-Point Guide to the Work of Francis Bacon," *AnOther Magazine*, 4 May 2016, https://www.anothermag.com/art-photography/8644/a-five-point-guide-to-the-work-of-francis-bacon.
9. Michael Sevastakis, *Giallo Cinema and Its Folktale Roots: A Critical Study of 10 Films, 1962–1987* (Jefferson, NC: McFarland, 2016), 47.

10. Fèlix Fanés, "Film as Metaphor," in Dali & Film, London: Tate Publishing, 2007. 32–51., p. 46.

11. Francis Bacon (Archimbaud, 1993, 16); quoted in Susan Felleman, "Two-Way Mirror: Francis Bacon and the Deformation of Film," in Film, Art, New Media, ed. Angela Dalle Vacche (Houndsmills: Palgrave Macmillan, 2012), 221.

12. See, for example: Kim Newman, "Un Chien Andalou Review," Empire, 28 April 2006, https://www.empireonline.com/movies/reviews/un-chien-andalou-review/.

13. Gillian McIver, op. cit., 144.

14. Matthew Collings, op. cit., 69.

15. Zuzanna Stanska, "A Study of Loneliness and Isolation: The Man in Blue," Daily Art Magazine, 20 May 2018, https://www.dailyartmagazine.com/man-in-blue-by-francis-bacon/.

16. The director is clearly a strong influence on this film; elsewhere, a scene where Carol is attacked by bats also has more than a passing similarity to Hitchcock's *The Birds* (1963).

17. Mikel J. Koven, op. cit., 54.

18. Monstrous lesbians are not rare in *giallo* cinema, such as the killer lesbian in *The Killer Is on the Phone* (*L'assassino... è al telefono*, Alberto De Martino, 1972) and extreme violence committed against lesbian characters as 'punishment' is also not unusual, as seen in *The Killer Reserved Nine Seats* (*L'assassino ha riservato nove poltrone*, Giuseppe Bennati, 1974) or Dario Argento's *Tenebrae* (1982). Both *The Killer is on the Phone* and *The Killer Reserved Nine Seats* will be discussed further in Chapter Fourteen.

19. Beginning in the late 1960s, Bolkan was in a twenty-year relationship with photographer and film producer Countess Marina Cicogna. In her capacity in the latter, Cicogna was involved in producing two key early Bolkan films, Elio Petri's experimental polizietteschi/giallo hybrid *Investigation of a Citizen Above Suspicion* (*Indagine su un cittadino al di sopra di ogni sospetto*, 1970), and Luigi Bazzoni's later giallo *Footprints on the Moon* (*Le Orme*, 1975). See: Vanessa Grigoriadis, "Countess Marina Cicogna, a Woman of the World," *The New York Times*, 31 October 2013, https://www.nytimes.com/2013/10/31/t-magazine/-countess-marina-cicogna-a-woman-of-the-world.html.

20. Hunt (1992), op. cit., 72.

21. Joseph E. Dwyer, "Returning to Gialloville," Diabolique Magazine, 15 October 2019, https://diaboliquemagazine.com/returning-to-gialloville/

22. While I do not believe it is interlinked as directly with *A Lizard in a Woman's Skin* as some of the paintings discussed here, it may on the exploitation front be worth briefly mentioning the notorious dog vivisection scene from this film, which almost resulted in Fulci being imprisoned for two years for animal cruelty. The magistrate famously only rejectd the charges when special effects maestro Carlo Rimbaldi physically reconstructed one of the dogs using his original puppets and materials from the film in the courtroom (For more on this, see: Stephen Thrower, op. cit., 69–70). While not perhaps a direct reference, we can speculate that the passivity of the audience of the extreme horror of live animal vivisection in Émile Édouard Mouchy's shocking painting *A Physiological Demonstration with the Vivisection of a Dog* (1832) may have been what Fulci was riffing on to some degree.

Chapter Five

1. Quoted in Stephen Thrower, op. cit., 153.

2. *Suspiria* (1977), *Inferno* (1980) and *The Mother of Tears* (*La terza madre*, 2007).

3. Mikel Koven identifies *The Stendhal Syndrome* as a giallo (op. cit., 100), while it has been described explicitly as a "rape-revenge *giallo*" by Colette Jane Balmain, "Genre, Gender, Gialloi: The Disturbed Dreams of Dario Argento," PhD thesis, University of Greenwich, January 2004 (p. 29), https://gala.gre.ac.uk/id/eprint/5795/5/Colette%20Jane%20Balmain%202004%20-%20redacted.pdf.

4. Travis Crawford, "Argento on Stendhal: The Maestro of Mayhem Discusses His Newest Film The Stendhal Syndrome," *European Trash Cinema* 15 (1997), 25–28. 25.

5. *Ibid.*

6. Michael Sevastakis, "A Dangerous Mind: Dario Argento's *Opera* (1987)," *Kinoeye: New Perspectives on European Film*, 2.12 (24 June 2002) www.kinoeye.org/02/12/sevastakis12.php.

7. Chris Gallant, "The Art of Allusion: Painting, Murder and the 'Plan Tableau,'" in *Art of Darkness: The Cinema of Dario Argento*, ed. Chris Gallant (Godalming: FAB Press, 2001), 64.

8. Maitland McDonagh, *Broken Mirrors/Broken Minds*, op. cit., 239.

9. Ronny Swennson, op. cit., 41.

10. Stephane Derderian, "Entretien avec Dario Argento," *L'avant-scene Cinema* (March 2007): 6–9. Interview republished in L. Andrew Cooper, op. cit., 154.

11. Ibid.

12. Ibid., 152.

13. L. Andrew Cooper, op. cit., 2.

14. See, for example, Jacinda Read's *The New Avengers: Feminism, Feminity and the Rape-Revenge Cycle* (Manchester, UK: Manchester Univerity Press, 2000) and Claire Henry's *Revisionist Rape-Revenge: Redefining a Film Genre* (New York: Palgrave Macmillan, 2014), as well as significant sections of books including Rikke Schubart's *Super Bitches and Action Babes: The Female Hero in Popular Cinema, 1970–2006* (Jefferson, NC: McFarland, 2007) and Sarah Projansky's *Watching Rape: Film and Television in Postfeminist Culture* (New York University Press, 2001).

15. I have written two books on rape-revenge cinema, *Rape-Revenge Films: A Critical Study* (Jefferson, NC: McFarland, 2011) and *Ms. 45* (New York: Columbia UP/Wallflower, 2017).

16. See: Ronan Farrow, "From Aggressive Overtures to Sexual Assault: Harvey Weinstein's Accusers Tell Their Stories," *The New Yorker*, 23 October 2017, https://www.newyorker.com/news/news-desk/from-aggressive-overtures-to-sexual-assault-harvey-weinsteins-accusers-tell-their-stories.

17. Graziella Magherini, *La Sindrome di Stendhal* (Firenze: Ponte Alle Grazie, 1989).

18. Vivian Sobchack, *Carnal Thoughts: Embodiment and Moving Image Culture* (Berkeley: University of California Press, 2004), 25.

19. As the name suggests, the Stendhal Syndrome takes its name from French author Henri Stendhal who wrote about a series of traumatic physical and psychological sensations after viewing frescoes in Florence sometime in the early nineteenth century.

20. Colette Balmain, "Female Subjectivity and the Politics of 'Becoming Other': Dario Argento's *La Sindrome di Stendhal (The Stendhal Syndrome*, 1996)," *Kinoeye: New Perspectives on European Film*, 12.2 (2004) http://www.kineye.org/02/12/balmain12.php.

21. Diane Wolfthal, *Images of Rape: The 'Heroic' Tradition and Its Alternatives* (Cambridge: Cambridge University Press, 1999), 10.

22. Ibid.

23. Linda Badley, "Talking Heads, Unruly Women and Wound Culture: Dario Argento's *Trauma* (1993)," *Kinoeye: New Perspectives on European Film*, 12.2 (2002) http://www.kinoeye.org/02/12/badley12.php.

24. Sigmund Freud, "Medusa's Head (excerpt)," *The Medusa Reader*, eds. Marjorie Garber and Nancy J. Vickers (New York: Routledge, 2003), 84.

25. Claire Raymond, *The Posthumous Voice in Women's Writing from Mary Shelley to Sylvia Plath* (Aldershot: Ashgate, 2006), 206.

26. Ibid., 133.

27. Louis Marin, "To Destroy Painting (excerpt)," in *The Medusa Reader*, eds. Marjorie Garber and Nancy J. Vickers (New York: Routledge, 2003), 147.

28. Ibid., 144.

29. Linda Badley, Ibid.

30. Walter S. Gibson, *Bruegel* (London: Thames and Hudson, 1977), 40.

31. Colette Balmain (2004), op. cit.

32. Egbert Haverkamp-Begemann, *Rembrandt: The Night Watch* (Princeton, NJ: Princeton Univerity Press, 1982), 95.

33. Travis Crawford, op. cit., 25.

Chapter Six

1. This is an enduring horror motif in genre films surrounding art and artists including but not limited to Roger Corman's *A Bucket of Blood* (1959), *Color Me Blood Red* (Herschell Gordon Lewis, 1965), Hideshi Hino's last film in the

notorious Japanese *Guinea Pig* series *Mermaid in a Manhole* (1988) and Dan Gilroy's *Velvet Buzzsaw* (2019).

2. Lucas Balbo, "*L'Uccello dale piume di cristallo*," Fantasy Film Memory, 4/5 (1991), 10.

3. Alan Jones (2004), op. cit., 21.

4. Lucas Balbo, op. cit., 10.

5. Michel Weemans, "Pieter Bruegel's *Hunters in the Snow* and *Insidious Auceps* as Trap Images," in *Pieter Bruegel the Elder and Religion*, eds. Bertram Kaschek, Jürgen Müller, and Jessica Buskirk (Leiden: Brill, 2018), 245.

6. *Ibid.*, 246.

7. *Ibid.*, 265.

8. Alexia Kannas (*Deep Red*, 2017), op. cit., 69–70.

9. *Ibid.*, 70–71.

10. *Ibid.*

11. The casting of Hemmings, as has been broadly noted, evokes strong associations between *Deep Red* and Michelangelo Antonioni's *Blow Up* (1966) which Hemmings also starred, both films centred on the fallibility of perception by amateur detectives. See: *ibid.*, 81–82.

12. Again courtesy of Carlo Rambaldi, famous for his later work on Steven Spielberg's *E.T.: The Extraterrestrial* (1982) perhaps, but for our purposes a familiar name for having worked on Fulci's *A Lizard in a Woman's Skin*, discussed previously.

13. As Kannas notes, there are various cuts of the film, and not all include this sequence, either due to pan-and-scanning or due to low quality image reproductions. See: Alexia Kannas (Deep Red, 2017), op. cit., 77.

14. *Ibid.*

15. Maitland McDonagh, *Broken Mirrors/Broken Minds*, op. cit., 114.

16. For more on Bartoli's donation to the film, see Antonio Nalli, "Profondo Rosso e i suoi quadri: l'arte del maestro Francesco Bartoli che stregò Dario Argento e lasciò con il fiato sospeso il mondo intero," Biro: Una penna che non scrive e una vita che non vive, 4 November 2012, https://antonionalli.wordpress.com/2012/11/04/profondo-rosso-e-i-suoi-quadri-larte-del-maestro-francesco-bartoli-che-strego-dario-argento-e-lascio-con-il-fiato-sospeso-il-mondo-intero/.

17. Discovered quite literally the day before I submitted the manuscript of this book to my publisher, Letícia Badan Palhares Knauer de Campos's 2017 master's dissertation "A cultura visual no cinema de Dario Argento" offers an in-depth exploration not only for Bartoli and Enrico Colombotto Rosso in regard to *Deep Red*, but on the visual arts on Argento's work more broadly. Despite my inability to read Portuguese this is clearly an impressive donation to Argento studies at the intersection of art history, and it is dearly hoped this work is translated into English. For those fortunate enough to read Portuguese, the thesis in full can be found online here "A cultura visual no cinema de Dario Argento," 2017, Universidade Estadual de Campinas, Instituto de Filosofia e Ciências Humanas, Campinas, Brazil http://repositorio.unicamp.br/jspui/bitstream/REPOSIP/322713/1/Campos_LeticiaBadanPalharesKnauerDe_M.pdf (and a sincere apology to the author that I did not have time to get her work translated in full to use further in this book!).

18. Daniele Abbiati, "Guanti, corvi, pupazzi: viaggio allucinante nelle tenebre di Dario Argento," *Il Giornale*, 2 February 2017 www.ilgiornale.it/news/spettacoli/guanti-corvi-pupazzi-viaggio-allucinante-nelle-tenebre-dario-1358585.htmlwww.ilgiornale.it/news/spettacoli/-guanti-corvi-pupazzi-viaggio-allucinante-nelle-tenebre-dario-1358585.html.

19. See: Frances K. Barasch, *The Grotesque: A Study in Meanings* (The Hague: Mouton, 1971).

20. Wilson Yates, "An Introduction to the Grotesque: Theoretical and Theological Considerations," in *The Grotesque in Art and Literature: Theological Reflections*, eds. James Luther Adams and Wilson Yates (Grand Rapids, MI: William B. Eerdmans Publishing Company, 1997), 2.

21. See: Mikhail Bakhtin, *Rabelais and his World* (Bloomington: Indiana University Press, 1984).

22. While there are many examples of this, the collection *Transnational Horror Cinema: Bodies of Excess and the Global Grotesque* edited by Sophia Siddique, Raphael Raphael (London: Palgrave

Macmllan, 2016) perhaps most immediately demonstrates its diversity.
23. Paul Wells, *The Horror Genre: From Beelzebub to Blair Witch* (London and New York: Wallflower, 2000), 114.
24. As Adrian Luther Smith also notes, *My Dear Killer* also predates a "repellent child-killer theme with the following year's Don't Torture a Duckling and Who Saw Her Die," op. cit., 77.

Chapter Seven

1. Kamilla Elliott, *Portraiture and British Gothic Fiction: The Rise of Picture Identification 1764–1835* (Baltimore: The John Hopkins University Press, 2012), 2.
2. *Ibid.*
3. *Ibid.*, 5.
4. *Ibid.*
5. *Ibid.*, 6.
6. Michael Walker, *Hitchcock's Motifs* (Amsterdam University Press, 2005), Ebook (no page).
7. Steven Jacobs and Lisa Colpaert, op. cit.
8. Susan Felleman (2006), op. cit., 17.
9. *Ibid.*
10. *Ibid.*, 24.
11. Robert Mahoney "The Legend Picture in *Red Queen Kills Seven Times* (1972): An Example of the Instrumentation of 'Vigilogogy,'" rmarts: reviews of contemporary art, culture and agency theory, 26 November 2017, https://rjamahoncy.wordpress.com/2017/11/26/the-legend-picture-in-red-queen-kills-seven-times-1972-an-example-of-the-instrumentation-of-vigilogogy/.
12. *Ibid.*
13. *Ibid.*
14. *Ibid.*
15. Kat Ellinger, *All the Colours of Sergio Martino*, op. cit, 25.
16. *Ibid.*, 24.
17. The cat in Michele Soavi's *Stage Fright (Deliria*, 1987) is called Lucifer, perhaps a subtle reference to Martino's earlier film.
18. Kier-La Janisse, *House of Psychotic Women: An Autobiographical Topography of Female Neurosis in Horror and Exploitation Film* (Godalming: FAB Press, 2012), 42.

Chapter Eight

1. For more on this category, see Austin Fisher (2016), op. cit.
2. Particularly Viktor Shklovsky, *Theory of Prose* (Elmwood Park, IL: Dalkey Archive Press, 1993). First published in 1925.
3. Carlo Ginzburg, "Making It Strange: The Prehistory of a Literary Device," in *Wooden Eyes: Nine Reflections on Distance* (New York: Columbia University Press, 2001), 7.
4. Anne Billson, op. cit.
5. This is, I believe, the direct Italian translation, rather than that which appears on subtitled English language versions.
6. Mikel J. Koven, op. cit., 120.
7. *Ibid.*
8. Valentina Liepa, "The Image of Saint Sebastian in Art," *Acta Humanitarica Universitatis Saulensis*, 8 (2009), 455–6.
9. *Ibid.*, 456.
10. *Ibid.*
11. Bill Goldstein, "Castanets in a Snowstorm," *The New York Times*, 18 November 2001, https://www.nytimes.com/2001/11/18/books/castanets-in-a-snowstorm.html.
12. See: Charles Darwent, "Arrows of Desire: How Did St Sebastian Become an Enduring, Homo-erotic Icon?," *The Independent*, 10 February 2008, https://www.independent.co.uk/arts-entertainment/art/features/arrows-of-desire-how-did-st-sebastian-become-an-enduring-homo-erotic-icon-779388.html.
13. Richard Dyer, "The House with the Laughing WIndows" in *Directory of World Cinema: Italy*, ed. Louis Bayman (Bristol: Intellect Books, 2011), 144.
14. Mikel J. Koven, op. cit., 108.
15. Richard Dyer, op. cit., 144.

Chapter Nine

1. Susan Felleman (2006), op. cit., 140.
2. Doris Berger, *Projected Art History: Biopics, Celebrity Culture, and the Popularization of American Art* (New York: Bloomsbury, 2014), 1.
3. Vito Adriaensens, "Women, or

Wax? Eros, Thanatos, and Sculpture in Cinema," in *Sculpture, Sexuality and History: Encounters in Literature, Culture and the Arts*, eds. Jana Funke and Jen Grove (Basingstoke: Palgrave Macmillan, 2019), 96.
    4. *Ibid.*, 100.
    5. Quoted in Barry Schwabsky, "Little Resistance to Gravity: On Lynda Benglis and David Hammons," *The Nation*, 28 March 2011, https://www.thenation.com/article/little-resistance-gravity-lynda-benglis-and-david-hammons/.
    6. See: John-Paul Stonard "Abstract expressionism—not just macho heroes with brushes," *The Guardian*, 3 September 2016., https://www.theguardian.com/artanddesign/2016/sep/03/abstract-expressionism-not-just-macho-heroes-with-brushes.
    7. Tyler Coates, "When Hitchcock Went Gay: 'Strangers On A Train' and 'Rope,'" *Decider*, 11 August 2014, https://decider.com/2014/08/11/alfred-hitchcock-gay-strangers-on-a-train-and-rope/.

Chapter Ten

    1. Nor is it purely fictional. Yoni art has long involved the use of menstrual fluid, an art practice recently updated and granted widespread media attention through the work of American artist Sarah Levy who paints portraits of President Donald Trump with her period blood. Carolee Schneemann used the artist's menstrual blood in her artwork *Blood Diary Work* (1972), and other artworks involving menstruation include Leslie Labowitz's performance piece *Menstruation-Wait* (1971) and Judy Chicago's *Red Flag* (1971) and *Menstruation Bathroom* (1972). New York artist Vincent Castiglia is also renowned for using human blood in his paintings.
    2. Griselda Pollock, "Artists, Mythologies and Media—Genius, Madness and Art History," *Screen*, 21.3 (Autumn 1980), 64.
    3. *Ibid.*, 65.
    4. *Ibid.*
    5. "The theory that achieving something great requires suffering dates back to ancient times. The Greek myth of Philoctetes tells the story of a man who as a result of a wound, is exiled on an island, and during that time he invents the bow and arrow from scraps of material he finds in a cave. His invention becomes an important weapon used by the Greeks in their battles. Philoctetes is a figure who exists in the margins, much like all artists. His wound (a symbol of his emotional suffering) is the reason he is excluded from society but also seen as the facilitator for his invention, which in turn fulfils his deep longing for social acceptance." See: Yashi Banymadhub "The Tortured Artist Is a Dangerous Myth. It's the Way Creative Workers Are Treated That Causes Breakdown," *The Independent*, Wednesday 10 October 2018, https://www.independent.co.uk/voices/world-mental-health-day-tortured-artist-dangerous-myth-pain-art-depression-suicide-a8576971.html.

Chapter Eleven

    1. In keeping with the giallo tradition to cast foreign actors in their films, Petri had initially considered Jack Nicholson for the role of Leonardo. See: Pasquale Iannone, "*Un tranquillo posto di campagna/A Quiet Place in the Country*," *Senses of Cinema*, 67 (July 2013) sensesofcinema.com/2013/uncategorized/un-tranquillo-posto-di-campagnaa-quiet-day-in-the-country/.
    2. "Journey Into Madness" featurette, *A Quiet Day in the Country*, Scream Factory home entertainment release (2017).
    3. Fernando Gabriel Pagnoni Berns and Leonardo Acosta Lando, "Translating Kafka into Italian: Kafkaesque Themes in Elio Petri's Films," in *Mediamorphosis: Kafka and the Moving Image*, eds. Shai Biderman and Ido Lewit (New York: Columbia University Press, 2016), 295–306. 295–6.
    4. "Elio Petri: Cinema Is Not for an Elite, But for the Masses," *Art Politics Cinema: The Cineaste Interviews*, eds. Dan Georgakas and Lenny Rubenstien (London: Pluto Press, 1984), 53.
    5. Fernando Gabriel Pagnoni Berns and Leonardo Acosta Lando, op. cit., 302.
    6. *Ibid.*

7. David Stuart Davies, "Introduction," in *The Dead of Night: The Ghost Stories of Oliver Onions* (Ware: Wordsworth Editions, 2010), ix.

8. Luciano Vincenzoni was a successful writer in his own right, having written over sixty screenplays in the second half of the twentieth century including perhaps most famously co-writing Sergio Leone's *For a Few Dollars More* (1965) and *The Good, the Bad and the Ugly* (1966).

9. Anthony J. Fonesca, "Beckoning Fair One, The," in *Ghosts in Popular Culture and Legend*, eds. June Michele Pulliam and Anthony J. Fonseca (Santa Barbara: Greenwood, 2016), 19.

10. Fernando Gabriel Pagnoni Berns and Leonardo Acosta Lando, op. cit., 303.

11. *Ibid.*

12. *Ibid.*

13. *Ibid.*

14. Roberto Curti (2015), op. cit., 179.

15. For Larry Portis, "ostensibly, the film is about a successful artist in the abstract expressionist vein." See: Larry Portis, "The Director Who Must (Not?) Be Forgotten: Elio Petri and the Legacy of Italian Political Cinema, Part 1," *Film International*, 21 June 2011 filmint.nu/?p=2448.

16. "Journey Into Madness," op. cit.

17. Chris Nashawaty, "Murder, Italian Style: A Primer on the Giallo Film Genre," *Vulture*, 18 July 2019, https://www.vulture.com/2019/07/giallo-italian-film-guide.html.

18. David Charles Fox, "Comparing Abstract Expressionism and Pop Art," *DavidCharlesFox.com*, 14 October 2016, https://davidcharlesfox.com/comparing-abstract-expressionism-pop-art/.

19. Quoted in *The World Goes Pop*, eds. Jessica Morgan and Flavia Frigeri (New Haven: Yale University Press, 2015), 123.

20. Franco Nero shared more information about his work with Dine: "United Artists, which was the movie's global distributor, sent to Veneto, where we were shooting, a young American, a bit of an avant-garde painter, to tech me how to paint." He continues, "This painter, of course, was with me for a long time, and I would follow him. I remember him doing a painting, then he would put a shoe on it, then a shoelace—he was really strange, this painter. Well, anyway, working with him in the end, I became quite good at painting. At the end of the movie, the painter had completed about ten paintings. And he asked Elio Petri and me, "Do you want to buy them?" "How Much?" "$10,000." So, thousands of dollars each, and we are talking in '68. Obviously, we told him off. Actually, I even told him "I'm better than you, get lost!." Well, then the movie is released. Two years later I am in Paris at a gallery and I see his name. So I ask the gallery manager, "What about this one." "This one is a young American painter who is doing very well." A year later, I am in New York, in the Fifth Avenue. There is a big billboard, one of those banners they put in the streets, There was his name, Jim Dine. "Damn it," I said, "Imagine if I had bought those paintings!." Instead, the next year, I ended up buying some fake paintings and I lost everything." See: "Journey Into Madness," op. cit.

21. Quoted in Larry Portis, op. cit.

22. Quoted in Larry Portis, op. cit.

23. Larry Portis, op. cit.

24. Jean A. Gili, "Rencontre avec Elio Petri," in *Elio Petri*, ed. Jean A. Gili (Nice: Faculté des Lettres et Science Humaines, Section d'Histoire, 1974).

25. Larry Portis, op. cit.

26. "Elio Petri: Cinema Is Not for an Elite, but for the Masses," op. cit., 55.

27. *Ibid.*

28. *Ibid.*

29. *Ibid.*

Chapter Twelve

1. Tim Lucas, op. cit., 544.

2. With its Italian title literally translating to "The Girl with the Yellow Pajamas," Mogherini's film specifically refers to an Australian true crime case from the 1930s where an initially unidentified woman was put on public display in hopes of gaining information about her, notable only for her distinctive yellow pajamas. While her identity has since been debated, police identified her as Linda Agostini and her husband Antonio Agostini was convicted of the crime and deported back to Italy. For

more on the film and the case it is based on, see my previous works; my booklet essay "Stranger Than Fiction: Immigration, Alienation, and the Real Pyjama Girl" that was included with Arrow Video's 2018 Blu-ray release of the film, and "The Unknown Soldier of the War Against Women," *Overland Literary Journal*, 30 July 2014, https://overland.org.au/2014/07/the-unknown-soldier-of-the-war-against-women/.

3. Leon Hunt (1992), op. cit., 72.

4. See: Alexandra Heller-Nicholas, *Suspiria* (Leighton Buzzard: Auteur, 2015), 73.

5. Alexia Kannas ("All the Colours of the Dark" 2017), op. cit., 174.

6. Rolando Caputo, op. cit., 58.

7. *Ibid.*

8. Stephen Thrower, op. cit., 64.

9. *Ibid.*

10. *Ibid.*

11. *Ibid.*

12. *Ibid.*

13. Gundrun D. Whitehead and Julia Petrov, "Introduction," in *Fashioning Horror: Dressing to Kill on Screen and in Literature*, eds. Julia Petrov and Gundrun D. Whitehead (London: Bloomsbury, 2018), 6.

14. *Ibid.*

15. Laura Mulvey, "Visual Pleasure and Narrative Cinema," in *The Sexual Subject: A Screen Reader in Sexuality* (New York: Routledge, 1992), 27. Originally published *Screen*, 16.3 (October 1975): 6–18.

16. Howard Hughes, *Cinema Italiano: The Complete Guide from Classics to Cult* (London: I.B. Tauris, 2011), 224–226.

17. Gundrun D. Whitehead and Julia Petrov, op. cit., 5–6.

18. Michael Sevastakis (2016), op. cit., 138.

19. Argento's segment in his 1990 horror collaboration with George A. Romero *Two Evil Eyes*—"The Black Cat"— also features a character based on the famous American photographer Weegee. Maitland McDonagh, *Broken Mirrors/Broken Minds*, op. cit., 246.

20. Anandi Ramamurthy, "Spectacles and Illusions: Photography and Commodity Culture," in *Photography: A Critical Introduction*, ed. Liz Wells (London: Routledge, 2003), 221.

21. A regular feature of the profiles that make up sadly now defunct *The Giallo Files* blog, for example, is the endlessly captivating "Fashion Moment" section that outlines the highlights the kitsch fashion highlight of each film. In the case of *Smile Before Death* (*Il sorriso della iena*, Silvio Amadio, 1974), for example, they write "Smile Before Death lets you know right off the bat that it's a giallo, by showing a wounded, bloody Dorothy writhing on the floor in this frilly yellow ("giallo") housecoat. Or maybe it's an evening gown. It's hard to tell." See: "Smile Before Death," *The Giallo Files*, June 2014, giallofiles.blogspot.com/2014/06/smile-before-death.html.

22. John Ingledew, *Photography* (London: Laurence King Publishing in Association with Central Saint Martins College of Art & Design, 2005), 66.

23. *Ibid.*

24. Rosetta Brookes, "Fashion Photography: The Double-Page Spread: Helmut Newton, Guy Bourdin & Deborah Turbeville," in *Chic Thrills: A Fashion Reader*, eds. Juliet Ash and Elizabeth Wilson (Berkeley: University of California Press, 1992), 17.

25. Susan Sontag, *On Photography* (London: Penguin Books, 2008), 7.

26. Gaby Wood, "Death Becomes Her," *The Guardian*, 14 April 2003, https://www.theguardian.com/theobserver/2003/apr/13/features.review27.

27. Natalia Borecka, "The Sinister Sexuality of Guy Bourdin, a Deeply Troubled Genius," *Lone Wolf Magazine*, 11 November 2014, https://lonewolfmag.com/sinister-sexuality-guy-bourdin-photographer/.

28. *Ibid.*

29. Donna de Ville, "Menopausal Monsters and Sexual Transgression in Argento's Art Horror," in *Cinema Inferno: Celluloid Explosions from the Cultural Margins*, eds. Robert G. Weiner and John Cline (Lanham: The Scarecrow Press, Inc. 2010), 71.

30. Leon Hunt (1992), op. cit., 72.

31. *Ibid.*

32. *Ibid.*

33. *Ibid.*

34. Michael Sevastakis (2016), op. cit, 192.

35. Christine Moneera Laennec, "The

'Assembly-Line Love Goddess': Women and the Machine Aesthetic in Fashion Photography, 1918–1940," in *Bodily Discursions: Genders, Representations, Technologies*, eds. Deborah S. Wilson and Christine Moneera Laennec (Albany: State University of New York Press, 1997), 81.

36. John Ingledew, op. cit., 66.
37. Alan Jones, "Argento," *Cinefantastique* 13.6/14.1 (1983): 20.
38. Élie Castiel, "Dario Argento," *Sequences: La Revue de Cinema* 167 (November-December 1993): 8–9. Republished in L. Andrew Cooper, op. cit., 150.
39. Alan Jones (2004), op. cit., 21.
40. Marcia Landy, op. cit., 101.
41. Michael Mackenzie, "Gender, Genre and Sociocultural Change in the giallo," PhD thesis, Department of Theatre, Film and Television Studies School of Culture and Creative Arts University of Glasgow August 2013 http://theses.gla.ac.uk/4730/1/2013Mackenziephd.pdf.
42. Ian Olney, op. cit., 121.
43. Ian Olney, op. cit., 11.
44. This is a central argument of my 2011 book *Rape-Revenge Films: A Critical Study* (Jefferson, NC: McFarland).
45. See: Patrik Aspers, *Markets in Fashion: A Phenomenological Approach* (New York: Routledge, 2006), 60.

Chapter Thirteen

1. Christopher Ames, *Movies About the Movies: Hollywood Reflected* (Lexington: The University of Kentucky Press, 1997), 3.
2. Tom Gunning, "The Cinema of Attraction[s]: Early Film, Its Spectator and the Avant- Garde," in *The Cinema of Attractions Reloaded*, ed. Wanda Strauven. Amsterdam: Amsterdam University Press, 2006), 382.
3. Fernando Ramos Arenas, "Towards a Generic Understanding of the Giallo: Crime-Horror Hybrids in Italian Cinema of the 1970s," in *Genre Hybridisation: Global Cinematic Flow*, eds. Ivo Ritzer and Peter W. Schulze (Marburgh: Schuren Verlag, 2013), 90.
4. Alan Jones (2004), op. cit., 159.
5. Michael Sevastakis (2016), op. cit., 174.
6. Marcia Landy, op. cit., 97.
7. Christopher Ames, op. cit., 3.
8. *Ibid.*, 5.
9. *Ibid.*, 6.
10. Adrian Luther Smith, op. cit., 23.
11. Mikel J. Koven, op. cit., 137.
12. Ian Olney, op. cit., 128.
13. The date of Festa's debut film *Gipsy Rose* is unclear; while Louis Paul dates it as 1994, IMDB.com has it as a 1990 release. Paul describes *Gipsy Angel* as "an overlong but admirable attempt at a romantic thriller in the *giallo* mold, but the quick cuts and music video–like editing distracts from the core plot about a disillusioned pop starlet who stumbles onto a deadly mystery." While his sophomore feature *Fatal Frames* therefore shares much with this previous effort, Paul is less enthusiastic about the end result; "At well over two hours, the film stumbles chaotically until its mind-blowing finale, which makes as little sense as everything that had come before. *Fotogrammi Mortali* is one of the most unusual and failed Italian horror films." Louis Paul, op. cit., 204.
14. Christopher Ames, op. cit., 8.
15. Louis Paul, op. cit., 55.
16. Ruby Helms, "It's a Man's World: Marlene Dietrich and Her Cross-Dressing Wardrobe," *The Costume Society*, 24 June 2016 costumesociety.org.uk/blog/post/-its-a-mans-world-marlene-dietrich-and-her-cross-dressing-wardrobe.
17. "MIFF Talks | Peter Strickland In Conversation," Melbourne International Film Festival, Wheeler Centre, Melbourne, 4 August 2019. Posted to YouTube, 3 September 2019, https://www.youtube.com/watch?v=yKSgwn7EScY.
18. Basia Lewandowska Cummings, "Foley Cow! Berberian Sound Studio Director Peter Strickland Interviewed," *The Quietus*, 31 August 2012, https://thequietus.com/articles/09874-peter-strickland-interview-berberian-sound-studio.
19. *Ibid.*
20. *Ibid.*
21. Christopher Ames, op. cit., 6.

Chapter Fourteen

1. André Loiselle, *Theatricality in the Horror Film: A Brief Study on the Dark*

Pleasures of Screen Artifice (London: Anthem Press, 2020), 49.

2. *Ibid.*, 8.

3. A short note on the word "actress"; while I personally believe job titles should not be indiscriminately gendered between actor/actress (we do not, for example, talk about teacheresses, doctoresses or bakeresses), within the film itself Eleanor's job is described in the English translation as an "actress" and I have kept this loyal to the original text. It is also of note that in my own experience as a film journalist, many women in the profession prefer the term "actress" over "actor" and thus it is respectful not to change the term if it is clear one is preferred over the other.

4. Samm Deighan, "31 Days of Gialloween: *The Killer Is on the Phone* (1972)," *Diabolique Magazine*, 15 October 2018, https://diaboliquemagazine.com/31-days-of-gialloween-the-killer-is-on-the-phone-1972/.

5. The lesbian "twist" at the end of *The Killer Is on the Phone* is no doubt building on Heywood's reputation for queer film subjects based on her most famous film role, the controversial 1967 Mark Rydell film *The Fox* co-starring Sandy Dennis, a screen adaptation of D.H. Lawrence's 1923 novella of the same name. Heywood would appear in a number of other Italian exploitation films during this period including the horror movie *Ring of Darkness* (*Un'ombra nell'ombra*, Pier Carpi, 1979) and, perhaps most famously, nunsploitation films such as *The Nun and the Devil* (*Le monache di Sant'Arcangelo*, Paolo Dominici, 1973) and *The Nun of Monza* (*La monaca di Monza*, Eriprando Visconti, 1969).

6. Samm Deighan, "31 Days of Gialloween," op. cit.

7. Erik Piepenburg, "Evil Stalks the Stage: It's Curtains!," *New York Times*, 15 May 2014, https://www.nytimes.com/2014/05/18/movies/horror-films-set-in-the-world-of-theater.J.html.

8. Mikel Koven discusses the influence of *gialli* on slashers at length in the final chapter of *La Dolce Morte: Vernacular Cinema and the Italian Giallo Film* (2006).

9. André Loiselle, "*Cinéma du Grand Guignol*: Theatricality in the Horror Film," in *Stages of Reality: Theatricality in Cinema*, eds. Loiselle, André, and Jeremy Maron (University of Toronto Press, 2000), 65.

10. *Ibid.*, 75.

11. Kat Ellinger, "31 Days of Gialloween: Stage Fright (1987)," *Diabolique Magazine*, 8 October 2018, https://diaboliquemagazine.com/31-days-of-gialloween-stage-fright-1987/.

12. I have written extensively on the specific use of the owl as a symbol in *Stage Fright* in my book *Masks in Horror Cinema: Eyes Without Faces* (Cardiff: University of Wales Press, 2019).

13. This is not the first time the Hollywood icon has appeared in a Lamberto Bava film. In *You'll Die at Midnight* (*Morirai a mezzanotte*, 1986) a large blown-up photograph features in an apartment living room (the same location is also used in Ruggero Deodato's *Phantom of Death*, which also emphasizes the Monroe mural as its central, striking *mise-en-scène* element).

14. As Carol J. Clover defines the Final Girl, "She is the one who encounters the mutilated bodies of her friends and perceives the full extent of the proceeding horror and her own peril; who is chased, cornered, wounded; whom we see Scream, stagger, fall, rise and Scream again. She is abject terror personified. If her friends knew they were about to die only seconds before the event, the Final Girl lives with the knowledge for long minutes or hours. She alone looks death in the face, but she alone also finds the strength either to stay the killer long enough to be rescued (ending A) or kill him herself (ending B)." Clover, Carol J., *Men, Women and Chainsaws: Gender in the Modern Horror Film* (New Jersey: Princeton University Press, 1992), 35.

15. André Loiselle (2000), op. cit., 74.

16. *Ibid.*

17. *Ibid.*

18. *Ibid.*

19. In true slasher style, however, the seemingly dead Wallace is shown opening his eyes suddenly just before the film finishes, cutting back to an image of the saxophone playing Monroe look alike, the image that the film's credits run over. This is, after all, Soavi seems to be reminding us, a film about not just the fantastic in

Chapter Fifteen

1. "Remembering She—A Cathedral 3.6.2018–10.32019," Moderna Museet, no date, https://www.modernamuseet.se/stockholm/en/exhibitions/remembering-she-a-cathedral/.
2. Ibid.
3. Annika Öhrner, "Niki de Saint Phalle Playing with the Feminine in the Male Factory: HON—en katedral," Stedelijk Studies, 7 (Fall 2018), https://stedelijkstudies.com/journal/niki-de-saint-phalle-playing-with-the-feminine-in-the-male-factory-hon-en-katedral/.
4. "Remembering She—A Cathedral 3.6.2018–10.32019," op. cit.
5. Rudolf Arnheim, "Film and Reality," in *Film Theory and Criticism—Introductory Readings*, ed. Leo Braudy, 5th edition (New York: Oxford University Press, 1999), 312–321. https://culturetechnologypolitics.files.wordpress.com/2015/11/arnheim-film-and-reality.pdf.
6. Luca M. Palamerini and Mistretta Gaetano, *Spaghetti Nightmares: Italian Fantasy-Horror as Seen Through the Eyes of their Protagonists* (Key West: Fantasma Books, 1996), 47.
7. Adrian Luther Smith, op. cit., 89.
8. Benjamin Halligan, "The Perfume of the Lady in Black (1974)," in *Eaten Alive: Italian Cannibal and Zombie Movies*, ed. Jay Slater (London: Plexus, 2002) pp. 54–55.
9. Samm Deighan also suggests that the film may be "a riff on Patrick Hamilton's play *Gaslight* (1938)—adapted to the screen by Thorold Dickinson in 1940 and George Cukor in 1944—where a woman's husband slowly, subtly begins to isolate her and drive her mad. Mimsy Farmer played a number of these fragile characters pushed to the brink of madness, as in Dario Argento's *4 mosche di velluto grigio* (*Four Flies on Grey Velvet*, 1971) and Armando Crispino's *Macchie solari* (*Autopsy*, 1975). In these roles, her characters are intimately connected with violence, childhood trauma and abusive parent–child relationships."

Samm Deighan, "All Mimsy Were the Borogoves: The Spectre of Lewis Carroll in Francesco Barilli's *The Perfume of the Lady in Black* (1974)," *Senses of Cinema*, 86 (March 2018 sensesofcinema.com/2018/alice-in-wonderland/all-mimsy-were-the-borogoves-the-spectre-of-lewis-carroll-in-francesco-barillis-the-perfume-of-the-lady-in-black-1974/.
10. For more information, see the collection *Eaten Alive! Italian Cannibal and Zombie Movies* edited by Jay Slater (London: Plexus, 2005).
11. Terry Hale, "Afterword," in Gaston Leroux, *The Perfume of the Lady in Black* (Sawtry: Dedalus, 1998), 245. These masterworks in this category are of course Edgar Allan Poe's *The Murder in the Rue Morgue* (1841) and Arthur Conan Doyle's *The Adventure of the Speckled Band* (1892) and *The Adventure of the Crooked Man* (1893).
12. Gaston Leroux, *The Perfume of the Lady in Black* (Sawtry: Dedalus, 1998), 103.
13. Ibid., 150.
14. Ann C. Hall, *Phantom Variations: The Adaptations of Gaston Leroux's Phantom of the Opera, 1925 to the Present* (Jefferson, NC: McFarland, 2009), 15.
15. Samm Deighan, "All Mimsy Were the Borogoves," op. cit.
16. Kier-La Janisse, op. cit. 57.
17. Mario Terci, "What Is Alice, What Is This Thing, Who Are You?: The Reasons of the Body in Alice," in Rachel Fordyce and Carla Marella (eds.), *Semiotics and Linguistics in Alice's World* (Berlin: Walter de Gruyter & Co., 1994), 70.
18. Quoted in the featurette "Ritrato in Nero" on the 2004 Raro Video home entertainment release of *The Perfume of the Lady in Black*.
19. Kamilla Elliot, Rethinking the Novel/Film Debate (Cambridge: Cambridge University Press, 2003), 187.
20. Ibid., 186.
21. Samm Deighan, "All Mimsy Were the Borogoves," op. cit.
22. Ibid.
23. "Ritrato in Nero," op. cit.
24. "Ritrato in Nero," op. cit.
25. Samm Deighan, "All Mimsy Were the Borogoves," op. cit.
26. "Ritrato in Nero," op. cit.
27. "Ritrato in Nero," op. cit.

Conclusion

1. Jim Harper, *Legacy of Blood: A Comprehensive Guide to Slasher Movies* (Manchester: Critical Vision, 2009), 9.
2. Nicholas Caruso, "Celebrating 'Style Over Substance' in Horror," *Birth.Movies.Death*, 29 November 2018, https://birthmoviesdeath.com/2018/11/29/celebrating-style-over-substance-in-horror.
3. Virginie Sélavy, "Interview with Hélène Cattet and Bruno Forzani," *Electric Sheep: A Deviant View of Cinema*, 10 April 2014 www.electricsheepmagazine.co.uk/2014/04/10/interview-with-helene-cattet-and-bruno-forzani/.
4. *Ibid.*
5. *Ibid.*
6. *Ibid.*
7. *Ibid.*
8. Alexandra Heller-Nicholas, "MIFF Talks | Peter Strickland In Conversation," op. cit.
9. Anton Bitel, "Interview: Bruno Forzani and Hélène Cattet," *Projected Figures*, 2 July 2014, https://projectedfigures.com/2014/07/02/interview-bruno-forzani-and-helene-cattet.
10. *Ibid.*
11. *Ibid.*
12. As noted previously, Mikel J. Koven examines this connection in-depth in the final chapter of *La Dolce Morte: Vernacular Cinema and the Italian Giallo Film*, op. cit.
13. Donald Clarke, "The Neon Demon review: Ban this slick filth!," *The Irish Times*, 7 July 2016, https://www.irishtimes.com/culture/film/the-neon-demon-review-ban-this-slick-filth-1.2713514.
14. Henry Fuseli, "Aphorisms on Art," in *The Gothic Reader: A Critical Anthology*, ed. Martin Myrone; consultant ed. Christopher Frayling (London: Tate Publishing, 2006), 242.

Bibliography

Adriaensens, Vito. "Women, or Wax? Eros, Thanatos, and Sculpture in Cinema," in *Sculpture, Sexuality and History: Encounters in Literature, Culture and the Arts*, eds. Jana Funke and Jen Grove (Basingstoke: Palgrave Macmillan, 2019), 81–101.
Allen, Brian T. "'Bruegel: The Hand of the Master' Makes Its Debut," *National Review*, 22 December 2018, https://www.nationalreview.com/2018/12/art-review-pieter-bruegel-vienna-showcase-a-success/#slide-1.
Allen, Steven, and Laura Hubner. "Introduction," in *Framing Film: Cinema and the Visual Arts*, eds. Steven Allen and Laura Hubner (Bristol: Intellect, 2012), 1–36.
Ames, Christopher. *Movies about the Movies: Hollywood Reflected* (Lexington: University of Kentucky Press, 1997).
Andersen, Nathan. *Shadow Philosophy: Plato's Cave and Cinema* (Abingdon, UK: Routledge, 2014).
Andrew, Dudley (ed.). *The Image in Dispute: Art and Cinema in the Age of Photography* (Austin: University of Texas Press, 1997).
Arenas, Fernando Ramos. "Towards a Generic Understanding of the Giallo: Crime-Horror Hybrids in Italian Cinema of the 1970s," in *Genre Hybridisation: Global Cinematic Flow*, eds. Ivo Ritzer and Peter W. Schulze (Marburgh: Schuren Verlag, 2013), 81–91.
Arnheim, Rudolf. "Film and Reality," in *Film Theory and Criticism—Introductory Readings*, ed. Leo Braudy, 5th edition (New York: Oxford University Press, 1999), 312–321, https://culturetechnologypolitics.files.wordpress.com/2015/11/arnheim-film-and-reality.pdf.
Aspers, Patrik. *Markets in Fashion: A Phenomenological Approach* (New York: Routledge, 2006).
Badley, Linda. "Talking Heads, Unruly Women and Wound Culture: Dario Argento's *Trauma* (1993)," *Kinoeye: New Perspectives on European Film*, 12.2 (2002) http://www.kinoeye.org/02/12/badley12.php
Bailey, Anthony. *A View of Delft: Vermeer Then and Now* (London: Chatto & Windus, 2001).
Bakhtin, Mikhail. *Rabelais and his World* (Bloomington: Indiana University Press, 1984).
Bal, Mieke. *Looking In: The Art of Viewing* (Amsterdam: G+B Arts, 2001).
Balbo, Lucas. "*L'Uccello dale piume di cristallo*," Fantasy Film Memory, 4/5 (1991), 10–12.
Balmain, Colette. "Female Subjectivity and the Politics of 'Becoming Other': Dario Argento's *La Sindrome di Stendhal* (*The Stendhal Syndrome*, 1996)," *Kinoeye: New Perspectives on European Film*, 12.2 (2004) http://www.kineye.org/02/12/balmain12.php.
Balmain, Colette Jane. "Genre, Gender, Gialloi: The Disturbed Dreams of Dario Argento," PhD thesis, University of Greenwich, January 2004, https://gala.gre.ac.uk/id/eprint/5795/5/Colette%20Jane%20Balmain%202004%20-%20redacted.pdf.
Balun, Chas, and John Gullide. "Michele Soavi: Under the Influence," *Giallo Pages*, 1 (Spring 1993): 7–9.

Banymadhub, Yashi. "The Tortured Artist Is a Dangerous Myth. It's the Way Creative Workers Are Treated That Causes Breakdown," *The Independent*, Wednesday 10 October 2018, https://www.independent.co.uk/voices/world-mental-health-day-tortured-artist-dangerous-myth-pain-art-depression-suicide-a8576971.html.
Barasch, Frances K. *The Grotesque: A Study in Meanings* (The Hague: Mouton, 1971).
Baschiera, Stefano, and Francesco Di Chiara. "Once Upon a Time in Italy: Transnational Features of Genre Production 1960s–1970s," *Film International*, 8.6 (2011): 30–39.
Baschiera, Stefano, and Russ Hunter. "Introduction," in *Italian Horror Cinema*, eds. Stefano Baschiera and Russ Hunter (Edinburgh: Edinburgh University Press, 2016), 1–14.
Bauman, Richard. *A World of Others' Words: Cross-cultural Perspectives on Intertextuality* (London: Wiley-Blackwell, 2007).
Bazin, André. "Painting and Cinema," in *What Is Cinema?* Essays selected and translated by Hugh Gray (Berkeley: University of California Press, 1967), 164–169.
Benjamin, Walter. "The Work of Art in the Age of Mechanical Reproduction," *Marxists.org*, https://www.marxists.org/reference/subject/philosophy/works/ge/benjamin.htm.
Berger, Doris. *Projected Art History: Biopics, Celebrity Culture, and the Popularizing of American Art* (New York: Bloomsbury, 2014).
Berns, Fernando Gabriel Pagnoni, and Leonardo Acosta Lando. "Translating Kafka into Italian: Kafkaesque Themes in Elio Petri's Films," in *Mediamorphosis: Kafka and the Moving Image*, eds. Shai Biderman and Ido Lewit (New York: Columbia University Press, 2016), 295–306.
Betti, Claudia, and Teel Sale. *Drawing: A Contemporary Approach* (Belmont, CA: Thomson Wadworth, 2008).
Billson, Anne. "Violence, Mystery and Magic: How to Spot a Giallo Movie," *The Telegraph*, 14 October 2013, https://www.telegraph.co.uk/culture/film/10377468/-Violence-mystery-and-magic-how-to-spot-a-giallo-movie.html.
Bitel, Anton. "The Gender(s) of Genre in Cattet and Forzani's Ambisexual Cinema," *Senses of Cinema*, 87 (June 2018) sensesofcinema.com/2018/split-screen-cattet-forzani/the-genders-of-genre-in-cattet-and-forzanis-ambisexual-cinema/.
———. "Interview: Bruno Forzani and Hélène Cattet," *Projected Figures*, 2 July 2014, https://projectedfigures.com/2014/07/02/interview-bruno-forzani-and-helene-cattet/.
Borecka, Natalia. "The Sinister Sexuality of Guy Bourdin, a Deeply Troubled Genius," *Lone Wolf Magazine*, 11 November 2014, https://lonewolfmag.com/sinister-sexuality-guy-bourdin-photographer/.
Borstlap, John. *The Classical Revolution: Thoughts on New Music in the 21st Century* (Lanham, MD: The Scarecrow Press Inc., 2013).
Bourdieu, Pierre. *Distinction: A Social Critique of the Judgement of Taste* (Cambridge: Harvard University Press, 1984).
Brookes, Rosetta. "Fashion Photography: The Double-Page Spread: Helmut Newton, Guy Bourdin & Deborah Turbeville," in *Chic Thrills: A Fashion Reader*, eds. Juliet Ash and Elizabeth Wilson (Berkeley: University of California Press, 1992), 17–24.
Bruschini, Antonio, and Stefano Piselli. *Giallo and Thrilling All'Italiana (1931–1983)* (Florence: Glittering Images, 2010).
Caputo, Rolando. "Blood and Black Celluloid: Some Thoughts on the Cinema of Mario Bava," *Metro*, 10 (1997): 55–59.
Castagno, Paul C. "The Mannerist Space in Early Commedia dell'Arte Iconography," in *Theatrical Spaces and Dramatic Places: The Reemergence of the Theatre Building in the Renaissance. Theatre Symposium; A Journal of the Southeastern Theatre Conference*. Volume 4 (Tuscaloosa: University of Alabama Press, 1996), 109–124.
Cherry, Brigid "Beyond Suspiria? The Place of European Horror Cinema in the Fan Canon," in *European Nightmares: Horror Cinema in Europe Since 1945*, eds. Patricia Allmer, Emily Brick, and David Huxley (London: Wallflower Press, 2012), 25–34.
Christie, Ian. "Painting and the Visual Arts," in *Encyclopedia of Early Cinema*, ed. Richard Abel (Abingdon, Oxfordshire, United Kingdom, Taylor & Francis Ltd., 2005), 695.

Bibliography 233

Clarke, Donald. "The Neon Demon Review: Ban this Slick Filth!," *The Irish Times*, 7 July 2016, https://www.irishtimes.com/culture/film/the-neon-demon-review-ban-this-slick-filth-1.2713514.
Clover, Carol J. *Men, Women and Chainsaws: Gender in the Modern Horror Film* (Princeton, NJ: Princeton University Press, 1992).
Coates, Tyler. "When Hitchcock Went Gay: 'Strangers on a Train' And 'Rope,'" *Decider*, 11 August 2014, https://decider.com/2014/08/11/alfred-hitchcock-gay-strangers-on-a-train-and-rope/.
Collings, Matthew. *This Is Modern Art* (London: Weidenfeld & Nicolson, 1999).
Conterio, Martyn. *Black Sunday* (Leighton Buzzard: Auteur, 2015).
Cooper, L. Andrew. *Dario Argento* (Urbana: University of Illinois Press, 2012).
Crawford, Travis. "Argento on Stendhal: The Maestro of Mayhem Discusses His Newest Film The Stendhal Syndrome," *European Trash Cinema* 15 (1997), 25–28.
Curti, Roberto. "Francesco Barilli Interview: Cinema Between Brush Strokes," *Offscreen*, 15.12 (December 2011), https://offscreen.com/view/francesco_barilli_interview.
_____. *Italian Gothic Horror Films, 1957–1969* (Jefferson, NC: McFarland, 2015).
D'Adda, Roberta. *Vermeer* (New York, Rizzoli, 2005).
Dalle Vacche, Angela. *Cinema and Painting: How Art is Used in Film* (Austin: University of Texas Press, 1996).
Darwent, Charles. "Arrows of Desire: How Did St Sebastian Become an Enduring, Homo-erotic Icon?," *The Independent*, 10 February 2008, https://www.independent.co.uk/arts-entertainment/art/features/arrows-of-desire-how-did-st-sebastian-become-an-enduring-homo-erotic-icon-779388.html.
Davies, David Stuart. "Introduction," in *The Dead of Night: The Ghost Stories of Oliver Onions* (Ware: Wordsworth Editions, 2010), vii–xii.
Defining Cult Movies: The Cultural Politics of Oppositional Tastes, eds. Mark Jancovich, Antonio Lázaro Reboli, Julian Stringer and Andrew Willis (Manchester: Manchester University Press, 2003).
Deighan, Samm. "All Mimsy Were the Borogoves: The Spectre of Lewis Carroll in Francesco Barilli's *The Perfume of the Lady in Black* (1974)," *Senses of Cinema*, 86 (March 2018 sensesofcinema.com/2018/alice-in-wonderland/all-mimsy-were-the-borogoves-the-spectre-of-lewis-carroll-in-francesco-barillis-the-perfume-of-the-lady-in-black-1974/.
_____. "31 Days of Gialloween: *The Killer is on the Phone* (1972)," *Diabolique Magazine*, 15 October 2018, https://diaboliquemagazine.com/31-days-of-gialloween-the-killer-is-on-the-phone-1972/.
Del Valle, David. "When Sex and Death Are Indissoluble: Riccardo Freda's *L'Orribile segreto del dottor Hichcock (The Horrible Secret of Dr Hichcock / Raptus*, 1962)," *Kino-eye: New Perspectives on European Film*, 3.12 (27 Oct 2003) http://www.kinoeye.org/03/12/delvalle12.php.
de Quincey, Thomas. "Thomas de Quincey," *Project Gutenberg* (2004), https://www.gutenberg.org/files/10708/10708-8.txt.
de Ville, Donna. "Menopausal Monsters and Sexual Transgression in Argento's Art Horror," in *Cinema Inferno: Celluloid Explosions from the Cultural Margins*, eds. Robert G. Weiner and John Cline (Lanham, ND: The Scarecrow Press, 2010), 53–75.
Di Chiara, Francesco. "Domestic Films Made for Export: Modes of Production in the 1960s Italian Horror Film," in *Italian Horror Cinema*, eds. Stefano Baschiera and Russ Hunter (Edinburgh: Edinburgh University Press, 2016), 30–44.
Dixon, Wheeler Winston. "Surrealism and Sudden Death in the Films of Lucio Fulci," *Film International*, 24 December 2012 filmint.nu/?p=6616.
Dwyer, Joseph E. "Returning to Gialloville," *Diabolique Magazine*, 15 October 2019, https://diaboliquemagazine.com/returning-to-gialloville/.
Dyer, Richard. "The House with the Laughing WIndows" in *Directory of World Cinema: Italy*, ed. Louis Bayman (Bristol: Intellect Books, 2011), 143–144.
Ebert, Roger. "Four Flies on Grey Velvet," RogerEbert.com, 18 October 1972, https://www.rogerebert.com/reviews/four-flies-on-grey-velvet-1972.

Ehrlich, Linda C., and David Desser. *Cinematic Landscapes: Observations on the Visual Arts and Cinema of China and Japan* (Austin: University of Texas Press, 1994).

"Elio Petri: Cinema is Not for an Elite, But for the Masses," *Art Politics Cinema: The Cineaste Interviews*, eds. Dan Georgakas and Lenny Rubenstien (London: Pluto Press, 1984), 53–63.

Ellinger, Kat. *All the Colours of Sergio Martino* (Shenley: Arrow Books, 2018).

_____. "31 Days of Gialloween: Stage Fright (1987)," *Diabolique Magazine*, 8 October 2018, https://diaboliquemagazine.com/31-days-of-gialloween-stage-fright-1987/

Elliott, Kamilla. *Portraiture and British Gothic Fiction: The Rise of Picture Identification 1764–1835* (Baltimore: The John Hopkins University Press, 2012).

_____. *Rethinking the Novel/Film Debate* (Cambridge: Cambridge University Press, 2003).

Farrow, Ronan. "From Aggressive Overtures to Sexual Assault: Harvey Weinstein's Accusers Tell Their Stories," *The New Yorker*, 23 October 2017, https://www.newyorker.com/news/news-desk/from-aggressive-overtures-to-sexual-assault-harvey-weinsteins-accusers-tell-their-stories.

Felleman, Susan. *Art and the Cinematic Imagination* (Austin: University Press of Texas, 2006).

_____. "Two-Way Mirror: Francis Bacon and the Deformation of Film," in *Film, Art, New Media*, ed. Angela Dalle Vacche (Houndsmills: Palgrave Macmillan, 2012), 221–238.

"Figure with Meat" (1954)," Art Institute of Chicago, no date, https://www.artic.edu/artworks/4884/figure-with-meat.

Fisher, Austin. "Italian Popular Film Genres," in *A Companion to Italian Cinema*, ed. Frank Burke (Malden; John Wiley & Sons, 2017), 250–266.

_____. "Political Memory in the Italian Hinterland: Locating the 'Rural Giallo,'" in *Italian Horror Cinema*, eds. Stefano Baschiera and Russ Hunter (Edinburgh, UK: Edinburgh University Press, 2016), 160–174.

Fleming, Elizabeth A. "Britain," *Encyclopedia of Interior Design*, ed. Joanna Banham (London: Routledge, 1997), 175–189.

Fonseca, Anthony J. "Beckoning Fair One, The," in *Ghosts in Popular Culture and Legend*, eds. June Michele Pulliam and Anthony J. Fonseca (Santa Barbara, CA: Greenwood, 2016), 19–20.

Forshaw, Barry. "Giallo," in *Directory of World Cinema: Italy*, ed. Louis Bayman (Bristol: Intellect Books Ltd., 2011), 133–153.

Fox, David Charles. "Comparing Abstract Expressionism and Pop Art," *DavidCharlesFox.com*, 14 October 2016, https://davidcharlesfox.com/comparing-abstract-expressionism-pop-art/.

"Francis Bacon: Invisible Rooms," *Tate*, 22 January 2016, https://www.tate.org.uk/press/press-releases/francis-bacon-invisible-rooms-0.

Frayling, Christopher. "We Live in Gothic Times…," in *The Gothic Reader: A Critical Anthology*, ed. Martin Myrone, consultant ed. Christopher Frayling (London: Tate Publishing, 2006), 12–20.

Freud, Sigmund. "Medusa's Head (excerpt)," *The Medusa Reader*, eds. Marjorie Garber and Nancy J. Vickers (New York: Routledge, 2003), 84–86.

Fuseli, Henry. "Aphorisms on Art," in *The Gothic Reader: A Critical Anthology*, ed. Martin Myrone; consultant ed. Christopher Frayling (London: Tate Publishing, 2006), 242.

Gallant, Chris. "The Art of Allusion: Painting, Murder and the 'Plan Tableau,'" in *Art of Darkness: The Cinema of Dario Argento*, ed. Chris Gallant (Godalming: FAB Press, 2001), 65–74.

Gaskell, Ivan. *Vermeer's Wager: Speculations on Art History, Theory and Art Museums* (London: Reaktion Books, 2000).

Gibson, Walter S. *Bruegel* (London: Thames and Hudson, 1977).

Gili, Jean A. "Rencontre avec Elio Petri," in *Elio Petri*, ed. Jean A. Gili (Nice: Faculté des Lettres et Science Humaines, Section d'Histoire, 1974).

Ginzburg, Carlo. "Making It Strange: The Prehistory of a Literary Device," in *Wooden Eyes: Nine Reflections on Distance* (New York: Columbia University Press, 2001), 1–23.

Bibliography 235

Goldstein, Bill. "Castanets in a Snowstorm," *New York Times*, 18 November 2001, https://www.nytimes.com/2001/11/18/books/castanets-in-a-snowstorm.html.
Gombrich, E.M. *The Sense of Order: The Study in the Psychology of Decorative Art* (Ithaca: Cornell University Press, 1979).
Gracey, James. *Dario Argento* (Harpenden: Kamera Books, 2010).
Grigoriadis, Vanessa. "Countess Marina Cicogna, a Woman of the World," *New York Times*, 31 October 2013, https://www.nytimes.com/2013/10/31/t-magazine/countess-marina-cicogna-a-woman-of-the-world.html.
Gromaire, Marcel. "A Painter's Ideas About the Cinema," in *French Film Theory and Criticism: A History/Anthology, 1907–1939. Voume 1: 1907–1939*, ed. Richard Abel (Princeton, NJ: Princeton University Press, 1988), 174–182.
Guins, Raiford. "Blood and Black Gloves on Shiny Discs: New Media, Old Tastes, and the Remediation of Italian Horror Films in the United States," in *Horror International*, eds. Steven Jay Schneider and Tony Williams (Detroit: Wayne State University Press, 2005), 15–32.
Gunning, Tom. "The Cinema of Attraction[s]: Early Film, Its Spectator and the Avant-Garde," in *The Cinema of Attractions Reloaded*, ed. Wanda Strauven. Amsterdam: Amsterdam University Press, 2006), 381–388.
Hale, Terry. "Afterword," in Gaston Leroux, *The Perfume of the Lady in Black* (Sawtry: Dedalus, 1998), 245–252.
Hall, Ann C. *Phantom Variations: The Adaptations of Gaston Leroux's Phantom of the Opera, 1925 to the Present* (Jefferson, NC: McFarland, 2009).
Hallam, Lindsay. "Touching the Colour and Sound of Your Body's Tears: Affect and Homage in the Neo-Giallo," *16:9 Filmtisskrift*, 22 October 2017, www.16-9.dk/2017/10/touching-the-colour/.
Halligan, Benjamin. "The Perfume of the Lady in Black (1974)," in *Eaten Alive: Italian Cannibal and Zombie Movies*, ed. Jay Slater (London: Plexus, 2002), 54–55.
Harper, Jim. *Legacy of Blood: A Comprehensive Guide to Slasher Movies* (Manchester, UK: Critical Vision, 2009).
Harris, Alana. "Introduction: The Summer of '68 - Beyond the Secularization Thesis," in *The Schism of '68: Catholicism, Contraception and Humanae Vitae in Europe, 1945–1975*, ed. Alana Harris (Basingstoke: Palgrave MacMillan, 2018) 1–20.
Hassard, John. Mihaela Kelemen and Julie Wolfram Cox, *Disorganization Theory: Explorations in Alternative Organizational Analysis* (London: Routledge, 2008).
Haverkamp-Begemann, Egbert. Rembrandt: The Night Watch (Princeton, NJ: Princeton Univerity Press, 1982).
Heller-Nicholas, Alexandra. *Masks in Horror Cinema: Eyes Without Faces* (Cardiff: University of Wales, 2019).
———. (moderator) "MIFF Talks | Peter Strickland in Conversation," Melbourne International Film Festival, Wheeler Centre, Melbourne, Australia, 4 August 2019. Posted to YouTube, 3 September 2019, https://www.youtube.com/watch?v=yKSgwn7EScY.
———. *Ms. 45* (New York: Columbia UP/Wallflower, 2017).
———. *Rape-Revenge Films: A Critical Study* (Jefferson, NC: McFarland, 2011).
———. "Stranger Than Fiction: Immigration, Alienation, and the Real Pyjama Girl," booklet essay, *The Pyjama Girl Case* (Arrow Video, 2018).
———. *Suspiria* (Leighton Buzzard: Auteur, 2015).
———. "The Unknown Soldier of the War Against Women," *Overland Literary Journal*, 30 July 2014, https://overland.org.au/2014/07/the-unknown-soldier-of-the-war-against-women/.
Helms, Ruby. "It's a Man's World: Marlene Dietrich and her Cross-Dressing Wardrobe," *The Costume Society*, 24 June 2016. costumesociety.org.uk/blog/post/its-a-mans-world-marlene-dietrich-and-her-cross-dressing-wardrobe.
Henry, Claire. *Revisionist Rape-Revenge: Redefining a Film Genre* (New York: Palgrave Macmillan, 2014).
Hess, Barbara. *Willem de Kooning, 1904–1997: Content as a Glimpse* (Cologne: Taschen, 2004).

Hilwig, Stuart J. *Italy and 1968: Youthful Unrest and Democratic Culture* (Houndmills: Palgrave MacMillan, 2009).
Hollander, Martha. "Vermeer's Empty Room," *Raritan* 10 (Fall 1990): 1–17.
Houpt, Simon. *Museum of the Missing: A History of Art Theft* (New York: Sterling Publishing Co. Inc., 2006).
Huber, Christoph. "A Language of Their Own: An Introduction to Hélène Cattet and Bruno Forzani," *Senses of Cinema*, 87 (June 2018), sensesofcinema.com/2018/split-screen-cattet-forzani/introduction-to-helene-cattet-and-bruno-forzani/.
Hughes, Howard. *Cinema Italiano: The Complete Guide from Classics to Cult* (London: I.B. Tauris, 2011).
Hunt, Leon. "Burning Oil and Baby Oil: Bloody Pit of Horror," in *Alternative Europe: Eurotrash and Exploitation Cinema Since 1945*, ed. Ernest Mathjis and Xavier Mendik (London: Wallflower Press, 2004), 172–180.
_____. "Kings of Terror, Geniuses of Crime: Giallo Cinema and *Fumetti Neri*," in Italian Horror Cinema, eds. Stefano Baschiera and Russ Hunter (Edinburgh University Press, 2016), 145–159.
_____. "A Sadistic Night At the Opera: Notes On The Italian Horror Film," *The Velvet Light Trap*, 30 (Fall 1992): 65–75.
Hunter, Russ. "Preferisco L'Inferno: Early Italian Horror Cinema," in *Italian Horror Cinema*, eds. Stefano Baschiera and Russ Hunter (Edinburgh: Edinburgh University Press, 2016), 15–29.
Huntington Wright, Willard. *Modern Painting: Its Tendency and Meaning* (New York: John Lane, 1915).
Hutchings, Peter. "Bavaesque: The Making of Mario Bava as Italian Horror Auteur," in *Italian Horror Cinema*, eds. Stefano Baschiera and Russ Hunter (Edinburgh: Edinburgh University Press, 2016), 79–92.
Iannone, Pasquale. "*Un tranquillo posto di campagna/A Quiet Place in the Country*," *Senses of Cinema*, 67 (July 2013) sensesofcinema.com/2013/uncategorized/un-tranquillo-posto-di-campagnaa-quiet-day-in-the-country/.
Ingledew, John. *Photography* (London: Laurence King Publishing in Association with Central Saint Martins College of Art & Design, 2005).
Iwabuchi, Koichi. *Recentering Globalization: Popular Culture and Japanese Transnationalism* (Durham: Duke University Press, 2002).
Jacobs, Steven. *Framing Pictures: Film and the Visual Arts* (Edinburgh, UK: Edinburgh University Press, 2011).
Jacobs, Steven, and Lisa Colpaert. *The Dark Galleries: A Museum Guide to Painted Portraits in Film Noir, Gothic Melodrama, and Ghost Stories of the 1940s and 1950s* (Ghent: AraMER, 2013).
Janisse, Kier-La. *House of Psychotic Women: An Autobiographical Topography of Female Neurosis in Horror and Exploitation Film* (Godalming: FAB Press, 2012).
Jenson, Kristofer. "Season of 'The Witch': A Q&A with Robert Eggers and Anya Taylor-Joy," *Newsweek*, 19 February 2016, https://www.newsweek.com/interview-robert-eggers-anya-taylor-joy-witch-movie-428681.
Jones, Alan. "Argento" *Cinefantastique* 13.6/14.1 (1983): 20.
_____. *Profondo Argento: The Man, The Myths and the Magic* (Godalming: FAB Press, 2004).
Joselit, David. "Truth or Dare: The Art of Witnessing," *ArtForum*, September 2011, https://www.artforum.com/print/201107/truth-or-dare-the-art-of-witnessing-28804.
Joubert-Laurencin, Hervé. "André Bazin and 'Arts': The Reverse of a Theorem," Film Criticism, 39.1 (Fall, 2014): 81–99.
Kalbian, Aline H. *Sexing the Church: Gender, Power, and Ethics in Contemporary Catholicism* (Bloomington: Indiana University Press, 2005).
Kannas, Alexia. "All the Colours of the Dark: Film genre and the Italian giallo," *Journal of Italian Cinema & Media Studies*, 5.2 (2017): 173–190.
_____. *Deep Red* (New York: Columbia University Press/Wallflower Press, 2017).

Bibliography

_____. *GIALLO! Genre, Modernity and Detection in Italian Horror Cinema* (Albany: State University of New York Press, forthcoming).
_____. "No Place Like Home: The Late-Modern World of the Italian *Giallo* Film," *Senses of Cinema*, 67 (July 2013), sensesofcinema.com/2013/uncategorized/no-place-like-home-the-late-modern-world-of-the-italian-giallo-film/.
Koven, Mikel J. *La Dolce Morte: Vernacular Cinema and the Italian Giallo Film* (Lanham, MD: The Scarecrow Press, 2006).
Kristeva, Julia *Semeiotike: recherches pour une sémanalyse* (Paris: Editions du Seuil, 1969).
Laennec, Christine Moneera. "The 'Assembly-Line Love Goddess': Women and the Machine Aesthetic in Fashion Photography, 1918–1940," in *Bodily Discursions: Genders, Representations, Technologies*, eds. Deborah S. Wilson and Christine Moneera Laennec (Albany: State University of New York Press, 1997), 81–102.
Landy, Marcia. "The Argento Syndrome: Aesthetics of Horror," in *Italian Horror Cinema*, eds. Stefano Baschiera and Russ Hunter (Edinburgh University Press, 2016), 93–110.
Laseur, Carol. "Australian Exploitation Film: The Politics of Bad Taste," *Continuum*, 5:2 (1992): 366–377.
Léger, Fernand. "Painting and Cinema," in in *French Film Theory and Criticism: A History/Anthology, 1907–1939. Volume 1: 1907–1939*, ed. Richard Abel (Princeton, NJ: Princeton Univerity Press, 1988), 372–373.
Leroux, Gaston. *The Perfume of the Lady in Black* (Sawtry: Dedalus, 1998).
Lewandowska Cummings, Basia. "Foley Cow! Berberian Sound Studio Director Peter Strickland Interviewed," *The Quietus*, 31 August 2012, https://thequietus.com/articles/09874-peter-strickland-interview-berberian-sound-studio.
Lidwell, William, Kritina Holden, and Jill Butler. *Universal Principles of Design, Revised and Updated: 125 Ways to Enhance Usability, Influence Perception, Increase Appeal, Make Better Design Decisions and Teach Through Design* (Beverly: Rockport Publishers, 2010).
Liepa, Valentina. "The Image of Saint Sebastian in Art," *Acta Humanitarica Universitatis Saulensis*, 8 (2009), 455–462.
Loiselle, André. "*Cineima du Grand Guignol*: Theatricality in the Horror Film," in *Stages of Reality: Theatricality in Cinema*, eds. Loiselle, Andreì, and Jeremy Maron (Toronto: University of Toronto Press, 2000), 55–80.
_____. *Theatricality in the Horror Film: A Brief Study on the Dark Pleasures of Screen Artifice* (London: Anthem Press, 2020).
Lowenstein, Adam. "The Giallo/Slasher Landscape: Ecologia del delitto, Friday the 13th and Subtractive Spectatorship," in *Italian Horror Cinema*, eds. Stefano Baschiera and Russ Hunter (Edinburgh: Edinburgh University Press, 2016), 127–144.
_____. "Horror's Otherness and Ethnographic Surrealism: The Case of The Shout," *A Companion to the Horror Film*, ed. Harry M. Benshoff (Somerset: John Wiley & Sons, Inc., 2014), 519–535.
_____. *Shocking Representation: Historical Trauma, National Cinema, and the Modern Horror Film* (New York: Columbia University Press, 2005).
Lucas, Tim. *Mario Bava: All the Colors of the Dark* (Cincinnati: Video Watchdog, 2007).
Luzzi, Joseph. *A Cinema of Poetry: Aesthetics of the Italian Art Film* (Baltimore: John Hopkins University Press, 2014).
MacKay, Andrew Stewart. "A Five-Point Guide to the Work of Francis Bacon," *AnOther Magazine*, 4 May 2016, https://www.anothermag.com/art-photography/8644/a-five-point-guide-to-the-work-of-francis-bacon.
Mackenzie, Michael. "Gender, Genre and Sociocultural Change in the giallo," PhD thesis, Department of Theatre, Film and Television Studies School of Culture and Creative Arts University of Glasgow August 2013, http://theses.gla.ac.uk/4730/1/2013Mackenziephd.pdf.
Magherini, Graziella. *La Sindrome di Stendhal* (Firenze: Ponte Alle Grazie, 1989).
Mahoney, Robert. "The Legend Picture in *Red Queen Kills Seven Times* (1972): An Example of the Instrumentation of 'Vigilogogy,'" *rmarts: reviews of contemporary*

art, culture and agency theory, 26 November 2017, https://rjamahoney.wordpress.com/2017/11/26/the-legend-picture-in-red-queen-kills-seven-times-1972-an-example-of-the-instrumentation-of-vigilogogy/.

Makuchowska, Ludmila. *Scientific Discourse in John Donne's Eschatological Poetry* (Newcastle upon Tyne: Cambridge Scholars Press, 2014).

Manders, Stanley. "Terror in Technicolor," *American Cinematographer* (February 2010), 68–76.

Marin, Louis. "To Destroy Painting (excerpt)," *The Medusa Reader*, eds. Marjorie Garber and Nancy J. Vickers (New York: Routledge, 2003), 135–60.

Martin, John. "Profondo Argento," *Giallo Pages*, 1 (Spring 1993): 4–6.

Martinez, Ricardo. "From Pop Surrealism to Lowbrow—Something Got Lost in Translation," Widewalls, 5 December 2015., https://www.widewalls.ch/pop-surrealism-lowbrow/.

McDonagh, Maitland. *Broken Mirrors/Broken Minds: The Dark Dreams of Dario Argento* (Minneapolis: University of Minnesota Press, 2010).

———. "Strip Nude for Your Killer," *Alliance of Women Film Journalists*, 11 July 2019., https://awfj.org/blog/2019/07/11/strip-nude-for-your-killer-review-by-maitland-mcdonagh/.

McIver, Gillian. *Art History for Filmmakers: The Art of Visual Storytelling* (London: Bloomsbury, 2016).

Met, Philippe. "'Knowing Too Much' About Hitchcock: The Genesis of the Italian Giallo," in *After Hitchcock: Influence, Imitation, and Intertextuality*, eds. David Boyd and R. Barton Palmer (Austin: University of Texas Press, 2006), 195–214.

Millner Kahr, Madlyn. "Vermeer's 'Girl Asleep': A Moral Emblem," *Metropolitan Museum Journal*, 6 (1972): 115–132.

Mitry, Jean. *The Aesthetics and Psychology of the Cinema*, translated by Christopher King (London: The Athlone Press, 1998).

Moliterno, Gino. *The A to Z of Italian Cinema* (Lanham, MD: The Scarecrow Press, 2009).

Morgan, Jessica and Flavia Frigeri (eds). *The World Goes Pop* (New Haven: Yale University Press, 2015).

Morrison, Robert. "Introduction to On Murder by Thomas De Quincey," in *Thomas De Quincey on Murder* (Oxford: Oxford University Press, 2006), vii–xxxvii.

Mulvey, Laura. "Visual Pleasure and Narrative Cinema," in *The Sexual Subject: A Screen Reader in Sexuality* (New York: Routledge, 1992), 22–34. Originally published in *Screen*, 16.3 (October 1975): 6–18.

Nashawaty, Chris. "Murder, Italian Style: A Primer on the Giallo Film Genre," *Vulture*, 18 July 2019, https://www.vulture.com/2019/07/giallo-italian-film-guide.html.

Nead, Lynda. "The Artist's Studio: The Affair of Art and Film," in Film, Art, New Media, ed. Angela Dalle Vacche (Houndsmills: Palgrave Macmillan, 2012), 23–38.

Nechvatal, Joseph. "How Alphonse Mucha's Smoking Designs Made Art Nouveau," *Hyperallergenic*, 9 January 2019, https://hyperallergic.com/478909/how-alphonse-muchas-smoking-designs-made-art-nouveau/.

Needham, Gary. "Playing with Genre: Defining the Italian giallo," Fear Without Frontiers: Horror Cinema Across the Globe, ed. Steven Jay Schneider (Godalming: FAB Press, 2003) 135–144.

Öhrner, Annika. "Niki de Saint Phalle Playing with the Feminine in the Male Factory: HON—en katedral," *Stedelijk Studies*, 7 (Fall 2018), https://stedelijkstudies.com/journal/niki-de-saint-phalle-playing-with-the-feminine-in-the-male-factory-hon-en-katedral/.

Olney, Ian. *Euro Horror: Classic European Horror Cinema in Contemporary American Culture* (Bloomington: Indiana University Press, 2013).

O'Neill, John. *Plato's Cave: Television and its Discontents* (Cresskill: Hampton Press, 2002).

Palmerini, Luca. "For Your Eyes Only: The Lucio Fulci Interview," *Giallo Pages*, 1 (Spring 1993): 35–39.

Palmerini, Luca M., and Mistretta Gaetano, *Spaghetti Nightmares: Italian Fantasy-Horror as Seen Through the Eyes of Their Protagonists* (Key West: Fantasma Books, 1996).

Panofsky, Erwin. *Problems in Titian: Mostly Iconographic* (New York: New York University Press, 1969).
Pasolini, Pier Paolo. "The Cinema of Poetry," in *Movies and Methods. Vol. 1*, ed. Bill Nichols (Berkeley: University of California Press, 1976), 542–558.
"The Passing Shows: Jackson Pollock," *Art News*, 44.4 (1 April 1945); 6.
Paul, Louis. *Italian Horror Film Directors* (Jefferson, NC: McFarland, 2005).
Peucker, Brigitte. *Incorporating Images: Film and the Rival Arts* (Princeton, NJ: Princeton University Press, 1995).
———. *The Material Image: Art and the Real in Film* (Standford, CA: Stanford University Press, 2007).
Pezzotti, Barbara. *Investigating Italy's Past Through Historical Crime Fiction, Films, and TV Series: Murder in the Age of Chaos* (New York: Palgrave, 2016).
Piepenburg, Erik. "Evil Stalks the Stage: It's Curtains!" *New York Times*, 15 May 2014, https://www.nytimes.com/2014/05/18/movies/horror-films-set-in-the-world-of-theater.html.
Pollock, Griselda. "Artists, Mythologies and Media—Genius, Madness and Art History," *Screen*, 21.3 (Autumn 1980): 57–96.
Pops, Martin. *Vermeer: Consciousness and the Chamber of Being* (Ann Arbor, University of Michigan Research Press, 1984).
Portis, Larry. "The Director Who Must (Not?) Be Forgotten: Elio Petri and the Legacy of Italian Political Cinema, Part 1," *Film International*, 21 June 2011 filmint.nu/?p=2448
Price, David. *Albrecht Dürer's Renaissance: Humanism, Reformation, and the Art of Faith* (Ann Arbor: University of Michigan Press, 2003).
Pritchard, Anna. "Envisaging the Possibilities for Art in the Age of Mechanical Reproduction, Consumer Culture and the Pervasiveness of the Media: Andy Warhol," *Deep South*, 6.3 (Spring 2000), https://www.otago.ac.nz/deepsouth/spring2000/pritchardone.html.
Projansky, Sarah. *Watching Rape: Film and Television in Postfeminist Culture* (New York: New York University Press, 2001).
Raitt, Suzanne. "Immoral Science in *The Picture of Dorian Gray*," in *Strange Science: Investigating the Limits of Knowledge in the Victorian Age*, ed. Lara Karpenko and Shalyn Claggett (Ann Arbor: University of Michigan Press, 2017), 164–178.
Ramamurthy, Anandi. "Spectacles and Illusions: Photography and Commodity Culture," in *Photography: A Critical Introduction*, ed. Liz Wells (London: Routledge, 2003), 193–244.
Raymond, Claire. *The Posthumous Voice in Women's Writing from Mary Shelley to Sylvia Plath* (Aldershot: Ashgate, 2006).
Read, Jacinda. *The New Avengers: Feminism, Feminity and the Rape-Revenge Cycle* (Manchester: Manchester University Press, 2000).
"Remembering She—A Cathedral 3.6.2018–10.32019" Moderna Museet, no date, https://www.modernamuseet.se/stockholm/en/exhibitions/remembering-she-a-cathedral/.
Roberts, Seb. "Strange Vices: Transgression and the Production of Difference in the Giallo," *Imagination: Journal of Cross-Cultural Image Studies*, 9.1 (29 October 2018) imaginations.glendon.yorku.ca/?p=10655.
Ross, Alex. "How Oscar Wilde Painted Over 'Dorian Gray.'" *The New Yorker*, 1 August 2011, https://www.newyorker.com/magazine/2011/08/08/deceptive-picture.
Schama, Simon. *Power of Art* (London: BBC Books, 2006).
Schoell, William. *Stay Out of the Shower: The Shocker Film Phenomenon* (London: Robinson Publishing, 1988).
Schubart, Rikke. *Super Bitches and Action Babes: The Female Hero in Popular Cinema, 1970–2006* (Jefferson, NC: McFarland, 2007).
Schwabsky, Barry. "Little Resistance to Gravity: On Lynda Benglis and David Hammons," *The Nation*, 28 March 2011, https://www.thenation.com/article/little-resistance-gravity-lynda-benglis-and-david-hammons/.

Sconce, Jeffrey. "'Trashing' the Academy: Taste, Excess, and an Emerging Politics of Cinematic Style," *Screen*, 36.4 (1995): 371–393.
Sélavy, Virginie. "Interview with Hélène Cattet and Bruno Forzani," *Electric Sheep: A Deviant View of Cinema*, 10 April 2014 www.electricsheepmagazine.co.uk/2014/04/10/interview-with-helene-cattet-and-bruno-forzani/.
Sevastakis, Michael. "A Dangerous Mind: Dario Argento's *Opera* (1987)" *Kinoeye: New Perspectives on European Film*, 2.12 (24 June 2002) www.kinoeye.org/02/12/sevastakis12.php.
_____. *Giallo Cinema and Its Folktale Roots: A Critical Study of 10 Films, 1962–1987* (Jefferson, NC: McFarland, 2016).
Shields, Chris. "Art/Form: Fulci's Brush with Death," *Film Comment*, 24 July 2017, https://www.filmcomment.com/blog/artform-fulcis-brush-death/.
Shipka, Danny. *Perverse Titillation: The Exploitation Cinema of Italy, Spain and France, 1960–1980* (Jefferson, NC: McFarland, 2011).
Shklovsky, Viktor. *Theory of Prose* (Elmwood Park: Dalkey Archive Press, 1993). First published 1925.
Sicinski, Michael. "The Gaze in Hélène Cattet and Bruno Forzani's *Amer* (2009)," *Senses of Cinema*, 87 (June 2018) sensesofcinema.com/2018/split-screen-cattet-forzani/the-gaze-in-helene-cattet-and-bruno-forzanis-amer-2009/.
Siddique, Sophia, and Raphael Raphael (eds). *Transnational Horror Cinema: Bodies of Excess and the Global Grotesque* (London: Palgrave Macmllan, 2016).
Skelly, Julia. *Radical Decadence: Excess in Contemporary Feminist Textiles and Craft* (London: Bloomsbury, 2017).
Slater, Jay (ed.), *Eaten Alive! Italian Cannibal and Zombie Movies* (London: Plexus, 2005).
Smith, Adrian Luther. *Blood & Black Lace: The Definitive Guide to Italian Sex and Horror Movies* (Liskeard: Stray Cat Publishing, 1999).
Smith, Otto Saumarez. "Painstakingly Perfect and Utterly Peculiar—The Drawings of Jean-Jacques Lequeu," *Apollo Magazine*, 18 February 2019, https://www.apollo-magazine.com/jean-jacques-lequeu-drawing-petit-palais/.
Snow, Edward. *A Study of Vermeer* (Berkeley: University of California Press, 1994).
Sobchack, Vivian. *Carnal Thoughts: Embodiment and Moving Image Culture* (Berkeley: University of California Press, 2004).
Soderman, Braxton. "'Don't Look ... Or It Takes You': The Games of Horror Vacui," *Journal of Visual Culture*, 14.3 (2015): 311–316.
Sontag, Susan. *On Photography* (London: Penguin Books, 2008). First published 1977.
Soren, David. *The Rise and Fall of the Horror Film: An Art Historical Approach to Fantasy Cinema* (Columbia: Lucas Brothers Publishing, 1977).
Squires, John. "Muschietti Talks Paintings that Inspired Nightmarish New 'IT' Creature," *Bloody Disgusting*, 10 September 2017, https://bloody-disgusting.com/movie/3458110/muschietti-talks-paintings-inspired-nightmarish-new-creature/.
Stabenow, Cornelia. *Rousseau* (Cologne: Taschen, 2001).
Stam, Robert. *Reflexivity in Film and Literature: From Don Quixote to Jean-Luc Godard* (New York: Columbia University Press, 1992).
Stanska, Zuzanna. "Gustav Klimt and His Love for Trees in Paintings," *Daily Art Magazine*, 9 October 2018, https://www.dailyartmagazine.com/gustav-klimt-trees-paintings/.
_____. "A Study of Loneliness and Isolation: The Man in Blue," *Daily Art Magazine*, 20 May 2018, https://www.dailyartmagazine.com/man-in-blue-by-francis-bacon/.
Steadman, Philip. *Vermeer's Camera: Uncovering the Truth Behind the Masterpieces* (Oxford: Oxford University Press, 2001).
Still, Judith, and Michael Worton. "Introduction," in *Intertextuality: Theories and Practices*, eds. Judith Still and Michael Worton (Manchester: Manchester University Press, 1990), 1–44.
Stonard, John-Paul. "Abstract Expressionism—Not Just Macho Heroes with Brushes," *The Guardian*, 3 September 2016, https://www.theguardian.com/artanddesign/2016/sep/03/abstract-expressionism-not-just-macho-heroes-with-brushes.
Swennson, Ronny. "Tenebre," *Fantasy Film Memory*, 4/5 (1991): 41.

Terci, Mario. "What Is Alice, What Is This Thing, Who Are You?: The Reasons of the Body in Alice," in *Semiotics and Linguistics in Alice's World*, eds. Rachel Fordyce and Carla Marella (Berlin: Walter de Gruyter & Co., 1994), 63–73.
Thompson, Kristin. "The Concept of Cinematic Excess," in *Narrative, Apparatus, Ideology. A Film Theory Reader*, ed. Philip Rosen (New York: Columbia University Press, 1986), 130–142.
Thrower, Stephen. *Beyond Terror: The Films of Lucio Fulci* (Godalming: FAB Press, 2002).
Totaro, Donato. "The Beyond: Lucio Fulci's Zombie Masterpiece," *Offscreen*, 1.2 (July 1997), https://offscreen.com/view/the_beyond.
———. "A Genealogy of Italian Popular Cinema: The Filone," *Offscreen*, 15.11 (November 2011), https://offscreen.com/view/genealogy_filone.
Ungaretti, Giuseppe. "Preface," in Roberta D'Adda, *Vermeer* (New York, Rizzoli, 2005), 11.
Vanelli, Marco. "Italian Cinema and Catholicism: From *Vigilanti cura* to Vatican II and Beyond," in *A Companion to Italian Cinema*, ed. Frank Burke (Malden: John Wiley & Sons, 2017), 104–119.
Walker, John A. *Art and Artists on Screen* (Manchester, UK: Manchester University Press, 1993).
Walker, Michael. *Hitchcock's Motifs* (Amsterdam University Press, 2005).
Weemans, Michel. "Pieter Bruegel's *Hunters in the Snow* and *Insidious Auceps* as Trap Images," in *Pieter Bruegel the Elder and Religion*, eds. Bertram Kaschek, Jürgen Müller, and Jessica Buskirk (Leiden: Brill, 2018), 245–276.
Wells, Paul. *The Horror Genre: From Beelzebub to Blair Witch* (London and New York: Wallflower, 2000), 114.
Whitehead, Gundrun D., and Julia Petrov. "Introduction," in *Fashioning Horror: Dressing to Kill on Screen and in Literature*, eds. Julia Petrov and Gundrun D. Whitehead (London: Bloomsbury, 2018), 1–24.
Wiegand, Daniel. "The Unsettling of Vision: Tableaux Vivants, Early Cinema, and Optical Illusions," in *The Image in Early Cinema: Form and Material*, eds. Scott Curtis, Philippe Gauthier, Tom Gunning and Joshua Yumibe (Bloomington: Indiana University Press, 2018), 26–35.
Wolfthal, Diane. *Images of Rape: The 'Heroic' Tradition and Its Alternatives* (Cambridge: Cambridge University Press, 1999).
Wood, Gaby. "Death Becomes Her," *The Guardian*, 14 April 2003, https://www.theguardian.com/theobserver/2003/apr/13/features.review27.
Woolf, Virginia. "The Movies and Reality," *The New Republic*, 4 August 1926, https://newrepublic.com/article/120389/movies-reality.
Yates, Wilson. "An Introduction to the Grotesque: Theoretical and Theological Considerations," in *The Grotesque in Art and Literature: Theological Reflections*, eds. James Luther Adams and Wilson Yates (Grand Rapids, MI: William B. Eerdmans Publishing Co., 1997), 1–68.

Index

Abrakadabra 209
abstract expressionism 68–9, 134, 147–8
Aertsen, Pieter 54
Alice in Wonderland see Carroll, Lewis
Alighieri, Dante see Dante
All the Colors of the Dark (Tutti i colori del buio) 41, 42, 44, 62, 208
Amer 41, 55, 208, 209
American International Pictures 44
Amuck! (Alla ricerca del piacere) 43, 49, 55, 135
Animal Trilogy 40, 117; see also Argento, Dario; *The Bird with the Crystal Plumage*; *Cat O'Nine Tails*; *Four Flies on Grey Velvet*
Antonioni, Michelangelo 8, 40, 44, 63, 160, 222n
architecture 21, 49, 56, 78, 81, 85, 100
Argento, Asia 80–92
Argento, Dario 3, 4, 5, 13, 14, 16, 21, 27, 29, 32, 36, 37, 40, 43, 44–5, 46, 49, 54, 62, 63, 70, 80–92, 94–104, 116, 117, 119, 148, 154, 155, 160, 161, 163, 165, 168, 169, 171, 173, 177, 178, 193, 198, 207
Armani, Georgio 155
art nouveau 47, 49, 56, 57, 218
Atom Age Vampire (Seddok, l'erede di Satana) 35
Autopsy (Macchie solari) 160
Avati, Pupi see *The House with Laughing Windows*

Bacon, Francis 5, 19, 20, 54, 70–3, 75–79, 94, 149
Baker, Carroll 44, 47, 108
Barilli, Francesco 32, 188, 193–205
Bartoli, Francesco 103, 222n
Bava, Lamberto 5, 28, 32, 43, 47, 49, 160, 163, 173–5, 177, 198
Bava, Mario 4, 5, 29, 32, 35, 36, 42, 43, 44, 45, 47, 54, 55, 61, 70, 130, 132, 133, 155–61, 163, 164, 178, 196, 215n
Bazin, André 11–2
Beardsley, Aubrey 71
The Beckoning Fair One (novella) 144–6
Benjamin, Walter 46–7
Berberian Sound Studio 29, 41, 175–6, 208, 209
Bergonzelli, Sergio see *Blood Delirium*
Bertolucci, Bernardo 8, 193, 202
The Beyond (E tu vivrai nel terrore—L'aldilà) 63, 69, 70
The Bird with the Crystal Plumage (L'uccello dalle piume di cristallo) 4, 37, 43, 48, 80, 81, 92, 95–100, 104, 117, 131, 161, 176, 207; see also the Animal Trilogy
Black Belly of the Tarantula (La tarantola dal ventre nero) 46, 95, 160
Black Sabbath 35, 159
Black Sunday (La maschera del demonio) 29, 159, 215n
A Black Veil for Lisa (La morte non ha sesso) 37
A Blade in the Dark (La casa con la scala nel buio) 28, 38, 47, 48, 49, 173–6, 185
Blood and Black Lace (Sei donne per l'assassino) 4, 37, 40, 47, 55, 133, 154, 155–60, 161, 163
Blood Delirium (Delirio de sangue) 11, 131, 135–140
The Bloodsucker Leads the Dance (La sanguisuga conduce la danza) 177
Bloody Pit of Horror (Il boia scarlatto) 36
Blow Out 170, 174
Blow Up 222n
Boccaccio, Giovanni 32
Böcklin, Andre 24
Bolkan, Florinda 71, 72, 75, 79, 220n
Bosch, Hieronymus 15, 80, 81, 99
Botticelli, Sandro 86–7, 88, 94, 99, 108

243

244　　　　　　　　　　　　Index

Bourdieu, Pierre 3, 9
Bourdin, Guy 162–5
Bruegel, Pieter (the elder) 15, 24, 90–91, 99–100
Busiri, Saverio 49

The Cabinet of Dr. Caligari 1, 16
Il cadavere di marmo 35
Calling All Police Cars (...a tutte le auto della polizia...) 160
Caltiki, The Immortal Monster (Caltiki, il mostro immortale) 35
cannibalism 194–5, 198, 203–5
Capucine 163–4
Caravaggio, Michelangelo Merisi da 32, 63, 80, 88–9, 94, 99
Carracci, Annibale 54
Carroll, Lewis 194–204
The Case of the Bloody Iris (Perché quelle strane gocce di sangue sul corpo di Jennifer?) 43, 156, 162, 164
The Castle of Terror (La danza macabre) 35
Cat O' Nine Tails (Il Gatto a Nove Code) 40, 43, 81, 117, 117, 161; see also the Animal Trilogy
Cattet, Hélène 41, 55–8, 208–9
Cemetery Man (Dellamore Dellamore) 55, 187
Christie, Agatha 5, 33
City of the Living Dead (Paura nella città dei morti viventi) 63
Cixous, Hélène 89
Clap, You're Dead (Ciak si muore) 28, 170–2, 174, 175, 177, 185
class 35, 38, 46, 47, 73, 79, 105, 151, 158–9
Closed Circuit (Circuito chiuso) 170
Cold Eyes of Fear (Gli occhi freddi della paura) 28
comics 33, 49, 157; see also *fumetto*

Dagger Eyes (Mystere) 46–7, 161
Dalí, Salvador 5, 70, 73–8, 94, 149, 150, 166
Dallamano, Massimo 17, 18, 37, 42, 43, 153
Dante 31, 32
David, Jacques-Louis 149
Da Vinci, Leonardo 32, 104, 115
The Dead Are Alive (L'etrusco uccide ancora) 160
Death Carries a Cane (Passi di danza su una lama di rasoio) 46, 49, 130, 160
Death Laid an Egg (La morte ha fatto l'uovo) 37

Death Walks at Midnight (La morte accarezza a mezzanotte) 47, 49, 130, 155, 160
Deep Red 3, 4, 11, 14, 19, 29, 32, 43, 44, 48, 49, 58, 61, 74, 77, 80, 81, 83, 94, 95, 96, 97, 100–4, 130, 147, 160, 171, 173, 177, 207, 209
Deep Sleep (Sonno Profondo) 209
Delacroix, Eugene 149
Delirium (Le foto di Gioia) 156, 160, 163–4
Delitto d'autore 55
De Palma, Brian 13, 49, 170, 174, 209
de Quincey, Thomas 19, 95, 163
The Devil's Commandment (I vampiri) 35
Dine, Jim 149, 225n
Do You Like Hitchcock? 45
Don't Torture a Ducking (Non si sevizia un paperino) 117
Dorian Gray (Il dio chiamato Dorian) 18
Dressed to Kill 49

The Editor 41, 209
Ercoli, Luciano 5, 47, 49, 130, 154, 155, 179
Evil Eye (Malocchio) 62
excess 8–26, 29, 36, 48, 55, 74, 118, 125, 136, 138, 139, 143, 167, 168, 169–70, 171, 172, 176, 181, 183, 187, 189, 193, 199, 203, 205, 207–10.
The Exorcist 13, 16
Eye of the Labyrinth (L'occhio nel labirinto) 46, 130
Eyeball (Gatti rossi in un labirinto di vetro) 55, 161
Eyes Behind the Wall (L'occhio dietro la parete) 49
Eyes of Laura Mars 162, 209

Farmer, Mimsy 44, 193, 201, 219n
fashion 5, 47 48, 110, 154–167, 169, 175, 209
Fashion Crimes (La morte è di moda) 154
Fassbinder, Rainer Werner 9, 52
Fatal Frames (Fotogrammi mortal) 95, 171–3, 175, 176, 227n
Feast of Satan (Las amantes del diablo) 62
Fellini, Federico 8, 40, 129, 197
Fenech, Edwige 48, 54, 113, 155, 161, 162, 164, 178, 209
Fenoglio, Pietro 49
The Fifth Cord (Giornata nera per l'ariete) 46, 155
filone 38

Index 245

Five Dolls for an August Moon (*5 bambole per la luna d'agosto*) 47, 54, 130, 155, 178
The Flower with the Petals of Steel (*Il fiore dai petali d'acciaio*) 49
The Forbidden Photos of a Lady Above Suspicion (*Le foto proibite di una signora per bene*) 155, 160, 178
The Forbidden Room (*Anima Persa*) 58–61, 68, 130, 177
Forzani, Bruno 41, 55–8, 208–9
Four Flies on Grey Velvet (*4 mosche di velluto grigio*) 4, 14, 40, 43, 49, 80, 117, 130, 154, 177
Freda, Riccardo 28, 29, 35, 42, 46; *see also* the Animal Trilogy
The French Sex Murders (*Casa d'appuntamento*) 42
Friedrich, Caspar David 8, 16
Frontoni, Angelo 164
Fulci, Lucio 5, 20, 32, 37, 40, 42, 45, 49, 55, 58, 61–9, 70–9, 80, 94, 116, 117, 119, 130, 162, 165, 170, 193, 207
fumetti neri see *fumetto*
fumetto 33, 157; *see also* comics
Fuseli, Henry 210

Gabrielle d'Estrées et une de ses sœurs (painting) 54
Gainsbourg, Serge 42
Garnett, Eleanora 159
genre 38–9
Gentileschi, Artemisia 19
The Ghost (*Lo sprettro*, 1963) 35
Giacometti, Albert 232
Giallo (1934 film) 27–29, 170, 185
Giallo (2009 film) 27, 161, 171
giallo-fantastico see supernatural giallo
The Girl Who Knew Too Much (*La ragazza che sapeva troppo*) 4, 36, 43, 44–5, 159
Goblin (band) 101
Gogol, Nikolai 21
The Goodbye Kiss (*Arrivederci amore, ciao*) 46, 49
gothic 16, 29, 43, 105, 110, 113, 181
Goya Francisco 16, 149
Granger, Farley 43, 55, 130–5
Grani, Tina 159
Greenaway, Peter 9, 53
grotesque art 32, 71 193

The Haller Case (*Il Caso Haller*) 35
Hatchet for the Honeymoon (*Il rosso segno della follia*) 42, 61, 133
Hemmings, David 43, 101, 102, 160, 222*n*

Hitchcock, Alfred 9, 15, 16, 44, 45, 78, 106, 177
Hogarth, William 16
Hopper, Edward 16, 100
The Horrible Secret of Dr. Hichcock (*L'orribile segreto del dottor Hichcock*) 35
Horror Castle (*La vergine di Norimberga*) 36
horror vacui 23–6, 207
The House with Laughing Windows (*La Casa dalefinestre che ridono*) 5, 48, 95, 116, 117–27

The Iguana with the Tongue of Fire (*L'iguana dalla lingue difuoco*) 42, 46
In the Folds of the Flesh (*Nelle pieghe della carne*) 46
Inferno 21; *see also* Three Mothers trilogy
L'Inferno 35
intertextuality 5, 20–21

J&B Whiskey 41–2

Kendall, Suzy 44, 96, 108, 115, 176
Kill, Baby ... Kill! (*Operazione paura*) 29, 61, 132, 159, 196, 197
The Killer Is on the Phone (*L'assassino ... è al telefono*) 42, 177, 179–81, 220
The Killer Reserved Nine Seats (*L'Assassino ha riservato nove Paltrone*) 62, 79, 108, 131, 177, 181–5, 220
The Killer Wore Gloves (*La muerte llama a las 10*) 160
Knife+Heart (*Un couteau dans le cœur*) 209
Knife of Ice (*Il coltello di ghiaccio*) 47, 131
Krimi films 36, 44, 157

Lado, Aldo 5, 40, 42, 60, 62, 170
The Lady in Black (*Damen i svart*) 154
The Last Fashion Show (*Sotto il vestito niente—L'ultima sfilata*) 166
The Laughing Woman (*Femina Ridens*) 49, 133, 160, 188–93
Le Fanu, Sheridan 21
Lenzi, Umberto 1, 5, 40, 46, 47, 49, 55, 94, 107–108, 133, 149, 161, 193, 195, 203
Leroux, Gaston 178, 194–6, 198, 201–2, 204
Libido 37
Lisa and the Devil (*Lisa e il diavolo*) 29
A Lizard in a Woman's Skin 5, 20, 40, 42, 55, 69, 71–9, 130, 207, 220*n*
Lotto, Lorenzo 55
Lovecraft, H.P. 14, 144

246 Index

lowbrow art 9, 24, 60; see also paracinema

Magherini, Graziella 85
Magritte, Rene 16, 55, 81, 83, 148–9, 187
Malombra 35
Manhattan Baby 71
The Mannequin in Red (Mannekäng i rött) 154
Martino, Sergio 5, 42, 49, 55, 62, 95, 104, 112–116, 119, 154, 155, 160, 162, 177, 179, 193, 195, 208
Medusa 88–91
Michelangelo 32, 44, 63, 137
Mill of the Stone Women (Il mulino delle donne di pietra) 29, 35
Miraglia, Emilio 55, 95, 110–2, 116
modernism 1, 7, 20, 53, 173
Modigliani, Amedeo 16, 86
Mondadori (publisher) 5, 27, 33
Mondo films 9, 36, 195
Mondrian, Piet 57, 149
Morricone, Ennio 72, 77, 86, 89, 143, 148
Il mostro di Frankenstein 35
Mozart Is a Murderer (Mozart è un assassin) 49
Mucha, Alphonse 47, 56, 57
Mulvey, Laura 158, 164
Munch, Edvard 14, 16, 19, 102
Murder by Appointment (Omicidio per appuntamento) 32
Murder Rock (Murderock—uccide a passo di danza) 49, 130
My Dear Killer (Mio caro assassin) 104, 198, 223n

national cinema 39–45
neo-giallo 29, 41, 49, 56, 175, 181, 209, 215
The Neon Demon 209
The New York Ripper (Lo squartatore di New York) 42, 165, 170
The Night Evelyn Came Out of the Grave (La notte che Evelyn uscì dalla tomba) 106, 110–1, 132
Nothing Underneath (Sotto il vestito niente) 154

Oasis of Fear (Un posto ideale per uccider) 47
Obsession (Ossessione) 37
Once Upon a Time in the West (C'era una volta il West) 96
opera 21, 49, 80, 168–70

paracinema 9–10, 23, 25; see also taste
Paranoia (Orgasmo) 40, 47, 55, 108, 131

peplum films 36
The Perfume of the Lady in Black (novel) 194–6, 197, 198, 201–2, 204
The Perfume of the Lady in Black (Il profumo della signora in nero) (film) 32, 188, 193–205
Perugino, Pietro 55, 115, 122
Petri, Elio see A Quiet Place in the Country
Phantom of Death (Un delitto poco comune) 49, 228n
The Phantom of the Opera (film) 21
The Phantom of the Opera (novel) 178, 195
Phenomena 46, 62, 155
photography 5, 48, 78, 154–167, 209
Picasso, Pablo 19, 86, 149
The Picture of Dorian Gray 16–9
Play Motel 43, 160
The Playgirls and the Vampire (L'ultima preda del vampire) 35
Poe, Edgar Allan 14, 67, 69, 114, 146
Police Grope in the Dark (La polizia brancola nel buio) 160
poliziotteschi 34, 141, 164, 220n
Pollock, Jackson 24, 135
pop art 147–50, 157; see also Warhol, Andy
Pope John XXIII 34
portraiture 103, 105–16, 113, 215n
postmodernism 20, 52, 173
Puzzle (L'uomo senza memoria) 49
The Pyjama Girl Case (La ragazza dal pigiama giallo) 42, 43, 154

A Quiet Place in the Country (Un tranquillo posto di campagna) 10, 55, 108, 131, 141–51, 219n

rape-revenge film 80–92, 166, 220n
The Red Headed Corpse (La rossa dalla pelle che scotta) 11, 43, 130–6
The Red Light Girls (Prostituzione) 160
Rembrandt 60, 80, 86, 91–2, 98, 149
Risi, Dino 58–61, 68, 130, 177
Rosso, Enrico Colmbotto 111
Rothko, Mark 68–9, 135
Rubens, Peter Paul 55, 63
Russo, Renzol see The Red Headed Corpse

Saint Phalle, Niki de 71, 190–3
Saint Sebastian 115–116, 117–26
Scerbanenco, Giorgio 33
Schifano, Mario 70–1
Sciascia, Leonardo 33

Index

Sconce, Jeffrey *see* paracinema
sculpture 5, 32 48, 49, 80, 81, 133, 143, 188, 190, 191
Second Vatican Council 34
The Sect (La Setta) 32
Seven Blood Stained Orchids (Sette orchidee macchiate di rosso) 46, 94
Seven Deaths in a Cat's Eye (La morte negli occhi del gatto) 42
Seven Murders for Scotland Yard (Jack el destripador de Londres) 42
Seven Shawls of Yellow Silk (Sette scialli di seta gialla) 55, 155
Sexy Cat 49
Short Circuit (Cortocircuito) 37
Short Night of Glass Dolls (La Corte Notte Delle Bambole Di Vetro) 40, 42, 62
Sleepless (Non ho sonno) 21, 80
Snapshot of a Crime (Istantanea per un delitto) 160
snuff film 8, 121, 171
So Sweet, So Dead (Rivelazioni di un maniaco sessuale al capo della squadra mobile) 43, 135, 160
So Sweet... So Perverse (Cosi Dolce, Cosi Perversa) 40
Soavi, Michele 32, 47, 49, 55, 174, 177, 185–7, 204, 223*n*
Solari, Andrea 19
Something Creeping in The Dark (Qualcosa striscia nel buio) 43, 135
Sontag, Susan 163
Spasmo 1, 2, 3, 54, 55, 107–8, 130, 133, 149
Special Broadcasting Service (SBS) (Australian television network) 4
The Spider Labyrinth (Il nido del ragno) 62
Stage Fright 177, 178, 185–7, 204, 223*n*
Steele, Barbara 29, 44
The Stendhal Syndrome (La Sindrome di Stendhal) (film) 80–92, 97, 98, 99, 130, 148, 207
Stendhal Syndrome (psychological condition) 81, 83, 85
The Strange Colour of Your Body's Tears (L'étrange couleur des larmes de ton corps) 41, 55–7, 208, 209
Strickland, Peter 29, 41, 134, 175–6, 208, 209
Strip Nude for Your Killer (Nude per l'assassino) 48, 154, 161–2
supernatural *giallo* 46, 61, 136, 155, 162, 181
surrealism 16, 32, 81, 103, 112, 141
Suspiria 21, 37, 81, 95, 200*n*; *see also* Argento, Dario; the *Three Mothers* trilogy
The Sweet Body of Deborah (Il dolce corpo di Deborah) 37

tableau vivant 53–5, 77, 100, 119, 164, 187
taste 2, 8–9, 24, 39
A Taste for Fear (Pathos—Segreta inquietudine) 160
Tenebrae 4, 21, 37, 49, 80, 198, 220*n*
Terror Creatures from the Grave (Cinque tombe per un medium) 36
Terror in the Crypt (La cripta e l'incubo) 29
Three Mothers trilogy 21, 80; *see also* Argento, Dario
Tiepolo, Giovanni Battista 55
Tinguely, Jean 190
Tomb of Torture (Metempsyco) 29
Too Beautiful to Die (Sotto il vestito niente II) 166–7, 172
Torso (I corpi presentano tracce di violenza carnale) 55, 104, 115, 119, 140, 154, 176
Trhauma 43, 161
Trussadi 155

Uccello, Paolo 86–7
Ultovedt, Per Olof 190

Valli, Alida 95, 135, 172
The Vampire and the Ballerina (L'amante del vampire) 35
Van Dine, S. S. (author) 33
van Schijndel, Meike 49
The Vengeance of Lady Morgan (La vendetta di Lady Morgan) 36
Vermeer, Johannes 52–69, 130, 177
Visconti, Luchino 37, 135

Wallace, Edgar 5, 27, 28, 33
Walter, Eugene 126
Warhol, Andy, 46–7, 86
Watch Me When I Kill (Il gatto dagli occhi di Giada) 49
What Have They Done to Your Daughters? (La polizia chiede aiuto) 43
What Have You Done to Solange? (Cosa avete fatto a Solange?) 42
A White Dress for Marialé (Un bianco vestito per Marialé) 154
Who Saw Her Die? (C'ha vista morire?) 40, 44, 60, 170
Wilde, Oscar *see The Picture of Dorian Gray*

Woolf, Virginia 1, 3
World War II 33–5, 45–6, 95, 144
Wright, Willard Huntington 33; see Van Dine, S.S.

Years of Lead (*anni di piombo*) 34
You'll Die at Midnight (*Morirai a mezzanotte*) 43, 198, 228*n*

Your Vice Is a Locked Room and Only I Have the Key (*Il tuo vizio è una stanza chiusa e solo io ne ho la chiave*) 49, 95, 104, 107, 113–5, 219*n*

Zapponi, Bernardino 58, 101

www.ingramcontent.com/pod-product-compliance
Ingram Content Group UK Ltd.
Pitfield, Milton Keynes, MK11 3LW, UK
UKHW041936140426
5217IPUK00014B/512